# PREFACE

THIS volume is a challenge, not a summary of fragile dubiosities. No mystery hangs over it. Underlying it is the assumption that science and the machine are two invincible facts with which all must reckon who write, teach, preach, lead, or practice the arts in our time. Those who refuse to face them are condemned in advance to sterility and defeat. While recognizing the evils brought by these modern engines—evils which weigh heavily in the minds of the authors—the volume as a whole rejects the pessimistic views of writers like Chesterton, Belloc, and Spengler. For visions of despair, it substitutes a more cheerful outlook upon the future of modern civilization, without at the same time resorting to the optimism of the real-estate agent.

A simple method has controlled the preparation of the volume. With the aid of friendly advice from many quarters, authorities of outstanding competence, possessing also the ability to present their ideas with clearness and vigor, were chosen to deal with the several phases of modern civilization. No limitations, save those of space, were laid upon them. Each writer was given a free hand. None of them was asked to assume any responsibility for the opinions of the others. The editor has not altered their copy, smoothed out contradictions, or taken on the duty of defending everything that appears in these pages. If the principle of liberty had not commanded this, the distinction of the co-operating authors would have made it imperative.

The editor's debt to Mr. Frank Ernest Hill, of Longmans, Green and Co. for editorial assistance passes all calculation.

CHARLES A. BEARD

*New Milford, Conn.*
*August, 1928*

# CONTENTS

# WHITHER MANKIND

## A PANORAMA OF MODERN CIVILIZATION

EDITED BY

### CHARLES A. BEARD

CO-AUTHOR OF "THE RISE OF AMERICAN CIVILIZATION"

LONGMAN

NEW YORK

## INTRODUCTION

### By Charles A. Beard

I

ALL over the world, the thinkers and searchers who scan the horizon of the future are attempting to assess the values of civilization and speculating about its destiny. Europe, having just passed through a devastating war and already debating the hour for the next explosion, wonders whether the game is worth the candle or can be played to the bitter extreme without inviting disaster so colossal as to put an end to civilization itself. In America, where Europeans have renewed their youth, conquered a wilderness, and won wealth and leisure in the sweat of their brows, the cry ascends on all sides: "Where do we go from here?" *Vivere deinde philosophari*—the stomach being full, what shall we do next? Far away in Japan, the younger generation, still able to see with their own eyes vestiges of a feudal order abandoned by their elders, are earnestly inquiring whether they must turn back upon their path or lunge forward with renewed energy into the age of steel and electricity. So for one reason or another, the intellectuals of all nations are trying to peer into the coming day, to discover whether the curve of contemporary civilization now rises majestically toward a distant zenith or in reality has already begun to sink rapidly toward a nadir near at hand.

On casual thought, names of anxious inquirers from every land come to mind: Ku Hung Ming and Hu Shih in China; Gandhi and Tagore in India; Yusuke Tsurumi and the late Arishima in Japan; Ferrero and Croce in Italy; Spengler and Kayserling in Germany; Fabre-Luce, Demangeon, and Georges Batault in France; Wells,

Chesterton, Belloc, Shaw, and Dean Inge in England; Unamuno in Spain; Trotzky in Russia; Ugarte in Argentina. The very titles of the books having a challenging ring: "The Decline of the West," "Mankind at the Crossroads," "The Rising Tide of Color," "The Revolt of the Unfit," "The Tragic Sense of Life," "The Decline of Europe," "War the Law of Life," and "The Destiny of a Continent."

It is not alone the philosophers who display anxiety about the future. The policies of statesmen and the quest of the people in circles high and low for moral values reveal a concern about destiny that works as a dynamic force in the affairs of great nations. In Italy, the Fascisti repudiate both democracy and socialism, bring about the most effective organization of capital and labor yet accomplished in any country, and prepare the way for the cooperation of these two forces or for a class war all the more terrible on account of the social equipment of the contending parties. In Russia, the Bolsheviki join the Italians in rejecting democracy but attempt to create a communist state which, if a success, would be a standing menace to all the governments of the world founded on different principles. Germany writhes and turns, torn by an inner *Zerrissenheit*, with Nationalists cursing international capitalism and longing for buried things, with Socialists and Communists still active if shorn of their former confidence, and with the mass of the people once more absorbed in the routine of the struggle for existence, yet dimly aware that the Faustian age may not be closed after all. In an hour of victory, France reckons the terrible cost and stirs restlessly, wondering about the significance of the ominous calm. Likewise triumphant, England sits as of yore enthroned amid her Empire, with all her old goods intact and valuable additions made; but the self-governing dominions assert an unwonted independence; top-heavy capitalism, having devoured domestic agriculture, feverishly searches for new markets among the half-civilized and backward races of the earth, hoping to keep its machinery turning and its profits flowing, while American and German competition in the same enterprise presses harder and harder upon the merchants of London, Manchester, and Liverpool.

Apparently secure between two seas, and enriched by the fortunes of the European war, America reaches out ever more vigorously, huckstering and lending money, evidently hoping with childlike faith that sweet things will ever grow sweeter; but critics, foreign and domestic, disturb the peace of the new Leviathan. Einstein frankly sneers at American intelligence; Siegfried finds here sounding brass, tinkling cymbals, noise, and materialism. If many are inclined to discount the aspersions of the alien, they are immediately confronted by a host of domestic scoffers. The appearance and success of the *American Mercury*, the weekly, nay, almost daily, blasts of H. L. Mencken, so deeply stir the Rotarians and Kiwanians that one of the richest chemical companies buys space in his magazine to make fun of the editor. In a milder vein, but perhaps still more ruinous to the counsels of perfection, the *Saturday Review of Literature*, edited by H. S. Canby, steadily undermines naïve valuations of every sort, bringing artistic judgments ever nearer to the test of realism. And still more ruthless in dealing with moss-grown conventions, V. F. Calverton, with too much assurance perhaps, slashes at the preciosities of American art and thought, threatening them all with the cruel touch of economic appraisal. The age of Victorian complacency has closed everywhere; those who are whistling to keep up their courage and deceive their neighbors merely succeed in hoodwinking themselves.

## II

THIS inquisitive wondering about civilization is no fitful fever of a day, likely to pass soon, to be followed by the calm satisfaction of an Indian summer. On the contrary, its emotional sources lie deep in the nature of things. While the doubts and pessimism raised by the World War might pass with the flow of time if the "normalcy" craved by the late President Harding could really be recovered, the prospects for "healing and serenity" are not good and the situation in which the world finds itself is not encouraging to advocates of seraphic peace and benevolence. Although the League of Nations and the inevitabilities of Locarno give promise of a respite, the restlessness of Italy, whose swelling population overflows her narrow borders, the hundred sources of unending friction in the Balkans, the discontent of Germany with a treaty that makes her a guilty criminal and tears from her side six or eight million German citizens, the turmoil of the Orient, and the constant menace of Russia to the imperialist powers of Europe, all tend to keep alive the interest of mankind in the future of modern civilization.

To these are added even more potent irritants, disturbing humanity with threats of destiny. It is not to be supposed that the revolutions in Russia and Italy, flouting as they do the whole bourgeois scheme of things, will pass, if they pass, without leaving scars in the mind of the race. Nor will the antagonism between socialism and capitalism struggling for the possession of the helm of state disappear soon in a wave of brotherly affection. Each school regards the other as the foe of civilization and continually stirs the stream of speculation. Spengler, as he admits in his introduction to "Prussianism and Socialism," derived from that collision the emotions which flowered, through sophistication, into the enormous philosophic pile, "The Decline of the West." And while socialism and capitalism stand face to face, the issue of civilization will abide.

Interwoven with this economic conflict, is the perennial struggle between Catholics and Protestants, the former idealizing the middle ages of papal supremacy—the age of feudalism, agriculture, handicrafts, miracles, and clericalism—and thus assailing capitalism, even where forced to yield to its economic exigencies. Conforming in many respects with the same substantial patterns, is the much discussed conflict between Latin and Nordic cultures—Italy, Spain, and France against Germany, England, and the United States—civilizations essentially agricultural against civilizations essentially industrial, Catholicism against Protestantism, mystery against science, adding thus racial antipathies to national, economic, geographical, and climatic contrasts.

Even if Europe could resolve her conflicts and let the war of the books over civilization die away there in peace and prosperity, the rise of the United States would perhaps keep the old question still open to debate. The passage of America from a provincial, agricultural status to the position of the premier capitalist power in international politics, with a navy hardly second to that of England, is itself an inescapable fact for those who speculate on cultural destinies. American civilization, the full flower of the machine apotheosized, with few traces of feudalism in its make-up, even more than Russia challenges the contemporary régime of Europe, particularly the Latin countries. If once the peasants, farmers, and laborers of the Old World should get it into their heads that more material goods would flow from machinery, science, efficiency, and capitalism triumphant, the result would be the abandonment of whole provinces of the ancient heritage, even in remote districts.

Beyond America lies Asia, presenting a sharp antithesis and challenge to the West. If it were possible to subdue the United States to the sublimated feudo-clerical civilization of Europe through education, cultural transference, and the intermarriage of aristocratic and capitalistic families, Asia would still remain— inscrutable to those who never visited the continent. This does not mean that there is in fact an Oriental civilization to be sharply contrasted with that of the Occident, or that the so-called color antagonism is likely to be a factor in the future of Western civilization; far from it. It just so happens, however, that the Orient is a scene of operation for four western empires, English, Russian, French, and American—the seat of an imperialist collision which will of necessity burn around the world if the friction reaches the point of combustion. Furthermore, the Orient is the home of one first-class power on the Western model, Japan, the only non-Caucasian people that has been able to use steel and gunpowder efficiently in self-defense and is rapidly transforming its feudal civilization into an industrial order. Chinese nationalism cannot find its goal and Japanese economic necessity attain its fruition without disturbing violently one or more of the Western imperial adventurers contending for mastery in the East. These two forces, rather than Gandhi's vain longing for a return to the hand loom and spinning wheel—in defiance of science and machinery—will serve to keep alive indefinitely the interest of the world in the contrast, real and imaginary, between the East and the West.

To these springs of emotion that feed the present concern about the problems of civilization, nationalism rampant adds another. The passion for self-determination, for democracy, which flamed so high during the World War, served to accentuate rather than smooth away the differences between cultures. For many a year, each of the nationalities composing the world's complex of self-governing communities is likely to continue to look upon its own institutions as indicating a certain moral superiority in the possessor. The spirit is very old.

Long ago, a Wahhabee preacher, while praising the people of Riad, to whom he belonged, remarked that the followers of Mohammed were to be divided into seventy-three sects—seventy-two being destined to hell-fire and only one to heaven, and then added in solemn measure: "And that, by the mercy of God, are we the people of Riad." In a tone less theological but with an assurance equally firm, the historian Macaulay informed mankind in 1835 that the English "have become the greatest and most highly civilised people that ever the world saw, . . . have produced a literature which may boast of works not inferior to the noblest which Greece has bequeathed to us, have discovered the laws which regulate the motions of the heavenly bodies, have speculated with exquisite subtilty on the operations of the human mind, have become the acknowledged leaders of the human race in the career of political improvement."

Reverting to the religious strain of the Wahhabee, William II, a grandson of Queen Victoria, came to the conclusion that pre-eminence lay elsewhere. "God would never have taken such great pains with our German Fatherland and its people," said William in 1905, "if He had not been preparing us for something still greater. We are the salt of the earth."

Across the Rhine in France, of course, this gospel was not accepted. On the contrary, innumerable patriotic French writers have contended, with kindred emotions, that France was really the mother of modern civilization, the home of liberty, soulfulness, and artistic sensibilities. "Une cuisine et une politesse!

Oui, les deux signes de vieille civilisation et de mentalité d'élite!
Qui, en dehors des Chinois et des Français, peut se vanter de les
arborer? Les Italiens? Peut-être. Les Anglais? Ils se saoulent
et gardent leur casquette sur la tête devant une femme. Les
Americains? Les Allemands? Il n'en est pas question."

Nor do high American authorities give their assent to the creed
of William II. Quite recently, the committee on citizenship
formed by the American Bar Association put into its credo for
the salvation of America an article as follows: "I believe that
we Americans have the best government that has ever been
created—the freest and the most just for all people; . . . that as
an American citizen the Constitution of the United States ought
to be as actual a part of my life and my religion as the Sermon on
the Mount."

If each nationalistic variant on modern civilization is vaunted
as the best, then how can the students of destiny hope to find any
rest from unceasing labors?

### III

ANXIETY about the values and future of civilization is real. It
has crept out of the cloister and appears in the forum and market
place. It will not pass; it will endure and increase. Forces as
potent as the struggle for existence—economic, racial, and nationalistic—will continue to feed it. But while the controversy becomes more intense, the very diversity of the collisions that keep
it alive lends confusion to all discussions bearing on the nature and
destiny of civilization. So while our library shelves sink under
the weight of books on the subject, ambiguity rather than clarity
and frankness mark the trend of their arguments. Civilization,
like politics, makes strange bedfellows.

In various places in Europe, for example, we find Marxian communists, Roman Catholics, and violent Chauvinists united in condemning the megalopolitan civilization of modern capitalism,
all for different reasons, and certain to divide savagely on the nature and work of the order which they would substitute for it.
In Germany, the Nationalists turn against science, machine, and
industrialism all the sentiments, religious, patriotic, and class,

that spring from their practical situation. In England and America, a school of anti-imperialists, disgusted with the slums and sooty towns of the machine, imagine that the kingdom of heaven must be in the Orient and, under the guise of Oriental wisdom, assail the evils of capitalism at home.

This psychology, of course, is not new.  The account of Germany which Tacitus gave to the Romans nearly two thousand years ago may have been designed to hold up the mirror to Roman vices rather than to present a true picture of the tribes beyond the Rhine.   The war which Rousseau waged on the civilization of science and reason was conducted in the name of nature, the noble savage, and agriculture. When all the metaphysics and verbiage of Spengler's "Decline of the West" are put aside and the heart of the matter is revealed, it becomes evident that the author is really aiming to glorify an agricultural, as contrasted with a metropolitan, civilization.  What really gives him distress and causes him to think that the West is declining is the fact that the city is overcoming the country.  "In place of a people true to type," he says, "springing from the soil and reared on it, there now appears a new kind of nomad, loosely co-operating with instable and changing masses, the parasitical city-dweller, without traditions, without religion, concerned only with matters of fact; clever, sterile, and profoundly contemptuous of the countryman, in particular that highest type of agriculturalist, the country gentleman." Stripped of rhetorical paint, this merely reflects the grudge of the Prussian landed-proprietor against the Berlin or Hamburg banker, merchant, and manufacturer.

Nor is the confusion that exists among the contestants over the merits of particular "cultures" cleared up by those who speak either glibly or profoundly about the downfall of civilizations. Just what happened when Rome "fell" is nowhere clearly set forth in the immortal pages of Gibbon.  It is true, he shows us the unitary state (if a state ever beset by social war deserves the name) dissolving and great artists in letters giving place to sophists and stylists; but whether Roman civilization perished or merely passed over into the next period he leaves for the scholars to debate; whether the masses of the Roman empire, even those upstanding Roman citizens who lived like rabbits in the slums of the Eternal City and were sustained by bread and circuses, were happier, stronger, wiser, and nobler than the people of the so-called "dark-ages" which followed the blaze of Augustan days is nowhere made plain by the philosopher of London and Lausanne.

And it must be confessed that the case presented by Spengler is not much better on the side of explications. He does, no doubt, speak of the coming "transition from constitutional systems to the informal sway of individuals," of "wars of annihilation," of "imperialism," and of "primitive human conditions thrusting themselves upward into high civilized modes of living"; but just how this represents a "decline" and why it presents features more alarming than those of the ages past cannot be discerned from the text of his argument.

## IV

GIVEN the liveliness of the present discussion about civilization and the confusion that reigns among those engaged in inquiries respecting the subject, it seems worth while and pertinent to the thinking of our age to take stock, to clarify our notions by definitions and specifications, to invite those who talk with facility about it to deliver a bill of particulars. Such is the purpose of this book.

At the outset, certain questions seem relevant. What is meant intrinsically by the contrast between Western and Oriental civilizations? By the contrast between the modern, mediæval, and classical civilizations? What is "the West" that is threatened with a decline? What does a decline imply in terms of population, economy, art, government, literature, and life in general? Is the assumption supported by data or is it a mere hypothesis born of temperament and certain psychological situations induced by outward events such as defeats, disappointments, and adversities in general? If the decline is really imminent, can anything be done about it? If not, must philosophy despair and assume that the universe is meaningless, that the force which carries nations to high pinnacles will shortly become bankrupt itself?

Conceivably a master mind, a modern Aristotle, equipped with all the sciences of the time, could attempt the solution of this riddle, but the intense specialization of our age, the enormous mass of accumulated knowledge precludes any such unitary treatment. Hence the concurrence of many minds is necessary if any progress is to be made.

Beyond yielding the fruits of co-operation, such concurrence itself may be a contribution of some consequence to civilization. "The various forms of intellectual activity which together make up the culture of an age," remarks Walter Pater, "move for the most part from different starting points and by unconnected roads. . . . There come, however, from time to time, eras of more favorable conditions, in which the thoughts of men draw nearer together than is their wont and the many interests of the intellectual world combine in one complete type of culture. The fifteenth century in Italy is one of these happier eras, and what is sometimes said of the age of Pericles is true of that of Lorenzo: it is an age productive in personalities, many-sided, centralized, complete. Here artists and philosophers and those whom the action of the world has elevated and made keen do not live in isolation but breathe a common air and catch light and heat from each other's thought. There is a spirit of general elevation and enlightenment in which all alike communicate."

If Pater's thesis is sound, and it seems to be, then a search for the essence of civilization ought to advance all the arts of the good life, reduce the social friction based upon misconceptions, illuminate the roads before us, and serve humanity in its struggle to get possession of the helm. A symposium on civilization, therefore, appears to be timely and it might possibly be a contribution of something to itself, if that is not an incredible paradox.

But a symposium may readily end in confusion rather than clarification, darkness rather than light, especially if no target is set up to give a general direction to the work of the participants. There is truth in the saying of the poet that everything written is in the nature of a confession. Nothing is more futile than a pretense to a kind of divine omniscience that leads readers by secret passages to predetermined ends.

The purpose of this book is, therefore, publicly admitted. It is not designed to bolster up the arguments of any economic, racial, religious, or nationalist school. It attempts to set forth clearly indubitable facts relevant to the consideration of the subject in hand. It proceeds from the conviction that history reveals no golden age in the past and the additional belief that the achievements of the past three hundred years, good and bad, are not the deeds of willful men and women who have perverted the perfection offered by the middle ages. While laying a firm emphasis on certain aspects of the problems before us, the book is not dominated by any facile optimism. It frankly concedes the force of numerous items in the bill of indictment lodged by critics against modern civilization—its darker and more dangerous features—without condemning it wholesale as a terrible error made through the neglect of the superlative wisdom of other times and places. At any rate, destiny seems to point to the future—not to the past.

v

WITH these preliminary admissions duly made, let us begin the discussion by recalling that a standard dictionary defines civilization as "the state of being reclaimed from the rudeness of savage life and advanced in the arts and learning." In origin, it derives immediately from the Latin word *civitas*, meaning in its concrete usage the rights and privileges of a Roman citizen, and figuratively a body of citizens, the state, commonwealth, or city. Now the rights and privileges of Roman citizens, as over against slaves and subject peoples, were realistic and economic, and it is of more than passing interest to note that in its deeper roots *civitas* comes from *quies*, repose from labor, perhaps that leisure enjoyed by ruling orders. Aside from all philological subtleties, civilization in its strict modern sense includes all these implements, devices, and practices by which men and women lift themselves above savages—the whole economic order, the system of leisure built upon it, the employment of that leisure, and all manifestations of religion, beauty, and appreciation.

Since the substructure of any civilization is the material fabric that frees mankind from the status of the savage, it follows that every civilization must depend in a large measure upon its geographical environment—rivers, mountains, seas, and natural resources—the state of its tools and industries, the occupations of the people, and the organization of society for the direction of industry. Civilization, therefore, is not a garment that can be put on or off by intellectuals at pleasure, transferred from a Frenchman or an Englishman to a Matabele or Zulu over night. Except for some of the minor decorative arts, a civilization cannot be borrowed without reproducing the accompanying economic order. And economic orders are not arrangements which nations can take on or discard at will without reference to their geographical situation or the competition of their neighbors. Japan, for example, if she is to survive, has no choice but the extensive adoption of the machinery and science employed by her rivals, and with that adoption go its social and artistic habiliments.

If this pattern of thought conforms with the facts, then the classification of civilizations by mere reference to longitude or to chronology is hardly short of absurd. The cultural status of a people is not determined by the element of time or by its position east or west of Greenwich. Many primitive societies have remained in substantially the same condition for thousands of years; where the modes of acquiring a living remain practically static, civilization preserves the same social designs. In the backward places of Europe are to be found numerous village communities which have carried forward into the twentieth century the whole cultural outfit of the middle ages. Hence the distinction between modern and mediæval civilizations, considered as the simple products of time, is intrinsically without meaning.

Nor is the geographical case much better—making astronomy rather than time the basis of calculation. In origin, the terms East and West are mere references to the dawning sun and its dusky resting place. Realistically considered, China and Japan, when compared with Europe of the fourteenth or fifteenth century, reveal more similarities than contrasts. Indeed early Christian missionaries in the Orient were so struck by the resemblance between Buddhist religious ceremonies and their own that they ascribed the former to the devices of the Devil. No doubt a meticulous scholar can discover many fine points of distinction between the feudalism of Japan and that of mediæval Europe, but for practical purposes the substance of the two orders was the same; the fighting men held the same supremacy in both geographical areas. There were differences between the lines and colors of the castle at Osaka and the castle at Warwick but they were both built of stone, their purposes were fundamentally the same, and the mode of life of their inhabitants strangely alike.

Proceeding from the definition given above and the argument thus sketched, it seems to follow that civilizations, apart from tribal and nomadic orders, when considered intrinsically, fall into three general types:

Agricultural—slave, feudal, peasant, or freehold.
Pre-machine urban—handicraft, mercantile, and
    political capitals.
Mechanical and scientific.

If it be urged that this is merely an economic classification which leaves out of account arts, religion, and learning, the reply is that these things are themselves bent to the order in which they thrive and have meaning and vitality only in relation to their economic substructure. Traces of previous orders no doubt survive or thrust themselves upward into new orders, but they thrive only in so far as they carry with them the soil that originally nourished them. Certainly there are more fundamental resemblances between the culture of a peasant in a remote village in Spain and that of a peasant in a remote village of Japan than between the culture of a Christian priest of the upper Pyrenees and that of a Baptist clergyman in a thriving manufacturing town in Illinois. A Buddhist monk from Horiugi would feel perfectly at home with a Catholic monk from Ravenna; but neither of them would enjoy the hospitality or approve the religion of a Methodist parson in Zenith.

WHAT is called Western or modern civilization by way of contrast with the civilization of the Orient or mediæval times is at bottom a civilization that rests upon machinery and science as distinguished from one founded on agriculture or handicraft commerce. It is in reality a technological civilization. It is only about two hundred years old, and, far from shrinking in its influence, is steadily extending its area into agriculture as well as handicrafts. If the records of patent offices, the statistics of production, and the reports of laboratories furnish evidence worthy of credence, technological civilization, instead of showing signs of contraction, threatens to overcome and transform the whole globe.

Considered with respect to its intrinsic nature, technological civilization presents certain precise characteristics. It rests fundamentally on power-driven machinery which transcends the physical limits of its human directors, multiplying indefinitely the capacity for the production of goods. Science in all its branches —physics, chemistry, biology, and psychology—is the servant and upholder of this system. The day of crude invention being almost over, continuous research in the natural sciences is absolutely necessary to the extension of the machine and its market, thus forcing continuously the creation of new goods, new processes, and new modes of life. As the money for learning comes in increasing proportions from taxes on industry and gifts by captains of capitalism, a steady growth in scientific endowments is to be expected, and the scientific curiosity thus aroused and stimulated will hardly fail to expand—and to invade all fields of thought with a technique of ever-refining subtlety. Affording the demand for the output of industry are the vast populations of the globe; hence mass production and marketing are inevitable concomitants of the machine routine.

For the present, machine civilization is associated with capitalism, under which large-scale production has risen to its present stage, but machine civilization is by no means synonymous with capitalism—that ever-changing scheme of exploitation.

While the acquisitive instinct of the capitalist who builds factories and starts mass production is particularly emphasized by economists and is, no doubt, a factor of immense moment, it must
not be forgotten that the acquisitive passion of the earth's multitudes for the goods, the comforts, and the securities of the classes
is an equal, if not a more important, force, and in any case is
likely to survive capitalism as we know it.  Few choose nakedness when they can be clothed, the frosts of winter when they
can be warm, or the misery of bacterial diseases when sanitation
is offered to them.  In fact, the ascetics and flagellants of the
world belong nowhere in the main stream of civilization—and
are of dubious utility and service in any civilization.

Though machine civilization has here been treated as if it
were an order, it in fact differs from all others in that it is highly
dynamic, containing within itself the seeds of constant reconstruction.  Everywhere agricultural civilizations of the pre-
machine age have changed only slowly with the fluctuations of
markets, the fortunes of governments, and the vicissitudes of
knowledge, keeping their basic institutions intact from century
to century.  Pre-machine urban civilizations have likewise retained their essential characteristics through long lapses of time.
But machine civilization based on technology, science, invention,
and expanding markets must of necessity change—and rapidly.
The order of steam is hardly established before electricity invades
it; electricity hardly gains a fair start before the internal combustion engine overtakes it.  There has never been anywhere in the
world any order comparable with it, and all analogies drawn from
the middle ages, classical antiquity, and the Orient are utterly
inapplicable to its potentialities, offering no revelations as to its
future.

### VII

GRANTED that these essential characteristics of so-called Western
civilization, namely, its mechanical and scientific foundations are
realistic, is it a mere "flash in the pan," a historical accident destined to give way to some other order based upon entirely different modes of life, lifting mankind "above the rudeness of the

savage"? Now, if the term "decline" in this connection means anything concrete, it signifies the gradual or rapid abandonment of the material modes of production prevailing in any particular age and the habits and arts associated with them. Conceivably the Prussianism of the Hohenzollerns described so well in Spengler's "Prussianism and Socialism," may decline—is declining. It is highly probable that the petty tenure system of the French peasantry, the now sadly diluted aristocracy inherited from the eighteenth century, the church of little mysteries and miracles may decline, but these things are not the peculiar characteristics of the West. They are the remnants of the agricultural complex which the machine is everywhere steadily subduing. The real question is this: can and will machine society "decline"?

It is generally agreed among historians that the decay of agriculture, owing to the lack of scientific management and fertilization, was one of the chief causes for the breakdown of the Roman state. Is it to be supposed that the drive of the masses of mankind for machine-made goods will fail, that large-scale production will be abandoned, that the huge literature of natural science will disappear in the same fashion as most of the literature of ancient Egypt, that the ranks of scientific men will cease in time to be recruited, that the scientific power to meet new situations will fail? An affirmative answer requires a great deal of hardihood. The scientific order is not recruited from a class, such as the patricians of ancient Rome; nor is scientific knowledge the monopoly of a caste likely to dissolve. Unless all visible signs deceive us, there is no reason for supposing that either machinery or science will disappear or even dwindle to insignificance. And they are the basis of the modern civilization.

If Western civilization does not break down from such internal causes, is there good reason for supposing that any of the races now inhabiting Asia or Africa could overcome the machine order of the West by any process, peaceful or warlike, without themselves adopting the technical apparatus of that order? No doubt, some of them are already borrowing various features of machine society, but slowly and with indifferent success. The most efficient of them, the Japanese, still rely largely upon the West for a substantial part of their mechanical outfit—for inventiveness and creative mechanical skill. Unless there is a material decline in Western technology—and no evidence of such a slump is now in sight—then it may be safely contended that none of the agricultural civilizations of Asia or Africa will ever catch up with the scientific development of the West. As things stand at present, none of them gives any promise of being able to overrun the West as the conquerors of Rome overran the provinces of that Empire. Certainly there is not likely to be, in any future that we can foresee, such an equality of armaments as existed between the best of the Roman legions and the forces of their conquerors. Hence the downfall of the West through conquest may fairly be ruled out of the possibilities of the coming centuries. If, in due time, the East smashes the West on the battlefield, it will be because the East has completely taken over the technology of the West, gone it one better, and thus become Western in civilization. In that case machine civilization will not disappear but will make a geographical shift.

Defining civilization narrowly in terms of letters and art, are the probabilities of a "decline" more numerous? Here we approach a more debatable, more intangible, topic. With reference to letters, taking into account the evidence of the last fifty years, there is no sign of a decay—at all events, a decay like that which occurred between the first and the sixth centuries in Roman history. Indeed, there are many cautious critics who tell us that the writers of the past hundred years, with the machine system at a high pitch, may be compared in number, competence, and power without fear with the writers of any century since the appearance of the Roman grand style. Granted that we have no Horace, Shakespeare, or Goethe, we may reasonably answer that literature of their manner has little meaning for a civilization founded on a different basis. Considered in relation to their environment rather than some fictitious absolute, the best of modern writers, it may well be argued, rank with the best of the middle ages and antiquity. If poetry sinks in the scale and tragedy becomes comical, it may be because the mythology upon which they feed is simply foreign to the spirit of the machine age—not because there has been a dissolution of inherited mental powers. The imagination of an Einstein, a Bohr, or a Millikan may well transcend that of a Milton or a Virgil. Who is to decide?

The case of the arts is on a similar footing. For the sake of the argument, it may be conceded that the machine age has produced nothing comparable with the best of the painting, sculpture, and architecture of antiquity and the middle ages. What does that signify? Anything more than a decline in the arts appropriate to an agricultural and market-city era? The machine age is young. As yet it can hardly be said to have created an art of its own, although there are signs of great competence, if not genius, about us—signs of a new art appropriate to speed, mechanics, motion, railway stations, factories, office buildings, and public institutions. Using the lowest common denominator in the reckoning, there is no evidence of a decay in artistic power such as appears in the contrast between the Pantheon of Agrippa and the rude churches of Saxon England. To say that the modern age has produced no ecclesiastical architecture comparable with that of the middle ages is to utter a judgment as relevant to our situation as a statement that the mediæval times can show no aqueducts or baths equal to the noblest structures of pagan Rome. It may be that the machine age will finally prove to be poor in artistic genius—a debatable point—but it can hardly be said that it has produced its typical art, from which a decline may be expected.

Passing to a more tangible subject, is it possible that machine civilization may be destroyed by internal revolutions or civil wars such as have often wrecked great states in the past? That such disturbances will probably arise in the future from time to time cannot be denied, and the recent Bolshevik revolution in Russia is often cited as a warning to contemporary statesmen. If the revolutions of antiquity be taken as illustrations, it must be pointed out that the analogies are to be used with extreme care in all applications to the machine age. When the worst has been said about the condition of the industrial proletariat, it must be conceded that as regards material welfare, knowledge, social consideration, and political power, it is far removed from the proletariat of Rome or the slaves of a more remote antiquity. The kind of servile revolt that was so often ruinous in Greece and Rome is hardly possible in a machine civilization, even if economic distress were to pass anything yet experienced since the eighteenth century. The most radical of the modern proletariat want more of the good things of civilization—not a destruction of technology. If the example of Russia be pressed as relevant, the reply is that Russia possessed not a machine, but an agricultural civilization of the crudest sort; peasant soldiers supplied the storm troops of the November revolution, and the Bolsheviki are straining every nerve to maintain their position by promising the peasants and urban dwellers that the benefits of a machine order will surely come. There will be upheavals in machine civilizations, no doubt, and occasional dictatorships like that in the United States between 1861 and 1865, but the triumph of a party dedicated to a deliberate return to pre-machine agriculture with its low standards of life, its diseases, and its illiteracy is beyond the imagination.

Finally, we must face the assertion that wars among the various nations of machine civilization may destroy the whole order. Probably terrible wars will arise and prove costly in blood and treasure, but it is a strain upon the speculative faculties to conceive of any conflict that could destroy the population and mechanical equipment of the Western world so extensively that human vitality and science could not restore economic prosperity and even improve upon the previous order. According to J. S. Mill, the whole mechanical outfit of a capitalistic country can be reproduced in about ten years. Hence the prospect of repeated and costly wars in the future need not lead us to the pessimistic view that suicide is to be the fate of machine civilization. We may admit the reality of the perils ahead without adopting the counsel of despair. If Europe and America were absolutely devastated, Japan with her present equipment in libraries, laboratories, and technology could begin the work of occupying the vacant areas, using the machine process in the operation.

For the reasons thus adduced it may be inferred: that modern civilization founded on science and the machine will not decline after the fashion of older agricultural civilizations; that analogies drawn from ages previous to technology are inapplicable; that according to signs on every hand technology promises to extend its area and intensify its characteristics; that it will afford the substance with which all who expect to lead and teach in the future must reckon.

VIII

SUCH appears to be the promise of the long future, if not the grand destiny of what we call modern civilization—the flexible framework in which the human spirit must operate during the coming centuries. Yet this view by no means precludes the idea that the machine system, as tested by its present results, presents shocking evils and indeed terrible menaces to the noblest faculties of the human race. By the use of material standards for measuring achievement, it is in danger of developing a kind of ignorant complacency that would make Phidias, Sophocles, Horace, St. Augustine, Dante, Michelangelo, Shakespeare, Lord Bacon, Newton, Goethe, Ruskin, and Emerson appear to be mere trifling parasites as compared with Lord Beaverbrook, Hugo Stinnes, John Pierpont Morgan, and Henry Ford. To deny the peril that lies in any such numerical morality would be a work of supererogation. More perilous still is the concentration on the production of goods that will sell quickly at the best price the traffic will bear and fall to pieces quickly—mass production of cheap goods—rather than concentration on the manufacture and exchange of commodities with the finest intrinsic values capable of indefinite endurance. What the creed of "give as little as you can for as much as you can get" will do to the common honesty of mankind, if followed blindly for centuries, can readily be imagined. Finally, it must be admitted that the dedication of the engines of state, supported by a passionate and uninformed chauvinism, to the promotion and sale of machine-made goods is creating zones of international rivalry likely to flame up in wars more vast and destructive than any yet witnessed.

To consider for the moment merely the domestic aspects of the question, the machine civilization is particularly open to attack from three sides.

On æsthetic grounds, it has been assailed for nearly a hundred years, England, the classical home of the industrial revolution, being naturally enough the mother of the severest critics—Ruskin, Carlyle, Kingsley, and Matthew Arnold. The chief article in their indictment, perhaps, is the contention that men who work with machinery are not creative, joyous, or free, but are slaves to the monotonous routine of the inexorable wheel. In a sense it is true that, in the pre-machine age, each craftsman had a certain leeway in shaping his materials with his tools and that many a common artisan produced articles of great beauty.

Yet the point can be easily overworked. Doubtless the vast majority of mediæval artisans merely followed designs made by master workmen. This is certainly true of artisans in the Orient today. With respect to the mass of mankind, it is safe to assume that the level of monotony on which labor is conducted under the machine régime is by and large not lower but higher than in the handicraft, servile, or slave systems of the past. Let anyone who has doubts on this matter compare the life of laborers on the latifundia of Rome or in the cities of modern China with that of the workers in by far the major portion of machine industries. Those who are prepared to sacrifice the standard of living for the millions to provide conditions presumably favorable to the creative arts must assume a responsibility of the first magnitude.

Indeed, it is not certain, so primitive as yet are the beginnings of machine civilization, that there can be no substitute for the handicrafts as æsthetic stimulants, assuming that mechanical industry is not favorable to the creative life. The machine régime does not do away with the necessity for designing or reduce the opportunities for the practice of that craft: it transfers the operation from the shop to the laboratory; and it remains to be seen whether great æsthetic powers will not flourish after the first storm of capitalism has passed. In any case, it must be admitted that the "cheap and nasty" character of machine-made goods, so marked everywhere, may really be due to the profit-making lust and the desire of the multitude to have imitations of the gewgaws loved by the patricians, not to the inherent nature of machine industry. Possibly what is lost in the merits of individual objects of beauty may be more than offset by city and community planning, realizing new types of æsthetic ideals on a vast, democratic basis. Certainly the worst of the æsthetic offences created by the machine—the hideous factory town—can be avoided by intelligent co-operative action, as the garden-city movement faintly foreshadows. In a hundred years the coal-consuming engine may be as obsolete as the Dodo and the Birminghams, Pittsburghs, and Essens of the modern world live only in the records of the historians. However this may be, the æsthetes of the future will have to work within the limitations and opportunities created by science and the machine, directed, it may be hoped, by a more intelligent economy and nobler concepts of human values.

Frequently affiliated with æsthetic criticism of the machine and science is the religious attack. With endless reiteration, the charge is made that industrial civilization is materialistic. In reply, the scornful might say, "Well, what of it?" But the issue deserves consideration on its merits, in spite of its illusive nature. As generally used, the term "materialistic" has some of the qualities of moonshine; it is difficult to grasp. It is the fashion of certain Catholic writers to call Protestantism materialistic, on account of its emphasis on thrift and business enterprise—a fashion which some radicals have adopted: Max Weber in Germany and R. H. Tawney in England, for example. With something akin to the same discrimination, Oswald Spengler calls all England materialistic, governed by pecuniary standards—as contrasted with old Prussia where "duty," "honor," and "simple piety" reigned supreme. More recently, André Siegfried, following a hundred English critics, with Matthew Arnold in the lead, has found materialism to be one of the chief characteristics of the United States, as contrasted with the richer and older civilizations of Europe, particularly France. And Gandhi consigns every one of them—England, Prussia, France, and America—to the same bottomless pit of industrial materialism. When all this verbiage is sifted, it usually means that the charge arises from emotions that have little or no relation to religion or philosophy—from the quarrels of races, sects, and nations.

If religion is taken in a crude, anthropomorphic sense, filling the universe with gods, spirits, and miraculous feats, then beyond question the machine and science are the foes of religion. If it is materialistic to disclose the influence of technology and environment in general upon humanity, then perhaps the machine and science are materialistic. But it is one of the ironies of history that science has shown the shallowness of the old battle between materialist and spiritist and through the mouths of physicists has confessed that it does not know what matter and force are. Matter is motion; motion is matter; both elude us, we are told. Doubtless science does make short shrift of a thousand little mysteries once deemed as essential to Christianity as were the thousand minor gods to the religion of old Japan, but for these little mysteries it has substituted a higher and sublimer mystery.

To descend to the concrete, is the prevention of disease by sanitation more materialistic than curing it by touching saints' bones? Is feeding the multitude by mass production more materialistic than feeding it by a miracle? Is the elimination of famines by a better distribution of goods more materialistic than prevention by the placation of the rain gods? At any rate, it is not likely that science and machinery will be abandoned because the theologian (who seldom refuses to partake of their benefits) wrings his hands and cries out against materialism. After all, how can he consistently maintain that Omnipotent God ruled the world wisely and well until the dawn of the modern age and abandoned it to the Evil One because Henry VIII or Martin Luther quarrelled with the Pope and James Watt invented the steam engine?

Arising, perhaps, from the same emotional source as æsthetic and religious criticisms, is the attack on the machine civilization as lacking in humanitarianism. Without commenting on man's inhumanity to man as an essential characteristic of the race, we may fairly ask on what grounds can anyone argue that the masses were more humanely treated in the agricultural civilization of antiquity or the middle ages than in the machine order of modern times. Tested by the mildness of its laws (brutal as many of them are), by its institutions of care and benevolence, by its death rate (that tell-tale measurement of human welfare), by its standards of life, and by every conceivable measure of human values, machine civilization, even in its present primitive stage, need fear no comparison with any other order on the score of general well-being.

Under the machine and science, the love of beauty, the sense of mystery, and the motive of compassion—sources of æsthetics, religion, and humanism—are not destroyed. They remain essential parts of our nature. But the conditions under which they must operate, the channels they must take, the potentialities of their action are all changed. These ancient forces will become powerful in the modern age just in the proportion that men and women accept the inevitability of science and the machine, understand the nature of the civilization in which they must work, and turn their faces resolutely to the future.

## IX

THE chapters which follow, in discussing the various aspects of modern civilization, develop more minutely the view thus presented and expand its implications in particular fields. On the other hand, while recognizing the validity of the general argument here advanced, they reflect an independent and critical spirit. If the tone of the volume seems positive, the defence may be offered that precision in error is useful to those who search for truth. At all events, by their very sharpness, the lines cut through the controversy over civilization will make it easier for the readers to share in the explorations of the symposium.

# I—THE CIVILIZATIONS OF THE EAST AND THE WEST

## By Hu Shih

IN RECENT years the despondent mood of a number of European writers has led to the revival of such old myths as the bankruptcy of the material civilization of the West and the superiority of the spiritual civilization of the Oriental nations. When I was in Germany last year, a German savant most solemnly assured me that the civilization of the East was based on spiritual principles. "In the East," said my enthusiastic friend, "even *souls* are selected on the basis of moral fitness. For does not the doctrine of the transmigration of souls imply the idea of moral selection?" Although these expressions represent nothing more than the pathological mentality of war-stricken Europe, they have already had the unfortunate effect of gratifying the vanity of Oriental apologists and thereby strengthening the hand of reaction in the East. In the West, too, one could see, as I have seen during my recent travels, that such loose thinking was leading not a few people away from a proper understanding of their own civilization which is fast becoming the world civilization. It is in the hope of furnishing a new point of view and a new basis of discussion that I now offer these few reflections on the civilizations of the East and the West.

I

As a true Chinese, I must begin with Confucius. According to Confucius, all implements of civilization are spiritual in origin: they all came from "ideas." "When conceived, they are called ideas. When materially embodied, they are called implements. When instituted for general use, they are called forms or patterns. When wrought into the everyday life of all the people, they marvel at them and call them the work of the gods." Confucius cited many examples to illustrate this point of view. Man saw wood floating on water and invented canoes and ships; he saw wood submerged under water and, caring for the preservation of the dead bodies of his parents, invented coffins and tombs. He saw rain fall from the heavens and, thinking probably of the work of time obliterating all traces of human memory, invented writing to take the place of knotted cords.

Needless to say, this view of Confucius was supported by Plato and Aristotle in the West. Human tools and institutions had their origin in the "ideas" or ideal patterns which Aristotle called the "formal causes." Confucius and Plato and Aristotle lived in those good old days when the human mind was not yet troubled by the mediæval dualism of matter and spirit and was therefore able to recognize the ideality underlying the material embodiment of human inventions.

Indeed there is no such thing as a purely material civilization. Every tool of civilization is produced by human intelligence making use of the matter and energy in the natural world for the satisfaction of a want, a desire, an æsthetic feeling or an intellectual curiosity. A clay pot is no more material than a love lyric; nor is St. Paul's Cathedral less material than the Woolworth Building. Indeed when man first made fire by accidentally drilling wood, the invention was regarded as such a spiritual thing as to be attributed to one of the greatest gods. In the East, all the legendary kings of China were not priest-philosophers, but inventors. Such, for example, were Sui-jen, the discoverer of fire, You-tsao, the first builder of houses, and Shen-nung, the first teacher of agriculture and medicine.

Our forefathers were quite right in deifying the creators of tools. Man is a tool-making animal, and it is tool-making which constitutes civilization. The invention of fire created a new epoch in the history of human civilization; agriculture, another; the invention of writing, a third; printing, a fourth. The great religions of the world may justly claim the credit for submerging the whole civilized world from the China Sea to the British Isles underneath the deluge of mediævalism.   But it was the invention of the telescope and the steam-engine and the discovery of electricity and radio activity that have made the modern world what it is to-day.   And if the priests of the Mediæval Age were justly canonized as saints, Galileo, Watt, Stephenson, Morse, Bell, Edison, and Ford certainly deserve to be honored as gods and enshrined with Prometheus and Cadmus.   They represent that which is most divine in man, namely, that creative intelligence which provides implements and makes civilization possible.

The civilization of a race is simply the sum-total of its achievement in adjusting itself to its environment.   Success or failure in that adjustment depends upon the ability of the race to use intelligence for the invention of necessary and effective tools.   Advancement in civilization depends upon the improvement of tools. Such names as the Stone Age, the Bronze Age, the Iron Age and the Steam and Electricity Age tell the tale of the development of civilization.   And what is true of the historical development of civilization, is no less true of the geographical distribution of the different civilizations.   The difference between the Eastern and Western civilizations is primarily a difference in the tools used. The West has during the last two hundred years moved far ahead of the East merely because certain Western nations have been able to devise new tools for the conquest of nature and for the multiplication of the power to do work.   The East, whence have come a number of the epoch-making tools of ancient civilization, has failed to carry on that great tradition and is left behind in the stage of manual labor while the Western world has long entered the age of steam and electricity.

This, then, is the real difference between the Oriental and Western civilizations.   The Oriental civilization is built primarily on human labor as the source of power whereas the modern civilization of the West is built on the basis of the power of machinery. As one of my American friends has put it, "each man, woman and child in America possesses from twenty-five to thirty mechanical slaves, while it is estimated that each man, woman and child in China has at his command but three quarters of one mechanical slave." [1]   An American engineer has stated the case almost in the same language:   "Every person in the United States has thirty-five invisible slaves working for him. . . . The American workman is not a wage slave, but a boss of a considerable force, whether he realizes it or not." [2]   Herein lies the real explanation of the difference between the two civilizations.   It is a difference in degree which in the course of time has almost amounted to a difference in kind.

II

IN JULY, 1926, I arrived at Harbin, in Northern Manchuria, on my way to Europe.   The modern city of Harbin was formerly a Russian Concession which grew up from a small trading centre into what is now called the "Shanghai of North China."   With the development of the Russian Concession, there has grown up, a few miles away, the native city of Harbin which was once only a group of peasant villages.   While I was touring through the city, I was struck by one interesting fact: whereas practically all the vehicles of locomotion in the native city were jinrickshas, or carriages pulled by human power, no 'ricksha was allowed to operate in the former Russian City which, though now under Chinese administration, still retained much of Russian influence and tradition.   Transportation and travelling in the modern city of Harbin were by tramways and taxicabs; 'rickshas carrying passengers from the native city must leave without a fare.

Here I made my great discovery in modern geography—I discovered the borderline between the Eastern and Western civilizations.   The city of Harbin separates the East from the West by separating the jinricksha (man-power-carriage) civilization from the motor-car civilization!

Let all apologists for the spiritual civilization of the East reflect on this.   What spirituality is there in a civilization which tolerates such a terrible form of human slavery as the 'ricksha

[1] Julean Arnold, "Some Bigger Issues in China's Problems," a booklet soon to be published by the Commercial Press, Shanghai.

[2] Thomas T. Read, "The American Secret," *The Atlantic Monthly*, March, 1927.

coolie? Do we seriously believe that there can be any spiritual life left in those poor human beasts of burden who run and toil and sweat under that peculiar bondage of slavery which knows neither the minimum wage nor any limit of working hours? Do we really believe that the life of a 'ricksha coolie is more spiritual or more moral than that of the American workman who rides to and from his work in his own motor-car, who takes his whole family outing and picnicking on Sundays in distant parks and woods, who listens to the best music of the land on the radio almost for no cost, and whose children are educated in schools equipped with the most modern library and laboratory facilities?

It is only when one has fully realized what misery and acute suffering the life of 'ricksha-pulling entails and what effects it produces on the bodily health of those human beasts of burden—it is only then that one will be truly and religiously moved to bless the Hargreaveses, the Cartwrights, the Watts, the Fultons, the Stephensons, and the Fords who have devised machines to do the work for man and relieve him from much of the brutal suffering to which his Oriental neighbor is still subject.

Herein, therefore, lies the real spirituality of the material civilization, of mechanical progress *per se*. Mechanical progress means the use of human intelligence to devise tools and machines to multiply the working ability and productivity of man so that he may be relieved from the fate of toiling incessantly with his unaided hands, feet, and back without being able to earn a bare subsistence, and so that he may have enough time and energy left to seek and enjoy the higher values which civilization can offer him. Where man has to sweat blood in order to earn the lowest kind of livelihood, there is little *life* left, letting alone civilization. A civilization to be worthy of its name must be built upon the foundation of material progress. As one of China's statesmen said twenty-six centuries ago, "when food and clothing are sufficiently provided for, honor and disgrace can be distinguished; and when granaries are full, the people will know good manners." This is not to drag in the so-called economic interpretation of history: it is simple commonsense. Picture a civilization where boys and girls and old women with bamboo baskets tied to their backs and with pointed sticks in hand, flock to every dumping place of garbage and search every heap of refuse for a possible torn piece of rag or a half-burnt piece of coal. How can we expect a moral and spiritual civilization to grow up in such an atmosphere?

Then people may point to the religious life in those regions where the material civilization is low. I shall not discuss those Oriental religions whose highest deities appear on roadsides in the shape of human sex organs. I shall only ask: "What spirituality is there, let us say, in the old beggar-woman who dies in the direst destitution, but who dies while still mumbling, '*Nama Amita Buddha!*' and in the clear conviction that she will surely enter that blissful paradise presided over by the Amita Buddha? Do we earnestly think it moral or spiritual to inculcate in that beggar-woman a false belief which shall so hypnotize her as to make her willingly live and die in such dire conditions where she ought not to have been had she been born in a different civilization?"

No! A thousand times No! All those hypnotic religions belong to an age when man had reached senility and felt himself impotent in coping with the forces of nature. Therefore he gave up the fight in despair and, like the disappointed fox in the ancient fable who declared the grapes sour because he could not reach them, began to console himself and teach the world that wealth and comfort are contemptible and that poverty and misery are something to be proud of. From this it was only a step to the idea that life itself was not worth living and that the only desirable thing was the blissful existence in the world beyond. And when wise men calmly taught these ideas, fanatics went further and practised self-denial, self-torture, and even suicide. In the West, saints prayed, fasted, lived on pillars, and whipped themselves at regular intervals. In mediæval China, monks prayed, fasted, and, feeding themselves daily with fragrant oil and tying their bodies with oiled cloth, gladly burned themselves to death as offerings to some deity of Mahāyāna Buddhism.

It was those religions of defeatism that sank the whole civilized world underneath the universal deluge of Mediævalism. It took over a thousand years for a portion of mankind to emerge from the civilization which glorifies poverty and sanctifies disease, and slowly build up a new civilization which glorifies life and combats poverty as a crime.   As we look around to-day, the religions of the Middle Ages are still there, the churches and cathedrals are still there, the monasteries and nunneries are still there.   How is it that the outlook upon life has so radically changed?   The change has come because in the last two centuries men have hit upon a few key-inventions out of which a vast number of tools and machines have been constructed for the control of the resources and powers in nature.   By means of these machines men have been able to save labor and reduce distance, to fly in the air, tunnel the mountains and sail underneath the deep seas, to enslave lightning to pull our carriages and employ "ether" to deliver our messages throughout the world.   Science and machinery seem to meet no resistance from nature.   Life has become easier and happier, and man's confidence in his own powers has greatly increased.   Man has become the master of himself and of his own destiny.   Thus a revolutionary poet sings:

> *I fight alone, and win or sink,*
> *I need no one to make me free;*
> *I want no Jesus Christ to think*
> *That he could ever die for me.*

Thus the new civilization of the new age has given to men a new religion, the religion of self-reliance as contrasted with the religion of defeatism of the Middle Ages.

### III

WE ARE all children of the past, and the distinctive types of civilization which we find to-day can be best understood in the light of the relationship they bear to their respective mediæval heritage.   The difference between the Eastern and Western civilizations is simply a degree of success or failure in the process of breaking away from the mediæval ideas and institutions which once ruled the whole civilized world.   The modern civilization of the West, as I have tried to show in the preceding paragraphs, represents a higher degree of success in the emancipation from mediævalism than any other cultural group has yet achieved. At the other end of the scale stands the civilization of India which is mediævalism made visible to-day. Between these two poles, we may arrange and grade all the other civilizations of the East.

A comparison between China and Japan will be most instructive in helping to drive home the point we are making. China started her fight against mediæval Buddhism at least twelve centuries ago. With the aid of the humanistic tradition of Confucianism and the naturalistic philosophy of the school of Laotse, China fought a long war against the mediæval religions. Mahāyāna Buddhism was replaced in the eighth century by Chinese Zennism which was only the naturalism of ancient China clothed in Buddhist terminology. By the ninth century, Zennism became iconoclastic and was hardly recognizable as a religious sect. A great revival of the secular philosophy of Confucianism began in the eleventh century. Since that time, Buddhism has gradually died out without a persecution. The Neo-Confucianism which began, naturally enough, as a scholastic philosophy, slowly developed a highly intellectualistic attitude and its slogan became: "Extend your knowledge by going to things and finding the reason thereof." By the middle of the seventeenth century, Chinese scholarship had developed a genuinely scientific method of study and investigation. Every philological reconstruction or textual criticism or historical research must be based upon evidences. With the aid of this new methodology, the scholarship of the last three hundred years became quite scientific and a number of historical sciences, notably philology, textual criticism, higher criticism and archæology reached a high stage of development.

Yet with all this achievement in the humanistic studies and with all the success in the gradual emancipation of philosophical thought from religion, China remains in her backward state where we find her to-day. She has overthrown the mediæval religions, but has not made life easier for the vast majority of the people; she has found a scientific method, but its application has been confined to books and documents; there has been an emancipation of the mind, but there has not been an equivalent subjugation of the material environment to sustain that intellectual emancipation and make it a reality in the ordinary life of the people. The thinkers of the seventeenth century lamented the fact that five hundred years of rational philosophy could not save the country from the fate of destruction by famine and banditry and final subjugation by a barbarian race. Thereupon they turned away from philosophizing and devoted themselves to what they considered to be "useful knowledge." Little did they dream that the three hundred years' diligent and scientific scholarship after them would also turn out to be only a new kind of scholasticism and would prove of little or no value in the salvation and uplifting of the life of the people!

On the other hand, Japan has achieved a modern civilization within a short period of time by an unreserved acceptance of the tools and machines of the Western civilization. When Perry knocked at the gate of Japan, she was deep in her mediæval slumbers. After a short period of resistance, she was forced to throw open her doors to Western influence. In the face of imminent dangers of national humiliation and ruin, she did not trouble about her mediæval religions and feudalistic morals, but went wholeheartedly into the work of equipping herself with all the new weapons of war, vehicles of commerce, machines of production, and methods of organization. In the course of half a century, Japan has not only become one of the greatest powers of the world, but has also solved a number of important problems which neither Buddhistic religion nor Chinese philosophy had been able to solve. Feudalism is gone forever, constitutional government by parliamentary representation has come to stay, and the mediæval religions are being rapidly undermined. Japan was the inventor of the 'ricksha; but to-day in the industrial centres of Yokohama and Tokio the 'ricksha coolie is rapidly disappearing. And his disappearance has not been brought about by the humanitarianism of the native or foreign religions, nor by the good offices of the ladies of the Society for the Prevention of Cruelty to Animals, but only by the advent of the "one-yen-within-the-city" Ford Car. And, with the increase of wealth and prosperity made possible by the mechanical and industrial civilization, the indigenous artistic genius of the nation has been able to develop in the course of time a new art and a new literature commensurable with the material progress in the country. Japan has to-day ninety institutions of scientific and technological research and thirty thousand engineers enrolled in the membership of her national engineering societies. Through these workers and instrumentalities a great modern civilization full of spiritual potentialities is being built up in the East.

The moral of the story is clear. Man began his career as the tool-making animal and built up his civilization by inventing new implements for the control of his material environment. Civilization sank into mediæval darkness when man became weary of the task of fighting his natural environment and sought refuge in the life of the spirit. It was science and the new technology which restored to man the sense of self-confidence and created the modern civilization of the West. It was the introduction of science and technology which transformed Japan and built up her modern civilization. And it will be the same science and technology which will transform the whole East and bring China and India into the world of modern civilizations.

IV

I BEGAN by pointing out the spirituality of the most material phase of modern Western civilization, namely, its technological phase. Modern technology is highly spiritual because it seeks, through human ingenuity and intelligence, to relieve human energy from the unnecessary hardships of life and provide for it the necessary conditions for the enjoyment of life. Whatever be the use man may make of the resultant comfort and leisure, the relief of suffering and hardship is in itself spiritual. We do not necessarily condemn God simply because some honest heretics were burned to death in His name.

I shall now try to show the spirituality of the other phases of the Western civilization. I shall leave out art, music, and literature, for it is evident to all that the West has its art and literature which are at least comparable with those found in the East, and its music which is certainly far more advanced than any which the Oriental countries can boast of.

Let us begin with Science. Whatever may be our divergent views regarding the exact definition of the life of the spirit, no one to-day will probably deny that the desire to know is one of the legitimate spiritual demands of mankind. Yet practically all the older civilizations have tried to suppress this intellectual longing of man. According to the Book of Genesis, the Fall of Man was caused, not by Woman, but by the acquisition of Knowledge. Most of the Oriental religions taught such slogans as "No knowledge, no desire"; "Know nothing and follow the plan of God"; "Abandon wisdom and shun sagacity." A great sage of the East declared: "Life is finite and knowledge is infinite. How hazardous it is to pursue the infinite with the finite!" Thereupon those teachers of man turned away from the strenuous path of knowledge-seeking and resorted to the various ways of introspection, meditation, and contemplation in search for what they conceived to be the "deeper wisdom." Some taught the ways of direct communion with God through devout contemplation. Others elaborated the four stages of *dhyāna* by means of which one might attain the six magic powers of the gods.

As recently as January, 1927, an Egyptian fakir tried to demonstrate to an American audience in Englewood, N. J., that he could prove the superiority of the spiritual civilization of the East by allowing himself to be buried alive for two hours and 52 minutes five feet under the ground. He bettered the record set by the great magician, Houdini, by 82 minutes, but failed to secure a vaudeville contract with the Loew's Company which feared that the theatre audience might not have the patience to sit three hours for the Oriental wise man to revive.

After all, there is very little spirituality in such small tricks of spiritualism, which are still commonly practised by mendicant priests of the East. Do not most animals succeed in doing this during their period of hibernation? On the other hand, there is genuine spiritual joy in the work of the scientists who seek to wring from nature her little secrets by means of rigid methods of study and experimentation.    Truth is deeply hidden and never reveals itself to those insolent souls who approach nature with unaided hands and untrained sense-organs.    Science trains our intelligence and equips it with necessary tools and methods.    It teaches us not to despair of the infinity of knowledge, for it is only through piecemeal accumulation of fragmentary information that we can hope to arrive at some knowledge of nature at all. Every piecemeal acquisition is progress, and every little step in advance gives to the worker a genuinely spiritual rapture.    When Archimedes, on jumping into the bath tub, suddenly found the solution of the scientific problem that had troubled him, he was so overjoyed that he ran naked into the streets and shouted to everybody: "Eureka!    Eureka!"    This has been the spiritual joy that has constantly visited every research-worker in science, every Galileo, Newton, Pasteur, and Edison—a state of rapturous spirituality totally unknown to the pseudo-prophets of the old civilization, who professed to seek the higher knowledge of the totality of things by inward contemplation and self-hypnotism.

For self-hypnotism it was which constituted the so-called spiritual pleasure of the practitioners of the older religions.    A great Chinese philosophical rebel in the seventeenth century thus recorded his own experience in one of his moods of spiritual "attainment": "It was a summer day.    Clad in cotton-padded coat, I was leading the mules carrying the wheat-crop from the field. When my hired laborer was unloading the mules and piling up the sacks, I sat alone under the willow-trees and looked at the blue skies.    The breezes were pleasant and the white clouds were gathering and regathering.    I sang aloud the famous song of the great philosopher Cheng-hao which began with the line 'Light clouds and light breezes a little before noon,' and I felt that I was very happy and my heart flew out as if it could embrace the whole heaven and earth, as if there were nothing else besides heaven and earth and myself.    Then I looked through the thick leaves with half-closed eyes, and the sun appeared like a brilliant pearl shining through a screen of green silk.    And the buzz of the invisible flies sounded like the divine music played in the court of the ancient sage-kings! . . ."    When the author of this episode,

Yen Yuen (1635–1704), in his later years revolted against all the empty philosophizing of Neo-Confucianism and founded the Northern school of Pragmatism which to this day bears his name, he allowed this record of his early folly to be preserved in his collected writings as a testimony to the unreal and self-deceptive character of the methods of the old semi-religious philosophies.

The most spiritual element in science is its skepticism, its courage to doubt everything and believe nothing without sufficient evidence. This attitude is not merely negative, although on the negative side it has performed very great service in liberating the human mind from slavish subjection to superstition and authority. The attitude of doubt is essentially constructive and creative: it is the only legitimate road to belief; it aims at conquering doubt itself and establishing belief on a new basis. It has not only fought the old beliefs with the irresistible weapon, "Give me evidence," but also raised new problems and led to new discoveries by the same insistence on evidence. It is this spirit of "creative doubt" which has made the biographies of the great scientists such as Darwin, Huxley, Pasteur, and Koch the most inspiring of all human records. Just as credulity has made our mediæval saints, so has doubt made our modern gods who overcame nature and blessed man.

## v

BUT the most spiritual phase of the modern civilization of the West is its new religion which, in the absence of a better name, I shall term the religion of Democracy.

Modern civilization did not begin with religion, but it has resulted in a new religion; it did not much trouble about morals, but it has achieved a new system of morals. The European powers of the fifteenth and sixteenth centuries were frankly states of piracy. The great heroes of the age, Columbus, Magellan, Drake, and their like, were great pirates who braved the stormy and unknown seas in search of gold, silver, ivory, spices, and slaves. Their adventures were usually supported by genuine royal or imperial patronage, and their glory and spoils were justly shared by their state and sovereign. They had no scruples for their religion which taught love for all men or for their morals which condemned even usury.

Those acts of piracy opened up the new continents to European trade and colonization which in turn greatly enhanced the material wealth and power of some of the European states and furnished tremendous stimulus to production and invention. The Industrial Revolution followed which fundamentally transformed the methods of production and multiplied the productive powers of the European states. With the increase in material enjoyment and the rise of a large middle class, there has been simultaneously an expansion in man's imaginative power and sympathy. And with the restoration of man's confidence in himself as the agent to control his own destinies, there have developed the various types of social consciousness and social virtues. All this leads to the rise of the new religion of democracy, by which I mean to include the individualistic ideals of the eighteenth century and the socialistic ideals of the last hundred years.

The new creeds of the eighteenth century were Liberty, Equality, and Fraternity. The new religion since the middle of the last century is socialism. All of which are spiritual forces rarely, if ever, dreamed of by the older civilizations. It is true that there were in the East religions which taught universal love and there were schools of thought which advocated equal distribution of land and property. But these have remained paper doctrines which never became real factors in social life and political organization.

Not so in the West. The ideals of Liberty, Equality, and Fraternity have become the war-cry of the American Revolution, the French Revolution, and the revolutions of 1848, and have vibrated through all the later revolutions. They have worked themselves into the constitutions of the new republics. They have brought about the downfall of monarchies, empires, and aristocracies. They have given to man equality before the law and freedom of thought, speech, publication, and religious belief. Above all, they have emancipated the women and made universal education a reality.

The ideals of Socialism are merely supplementary to the earlier and more individualistic ideas of democracy.    They are historically part of the great democratic movement.    By the middle of the nineteenth century, the *laissez-faire* policy was no longer sufficient to achieve the desired results of equality and liberty under the highly organized and centralized economic system.    Compulsory education was opposed as an infringement of liberty, and legislation regulating wages and factory conditions was branded as "class legislation."    The time had come for a new social and political philosophy which would meet the needs of the new economic life of the age.    Hence the rise of the socialistic movements which, when freed from their distracting theories of economic determinism and class war, simply mean the emphasis on the necessity of making use of the collective power of society or of the state for the greatest happiness of the greatest number.    In practice, the movement has taken two main directions.    On one hand, there has been the strong tendency to organize labor as the effective means for the protection of the interests of the working class, and collective bargaining and strikes have been the chief weapons.    On the other hand, there has been an equally strong tendency on the part of all modern governments to forestall the wasteful methods of class struggle by assimilating and putting into practice a number of socialistic ideas such as taxation on inheritance, progressive income tax, compulsory insurance of workmen against accident and old age, regulation of working hours, fixing of minimum wages, and others.    By one way or another or by both, many ideas which were once regarded as dangerously socialistic, have become an integral part of the legislative and governmental programme of every modern state.    One may still believe in the sacred right of property, but the tax on income and inheritance has become a most important source of revenue for most governments.    One may still condemn the idea of class war, but organized labor has become a fact and strikes are almost universally legalized.    England, the mother country of capitalism, has had a Labor Government and may soon have another.    The United States of America, the champion of individual liberty, is trying to enforce national prohibition.    The world is becoming socialistic without being aware of it.

This religion of Democracy which not only guarantees one's own liberty, nor merely limits one's liberty by respecting the liberty of other people, but endeavors to make it possible for every man and every woman to live a free life; which not only succeeds through science and machinery in greatly enhancing the happiness and comfort of the individual, but also seeks through organization and legislation to extend the goods of life to the greatest number —this is the greatest spiritual heritage of the Western civilization. Is it necessary for me to remind my readers that neither the emancipation of woman, nor democratic government, nor universal education has come from the so-called spiritual civilizations of the East? Is it necessary for me to add that, after all, there is not much spirituality in a civilization which bound the feet of its women for almost a thousand years without a protest, nor in that other civilization which long tolerated the practice of *suttee* or cremation of widows and has maintained the horrible caste-system to this day?

## VI

I CANNOT think of a more fitting conclusion to this lengthy discussion than proposing to reconsider the much misused and therefore very confusing phrases "spiritual civilization," "material civilization," and "materialistic civilization." The term "material civilization" ought to have a purely neutral meaning, for all tools of civilization are material embodiments of ideas and the wheelbarrow civilization of the East is no less material than the motorcar civilization of the West. The term "materialistic civilization," which has often been applied to stigmatize the modern civilization of the West, seems to me to be a more appropriate word for the characterization of the backward civilizations of the East. For to me that civilization is materialistic which is limited by matter and incapable of transcending it; which feels itself powerless against its material environment and fails to make the full use of human intelligence for the conquest of nature and for the improvement of the conditions of man. Its sages and saints may do all they can to glorify contentment and hypnotize the people into a willingness to praise their gods and abide by their fate. But that very self-hypnotizing philosophy is more materialistic than the dirty houses they live in, the scanty food they eat, and the clay and wood with which they make the images of their gods.

On the other hand, that civilization which makes the fullest possible use of human ingenuity and intelligence in search of truth in order to control nature and transform matter for the service of mankind, to liberate the human spirit from ignorance, superstition, and slavery to the forces of nature, and to reform social and political institutions for the benefit of the greatest number— such a civilization is highly idealistic and spiritual. This civilization will continue to grow and improve itself. But its future growth and improvement will not be brought about by returning to the spiritualistic ideals of the East, but only through conscious and deliberate endeavors in the direction of fully realizing those truly spiritual potentialities which the progress of this civilization has indicated.

## II—ANCIENT AND MEDIÆVAL CIVILIZATIONS

### By Hendrik Willem van Loon

G ENERALLY, very generally speaking, the human race can be divided into two parts: the few who "do" and the many who "classify" what the others have "done."

It was undoubtedly a member of the latter species, a convinced and avowed *homo classificans,* who bestowed upon us the unfortunate historical divisions by which the records of the past were forever to be separated into a "prehistoric era," an "ancient and classical period," an intermezzo entitled "the Middle Ages" and an indeterminable stretch of time which for some mysterious reason was to be known as the epoch of the "moderns."

As a result, instead of seeing the past as an inevitable entity—as a line that has neither beginning nor end—the average citizen, whenever the word History is mentioned, thinks of a rather jerky costume play—a long-drawn-out four-act drama, subdivided into endless dull scenes by an invisible stage-manager who knew that the last train for the suburbs left at twenty-seven minutes past eleven and that the final curtain should therefore be lowered not later than 10:45 sharp.

Since *homo classificans* is also a creature of habit, and since he outnumbers *homo agitans* a million to one, many brethren of our historical guild have argued that we are doomed to wear that absurd chronological harness for the rest of our planetary existence.

Perhaps so, but in patient anticipation of the happy day when the Assembled Historians shall speak *ex cathedra* and shall present us with the bull *Nunc autem chronologia antiquissima,* I beg to offer an humble suggestion of my own and here and now I propose that we divide the whole of the past into two parts and that we make the year of grace 1769 the great milestone of mankind.

For it was on the fifth of January of that ever memorable year that James Watt obtained a patent for his newly perfected "fire-machine."

It was on that day that the era of the *deus ex machina* came to an end and that the epoch of the *homo in machina* commenced.

It was on that day that man ceased to be a beast of burden and was given his first decent chance to become a human being.

THE history of the world (or what, in the pride of our own superior Western virtues, we are pleased to call the "history of the world") is the record of man in quest of his daily bread and butter.

I don't mean to speak slightingly of the pretty room in which he prefers to take his afternoon nap when he has reached a certain amount of affluence—of the book he reads when conversation with his beloved wife has run a little threadbare—of the musicians he occasionally hires to enliven a convivial gathering. All of these charming incidents of life fill an important part in civilized society. But first and foremost, with ninety-nine men out of a hundred, comes the problem of the hollow-bottomed dinner-pail.

In witness thereof I refer curious readers to the philosophy-of-life evolved by the young men who a few years ago were allowed to deliver the planet from the monster of autocracy and who in the discharge of their duties were changed (almost overnight) from modern citizens into counterparts of their Mousterian ancestors. Occasionally they sang songs about Home and Mother. They sometimes (less frequently) remembered the Girl They Left Behind Them. They never, unless compelled to do so by the spieler of the local Y.M.C.A., gave a thought to the country for which they were risking life and limb, and God Almighty was rarely referred to for purposes of a devotional nature. But under all and every circumstance, in the bowels of their darkened transports, amidst the stench-filled discomforts of their daily habitats, before battle, during battle, after battle, they gave expression to one single and all-over-powering thought and eagerly chanted the question, "When do we eat?"

IT IS a vulgar subject. It is a commonplace subject. But it is a subject from which even the best of us cannot escape for more than a few hours at a time.

There certainly never was an occasion upon which man's mind ought to have been as far removed from material considerations as on that famous afternoon when Jesus addressed his followers upon the Fatherhood of God and urged the people of Judea to love their neighbors as themselves. Yet no sooner had he ceased to talk than the problem of food became of such paramount importance that nothing short of a miracle was able to prevent a stampede for the bakeshops and fish-stores of the neighboring town of Capernaum.

Granted therefore that above and before all things man must eat, we come to our next question: "How will he try to satisfy his appetite?" and the answer is: "Man will invariably try to get a maximum of food with a minimum of effort."

Go to our public squares and see how true this is. The great leaders of the past who understood this principle are the heroes whose statues adorn our highways and byways.

All other benefactors of nations have to content themselves with footnotes in the text-books written for the benefit of graduate students and with solemn centenaries a hundred years after they starved to death.

"For greater glory hath no man in the eyes of his fellow-citizens than that he show them a short-cut to a well appointed porterhouse steak."

A WISE man once wrote that it was a comparatively easy task to find out what the people of ancient times knew. The difficulty began when we tried to make clear to ourselves what they did not know.

What holds good of our ancestors holds equally good of most of our contemporaries.

As a harmless and inexpensive sport, I have during the last four months conducted a series of private investigations into the minds of those humble menials whose path crossed mine and have tried to discover what the idea of "food" meant to them. As the problem of physical sustenance is almost as much interwoven with our daily existence as that of sex, it was quite easy to get the average person started upon the subject.

At first the question seemed to puzzle a good many. Why should any one be so foolish as not to know where one could get food?

Food was something that came from a store—from a delicatessen—a grocery-store—a butcher-shop—a bakery.

Food was something that came in tin cans—in paper parcels.

But why ask where people got this food? Food was something that was there—something that had always been there—that would always be there—something that was taken for granted as long as one had the money to pay for it.

That was something else again.

One had to pay for it.

One had to pay for it with money.

Now if I had only asked my friends how they were supposed to get that money, then they could have told me a different story, an interesting story, a story that filled all of their days and most of their nights with care and anxiety.

For in order to get money, etc., etc.

And I found out that our complex modern society had relieved the majority of the people from one sort of worry to make them the victims of another.

Food they took for granted with childlike simplicity.

The idea that there might not be food enough for all the people all the time never seemed to enter their minds. It was a self-evident and self-perpetuating commodity, like the postage-stamps in the home of our childhood. Of course, one might not have money enough to buy food, but the mere suggestion that food as such might give out, that there might be a shortage of the familiar rolls and bacon and coffee, all of them neatly done up in tin cans and paper bags—why the idea was silly, it was ridiculous, it was absurd.

Many of those humble men and women had never seen a grain-field. More of them had never seen a cow. How and in what manner beans and potatoes grew did not interest them in the least.

They knew only one thing—that they needed money.

The moment however they had enough money, there was not a single other problem in the world.

That little private excursion into the mysterious realm of present-day psychology was an interesting experiment.  But it did not make it any the easier for me to imagine myself back into a society where money was an absolutely unknown quantity and where food—food on the hoof and food in the fields and food in the water—was the one all-overpowering interest of the day.

And yet the human race has lived through hundreds of thousands of years when "food" in its most immediate and direct form was the paramount issue of existence.

What was the attitude of ancient man, of Egyptians and Babylonians and Greeks and Romans and Hebrews and Hittites, towards the ever-present and inevitable problem of nourishment?

Which brings us face to face with another problem, the problem of work.

WE LIVE in a society which lays great stress upon the blessings of "work."

We may not realize it, but that is a very novel idea.

Animals hate exertion.  All honest hunters will tell you that wild things never indulge in any form of labor for the fun of it.

They must fill their bellies and they can only get their bellies full by going through certain muscular motions, such as running or flying or swimming.

But the moment their hunger has been stilled, they are content to rest.

Of course they also need a certain amount of sexual satisfaction and they will indulge in terrific efforts to get themselves the right sort of mate.

But that urge is an occasional incident in their existence.  Once their appetite along that line has been satisfied, they experience only one other emotion, the desire to be properly fed.

I have never done any hunting myself, being one of those who are quite content to let Chicago do their slaughtering for them.

But as I said before all the disciples of Nimrod and the followers of the amiable Izaak inform me that a lion with a full tummy or a snake that has properly gorged himself or a fish that has absorbed a thousand minnows becomes comparatively a harmless creature, who has no other wish but to be left severely alone that he may enjoy his leisure in solitude.

Why and how and when we ever acquired the strange philosophy of life which makes "work" one of the cardinal virtues, I do not know.

Maybe the late and inevitable Dr. John Calvin had something to do with it. That queerly biassed and perverted person has a great deal to do with almost everything that concerns our daily American life.

Some day when he shall have become a mere historical curiosity, some learned person will submit the Calvinistic doctrines to a precise scientific examination and will be able to tell us at what moment "work" began to be regarded as a blessing.

The sainted Johannes probably found some basis for his dogma in Holy Writ. When one has lived long enough in the dreary town on the shores of the Lake of Geneva which was his home, one will probably be able to discover many things in the Old and New Testaments which more cheerful eyes have failed to notice.

But to a mere outsider, it seems difficult to connect the sacred scriptures with the ideal of a life spent in the pursuit of unnecessary toil.

For did not Jehovah in his righteous anger condemn man to the worst possible punishment of which he could think and was not that the punishment which doomed him to a life of labor?

"In the sweat of thy brow thou shalt gain thy daily bread." Surely those words did not imply that ancient Hebrews regarded work as a blessing.

"In the sweat of thy brow thou shalt gain thy daily bread." Simple words but, uttered as a threat, they express with singular clarity the feeling of most primitive people concerning the blessings of personal exertion.

Work was a curse. Work was a nuisance. The leisure of Paradise was the highest good that had ever been within the reach of

man.   Now Paradise was lost.   And as a result, man must work
to eat.

"Very well," man answered.   "I have been a wicked sinner.
I have heard my sentence.   Now let me see how I can get away
from this curse with the least possible exertion on my part."

And within twenty-four hours after he had departed from the
Garden of Eden, Adam had invented the spade.

It was the first labor-saving device.

It was the first bit of machinery.

It was the first blow for liberty of which history, as taught in
Tennessee, has retained the written record.

OUR knowledge about primitive man is of very recent date.
The "verboten" sign of the church kept all faithful Christians outside of the delectable realm of the Pre-Genesiac universe.

Very slowly, very gradually, very painfully we are at last pushing forth into the mysterious dark of those picturesque but indefinitely defined periods during which a creature, vaguely resembling
our noble selves, fought his first battles with the elements and ran
his desperate races with the ever-returning glaciers.

It may take centuries before those Heidelbergians and Piltdown-
ians (not to mention the little brother of the far-famed Dr.
Dubois) shall become something more than bits of curiously shaped
skulls and thigh-bones.   But we are finding things.   We are finding more and more things all the time.   And all of them tell of
man's terrific effort to invent implements, that would make his
daily toil less unbearable.

While I am writing this, two Germans have flown from Europe
to America.   The whole world is delighted with this latest triumph
of the Iron Man, the inanimate slave that becomes animate at
our bidding.   And yet what is a motor compared with the first
fish-hook or the first polished knife?

We are so self-contented.   We take so terribly much for granted.
Wheels, levers, tackles, oars, needles, hammers, nails, all the thousand and one necessities without which we should be obliged to eat
raw turnips and raw meat.   We use them and never give them a
thought.   They seem to be an integral part of a civilization that

has always existed and it is impossible for us to imagine a world that had to go after its food without the assistance of these incredibly simple objects.

And yet, such a world existed for hundreds of thousands of years. And I am convinced that the appearance of the first axe made of polished flint threw the shivering cave-dwellers of southern Europe into ecstasies of happiness which far surpassed our own delirious delight when Lindbergh flew across the ocean.

BUT the curse connected with the idea of work did not stop short at this side of the grave.

The dependence of primitive man upon his inanimate friends was so great that he could not imagine the hereafter without vast assortments of auxiliary hands and feet and he therefore buried his honored dead in the midst of a miniature hardware store which provided the future wanderers in Nirvana with everything they could possibly need from pots and pans to spurs and skewers.

During the last hundred years, we have discovered and explored vast store-houses of the departed in the valleys of the Nile and the Euphrates, in the marshes of the Scandinavian peninsula, and amidst the rocks of Peru.

Everywhere it is the same story. Everywhere the mummy or the corpse lies surrounded by an infinite variety of mechanical appliances. For one flute or harp we find a hundred implements of the hunt. One chair is offset by dozens of boats and baking-stoves and fishing-nets, and the average grave is nothing but a store-house for mechanical implements.

IT IS impossible to say what men of the ancient world would have done had they been given a few thousand more years of development. But after forty centuries of steady growth that early civilization came to an end and was succeeded by a different culture which suffered from the terrific disadvantage that it happened to be based upon slavery which is merely a living and human substitute for machinery.

Statistics upon the early subject of human bondage are scarce and unreliable.

But according to the best of our information, ancient Greece (in the widest geographical sense) was inhabited by five million freemen and twelve million slaves. Revaluated into the language of our own country, if we were Greeks instead of Americans, we would have more than three hundred million slaves to look after our daily needs.

We know nothing definite about the number of slaves in Rome but when we read that Spartacus, who drew most of his volunteers from among runaway gladiators, was able to assemble an army of 130,000 men in less than two weeks time, we get an idea of the number of helots who must have lived within the immediate vicinity of Rome in the year 73 B. C.

And when we realize that during the first century of our era, during the reign of the Emperor Nerva (the predecessor of the famous Trajan who turned all of eastern Asia into a slave reservoir for the benefit of his subjects), the city of Rome had water-works which covered a distance of more than four hundred and fifty kilometers, that the Romans built commercial and military highways of a total length of seventy-six thousand kilometers, when we remember that all those vast public edifices which served the daily needs of the Roman people were constructed by slave labor, we get a faint idea of the millions of human chattels that must have been at the disposal of these early masters of the Western world.

Incidentally those vast numbers of involuntary servants may explain the singular fact that both the Greeks and the Romans, who certainly were not lacking in intelligence, who regarded the whole of the universe as their experimental laboratory, accomplished so little in the field of practical inventions. The people of Mesopotamia and the people of the Nile had owned slaves, but in comparatively small quantities. They seem to have lacked the facilities for subjugating large masses of their neighbors. When the Romans grew tired of their Irish question and decided to make an end of the Jewish nation, they quietly and unobtrusively destroyed Jerusalem, reconstructed the city according to their own notions on top of the ancient ruins, killed a quarter of a million of the surviving Judæans and drove the rest into exile, and the whole expedition caused little more disturbance within the Empire itself than a Nicaraguan expedition under the consulate of Calvin creates within the confines of our own glorious Republic.

But the Egyptians and afterwards the Babylonians and the Persians were completely baffled by the Jewish problem and although they had to deal with a much smaller number of Hebrews than Titus, they did not in the least know how to get rid of them or make them obey their will.

Roman organization settled such difficulties with painful facility. And the Greeks, too, with their highly superior technique of battle, had found it a very easy matter to enslave as many of their neighbors as they needed for their immediate use.

It has been often said (and truthfully, methinks) that slavery is more disastrous for the slave-holder than for the poor serf himself, and the history of Greece and Rome bears out this contention.

It is a well known fact that the two billions of gold which were transported from the American continent to the Iberian peninsula destroyed the national character of its people because it gave the average Spaniard a profound contempt for any sort of physical or mental effort. He was no longer obliged to work for his daily bread. The ingots of the Incas did it for him.

A somewhat similar development took place in Greece. The Greeks of the age of Pericles had come to despise everything that was not connected with "pure thought." A free-born citizen devoted himself to the pursuits of the "mind"—everything done by the "hand" was left to the menial mercies of the slave. Even the great artists, the great sculptors and architects, did not escape this feeling of despisement. Pheidias may have been the greatest of all Greek sculptors, but his own contemporaries thought of him as we think of some Irish or Italian contractor who is digging away at a couple of miles of a subway. We happen (by mere chance and from a recently discovered Egyptian source) to know the name of the engineer who built the Hellespontine bridge across which Xerxes marched his armies into Europe. But about the men who were responsible for the temples and stadiums of Greece we know nothing but what they tell us through their own works and Vitruvius is almost the only Roman engineer whose name has come down to us. And in order to gain immortality he had to write a book.

To find a counterpart for this strange indifference, we must go two thousand years forward to the mysterious world of moving pictures. The modern followers of this anæsthetic pleasure hardly ever know the names of the men and women whose brains evolved the ideas upon which the story which delights their sluggish minds is based. They are familiar with the names of the poor mimes who forced through their paces on the screen, just as we happen to know the names of the utterly indifferent soldiers who first entered the city during the famous siege of Tyre, while we are completely ignorant about the personality of the mechanical genius who evolved the marvelous battering rams and ballistics that finally brought the Phœnician stronghold to terms.

And yet it is not difficult to discover the reason for this lack of respect for the power of the creative brain. The Greeks and the Romans could draw upon such enormous reservoirs of human talent (in the form of slaves) that sooner or later they were bound to find a man who could provide them with whatever they wanted. They therefore never needed to worry that a problem would go unsolved, that a marsh would remain undrained, that a bridge remain unbuilt. The modern ruler of the movie realm knows that the intellectual proletariat is so large and so hungry that he can always buy some convenient man or woman to do his thinking for him. Who that person happens to be does not interest him any more than it interested Cæsar to know whether his chief engineer was black or brown or a pale yellow.

That is probably the main reason why the moving picture with its incredible possibilities has remained a blot upon our civilization. It most certainly explains why the Greeks and the Romans contributed so little to the further development of the machine and of mechanical appliances in general. They did not have to exert themselves in that field of human endeavor. A centurion and a few hundred Veronese leather-necks turned loose in Gaul or Dacia would provide a whole countryside with enough workers to keep at least a dozen landlords happy and rich.

And although the Romans were not without a certain mechan-

ical aptitude (as was shown by the automatic marvels of the Colos-
seum, the disappearing and revolving stages of their public
theatres), in their daily lives they were comparatively indifferent
about mechanical improvements and they were indifferent because
necessity did not force them to be interested. Why should they
have bothered about installing an electric elevator in their houses
when it was so much cheaper and easier to maintain a dozen Par-
thian slaves for the special purpose of hoisting them to the second
story of their palace? Why invent dynamite when one can have
the tunnels of one's aqueducts dug by forced labor?

If this argument sounds a little too simple to be quite true, I
shall ask you to go to the patent-office and compare the number
of inventions registered during the first sixty years of the nineteenth century by citizens of the South and by citizens of the
North.

Would an Alabama land-owner of the year 1850 ever have
bothered about inventing a cotton-planting machine?

I doubt it.

Out of these observations I think that we can distill the general
observation that "the amount of mechanical development will always be in inverse ratio to the number of slaves that happen to be
at a country's disposal."

Prehistoric man and the Egyptians and the people of Mesopotamia had contributed largely to the mechanical development
of the world because most of the time they had been obliged to
help themselves.

The Romans and the Greeks had devoted themselves almost exclusively to the theoretical aspects of science and had neglected the
mechanical side of their civilization because their superior ability
at the business of war had made it possible for them to base their
culture entirely upon slave labor.

But this state of affairs came abruptly to an end when Europe
was overrun by savages whose proud boast it was that they were
free men and who at the same time handled the spear and the
sword with such dexterity that they were more than a match for
the Roman legionaries. And while they invaded the European
continent from the north-east, another force which was to contrib-

ute greatly to the disintegration of Rome was slowly moving westward from the east.

THE heathen of the modern world sometimes reproach the Christian church for its lukewarmness toward the miserable economic status of the majority of mankind. Let fashion decree a skirt that reaches only to the knees, let frightened statesmen whisper a word about the danger of over-population, and the church will be heard from by return mail. Bishops, chaplains, vestrymen, yea, even the overworked head of the Roman branch of the Christian faith will arise in their wrath and will denounce the wickedness of the flesh as manifested by gun-metal hose and methods of contraception as propounded by the advocates of birth control with a fury that seems to know no bounds.

But let an entire countryside starve to death as the result of a lock-out, let dozens of women and children be shot in consequence of a labor dispute, and the church will remain as mum as the proverbial clam.

This may seem regrettable on the part of an institution devoted to the dissemination of charity and brotherly love, but the fact is that the church only continues an age-old tradition and that the Holy Scriptures upon which her doctrines are based pay practically no attention to the serious problem of obtaining our daily sustenance.

It is true that the Lord's prayer mentions a request for the purveyance of a sufficient amount of "daily bread," but that is apparently a slightly erroneous translation. What Jesus seems to have meant was a request for daily "spiritual sustenance." For the rest, the Founder of the religion of the West remains almost completely silent upon the subject of economics. The admonition to render unto Cæsar what belonged to Cæsar sounds more like the attempt of a rather tired and slightly irritated man to avoid a debate upon a futile and ticklish subject than a positive expression of a well-defined economic creed.

No doubt the material needs of the young prophet were very slight and by avoiding the pitfalls of the material world he could devote himself all the more thoroughly to the noble task of making men realize the practical values of those suggestions he offered for the solution of our manifold ills.

An almost identical aloofness about the everyday affairs of our planet is found among the writings of the first of the great apostles.

Saul-Paul was an indefatigable commentator who expressed his opinion upon all subjects with Cadmanian sincerity. From matrimony to pedagogy he counseled, advised, and instructed. But of an interest in the practical problems of life, not a trace is to be found in those endless letters which he wrote to his followers in every part of the civilized world.

It would be foolish therefore to expect Christianity in its original form to have made the slightest attempt to ameliorate the fate of the toilers. As introduced into the West through the efforts of Saul-Paul, Christianity was and remained an oriental philosophy of life. It was essentially a man's religion. It originated in a world in which the male of the species was relieved from almost all drudgery by allowing his wives and his slaves and his female children to do his harvesting and plowing and watering and spading for him, and Pauline Christianity was very careful not to interfere with any of these popular male prerogatives.

To this day the pious among the Jews continue to thank a merciful Jehovah that he did not let them be born women. And to this very hour not a single theologian has been able to prove that Paul and his followers regarded the serf as anything but a two-footed piece of cattle.

To make matters still more complicated, or rather to make them still more simple, the followers of the new mystery believed seriously that the end of the world was near at hand and that it would be a sheer waste of time to attempt to improve man's lot. So why try?

Furthermore early Christianity was decidedly a proletarian and anti-intellectual movement. Its programme addressed itself primarily to the poor in purse and the poor in spirit. The rich and the powerful were not exactly excluded from the kingdom of Heaven but they were supposed to sneak in quietly through the well known Camel Gate. The razzias which the Christianized rabble held against the University of Alexandria, the lynching of philosophers who were suspected of unorthodoxy, all these brutal manifestations of cultural intolerance clearly showed the attitude of the average convert towards those who were supposed to know certain things that lay beyond his own reach.

And if Christianity had remained restricted to the Empire of the third century and had never passed beyond the countries that bordered the Mediterranean, it is doubtful whether European civilization could have survived the shock. Old and tired nations are like old and tired people. They cannot stand great emotional upheavals. Fortunately, the appearance of Christianity coincided with the conquest of Europe by young and vigorous barbarians.

The process of infiltration on the part of the eastern savages which eventually affected the whole of the Roman Empire was exceedingly slow. The Romans, vaguely conscious of what was happening, tried to stop this undesirable onrush with anti-immigration laws, with a strict military supervision of their frontiers, by the social ostracism of the "foreigner" within their gates. All of which of course did not in the least help them. Nature has always abhorred a vacuum. The Empire had gradually become dotted with innumerable territorial vacua. Others came and took what the Romans were no longer able to hold.

We can be pretty certain that these Goths and Vandals and Alamannians and Burgundians and Frisians were an unappetising lot, long-haired, smelly, and devoid of all the social graces. But they probably were not quite as bad as their unwilling hosts painted them. And above all things (the story about them which has become most widely spread) their primary object in life was not to destroy.

No doubt they could be as exasperating to people of discrimination as a traveling party of honest mid-western aborigines let loose in the Louvre or among the ruins of the Forum. But in their heart of hearts they resembled their twentieth century counterparts. In their heart of hearts they were so full of humble admiration before the older form of civilization that they could only express themselves by foolish and supercilious remarks.

No Irish peasant come to financial glory is half as pleased with a Papal title as a Gothic chieftain of the third century of our era was with the empty honor of being called a Roman senator. And quite frequently a diplomatically inclined emperor could avert an open break with these dread invaders by bestowing upon their rulers certain tokens of recognition which temporarily at least deadened that dreadful inferiority-pain which attacked the poor savages whenever they came within actual reach of the immortal city.

But alas, immortality is a virtue exclusively reserved for the gods. Human beings and human institutions are mortal. They grow, expand, and die with the regularity of trees and shrubs and after half a thousand years of slow decay the so-called classical world expired, and the Christian and the Barbarian who almost unwittingly had destroyed the old familiar civilization were forced to carry on.

At that juncture those who denied life as a burden were called upon to make common cause with those who accepted life as a glorious expression of wonderment and joy.

Out of their compromise of church and Barbarian grew the strange new world which we call the Middle Ages.

THE new occupants of the great European peninsula found themselves in an uncomfortable position. As long as the northern part of the continent remained a wilderness they could live on the proceeds of the forest. But when the forest came down, as was inevitable with the influx of more and more immigrants, the problem of daily sustenance was no longer so simple. And it was a problem they were obliged to solve by their own ingenuity. For the mechanical age introduced by the Egyptians and the Babylonians had come to an end during the period of Roman and Greek ascendancy when slave labor had taken the place of the machine and now the slave had become the master. And although Europe became the scene of a grandiose system of anarchy, it was an anarchy of free men and for a while at least slavery in its classical form was unknown.

After a few centuries the more powerful chieftains fell a victim to the old Roman delusion and bound their farm-hands to the soil.  But even during the worst era of feudalism, the serf was rarely reduced to the rank of a slave.  He was a stationary agricultural workman.  He was not an animated piece of machinery that could be bought and sold at will and that had no individual existence, like a plow or a barrow.

THE study of upheavals is interesting but difficult.  It is next to impossible to report a fair sized battle.  To describe a social encounter that lasted seven or eight centuries is beyond the grasp of the ordinary mind.

The period from the third to the ninth century will remain a mystery for a long time to come.  The best one can say of most people who lived during the first six centuries after the extinction of the older forms of culture is that they survived.  And they survived amidst surroundings that were as simple and as primitive as any that had ever been seen since the beginning of time.  They lived amidst ruins, they borrowed or stole from the past in a most shameless fashion.  They belonged to an intermediary period and had not yet found themselves.

For the moment it seemed that all experimental curiosity had become extinct.  The world was slipping backwards.  There still remained a few people with inquisitive brains, ready to plunge into the unknown and continue the task of letting nature do what man did not like to do for himself.  But they worked under a terrible disadvantage.

The defeatist strain inherent in all Eastern creeds (and therefore in Christianity) fought tooth and nail against a return to that ancient state of affairs in which man had been regarded as the highest expression of all creation.

The proud boast of "homo sum" of the first centuries had been discarded for the humbly whispered confession that one was only a miserable sinner, caught in the toils of one's own wickedness, a poor, helpless child of God imploring the interference of the *deus ex machina*.

The written pages of a book stood firmly between Man and the Universe.  A paper bulwark defied all people to inquire too closely into those secrets of nature which revaluated into terms of mechanical appliances might have saved millions of women and children from millions of hours of drudgery.

The struggle between the champions of human rights and the prophets of Heavenly prerogatives, which began in the fifth century, lasted for more than a thousand years and even then the victory was not complete.

The first great blow for the independence of the individual was struck with the invention of gun-powder. After the year 1300 the possession of fire-arms meant pretty much what the possession of money-in-the-bank means today. It protected the owner against sudden eventualities—it strengthened his feeling of self-reliance—it gave him a spiritual assurance based upon physical safety.

From that moment on, the enslavement of the inanimate forces of Nature for the benefit of the human race continued without further serious interruption. The curve of inventions took a sudden upward lift. It lagged behind in those countries where feudalism was successful and where people had other people to work for them. It showed the greatest developments in those regions where man was brought face to face with the realities of life—where he was called upon to do his own "digging" if he wanted to satisfy his hunger. Even the church was to feel the influence of this new spirit. Martin Luther, left to his own fate, would be known today as a courageous but misguided monk who had tried his hand at playing reformer and who had been burned at the stake for his troubles. Martin Luther, supported by a few landed proprietors, might have survived a few years longer, but sooner or later his political friends would have been forced to make peace with the Emperor and the Pope, and would have been obliged to surrender their spiritual adviser to the worldly hangman. Martin Luther, backed up by a prince who through the recent invention of new mining machinery had become one of the wealthiest individuals of northern Europe, was invincible.

I do not mean to imply that the Reformation did not have a spiritual side. But all the spirituality in the world would not have saved it from defeat without the practical aid of the silver mines of Thuringia.

The people of the Low Countries, rebelling against the tyranny of the Hapsburgs, would undoubtedly have fought as bravely as they did if they had only been poor fishermen or shepherds. But they would have suffered the fate of the German and French peasants if their enterprise had not been based upon a number of simple nautical innovations which had made their country the common carrier of a great many staple products of the European food market and had made them capitalists who need not spend fourteen hours of every day in the pursuit of eatables.

I might continue the list almost indefinitely.

In every conflict between the mechanically-minded inhabitants of the rapidly growing cities and their feudal enemies who based their wealth upon the possession of human chattels and continued the anti-mechanical traditions of ancient Rome, the citizens won out, until the difference between the mode-of-living of the towns and the way-of-subsisting of the countryside had become so marked that the ruling classes themselves began to desert their ancient homesteads and moved citywards. Occasionally they tried to continue certain of their ancestral habits for the purposes of sport, but the despised machine which had its home within the city walls contributed so much to their daily comfort that it was impossible for them to remain any longer amidst the simpler surroundings of their agricultural village and experience a feeling of satisfaction and happiness.

Nowadays we sometimes contemplate the crowded streets of our cities and ask ourselves the question: "Why don't these poor benighted fools leave their dark hovels and go and live in the country where there is plenty of air and sunlight and fresh green grass?"

The denizens of our slums know this just as well as we do. They too appreciate fresh air and sunlight and green grass. But they positively refuse to return to a state of civilization in which they are called upon to perform a great many tasks which they have come to regard as unworthy of human effort because they can be done just as well or better by machinery. And far from despising the Iron Man, they love him so dearly that whenever the machine goes forth to live in the country, large numbers of people will hasten to follow.

OF course it would be absurd to claim that our present form of civilization in which the machine is supreme is the last word in cultural perfection.   But that is our own fault.   Children with new toys with which they do not know how to play are a nuisance. Grown-up children, who suddenly find themselves possessed of flivvers and machine-guns and factories and who take these things seriously and render homage to steel contraptions as if they were mysterious gods instead of being merely servants, called upon to do our bidding and for the rest to "know their place," are bound to upset many pleasant old traditions.

But children have one great advantage.   Eventually they will grow up and sometimes even they will learn better.

It is unnecessary to repeat the well known lamentations about the low intrinsic quality of modern civilization.   Life, so it is said on all sides, has become dreary and standardized and shabby and shoddy.   All people wear the same clothes, think the same thoughts, eat the same food, partake of the same futile forms of amusement.   There is no high and no low.   There is only an intermediary form of drab mediocrity.   The exceptional man, like the exceptional artist or the exceptional musician, is given no chance to develop his talents.   Whatever the modern factory produces must be so utterly fool-proof that it has lost all individuality.

And so on and so forth.

But alas, that complaint is really the complaint of the ages.

Man, at the mercy of his own ignorance, has ever distrusted those influences which threatened to interfere with the safe and undisturbed pursuit of the one task with which he was fully familiar, the task of providing sufficient money or food for himself and his family.

To blame the machine for all the evils of our age is an easy but one-sided way of escape, which overlooks the real issue at the bottom of our problem.   And surely the history of the first fifty centuries of which we possess any reliable records shows us a very different story.

Far from despising the assistance of mechanical appliances in the pursuit of food and leisure, man ever since the beginning of time has done his utmost to develop and amplify those contraptions which were really nothing but extensions of his own hands and feet and eyes and ears and which he meant to use as such.

Upon a few occasions a superabundance of cheap forms of human labor made it unnecessary for him to exert himself as an inventor. But whenever he did not find himself possessed of slaves, he pondered deeply and cogitated furiously and experimented and devised and corrected until he had fabricated for himself still more inanimate servants and had set himself free from still other bits of labor that could be done just as well by steel or coal or gasoline.

In the fury of his eagerness, in his irrepressible desire to rid his own species of the curse of drudgery, he has unfortunately fallen a victim to the same error of judgment with which we became so unpleasantly familiar during the recent war when many honest citizens seemed to overlook the fact that war could never be an end in itself and was only justified as a means to bring about peace.

The machine too, we are at last beginning to understand, should never be an end in itself. On the other hand, as a means to one specified end (in this instance the delivery of mankind from the bondage of the larder and the kitchen) the machine should be given every possible chance to grow and develop.

That in a general way was the ideal towards which the civilizations of the past were striving whenever they were thrown upon their own resources and realized by daily experience how much human misery goes into the raising of a single acre of wheat.

It is of course fully possible that we shall prove less intelligent than our ancestors. Then the rôles will be reversed, we shall lose our freedom and shall have to work twice as hard as before to keep our mechanical servants from starving to death.

But that is another story.

It belongs to the chapter entitled "Suicide."

## III—SCIENCE

### By Bertrand Russell

W ESTERN civilization is derived from three sources: the Bible, the Greeks, and Science—the last operating chiefly through machines. The reconciliation between the Bible and the Greeks was a slow business, achieved in the course of centuries by the Catholic Church. The Renaissance and the Reformation undid the synthesis, and left the two elements again at war, as in antiquity. On the whole, Protestantism represented the Bible and free thought represented the Greeks. Pre-industrial America was biblical rather than Hellenic, and agricultural America has remained biblical, while industrial America is developing a new attitude, not hitherto known in the history of man. It is this new attitude that makes America interesting to the student of social science.

The effects of science are of two sorts, rather sharply separable. On the one hand, there is the scientific outlook as it exists in the man of science; on the other there is the transformation of ordinary life through the practical applications of scientific knowledge, more particularly through machines. The first is best seen in Germany; the second in America. Let us begin with the first, since historically it developed earlier than the other.

The Greeks are habitually praised by cultured persons on account of their literature and their art, but in these respects they were not very greatly superior to some other ancient nations, for example, the Chinese. Where they were unquestionably superior was in their invention of the deductive method and the science of geometry. Some few Greeks were scientific in the modern sense—notably Archimedes, who combined practice and theory, experiment and inference, in a thoroughly modern way. Some of the pre-Socratics, for example, Empedocles, were as scientific as was possible in the then state of knowledge. Aristotle is habitually praised for his extensive collection of facts, more especially in zoölogy; but the "Historia Animalium" shows that he was by no means careful to verify the tales brought him by those whom he employed, and that he did not realize the difficulty of accurate observation. Plato's influence was in the direction of emphasizing morals and metaphysics rather than experiment; and in later times this attitude prevailed more and more, so that Archimedes remained an isolated figure. Plato, one feels, was led by his aristocratic mentality to think it vulgar to do anything with one's hands, and the methods of the modern laboratory would have seemed to him beneath the dignity of a gentleman. These and other causes interfered with the development of experimental science in the ancient world, so that even what had been achieved came to be forgotten.

But there existed no such obstacles to the development of geometry. Until the work of Lobatchevsky in 1829, it seemed that the premises of geometry offered no difficulty, and that genuinely new knowledge about the actual world could be obtained by mere deduction. Consequently little attention was paid to premises and much to reasoning from them. This point of view dominated Greek philosophy and mediæval theology. To the outlook thus generated, particular facts were uninteresting except as the conclusions of syllogisms with general premises. The fact that Socrates was mortal was not ascertained from Plato's accounts of his last moments, but from the premise that all men are mortal. With the Renaissance, the actual was re-discovered: it became interesting on its own account, not as a mere instance of a general rule. There was at first a revolt against the intellectual tyranny of system, for example, in Montaigne, who hardly ever mentions general rules except to refute them by amusing exceptions. But men tired of intellectual anarchy, and invented a new discipline for the mind. The new discipline was the scientific method, which is already complete, as a method, in the writings of Galileo.

The essence of the scientific method is the discovery of general laws through the study of particular facts. It is thus a synthesis of the Greek and renaissance outlooks. Particular facts are the basis of the whole structure, but they are used for the purpose of induction, and when they have led to general laws inductively obtained, the Greek methods of deduction are applied to infer new particular facts from the laws. This method has had the most amazing success—amazing, because it is as indefensible intellectually as the purely deductive method of the Middle Ages. Hume long ago showed it up. All philosophy since his day has consisted of sophistical refutations of his arguments: the special skill of the philosopher has consisted in making his refutations so subtle and obscure that their fallacious character was not apparent. Men of science, meanwhile, have simply ignored Hume, and have marched from triumph to triumph. Gradually, however, more especially during the last thirteen years, the best men of science, as a result of technical progress, have been led more and more to a form of skepticism closely analogous to Hume's. Eddington, in expounding the theory of relativity, tends to the view that most so-called scientific laws are human conventions. Some of the leading authorities on the structure of the atom maintain explicitly that there are no causal laws in the physical world. And some philosophers hold the same view. "Superstition," says Wittgenstein, "consists of belief in causality."

This skepticism is a canker at the heart of science, affecting, as yet, only a few leaders, but capable, in time, of paralyzing the activities of the whole army of scientific workers. At least this would be the effect if men remained in the contemplative and intellectualistic mood. But science is becoming increasingly a manner of life, a way of behaving, and is developing a philosophy which substitutes for the old conception of knowledge the new conception of successful behavior. The more skepticism seems to result from a purely theoretic attitude, the more the practical pragmatic attitude triumphs. This is likely to become true throughout the world, but for the moment it is of course more true in a country like America, where the practical success of science is very evident, than in post-war Germany, where pessimism and disillusion fit in with the prevailing tenor of the national life. It is therefore not surprising that America is leading the way in the transition from science as knowledge to science as a set of practical habits. On this ground, whoever is interested in the future should especially study America. To my mind, the best work that has been done anywhere in philosophy and psychology during the present century has been done in America. Its merit is due not so much to the individual ability of the men concerned as to their freedom from certain hampering traditions which the European man of learning inherits from the Middle Ages.

Perhaps these traditions can be summed up in the one word *contemplation*. European universities were originally places for the training of monks; and monks, though they tilled the soil, existed primarily for the sake of the contemplative life. A modern European professor does not till the soil, but he continues to believe in contemplation. In him this belief takes the form of admiration for pure learning regardless of its practical applications. I am myself sufficiently mediæval to feel this admiration far more strongly than it is felt by the typical modern man. Nevertheless, I perceive that it is psychologically connected with an attitude of reverence towards the universe which is hardly compatible with the modern belief in man's omnipotence through the machine. We do not contemplate a flea; we catch it. The modern point of view is in its infancy, but we may foresee a time when it will lead men to regard the non-human world in general with as little reverence as we now feel towards the poor flea. This means that the philosophy of an industrial world cannot be materialism, for materialism, just as much as theism, worships the power which it believes to exist outside Man. Pious Russia, barely emerging from Byzantine ecclesiasticism, has become officially materialistic; probably the more pious portions of the American population will have to pass through this same phase. But sophisticated America, wherever it has succeeded in shaking off slavery to Europe (which is too common among the sophisticated), has already developed a new outlook, mainly as a result of the work of James and Dewey. This new outlook, embodied in the so-called instrumental theory of knowledge, constitutes the philosophy appropriate to industrialism, which is science in the sphere of practice.

The dominating belief of what may be called the industrial philosophy is that man is master of his fate, and need not submit tamely to the evils hitherto inflicted upon him by the niggardliness of inanimate nature or the follies of human nature. Man was in the past dependent upon the weather, which was beyond his control. This is still the case with peasants, who are usually pious, and still more so with fishermen, who are still more pious. It may be laid down broadly that the intensity of religious belief among sea-faring folk is inversely proportional to the size of their vessel. Accidents such as the sinking of the *Titanic,* however, tend to keep some measure of religion alive even in the largest ships. But this state of affairs is passing, and its passing is accelerated by every increase in the safety of navigation.

Man, since he became capable of forethought, has been dominated by fears—fear of natural phenomena such as lightning and tempest, fear of starvation, fear of pestilence, fear of defeat in war, fear of murder by private enemies. Elaborate systems, partly rational, partly magical, have been built up to minimize these dangers. In the early ages of agriculture men dealt with the fear of starvation by means of human sacrifice, which was supposed to invigorate the Corn Spirit. It is only very gradually that scientific agriculture has displaced this attitude. Inundations, except in China, were usually dealt with by prayer to the River God. There was a general tendency to regard misfortunes as due to the anger of invisible beings, who could be propitiated by suitable ceremonies. Pestilence was viewed superstitiously down to our own day, and is still so viewed in India. The fear of war has only just begun to be treated rationally, and those who so treat it still labor under the suspicion of being cranks. Our natural view of the causes of war is more consonant with Coleridge's:

> *Kubla heard from far*
> *Ancestral voices prophesying war.*

The fear of murder by private enemies is supposed to be dealt with by the criminal law. But the criminal law, also, was in its origin superstitious, being based upon the notion of blood pollution. Even now, our emotion towards an ancient crime, such as murder, is quite different from that towards (say) forgery, which has no roots in the superstitious past. And even now, the retributive element in punishment, which is superstitious, being based upon the rage inspired by fear of the criminal, prevents our criminal law from being as effective as it might be in the prevention of crime.

Few people realize how very modern is the influence of science upon the intellectual outlook of cultivated men, let alone the ordinary citizen of a civilized community. The Greeks, and the Romans in their best days, were, it is true, not dominated by fear. But their hopes had a different quality from ours. Compare Plato's "Republic" with any of Wells' Utopias. In Plato's hopes, men were to advance in virtue, and in a certain kind of wisdom; but he did not think of greater dominion over nature as an ingredient in the good life. Perhaps the reason for this was in part economic: where labor is performed by slaves, the free-man is not impressed with the importance of minimizing labor. But other more intellectual reasons played their part. Geometry led men to think that the truth could be discovered by reasoning, or, as Plato suggested, by reminiscence. Moral and æsthetic considerations were allowed an undue weight in framing hypotheses about the physical world: it was supposed that the physical world must be beautiful and intellectually agreeable to contemplate, which led to a preference for simple hypotheses, such as that the heavenly bodies moved in orbits which were circles or combinations of circles. As the intellectual vigor of the ancient world declined, authority became supreme, and commentaries took the place of fresh thought. Thus, although a few Greeks had achieved a scientific outlook, the ordinary cultivated man had a view of the world in which scientific investigation played no part.

This is no longer quite true of the Arabic civilization, which certainly had more scientific curiosity than the later Hellenistic centuries. But a great deal of superstition is mixed with science in all but the best of the Arabs. Alchemy, the search for the philosopher's stone, the attempt to discover the elixir of life, occupied many experimenters' thoughts to the exclusion of more genuine problems. In Europe, meanwhile, the over-emphasis on ethical considerations which is visible in all Greek post-Socratic philosophy, and the subsequent undue respect for authority which was both effect and cause of intellectual inferiority to earlier centuries, prevented almost all scientific investigation throughout the Middle Ages, except by those few men who, like Roger Bacon, had been stimulated by contact with the learning of the Moors. For all these reasons, science played hardly any part in life, even for the small learned minority, until the Renaissance.

The Renaissance was, of course, primarily a literary movement, involving, at first, not an emancipation from authority, but only a change, more especially from Aristotle to Plato. However, when men realized that the ancients had disagreed with each other, they were forced to think for themselves to decide which ancient author they should follow. Copernicus discovered in Italy that some of the Greeks had taught that the earth goes round the sun; if he had not known this, it may be doubted whether he would have had the courage to propound his theory, in favor of which he had no very solid scientific reasons to offer.

Kepler and Galileo represent the real beginnings of modern science; it is in them that we first find the patient and unbiassed observation of large numbers of particular facts, leading to the formulation of laws which they had not expected. The contemporaries of Galileo, especially the most learned, objected to his habit of ascertaining facts by looking at the world instead of at Aristotle. But the time was at last ripe for the victory of science. In an earlier age, Galileo might have been forgotten; as it was, a series of incredibly brilliant successors carried on his work quickly to its completion in Newton's "Principia."

Throughout the seventeenth and eighteenth centuries, though science had to fight against both theology and the humanities, it acquired an increasing ascendancy over the minds of educated men. But until after the end of this period science was conceived almost wholly from the standpoint of theoretical knowledge. It is true that Bacon had said "knowledge is power," and had viewed knowledge in relation to its practical uses. But astronomy, the dominating science of the time, had not much utility except for navigation, and there only in its elementary portions. The inventions which made physics and chemistry useful had not yet been made, or at any rate had not yet achieved success. The motive of men of science, accordingly, was to understand the world, not to change it. This is still the motive of those who make the great theoretical advances—Einstein, Planck, Bohr, and such men. But everybody now-a-days is aware that science is likely to have practical applications, and this has greatly modified the prevailing view of the purposes of science.

From the time when Charles II founded the Royal Society down to the outbreak of the French Revolution, science was associated with "enlightenment." At first, it was a cure for "enthusiasm," i. e., for the kind of fanaticism that had been displayed by the Puritans. Then, in France, in spite of the fact that both Jesuits and Jansenists had produced many admirable men of science, the pursuit of mathematical physics became gradually associated with materialism, with opposition to the Church, and with political radicalism. This movement culminated in the Revolution, which produced, throughout Europe, a temporary diminution in the rate of scientific progress.

It is only in the nineteenth century that science came to be commonly regarded as affording a means of improving the general level of human life, not by moral regeneration, and not by political reform, but by increasing man's command over the forces of nature. This point of view was, of course, due to the industrial revolution, and to various inventions, such as steamships, railways, and telegraphs. This view of science as the handmaid of industry has now become a commonplace. As already observed, it is now possible to hope that mankind may, to a very great degree, be freed from certain age-long terrors—pestilence, famine, drought, and flood, perhaps even war.

Science, in so far as it is successful, eliminates these various kinds of fear from our lives. It cannot, of course, altogether eliminate the fear of death, but it can and does cause us to live longer than our ancestors, and to this process no definite limit can be set. Fear of natural phenomena plays a very small part in modern urban life. Once in a way, some event such as the Tokyo earthquake reminds us that Nature is not yet wholly subdued. Taking a longer view, science assures us that our planet will not always remain habitable, and that, although we may migrate to Venus when the sun's heat diminishes, that can only put off the date of our extinction by a million years or so. These distant speculations, however, have no power to disturb the urban worker as he hurries for his morning train. His emotional world is a human one, trivial, boring, but safe—except from the anger of the boss. And so politics increasingly takes the place of religion, since it is in the sphere of politics that fear now finds its home.

It may be said that, while science has already greatly diminished the fear of nature, it has so far, if anything, somewhat increased men's fear of each other. Lightning conductors, which George III (rightly, as I think) regarded as impious, have destroyed fear of "the all-dreaded thunder-stone." But other inventions have enabled man to wield powers as destructive as those formerly wielded by Nature. And science has made society more organic, so that on the one hand the rebel finds it increasingly difficult to escape the vengeance of the holders of power, while on the other hand social chaos, when it occurs, becomes a much greater disaster than in more primitive communities. Perhaps for these reasons, the pressure of the herd and the fear of neighbors, are greater in America than in any other civilized country. While man collectively has been freed from bondage to the non-human world, men individually are held in bondage to their fellow-men more completely than in the pre-scientific ages.

Will science, in the end, deal also with this form of fear? I think it will. Hitherto, the practical applications of science have been mainly directed to modifications of our material environment. Whereas formerly the environment was a datum, something to be merely accepted and contemplated, it is now, so far as the surface of the earth is concerned, raw material for human manipulation. But human nature is still accepted as a datum. While we alter the environment to suit ourselves, we do not much alter ourselves to suit each other. The reason is, of course, that the sciences that deal with the formation of human character are far less developed than those that deal with the inanimate world. This, however, is rapidly changing. It is highly probable that in a hundred years we shall have acquired the same control over the characters of children that we now have over physical forces. We shall then, if we feel so disposed, be able to eliminate fear from the relations between human beings as we are already eliminating it from the relations of human beings with the world of nature. But what men will make of these powers when they come to possess them, it would be very rash to prophesy. Doubtless they will make something which, to our inherited standard of values, would seem horrible; but to them, one must suppose, it will seem good. Let us, then, console ourselves as best we may with Hamlet's dictum:

*There's nothing either good or bad but thinking makes it so.*

A good community is one that those who live in it think good; and that, at least, the scientific educators of the future will almost certainly be able to secure.

The philosophy inspired by industrialism is seeping away the static conception of knowledge which dominated both mediæval and modern philosophy, and has substituted what it calls the Instrumental Theory, the very name of which is suggested by machinery. In the Instrumental Theory, there is not a single state of mind which consists of knowing a truth—there is a way of acting, a manner of handling the environment, which is appropriate, and whose appropriateness constitutes what alone can be called knowledge as these philosophers understand it. One might sum up this theory by a definition: *To know something is to be able to change it as we wish.* There is no place in this outlook for the beatific vision, nor for any notion of final excellence.

This "dynamic" conception of knowledge and of value is so ingrained in most typical modern men that they are incapable of understanding the nostalgia which it produces in a sensitive European impregnated with the older culture. European countries (except Russia) differ far less from each other than all differ from the United States. It is perhaps worth while to consider this difference impartially, since any forecast of the development of machine civilization based upon European experience is likely to prove fallacious.

The last cantos of the "Divina Commedia" may serve to illustrate the point. In these the supreme bliss is represented as a combination of contemplation and love, both at the highest pitch of intensity, but wholly static, because perfection has been achieved and nothing is left to strive for. In Milton, more briefly, we find the same conception of heaven:

> *Where the bright seraphim in burning row*
> *Their loud uplifted angel trumpets blow,*
> *And the cherubic hosts in thousand quires*
> *Touch their immortal harps of golden wires.*

It is not suggested that the trumpets and harps should be of continually improved makes, or should be played by machinery to save the angels trouble and leave them free to increase the height of the buildings in the Golden City.

The modern European artist or man of learning knows that the beatific vision cannot constitute the whole of his life, and is skeptical of any life hereafter. But if he is sensitive, whether as an artist or a man of science, a lover or an explorer, he lives for the moments which approach nearest to the ultimate ecstasy, when he is "silent upon a peak in Darien." This is as true in the pursuit of knowledge as in that of beauty, for in a new theoretic insight he finds a rapture as intense as that of new love.

Such men, however, are to be regarded as strayed ghosts from an earlier epoch. Men do not always belong to their own time: eminent men are often psychologically ahead of this epoch, but are sometimes behind it. Dante, for example, sums up preceding centuries, and does not suggest the future in anything except his use of the Italian language. It is a curious speculation to consider what various men of past ages would think of our civilization if they were miraculously transported into it. Archimedes, I fancy, would find it wholly delightful. He would indefatigably visit factories, observatories, scientific instrument makers; he would read encyclopædias from cover to cover; he would be immensely impressed by wireless telegraphy, and beside himself with joy over aeroplanes. He would admire, above all things, our means of scientific warfare, but would be unable to understand why they are not used to exterminate the barbarians. He would master our science and our mathematics in a few years of intense study, but our politics would puzzle him—not so much what we do, but what we say, though what we do, also, would be in part unintelligible to him.

Aristotle, I fancy, would divide his time between Oxford Common Rooms and the Zoo. In the latter, he would question the keepers as to the habits of their animals, and would be led to amend what he says on cures for insomnia in elephants. In the former, his conversation on metaphysics would be better appreciated than anywhere else in the modern world, but he would be surprised by the lack of interest in zoölogy. He would make friends with explorers and statesmen, and would take a considerable interest in anthropology. But the mechanical aspects of our civilization would bore him, and he would be profoundly shocked by democracy. (So, indeed, would even the most democratic of the Greeks.) He would not use the subway unless he could have a special train for himself and his friends.

Plato, if he could return to this world, would make friends with Dean Inge and accept his views on modern civilization *in toto*.

Bacon would be appointed editor of the Encyclopædia Britannica, but would be dismissed for inserting advertising matter under the guise of articles. He would admire museums, card catalogues, and machine politicians. He would enthusiastically praise industrial technique, but would regard relativity and quantum theory as unduly subtle, and as fantastic speculations of no practical importance. He would have many friends among the eminent, and would feel thoroughly at home in our world as soon as he had acquired a comfortable fortune.

Newton, I fancy, would regret that he had ever allowed the world to become acquainted with his researches. He would be fairly happy so long as he remained within the gates of Trinity College, but motor cars and even bicycles would alarm him, and he would say that whenever he began to think about mathematics they ran into him. Machines, he would complain, have made present-day England less agreeable to the philosopher than the England of Queen Anne. And as Master of the Mint he would be inexpressibly shocked to find that paper had taken the place of gold.

I fear that a passion for psychological truth has led me to make these imagined reactions of distinguished ghosts more trivial than seems appropriate to their eminence, except in the case of Archimedes. Even the greatest men, however, are often influenced by very minor factors in forming their judgments; and this is an important fact, which should put us on our guard in attempting to sum up our own age. When we try to be as objective as possible in singling out the most important external differences between the present and the past before the nineteenth century, I think the following deserve emphasis.

First: greater mobility both of men and goods. From the time when the horse was first domesticated down to the invention of the locomotive, the greatest possible speed of land travel remained approximately constant. The Imperial Post in the Roman Empire travelled at about the same rate as Dickens' stage coaches. Trains made a rapid revolution, but soon achieved very nearly their present speed. Aeroplanes represent a new revolution. Sea travel, although there was a vast addition to geographical knowledge, did not very greatly increase in speed until the invention of steamboats.

Second: speed in sending messages. Here the three stages, so far, are the telegraph, the telephone, and wireless. It is theoretically impossible to surpass the speed of wireless, which is that of light. In this matter, therefore, we have, in a certain sense, achieved perfection.

Third: the substitution of machinery for handicrafts in industry, with the consequent enormous increase of material well-being in all classes.

Fourth: the improvement in public health, which has been particularly noteworthy since the beginning of the present century.

Fifth: the application of science to methods of warfare. But this is a trite theme, as to which I propose to say nothing further.

The intellectual changes brought about by science are in part considerably older than the above practical changes, but in part they also belong to the last hundred years. It may be said, broadly, that science has simultaneously, and in equal measure, increased man's power and diminished his pride. In the Middle Ages, the earth was the centre of the universe, and the human race was the principal object of divine solicitude. The first blow to this outlook, and perhaps the greatest, was the Copernican system, with the discovery that the earth is one of the smaller planets. The next blow was the doctrine of evolution, as to which traditionalists are still fighting a rearguard action. The next, which is only now beginning to be delivered, is the analysis of mind and soul by behaviorists and bio-chemists. I have heard it suggested by a bio-chemist that mysticism is due to excessive alkalinity of the blood. This particular doctrine may or may not be true, but some equally painful explanation of the mystic emotion is pretty sure to be found before long. Physics, biology, psychology, have each in turn passed over from superstition to science, and have each in turn demanded sacrifices dear to our human conceit. The increase of power which men derive from science has, however, made these sacrifices endurable, and has allowed the scientific outlook to triumph in practice even with those who continue to reject it in its general and speculative aspects.

Theoretical science itself has changed its character in the course of its development. Newton's "Principia" has a statuesque perfection; a modern man of science does not attempt to give his work this character. Final truth is no longer demanded of a scientific theory, or claimed for it by its inventor. There is no longer the same conception of "truth" as something eternal, static, exact, and yet ascertainable. Consequently even the best modern theories are more satisfying to the practical than to the theoretical side of our nature. The more physics advances, the less it professes to tell us about the external world. To the Greek atomist, an atom was a little hard lump, just like an ordinary body except that it was small. To the modern physicist, it is a set of radiations coming out from a centre, and as to what there may be in the centre nothing can be known. Even when we say that there are radiations coming out from a centre, we are saying something which, when correctly interpreted, is found to mean much less than it seems to mean at first sight. More and more, science becomes the art of manipulating nature, not a theoretical understanding of nature. The hope of understanding the world is itself one of those day-dreams that science tends to dissipate. This was not formerly the case; it is an outcome of the physics of the last twenty-five years. Undoubtedly it tends to strengthen the instrumentalist philosophy.

The influence of the theory of relativity has been in this same direction. Einstein's law of gravitation is better than Newton's, and represents an equal triumph of human genius; but its effect upon scientific mentality has been quite different. Both in England and in France, Newton's work led men to think that they had at last penetrated the secrets of the universe; fine ladies tried to understand the "Principia," and philosophers took pleasure in expounding it to them. But Einstein's work has, on the whole, made men think that they know less than they had supposed. It seems that, although physics enables us, within certain limits, to predict our own experiences, it gives us only an abstract and formal kind of knowledge concerning what lies outside. If we continue to use pictorial language, and say (for example) that the earth describes an orbit round the sun, we must not suppose that "earth" and "sun" and "orbit" mean what one naturally imagines them to mean—they are merely names for certain mathematical expressions. Einstein, therefore, has not brought men the same sense of triumph as Newton brought, although his work is just as remarkable. "Laws of nature" have turned out to be in some cases human conventions, in others mere statistical averages. This may not be always the case, but at any rate the old glad certainty is gone.

In conclusion, I wish to consider some of the social effects of science, and some of the hopes and fears for the future to which these effects give rise.

There is one regrettable feature of scientific civilization as hitherto developed: I mean, the diminution in the value and independence of the individual. Great enterprises tend more and more to be collective, and in an industrialized world the interference of the community with the individual must be more intense than it need be in a commercial or agricultural régime. Although machinery makes man collectively more lordly in his attitude towards nature, it tends to make the individual man more submissive to his group. Perhaps this is one cause of the fact that herd instinct is much more insistent in America than in England, and that individual liberty is less respected both politically and socially. I think, however, that a more important cause is the mixture of races and nationalities in the United States, which makes herd instinct a necessary unifying force. Even if a diminution of individual liberty be an essential feature of a scientific civilization, the mastery over nature is so great a boon that it is worth while to pay even a high price in order to achieve it. And it is probable that, as men's habits become more adjusted to the new régime, the interference with liberty will become very much less.

The omnipotence of man collectively and the feebleness of each individual man, which are features of a scientific civilization, should logically entail certain changes in values, religious, moral, and æsthetic. Belief in the infinite value of the individual soul arose as a consolation for the powerless subjects of the Roman Empire: ego-compensation had to be placed in another world, because the ordinary man had no share of political power. In the modern machine-world, owing to democracy and to the achievements of science, other compensations are possible, more especially nationalism, which identifies the individual emotionally with the power of his group. But in order that such compensations may satisfy, it is necessary to belittle the individual wherever he is not contributing to a totality. Lyric love, for example, which has inspired half the poetry of the world, has been a product of courts and aristocracies. Its revival after the Dark Ages was due to the Emperor Frederick II. The loves of an Emperor were events of public importance, and he saw nothing ridiculous in taking them seriously. His courtiers saw nothing ridiculous in imitating him. And so lyric love became a tradition. But in a civilization dominated by the machine, such seriousness about a mere emotion is impossible.

Changes in religion and morals come slowly, owing to our emotional resistance; yet they seem almost inevitable if a scientific civilization remains dominant for several centuries. In morals, we may expect a substitution of hope for fear, and an increase in the sense of the rights of the community as against the individual. Traditional morality, historically, was concerned with the relation of the individual soul to God. Political obligations formed part of the republican morality of Greece and Rome, but not of early Christianity, which grew up among populations without political power and therefore without political responsibility. This explains why many people still consider adultery a greater crime than acceptance of bribes by a politician or public official. Again: the State increasingly interferes between parents and children— for example, by insisting on education and forbidding physical cruelty. It would seem likely that this tendency will continue; more particularly, the State may be expected to assume the role of the father by taking over economic responsibility for the child, on the ground that many fathers cannot be trusted in this matter. If so, there will inevitably be a breakdown of the family, which must modify social psychology profoundly, producing, in place of individuals, well-drilled armies of intelligent but submissive Janissaries, without individual differences, and without loyalties other than their loyalty to the State.

There remains the question: Can a scientific society be stable? Or does it contain within itself some poison which must ultimately produce its downfall? The Greeks produced an admirable way of life, but it was incapable of survival. Something of what they created passed into the Roman Empire, and thence into the Catholic Church, but in a diluted form. So it may be that the intensity of the scientific element in life will have to be diminished before men arrive at a stable polity. This possibility is worth examining.

There is, to begin with, an intellectual inconsistency in the scientific outlook. The nominal practice of science is to accept nothing without evidence, to test all its assertions by means of facts. But in reality, as Dr. Whitehead has pointed out in "Science and the Modern World," science has dogmas as ill grounded as those of any theological system. All science rests upon induction, and induction rests upon what Mr. Santayana calls "animal faith." The proofs of the validity of induction are as numerous as the proofs of the existence of God; but not one of them is calculated to carry conviction to a candid mind. This will not impede the progress of science so long as most men of science remain genuinely unaware of their theoretical insecurity, but as soon as they have to practise a semi-deliberate shutting of the eyes, they will lose the ardor of fearless explorers, and will tend to become defenders of orthodoxy. If, on the other hand, the instrumental theory of knowledge prevails, and theoretical problems are put to one side as merely scholastic, the inspiration to fundamental discoveries will fail. I am not arguing that the instrumental theory is false; on the contrary, I incline to think that it is true. But I am arguing that it does not afford a sufficient incentive to the precarious labor of serious thinking. When Egyptian priests discovered the periodicity of eclipses, they did so because superstition had led them to record such phenomena with scrupulous care. A false belief may be an essential ingredient in discovery, and perhaps the progress of science will cease on the day when the men of science become completely scientific. If so, they will turn to superstition for relief, and the Dark Ages will return. All this, however, is no more than a doubtful speculation.

More serious is the effect of a scientific civilization upon population—not upon quantity, which is unimportant, but upon quality. The most intelligent individuals, on the average, breed least, and do not breed enough to keep their numbers constant. Unless new incentives are discovered to induce them to breed, they will soon not be sufficiently numerous to supply the intelligence needed for maintaining a highly technical and elaborate system. And new incentives will have to be far more powerful than any that seem politically feasible in any measurable future. In America and Great Britain, the fetish of democracy stands in the way; in Russia, the Marxian disbelief in biology. Wherever the Catholic Church is strong, mere quantity tends to be thought alone important. In France, the economic system that has grown up around the Code Napoléon makes any eugenic reform impossible.

Probably the best chance is in Germany, but even there it is small. Meanwhile, we must expect, at any rate for the next hundred years, that each generation will be congenitally stupider than its predecessor. This is a grave prospect.

In the ancient world, it is clear that Greece in the age of Pericles and Rome in the Augustan age were more intelligent than at later times; it is also fairly clear that the decay of Rome was primarily a decay of intelligence. Will this kind of decadence repeat itself? Not if biological science can obtain the same hold over men's minds as physical and mechanical sciences have now. In that case, by positive and negative eugenics the average intelligence can be increased in each generation, instead of being diminished, as at present. Unfortunately the concern of biology is with the most intimate part of human life, where emotions, morals, and religion alike stand in the way of progress. It may be doubted whether human nature could bear so great an interference with the life of instinct as would be involved in a really effective application of eugenics. Whatever may be thought disagreeable in the machine age would be greatly intensified by the application of science to parenthood, and men might well think the price not worth paying.

What does seem clear is that we cannot stand still with the measure of science that exists at present in western civilization. We must either have more science, in particular biological science, or gradually become incapable of wielding the science we already have. In that case the forces of ignorance and obscurantism will gradually creep back into power. For a while, the old machinery will survive, just as Roman aqueducts survived in the sixth and seventh centuries; but gradually there will be an increasing collapse, until the skyscrapers become as strange as Maya ruins in Yucatan. Let us not flatter ourselves that this is impossible; all past history proves the reverse.

In the course of this chapter, I have not sought to minimize what may be considered the defects of the machine civilization. I do not doubt, however, that its merits far outweigh its defects. Take two items alone: the diminution of poverty, and the improvement in public health. These two alone represent an almost incalculable increase in average happiness, and each of them is capable of being carried very much further than has yet been done.

The remedy for the one-sidedness and harshness of our present civilization is to be sought, not in less science, but in more. Psychology, physiology, and the study of heredity have much to contribute. But if they are to add to human happiness, it is essential that we should learn to use the machine without worshipping it. Studies of industrial fatigue with a view to facilitating a greater output are not the most important part of psychology. The effect of stimulants in diminishing work on Monday morning is not their only effect deserving of study. Nor is suitability as a factory hand the only quality the eugenist should aim at producing. The machine was made for man, not man for the machine. The important thing about work is that it affords leisure for play; if it does not do this, it is not fulfilling its social purposes. When the same scientific acumen comes to be applied to human nature as has already been applied to the physical world, it may be expected, with some confidence, that the importance of happiness will no longer be forgotten. And evidently the honeymoon intoxication of the machine age will pass soonest in the countries which have been the first to experience it. I look, therefore, to the western nations, and more particularly to America, to establish first that more humane, more stable, and more truly scientific civilization towards which, as I hope, the world is tending.

## IV—BUSINESS

### By Julius Klein

WHAT place has "business" in this symposium on Western civilization? After all, the intelligentsia continue to remind us cynically that "business is still business," and, if it has added anything to our civilization, its contributions have been but mercenary detractions from the loftier aspirations of mankind. Is the Moloch of modern industrialism anything but enthroned avarice? How can the metallic notes of clinking coins mean anything but discord with the more exalted strains of higher idealism? Can there be anything of real value to culture and civilization in its broader sense in the "babblings of the Babbittry" in the market place? As business emerged from the darkness of mediævalism with the tawdry pageantry of the guilds and of the princelings who capitalized the trade rivalries of the cities, did it not leave behind a tragic trail of ruthless exploitation, of warfare, and the debauching of civic honor? Does not business—the urge for commercial development—bear to this day the grave responsibility for that insatiable thirst for Empire, for politico-economic conquest, which has been so repeatedly the cause of ghastly holocausts throughout all history?

Can such an element be rated as a truly constructive factor in Western civilization? Have we not progressed in spite of this malevolent force rather than because of it? What has it really contributed aside from crass materialism and the debasements incident to its pursuit?

I

AT THE outset, the case for business raises the counter query: how much of Western civilization would have been possible had there been no solid foundation of material prosperity in each successive age upon which the lofty edifices of our culture could have been erected? To put it more concretely with an example from one of the golden eras of Western history, the glories of Gothic architecture, which have immortalized the best of mediæval idealism for us, rose primarily from the organizing ability, the industrial ingenuity, and, above all, the solid earnings—sordid perhaps at times, but none the less substantial and indispensable—of craftsmen who were progenitors of the business world of today.

One wonders what would have been the fate of latent genius in all the fields of art and letters throughout the ages had it not been for the continued and still continuing patronage of these "mercenary magnates" whom the present-day literati delight to lampoon. Many of the brightest names enumerated elsewhere in this volume as typifying the heights of achievement in painting, poetry, sculpture, architecture, science, and medicine would have disappeared without record, and Western civilization would have unknowingly been the poorer had there not been some affluent patron ready to divert his earnings to immortalize the genius of some master. Nor should we omit the inspiring and invaluable works in philanthropy and social service which have brightened many an otherwise dark page of arrogance and selfishness in Western history, which the world owes to these same "materialists," from the days of the great Fuggers of Augsburg down to their counterparts of our own day. Granted, the motive may all too frequently have been the shallowest vanity, but the world is none the less their debtor.

In order to be both just and accurate, we must appraise the place of business in this picture, not simply as a thing of material substance, but as a vehicle for the progress of humanity in all directions. The world of business is not simply made up of machines and merchandise, of counting houses and factories. It is the expression of, indeed the very means of existence for, civilization. As Secretary Hoover once expressed it in speaking of American business advancement, "we are a nation of men, women, and children. Our industrial system and our commerce are simply implements for their comfort and happiness. When we deal with those great problems of business and economics, we must be inspired by the knowledge that we are increasing and defending the standards of living of all our people. Upon this soil grow those moral and intellectual forces that make our nation great."

These same considerations are applicable not simply to the business life of each nation; they bind the world of international commerce and industry in one compact unit, whose economic interdependence is more and more evident with each new stage in the advancement of our civilization.

Time was when business was inseparably linked with the agencies of international discord and destruction; and in the earlier ages when nationalities were but vaguely defined and political units were reduced to hundreds of petty principalities and city states, the exploitation of their rivalries by merchant princes was widespread. Indeed, it was but the inevitable commercial reflex of the primitive principles of all relations between individuals that the ominous warning of *caveat emptor* was ever in the ears of every prospective buyer. Even after the well-organized city fairs—the international market places of that earlier age—and the strict regulations of the various guilds had established certain elementary rules of commercial ethics, the cloud of suspicion and fear still darkened the practices of trade. Although in some quarters this principle survives to this day, it is being more widely realized that the only permanent foundation for business operations is to be found in the mutuality of advantage in each transaction for both parties. Business today rests predominantly on credit, but another name for confidence, which, of course, perishes instantly in the presence of that sinister mediæval warning that the buyer must beware.

## II

BUT let us get down to specific details and review some of the outstanding contributions of business throughout Western history, in terms not so much of their meaning in the narrower limits of economics, but in the broader sphere of general well-being.

The threads of business run throughout the fabric of the recorded annals of Western civilization. Without the urge, and indeed the resources of trade and industry, not only would many of its brightest segments have been unwoven, but the very texture itself simply could not have survived. In the dreary records of the decline of one state after another, a conspicuous factor has been the laxity of business morale, the weakening of commercial acumen and fibre. In some cases, these once prosperous commonwealths have faded from history because of the failure of some vital trade advantage, as in the case of the mighty Hanseatic League of the North and the powerful city states of the Mediterranean.

The gradual spread of civilization moved with the tide of trade. The Phœnicians were the pioneers as they felt their way cautiously from one sheltered haven to another along the shores of the inland sea, ever searching for new commodities, new markets. Finally, they boldly ventured forth on the vast wastes beyond the Pillars of Hercules and left the evidences of their barterings from the quarries of Cape Spartel to the stannaries of Cornwall—mere vestiges of sordid business, if you will, but also the sources of the very fuel for the light of civilization, for with the records of their trafficking they brought to Western civilization the alphabet.

Then in their wake came their commercial heirs and colonial descendants, the Carthaginians and Greeks, with their substantial market centres at a dozen strategic points, exploiting hitherto unknown raw materials and stimulating new industries, many of which ultimately became the foundations of mediæval society. Thus was the dark curtain of barbarism gradually pushed back as civilization, in the persons of the lowly trader and hardy mariner, slowly groped along its way westward and northward, establishing its market posts, its primitive industries, its standards of barter with the natives. Imperial Rome, with her panoply of military and majestic splendor, felt herself far from demeaned by the activities of her merchants. The network of roads which she spread everywhere for the feet of her conquering legions were also the highways of her traders, whose operations she shrewdly appraised as a binding force of her power quite as potent as the achievements of her soldiery. The *Pax Romana* was the shield, not simply of her far-flung political institutions, but particularly of her caravans and shipping. The visible vestiges of her Empire may suggest primarily the breadth of her military power—from Hadrian's Wall in North Britain to the great camp of the Ninth Legion at Mérida in Western Spain, the barracks of Timgad, and farther Asia Minor. But more enduring and far more vital in their reactions on the world's civilization were her codes of business law, which to this day are factors in the affairs of trade and industry throughout the Latin lands of the Old World, and in the New, from Argentina to California and Louisiana.

As the Gothic hordes poured out of the wilds of northern and northeastern Europe, the "Roman Peace" was ended and darkness closed down upon the Western world. Business reverted to the primitive stages of nomadic barbarism, of furtive bartering in constant fear of swarthy Saracen raiders or the rapacious Viking seahawks. But even with the threats of these two menaces from North and South, there came a constant stream of commercial and industrial contributions to the revival of civilization: wool, dye woods, and spices from Africa and the Near East—to say nothing of those invaluable Arabic contributions of mathematical and classical lore—and numerous commodities and shipping experiences with each visitation of the Northmen.

The first glimmers of a more pretentious commercial revival came in the commissaries of the Crusaders, who were soon followed by the merchant fleets of Venice and her rivals. The development of their lucrative trade with the Near East not only inspired many phases of architectural and literary accomplishment in Western Europe but provided the foundation of riches for the patronage of art and literature in Northern Italy during the generations of their greatest achievements. Once more the crass materialists of business sheltered and made possible the works of many of the immortals of Western culture.

These merchant princes valued law and order; in fact, their fortunes were vitally dependent upon security; and, though the world of politics was riven with petty rivalries and clashing ambitions, the business life of the Middle Ages gradually evolved a comprehensive but effective series of international agreements and standards of commercial and industrial behavior, which laid the foundations for the restoration of Western civilization after its dismal depression in the Dark Ages. The formulation of such thirteenth and fourteenth century sea codes as that of the Hanseatic stronghold of Visby in the Baltic, of the island of Oléron in the English Channel, and of the Catalan *consolat del mar* in the Mediterranean, maintained for centuries the basis of international shipping practice, integrity, and mutual confidence. Similarly the trade standards and usages of the guilds and of the great international fairs at Medina, Lyons, Leipzig, Frankfort, and elsewhere, which gradually crystallized into written ordinances, provided foundations for modern municipal institutions and for commercial and financial codes, many of which survive to this day. These were the symbols of that mutual trust which has always been the indispensable factor in all enduring business relations—the spirit which found expression in those early days in such usages as the phrase "easterling," or "sterling," as applied in confident acceptance at face value of the silver offered in trade at the London Steelyard by the "easterlings" from the Hanseatic towns around the Baltic and the North Sea.

Thus there gradually emerged the steadily strengthening demand of the business world for orderly, peaceful relations, which gave powerful impulse to the movement toward the abolition and consolidation of countless petty principalities and the development of solid national growth. The abiding and compelling convictions of the merchant world thus left upon the every-day lives of men and women throughout the civilized world an enduring mark which was far more real and immediate to them than the lofty, sonorous thunderings of emperors, whose glamours so dominate the pages of orthodox historians.

It was only as these business agencies strayed from their proper fields and wandered along the devious paths of political aspirations that their usefulness and solid worth began to crumble. When the guild rules no longer reflected the conditions and standards of living and slowly caked down as a deadening restraint upon the freedom of enterprise and initiative, and particularly when they injected themselves into local and even national politics—even as business has done, to its shame and degradation, in many a later day—the influence of these once guiding spirits upon mediæval industrial and commercial life began to fade. When the Hanseatic League, once the proud mentor of trade standards throughout Europe, whose counting houses from Bergen to Venice, from London to the Lower Danube, stood for sterling integrity and impeccable reliability, began to intrude upon the affairs of state, upon the bickerings of political factions, and the rivalries of petty dukedoms, its power as an agency for business morality and goodwill soon dwindled.

### III

THE dramatic episode of the discovery of America has been ascribed to a variety of impulses—the super-emotional expression of the new era of the Renaissance and the urge for new outlets for the adventurous spirit and religious ardor, which had been rampant in Spain for more than seven centuries. The golden age of exploration and discovery, which dawned during the late fifteenth century and reached its zenith during the first half of the sixteenth, comprised a series of the most brilliant achievements ever attained in the recorded chronicles of grand adventure. We think of this epoch usually in just those terms—a bewildering story of astounding valor, incredibly fantastic daring, and truly prodigious energy. It would seem at first to be the sheerest sacrilege even to suggest the possible contamination of this immortal epic by any such lowly influence as commerce, and yet it was there, constantly and potently.

In appraising even the most exalted inspirations of men, such as this era of glorious adventure, it is folly to ignore that most prosaic of impulses, the need of food. And so, in searching for the motivating forces which so profoundly changed the current of Western civilization and enriched its annals with a hundred Odysseys, we must not ignore the yellowed pages of the cook-books of the time. They have none of the glittering lustre of royal decrees or the illuminated splendor of papal bulls, but surely there could be no more immediate contact with the every-day life of humanity than this literature of its daily bread.

The urge that drove the Portuguese down the West Coast of Africa, leading to the accidental discovery of Brazil en route, the impulse that sped Columbus on that hazardous adventure across the dark wastes of the Atlantic, and the inspiration of the frantic efforts to break through the fogs of the Northwest passage and of the countless subsequent drives to penetrate the unknown wilderness of the new continent—nearly all of these immortal episodes had as their chief objectives the attainment of new trade routes to the precious stores of spices in the East.

Pepper, cloves, and cinnamon were absolutely indispensable for the heavily predominant meat diets of Western Europe. Vegetables, in the opinion of those whose opinion counted, were fit only for the crude board of the peasantry. The tables of the rest of society groaned under endless courses of meat, fish, and game; hence, the elaborate laws of the time regarding poaching, forestry, hunting, etc. The only substitute for refrigeration was a profusion of spices; and if there had been no such emphatic demand for them, issuing with increasing emphasis from every kitchen in Western Europe as living standards improved, one wonders whether there would have been any abiding persistence, any lasting accomplishment, in all of the adventuring, all of the fervid revival of the Crusader's spirit, all of the hunting for the hated Moslem in the Orient.

When the *Victoria*, the lone survivor of Magellan's little fleet, finally tied up on the bank of the Guadalquivir at Triana, her precious cargo of cloves not only paid for the entire expedition but inspired quite as much jubilation as the astounding contribution to the world's geographic lore. Business had its part, and a vital one it was, in that memorable stride in the advancement of Western civilization literally in its very first world-wide effort.

Later, as the era of colonization came on, we find once again that the longing for religious and political liberty was not the sole impulse which inspired that great effort in projecting Western civilization across the seas to the New World. The diaries of the early governors of the Plymouth colony are dotted with references to the sums they "cleaned up," to use their own good Elizabethan phrase, on beaver skins and lumber. The first seeds of that sturdy growth, which was later to rise as the towering forest of modern American business, were planted by those stern devotees of Calvinistic frugality. The dazzling riches of Aztec and Inca focused attention on the exploitation of those mainland sections of the Spanish empire, but, as their easily accessible treasures dwindled away, the more lowly commodities of the island colonies came to the front. The French physician, Jean Nicot, had introduced Europe to the allurements of "those curious incense burners of the West Indies called *tabacos*" and had given his name to the distinctive ingredient of the weed. And so trade in tobacco, and, far more notably, that in sugar, came to inspire the struggles for empire which were waged in those waters for two centuries—struggles which wrought ultimately the dismemberment of the vast domains of Spain, at one time the greatest ever held under one flag—followed by the passage of supremacy from one dominant trading nation after another.

Portugal, Spain, Holland, France, and England, each contributed its quota to the advancement of civilization in the New World and the Orient, and the annals of those contributions are inseparably linked with the business records of the time: the fleet system of the galleons, merchant adventurers, East and West Indian companies, the Hudson's Bay Company, the Darien Company, the Guipuzcoa Company, and many others of lesser fame. All of them obviously had their political aspects. Indeed the conquests of government and business went hand in hand and shared jointly in the countless episodes which stand high on the honor pages of our Western history and also, be it added in frankness, in more than one shameless atrocity of exploitation and vicious deviltry. The sordid association of business and politics is not solely a phenomenon of our own time.

With all of these world-wide searchings for new trade routes and exotic products there poured in upon the Old World an ever-increasing tide of raw materials and riches, of hitherto undreamed contributions to every-day comfort, not simply of the finery of

Oriental fabrics, rare jewels, ivory, and gold, but lowly vegetables which were to change and vastly improve the diets of countless thousands—the potato and tomato from Peru and Chile, chocolate from Mexico, to say nothing of far greater quantities of sugar and coffee than had ever been available at moderate prices from the meagre stream which had hitherto trickled to Europe through the Near East. Later also there came new cabinet woods, rubber, tobacco, vegetable dyes, cotton, numerous other fibres, and new base metals, all of which reacted profoundly upon the industrial development of the Old World. With these new riches and comforts there came the resultant new desires for better things and simultaneously the means for their gratification.

IV

Out of it all there emerged from the antiquated guild crafts, first the crude domestic industries, then the industrial revolution, and finally the factory system—the successive foundation stones of modern business. Through them was industry emancipated from the mediævalism of the guild system with all of its rigid regulations and stern, archaic restrictions. A new era of business had come into being with far broader horizons, world wide in their scope. The autocracy of the craft hierarchies of the Middle Ages was gradually displaced first by the domestic or "putting out" system of fabrication, the hybrid link between the home crafts and what was to follow, and finally by the full-fledged new element of the factory system. Democratic in its origins, springing as it did from the very roots of the social order, it was soon to be transformed into the ruthless tyranny of the new factory magnates, who bestrode the life, political as well as social, of the later eighteenth and early nineteenth centuries with inexorable power.

In two brief generations, from 1770 to 1840, they had created a new empire in England, which was soon to have its prototypes on the Continent and across the Atlantic, an empire of mills and foundries, of railroads and canals, and with it all a formidable array of sordid problems profoundly affecting the lives of millions yet unborn. The host of new mechanical devices upon which they rode into power over the old industrial order became the symbol of their cold, calculating régime. They dominated the national drama of each major commonwealth in succession, even though they may not have been out in the centre of the stage in every scene.

The factory chimneys of Manchester were indeed the guns that won the battle at Waterloo. The craving for empire was the theme of the Napoleonic era, but the means of its attempted gratification on the one hand and of its final frustration on the other originated in the grimy ranks of industrial and commercial cities, whence came not only the physical equipment of warfare but the equally invaluable weapons of embargoes, blockades, and, above all, fiscal resources. England's iron output rose from 17,000 tons in 1740 to 125,000 in 1796. This mighty volume of raw stuff for the sinews of the war machine was ready to make its truly decisive contribution when the great need came to curb the menace of the Napoleonic legions.

Had industrial history been just a generation ahead of this schedule there is no telling what would have happened to the gaunt, scattered bands of colonial soldiery of 1776 and to their precious cause. Once again the evolution of business—fortunately retarded in this period—played, in a negative way, a vital part in the development of Western civilization.

After these spectacular, epoch-making transformations, the progress of the world's business during the first half of the nineteenth century seemed drab and lethargic. The heavy losses of warfare and of various crises in the Old World and New, aggravated by the inevitable nationalistic ardor which has followed in the wake of every war in modern history, considerably modified the progress of international economic affairs. The aggregate trade of all commercially active nations rose slowly in value from about 1.4 billions of dollars in 1800 to 4 billions in 1850, which meant a per capita growth from $2.31 to $3.76, according to Day's estimates. After the necessary allowance for price changes during this period, the net result would seem to show practically no per capita increase in actual volume. In the field of industry the showing was distinctly better; evidently each of the newly organized nations, as well as older ones which had weathered the severe storms of previous decades, was concentrating its strength primarily upon the development of resources toward self-sufficiency. The world's pig-iron production rose during the first half of the century from 800,000 tons to 4.7 millions, and coal from 11.6 millions to 81.4. The gains in these two essential staples were particularly accelerated from 1835 onward; evidently it took two decades for the world of business to bind up its wounds and convalesce from the wars of the Napoleonic generation.

The latter half of the century saw the accumulated momentum gathering speed with each swiftly passing decade. International commerce rose from 7.2 billion dollars in 1860 to 20.1 billions in 1900, a per capita increase from $6.01 to $13.02. Even with rising prices—and there were considerable dips as well as ascents in the price curve during the later years of the century—this represented a most substantial gain in volume of trade. Industrial output grew at an incredible speed: the world's pig-iron yield was 7.2 million tons in 1860 and 40.4 million tons in 1900, while coal production rose impressively from 142.3 million tons to 800 million.

Then came the thirteen years of the new century before the storm broke in the summer of 1914, a period of prodigious commercial and industrial expansion during which the business world, as in the years just before the Napoleonic wars, seemed to be unconsciously preparing itself for the frightful losses of 1914–18.

v

WHEN we come to interpret these monotonous rows of figures in terms of their reactions on human living and civilization, the task is indeed a formidable one. Each age is fond of ascribing to itself the favored position as the "turning point" or "crucial period" of the trend of history. Day quotes the American historian, Adams, and the economist, Wells, who expressed in 1871 and in 1890, respectively, their conviction as to the "unique and startling achievements" of the closing decades of the century, a period whose importance was undoubtedly "second to but very few and perhaps to none of the many similar epochs in time in any of the centuries that have preceded it."

Looking back upon that period, however, and particularly on the record of the relationship of business to the larger problems of society, it seems to be somewhat obscured by various questionable tendencies. True, it was an age of astounding advancement in volume of material achievement; but in the intangible, though far more lasting, aspects of its record, there is less cause for gratification. The gross offenses of monopolistic aggression, both of railroads and industry, in the United States soon brought business before the bar of an outraged public opinion. The results were the Interstate Commerce Commission and the Sherman Anti-trust Law. More potent even than these and similar stern mandates in the written statutes of the eighties and nineties was the chastened spirit of business itself. From the cynical, mercenary devotees of trickery, connivance, deceit, and general "public-be-damned" attitude, who had been so completely dominant in fixing the low standards of business morality, there gradually emerged a recognition that in self-defense business must shift its tenets to higher levels. The rigors of increasingly intensive competition made the consuming public the master; the rule of high-handed autocracy, which dated back a century to the industrial revolution, was distinctly at an end. Business became a thing of morals; its pursuit became a profession, which at last took its place with equal dignity and self-respect beside the law, medicine, and the ministry. The Wharton School of Finance was established at the University of Pennsylvania in 1881, and the Harvard Business School in 1908—a century or so after the first law and medical schools of the country and almost three hundred years after the first theological seminaries. "Is one to conclude," asks Owen D. Young, "that Harvard was fearful of an illiterate ministry of religion in 1636 but was not apprehensive of an illiterate ministry of business until 1908?"

The factors that entered into this amazing transformation in the soul of business are the basic themes of its history during our own generation, the truly vital contributions which it has made to the civilization of our time. The part played by business in the up-building of society to its present levels has been along widely divergent lines. First, and most obvious, is its contribution to the material comforts of mankind through a never-ending succession of inventions, each apparently more ingenious than its predecessor, each contributing an item which today may seem the sheerest luxury, but tomorrow may be an imperative necessity. The resultant transformation in our entire social order has been profoundly significant.

The almost unbelievable improvements in the means of transporting both things and thoughts within the past two decades have made the whole world one closely knit unit. Distance has been annihilated and with it the host of suspicions and hostilities that go with estrangement. In 1914 the combustion engine supplied only five per cent of the horse-power in the United States; today it contributes more than all other sources of power combined. It has completely remade our methods of business and the lives of our people on farms and in cities. It has created a host of entirely new industries and fields for service. It has made lighter the burdens of thousands; it has bound together all sections of the country, however remote, with broad bands of concrete, and, be it said with regret, has plastered the countryside with billboards, gasoline stations, and road houses.

The world's telephone wire mileage was about 33.7 millions in 1913; it was more than 84.5 millions in 1925. During the same period the number of pieces of mail carried increased from fifty billions to seventy-one billions, while the passengers carried on the world's railway systems rose from seven billions to ten billions. Scores of other figures might be cited on these vital factors of the new age of transportation and communication, showing the astounding increase of international cables, the magic growth of the radio, the incredible advancement of aviation, trans-oceanic wireless telephony from San Francisco to Stockholm, from Berlin to Buenos Aires, the significant economies and increased efficiency of petroleum burners, of the Diesel engine, and of the electrification of industry and transportation.

From the point of view of business, this tightening of the network of bonds of contact and communication around the globe has effected stupendous savings through the speeding up of valuable papers and commodities in transit. The newly established combination air and fast steamer mail service between Paris and

Buenos Aires, cutting the schedule from twenty-one days to ten, will save millions in interest charges each year. The most highly perishable "commodity" today is commercial intelligence, and the usable supply of it has, therefore, been vastly increased by every new medium for expedited transmission of trade information and the means of its translation into values.

It is true that with all of this speed, close contact, and resultant familiarity has come the disappearance of much that is romantic; distance lends enchantment and consequently all such space-annihilation has robbed our present-day business life of much of the leisurely charm and picturesqueness of the old days of the post-road and the clipper ship. Some cynics have even wondered whether Sarajevo could have brought on the holocaust of 1914 without the radio and telegraph flashing with blinding speed each hasty impulse and momentary passionate outburst from capital to capital, which urged on the fateful, irretrievable decisions, or whether the cataclysm of 1870 could have happened without the "telegram from Ems."

Today, instead of dreaming in peaceful isolation, each industry or trade is almost instantly responsive to impulses generated far beyond the horizon. Never before has the business of all peoples been so completely, so literally internationalized, so entirely inter-dependent. The textile mills in a small New England town come upon hard days; their principal market in far-off North China has dwindled because the sole industry of those remote Mongolian villages has collapsed, thereby destroying the buying power of their poverty-stricken inhabitants. The reason? Their livelihood was gained from making hair nets; the sudden shifts of feminine fancy brought on the bobbed hair "wave," and the once thriving Chinese hair net industry now lies buried under 400,000 tons of long locks, which have been shorn since the fashion started—whence comes at least a portion of the distress in the New England textile mills.

Of course, this despair of the modern business man in the presence of terrifying devastations due to changes in fashions is by no means a new phenomenon. In the year A. D. 22, Tiberius made these bitter observations to the Roman Senate: "If a reform (in dress) is in truth intended, where must it begin? And how am I to restore the simplicity of ancient times? . . . How shall we reform the taste of dress? . . . How are we to deal with the peculiar articles of feminine vanity, and, in particular, with that rage for jewels and precious trinkets which drains the Empire of its wealth and sends in exchange for baubles the money of the commonwealth to foreign nations, and even to the enemies of Rome?"

By these world-wide transmissions of impulses which react instantaneously upon trades and industries, tens of thousands of miles apart, business has become infinitely more complicated. The merchant or manufacturer of today can no longer exist in comfortable isolation even if he wants to. He must know what is going on not simply locally, but in remote parts of the world, if he is to carry on his operations profitably. He must prepare for repercussions upon his establishment from outposts of civilization whose very existence was entirely beyond the comprehension or interest of his immediate predecessors.

## VI

In the face of this complete transformation of the world of industry and trade, it is the sheerest folly to contemplate the "return to pre-war normalcy," as is still the practice in some quarters. As a matter of fact, the business world realizes now, as never before, that nothing could be more disastrous than a reversion to the utterly mediæval business practices and levels of 1913. To suggest that we scrap all of this astounding post-war economic revolution and build our hopes and plans on 1913 specifications is simply babbling, antiquated twaddle. For some years immediately after the War, it was customary among statisticians to base their calculations on pre-war index numbers, usually taking 1913 as one hundred or perhaps the annual average for the last five pre-war years. Today the United States Department of Commerce is basing practically all of its statistical indices on the average of the years 1923-25 inclusive, which is taken as a typical intermediary point in the post-war period.

The usual observation in some business circles about reversion to normalcy presupposes a fixed normal level which might be regarded as a desirable attainment for business. Nothing could be more seriously misleading. If business is as awake and progressive as it ought to be, it should obviously be readjusting its goal on a steadily advancing schedule. The last thing it can have in mind in this day of blinding speed and kaleidoscopic transformation is any firmly solidified objectives. The great reason why American business has progressed at such an incredible rate since the War has been its appreciation of the very fact that it must get away from the old and endeavor to attain steadily rising levels. The greatest monument to American industrial and commercial achievement is the enormous junk heap of abandoned practices, methods, and ideals, all of which were once "normal," but which today are the most useless relics of antiquity. Perhaps American business has been wasteful, but it would have been even more disastrously profligate had it remained shackled to the sanctified precedents of its mummified past.

Indeed, throughout the world wherever an industry or trade has been conspicuously successful in these recent years, it has been because its idea of "normalcy" has been the attainment of the abnormal, of the supposedly unattainable.

Now this does not by any means imply that the devotion of European industry to the honored traditions of its past have been an obstacle to its progress. Such may have been the case in some instances, but the vastly different circumstances of European industrial growth make comparison with the corresponding developments in the New World extremely difficult and misleading. European industry still rests in many respects upon individual craftsmanship, the skill of artisans handed down sacredly from generation to generation. American industrial growth is in the main a matter of steadily advancing machine technique, of superorganization, and of management, engineering, and equipment efficiency, all of which are factors susceptible of continued rapid advancement and change. In the delicate refinements, however, of the craftsman's skill, the development is apt to be much more gradual.

In general, the whole environment of American industry— labor scarcity, abundant raw materials, large domestic markets—

has created a combination of circumstances vastly different from those prevailing in Europe. It is, therefore, only with the greatest caution and reserve that one can contemplate the transfer of American methods of efficiency, mass production, and rationalization to the industrial communities of Europe. Such a transfer would inevitably involve the dislocation not simply of manufacturing, but of labor conditions, which would be bound to have profound social and political repercussions.

Indeed it is evident that those who have been prominent in proposing such a transplanting of American industrial technique to the Old World have overlooked the fundamental importance in the American scheme of the element of mass consumption as well as of mass production. The development of American industry has been a matter not simply of machines and highly intricate factory organization; it rests upon a vast and steadily increasing purchasing power within a market unincumbered by local trade barriers, racial or nationalistic antagonisms, and all the other hindrances which impede intra-European commerce.

A conspicuous feature of this improved standard of living and buying power is the increasing tendency of larger industries to open the way for employee stock ownership. This has been described of late as an economic revolution of major significance. Certainly it has made for a democratization of industry in a manner totally different from, and probably in a large part impossible in, Europe at least in the immediate present. It has given labor such an inseparable part in management and in the profits of industry that the doctrine of curtailment of output has made no headway in the labor movement in this country.

One of the inevitable costs of progress in all waste elimination in production methods has been the displacement of labor as indicated above. This would involve in Europe a factor of major importance, particularly because of the relatively less elastic conditions in industries and business in general—the greater difficulty of launching new practices, new enterprises, new consumer habits, etc. In America the problem has, of course, often been to the fore, especially in recent years, but there is here a vast advantage of new opportunity, of rapidly advancing buying power, of constant economic resilience, all of which have provided facilities for taking up at least some of the labor slack incident to the general improvement in manufacturing technique.

Throughout the history of the machine age this problem of the repercussions of greater manufacturing efficiency has been ever recurring. American steel production has increased fifty per cent per worker since 1913 and the efficiency of each operative in shoe factories has been enlarged sixteen per cent. In our automobile industry each employee is now turning out 11.5 units (cars, trucks, etc.) a year as against 7.2 in 1913. In other words, the need for labor in that industry has decreased more than fifty per cent in ratio to the output. This advancing efficiency, plus the deflation of America's wartime industrial abnormality, has resulted in a net decrease in employees in our factories of something like 917,000 since 1920. This substantial figure, if added to the 800,-000 represented in the decline of employees in agriculture (partly due to more efficient methods, the use of machinery, automotive traffic, etc.) and the 240,000 relieved from the railroads (likewise due in the main to better operation and greater efficiency in labor) since the War, gives a formidable total of nearly two millions in these groups.

If our observation were to stop at that point—and, unfortunately, several recent commentators have been so overwhelmed with that figure that their emotion has not permitted them to go any further—the business of the country would indeed be in a grave situation. In fact, more than one scathing indictment of this manifestation of the modern machine age has been drawn by social reformers.

There has, however, been a most helpful corrective, which has taken up most, though perhaps not all, of the slack, namely, the astonishing increase in non-manufacturing trades and pursuits. For example, since 1920, there has been an increase in the number of workers in automobile servicing and driving of nearly 760,000, including nearly 100,000 chauffeurs of buses, a vocation which scarcely existed before 1914. There are nearly 100,000 more insurance agents clamoring at our doors today than in 1919. The needs of the new electric refrigeration, light and power, and oil-heating establishments have required an increase of 100,000 in their service employees. Another hundred thousand addition to personnel has been required since the War in the management and general direction of construction work (exclusive of actual manual labor on building projects). There are 232,000 more teachers and professors required to look after the country's flaming youth of the present day than in 1919. The increase in the number of motion-picture servitors (again exclusive of production employees) accounts for another 125,000 names added to the payrolls of that exuberant industry since the War. It is not hard to explain the increase of 170,000 barbers and hairdressers during the same period. One of the most impressive figures is that in the service branches of hotels and restaurants, whose personnel has increased by no less than 525,000 (some estimates run as high as a million) since 1920—a vivid commentary upon the social transformation which has accompanied this post-war development of American business.

These new service functions not only counteract in large part the harmful unemployment effects of displacing manual labor by machinery; they are an encouraging indication of the higher per capita earning power of the operatives of the machines; they are a definite indication of better living standards and of the greater margin of general comfort made possible by lifting many of the burdens of drudgery from the backs of men and laying them on the steel frames of machines. As defined in the recent observations of a British visitor, "the objective of American democracy is to create an economic system which will assure to everybody who is prepared to work not simply food, clothing, and shelter, but a university education, a motor-car, a good annual holiday, and all of the amusement within reach, and which will then set to work either to increase his wages or shorten his hours from eight to seven and then to six or five so that more and more of his life will be spent in those leisure hours when he is master of his own time and fate."

And so, the harnessing of machinery and of factory technique in its most scientific form goes on apace. Nearly seventy per cent of the power used in the United States today is electrical. According to the latest available figures about $6,000 of capital is invested in the equipment and plant of American factories for every worker employed. This substantial sum—a margin far beyond the corresponding figure in leading European nations—accounts largely for the fact that the output per man per hour has increased since 1900 about eighty per cent.

There is a further social consequence of this changing era in the evolution of industry. In order to keep pace with the stream of economic changes that are engulfing one trade after another, business has in self-defense been compelled to resort to much more aggressive educational campaigns for the building up of trained personnel. The great technical schools in Europe have in recent years been materially strengthened, although their personnel and resources suffered sadly during the War and in the depression of 1921–23. The number of pupils in American vocational schools has risen from 265,000 in 1920 to more than 752,000 in 1926. Industry has taken upon itself not only the endowment of such establishments, but also the advancement of educational efforts within its own ranks through research laboratories on a vastly larger scale today than before the War, through trade papers, whose circulation in the United States exceeds two millions, through trade associations, of which there are more than two thousand in this country, and through close collaboration with various governmental bodies engaged in the advancement of industrial learning. All this has led to a host of new approaches to business problems through more intelligent, far-sighted preparation for their solution.

Industrial strategy is no longer a matter of momentary tactics, of sudden opportunistic shifts with each new situation. Business today is operating more and more on long-view planning, upon shrewd, broad-visioned appraisal of situations and prospects, all of which has greatly modified the dangerous variables of risks. The slide-rule has indeed displaced the rule-of-thumb. The gyrations of the business cycle have been lessened in severity, so that the strain on the economic machine is greatly modified. Closer contacts with demand and shrewder appraisal of its possible trends have lessened the strain on inventories and stocks, thereby modifying greatly the overhead burdens of business. The American

Federal Reserve System, whose counterpart is beginning to appear in many lands of Latin America and the Old World, has further contributed toward the same stabilizing process by more effective control of the flow of credit.

Conspicuous among these newer forces of control is the vastly increased co-operative and collaborative element in modern business. As Secretary Hoover has vividly expressed it, "We are, almost unnoticed, in the midst of a great revolution, or perhaps a better word, a transformation in the whole super-organization of our economic life. We are passing from a period of extremely individualistic action into a period of associational activities." These comprise a vast range of organizations embracing every conceivable phase of economic interest. There are perhaps twenty-five thousand of them in the United States alone. Although in the case of the European organizations, their ancestry is traceable back to the mediæval craft guilds in many cases, the present-day association is vastly different in its interests and significance. The purposes of some of them are admittedly sinister, but there can be no doubt that in the main their efforts are concentrated upon the modification of the destructive elements in our business life.

They stand for the adoption of codes of commercial ethics, for the standardization of grades of merchandise and accepted business practices, for the elimination of malicious competition, the curtailment of costly litigation through the spread of arbitration, and the interchange of ledger experience as a means of stabilizing credit practices. Perhaps the instinctive gregariousness of the American business man, his recognition of his own inadequate experience, and the general democratic congeniality of life in newer social environments have all contributed toward the relatively greater advancement of such trade organizations in America than in Europe.

Nevertheless, business in the Old World is also groping toward the same broad line of development, though with a degree of patronage and control from governments which has not been tolerated in the United States. The European chambers of commerce are usually semi-official bodies, occasionally with compulsory membership, and always with some intimate association with political authority. Their proceedings, therefore, have many of the sanctions of law in dealing with problems which are solved in America by voluntary restraint and informal collaboration. This contrast does not, of course, necessarily involve a judgment as to inferiority; it is simply the result of contrasts in environment, of entirely different social and political institutions, which probably would make difficult the injection of such American practices into Old World conditions.

The fundamental theme of the early factory system was its autocracy, a characteristic which has regrettably survived to this day in a minority of certain industries and localities. The new development of democracy through employee participation in management and ownership and broad collaborative effort, particularly among small establishments, through trade associations, is perhaps the outstanding element in the present-day transformation of business. Incidentally, these changes have greatly modified the once widespread custom of condemning industrial and commercial enterprises merely because of their size. The rapid advance in employee-owner collaboration in the large concerns on the one hand and the activity of trade association campaigns to clear up trade abuses among small establishments on the other have indicated that there is no essential relationship, in inverse ratio, between the virtue and the vastness of business enterprises. A substantial contributor to this change in the public mind has been the ever strengthening conviction within business circles that goodwill is after all the *sine qua non* of survival and that one of the most effective means for the attainment of that goodwill is through collaborative effort in building up accepted standards of sound trade ethics.

Until business can cure its own abuses from within through such commendable means, it need expect no mercy from the public and its authorized governmental agencies. Unfortunately, the experience of the past generation reveals all too many illustrations that such governmental intrusion upon the affairs of trade inevitably implies, especially in a democracy, the most dangerous temptations to bureaucracy and demagogy. And when the business relationships involved are international in scope, the perils are vastly multiplied. The additional phase of diplomacy and world-wide intrigue then begins to appear, with consequent problems of the utmost gravity. The cause of goodwill and friendly international relations is not encouraged by injecting the bickerings of the market-place into the counsels of ministries of foreign relations; nor does business itself stand to profit by being made the football of international politics—as has happened on several recent occasions when governments have undertaken active participation in affairs of trade.

Post-war policies of nationalistic economic self-sufficiency and the general need of replenishing sadly depleted stocks of raw materials led to a widespread campaign for the further development and control of trade in essential crude commodities. These factors, coupled with the collapse of prices during the 1921 depression, resulted in the launching of several schemes to manipulate through governmental agencies the trade in such essentials as rubber, coffee, nitrate, sisal, potash, quinine, and several others. In some cases this involved renewal of old pre-war price-fixing devices. This widespread injection of government into business may in some cases have had a momentary justification, but, as is invariably the case, the embarrassments of retirement, once such a step had been taken, have proved in most cases to be insurmountable. The situation of the producers in each case was temporarily aided, but the tendency toward further exploitation of the consumers, particularly through unscrupulous and irresponsible market operators who thrive only on erratic price changes, resulted in considerable friction and emphatic protest, particularly from American industries, which in most cases are the largest consumers of these products.

However, the inevitable cycle set in. Artificially stimulated prices far beyond equitable limits, arbitrary regulatory impediments to trade, and other defects in government operation encouraged the use of substitutes—of synthetic nitrates for the monopolized Chilean natural product, of other fibres in place of sisal, of various beverages substituted for coffee, and of reclaimed rubber and more economical uses of the crude product—each of these at one time or another, and in some instances permanently, resorted to by protesting consumers as effective weapons of defense.

The net result has been a thoroughly disturbed business situation in each case, much unnecessary animus and ill will, which have been promptly capitalized by professional agitators, and even more fundamentally a retarded introduction of the sound principles of accepted business practice, namely, large volume consumption at lowest prices consistent with stable fair profits.

Such distortions of distribution bring up all too clearly the fact that among the outstanding problems confronting business today one of the most conspicuous is the need for improvement in this broad field of economies in selling methods. In contrast with production, this aspect of the world's post-war economic development has been given far less scientific attention and intensified effort. The first problem after the termination of the struggle of 1914–18 was the rehabilitation of productivity to fill the gaps in world supplies of goods and equipment. Questions of economy in distribution, of eliminating wastes in selling costs, have only very recently received the attention which they deserve among business leaders. The world as a whole is still obviously in the earliest experimental stages with installment selling, with such mass distributive apparatus as chain stores and mail-order establishments, and with problems of more accurate market appraisals, calculations of potential buying power, etc. It is along these lines of more economical and generally less wasteful selling that business is likely to make its greatest progress in the immediate future.

In this connection, one of the phases of newer distributive changes in Europe has been the active exploitation of the international cartel, a revival in a more comprehensive form of an old pre-war institution. These organizations, which roughly may be described as marketing pools, now operate in dominating the European trade in some fourteen staple commodities, usually through the allocation of trade territories, sales quotas, and the establishment of uniform price policies. Ostensibly, their chief aim is to eliminate distributive wastes and excessive competition and to stabilize prices. As a matter of fact, they are, of course, still subject to all the usual faults of monopolies, notably a tendency to protect and sustain inefficient units in the trade and an inclination toward the exploitation either of consumers on the one hand or of labor on the other. Though not organized primarily as offensive weapons against the United States, it is obvious that their success will encourage them toward more aggressive competition with corresponding trades in this country. For the time being, their chief purpose is the elimination of abnormalities in European business and the introduction of more orderly trading conditions on the Continent. They are part of the general trend toward greater cohesion among Old World interests, both economic and political, and reflect the increasing belief that collaboration is indispensable if Europe is to be saved. The cartels have undoubtedly contributed some elements of stability to the world's trade in certain respects, thereby assisting the marketing of similar American products. Their further competitive development and possible antagonism to American business practices, however—especially in connection with their association with governmental authority—will undoubtedly be most carefully observed from this side of the Atlantic.

VII

WITH this widespread growth of more and more associated effort in all aspects of business, the question is frequently raised as to whether we are not witnessing the rapid construction of a great Moloch of organized industry and commerce completely dominating and overwhelming the finer elements of individual initiative, the spirit of enterprise and originality.

But whatever the machine age has done for us, it must be granted that it has spared humanity from the interminable and insufferable detailed, repetitive routine. The old Periclean law gave each Athenian the right to own five slaves. It has been calculated that every inhabitant of the United States has today at his disposal the power equivalent of 150 slaves. Surely there could be no more impressive indication of the contribution that machinery and its directive force, modern business, have made in easing the burdens of drudgery, in sparing the costs of countless tasks, and in making available a larger leisure for the enjoyment of those finer comforts which in earlier ages were the exclusive prerogatives of a few.

Some writers, such as Aldous Huxley, for example, have questioned the benefits of our business progress and wondered whether it is not being accelerated at the expense of future generations. The population of the earth has increased two and one-half times during the nineteenth century, while coal production has grown one hundred and ten times, iron eighty, cotton twenty, the volume of the world's commerce forty, and so on. But does this piling up of mass output mean a better civilization? These critics quote Ben Jonson's observation that

> *It is not growing like a tree*
> *In bulk doth make men better be.*

Unless these mighty works of modern industry and managerial genius really contribute to improved comfort and welfare for masses of human beings, business cannot claim to have advanced in fundamental social value since the primitive days of the industrial revolution. But most assuredly the business world has awakened to a new consciousness of its responsibilities in that direction and to a realization that only by assuming them can it play its part in restoring the fabulous losses of the War and the post-war economic chaos.

## V—LABOR

*By* SIDNEY AND BEATRICE WEBB

THE APPLICATION to industry of scientific discoveries and inventions, with the consequent great development of machinery and of every form of capital during the past two centuries, have wrought, as is well known, a marvellous increase in the production of nearly every kind of commodity desired by man. This increase in every form of material wealth is definitely distinctive of Western civilization. What is not so commonly realized is that the Industrial Revolution, as it is termed, effected equally substantial changes in the daily lives of the hired men and their families, who came gradually to form the bulk of the whole community—constituting in fact, at the present day, in the nations in which the changes have gone farthest, four-fifths of the population. It is the thesis of this chapter that the Industrial Revolution, whilst ultimately of great social advantage, did, at the outset, in every country create considerable evils. These evils have been, during the past century, very largely prevented and remedied by appropriate collective action, differing in details from country to country, and varying in the degree of success yet attained; but everywhere steadily increasing in volume and range. An analysis of these changes in the life and labor of the people, from decade to decade, and from country to country, will, we think, best reveal the present value and the future prospects of Western civilization.

I

LET US note, to begin with, that the application of science and machinery to wealth-production, which is so characteristic of Western civilization, has no necessary relation to the Capitalist organization of industry, on the one hand, or to any particular status of the manual worker, on the other. As Dr. Beard points out in the Introduction to this volume, "Machine civilization is by no means synonymous with capitalism." The owners and ultimate directors of the instruments of production are not necessarily private persons or corporations of private persons, whose "acquisitive instincts" have led them to "build factories and start mass production," for the purpose of making profit. Quite apart from possibilities of the future, there is, in the world of to-day, no small aggregate of capital embodied in large masses in great undertakings, in which there is neither private ownership nor private profit. We may instance, in one or other nation, great governmental systems of internal transportation and communication (railways, roads, and canals; the postal, telegraph, and telephone services; even radio broadcasting); innumerable national and municipal institutions of public character (schools and colleges, hospitals, and museums); the supply of water, gas, electricity, and hydraulic power; the tramway and motor omnibus service; the provision of dwellings, pleasure grounds and parks; the administration of vast areas of forest; even governmental concerns of magnitude dealing with such transactions of finance as banking, insurance, investments, and remittance. In Great Britain, Germany, Scandinavia, and other European countries there are extensive "Democracies of Consumers" (the Co-operative Movement), conducting, through a hierarchy of salaried officials, "big business" of amazing bulk and variety, including banking, insurance, growing, mining, manufacturing, importing and exporting, together with both wholesale and retail distribution—all instituted and administered without any thought of "profit on price." There are, in fact, to-day States of magnitude in which as many as one tenth of all the families are on the public payroll, directly enrolled in either the national, the municipal, or the co-operative service.

Moreover, the masses of men and women who pass their working lives in this associated production with the "machines," or other forms of capital—who become more and more nearly coextensive with the "Industrial State"—are not necessarily "free." They have been in the recent past (as in parts of the United States down to 1865, and, here and there in Africa, even nearer to our own day) actually chattel slaves. They have been semi-slaves or unenfranchised serfs to the end of the eighteenth century (as in Scottish salt- and coal-mines); or down to 1860 (as in government factories in Czarist Russia); or even (in parts of Asia and Africa) down to the present day. But in the modern industrial States of Europe, Australia, and America, as in Japan, and in the parts of continental Asia and Africa in which Western civilization has already become dominant, the men and women laboring with the masses of capital are free wage-earners, working under contracts of service voluntarily entered into, which run usually for short periods, and are always terminable at the will of either party to the contract.

## II

THE initial effects of the Industrial Revolution on the lives of those wage-earners who were brigaded in the mines, the factories, and the other forms of highly capitalized industry, were twofold. As compared with the life of the individual producer in handicraft or agriculture, the factory operative found his work simplified, systematized, and regulated. Instead of working when he liked, and producing what he chose, in whatever way he preferred, the handloom weaver or the agricultural peasant who entered the cotton mill or the mine was required to be in attendance every day, at a prescribed hour, and to continue at the task dictated to him for a fixed working period. In the England of the eighteenth century this involved, we believe, for large masses of workers, a gain in the diminution of loose living, hard drinking, and spells of idleness and ill-health.

But the second and more general effect was wholly disadvantageous. Though the application to industry of power-driven machinery, and the more organized production which it necessitated, poured forth a vastly increased aggregate of commodities, it soon appeared that the increase in wealth meant often no improvement of material conditions for the wage-earners, but very much the opposite. This happened, not so much from the thoughtlessness and inhumanity of the owners of the new machine industries, as from the economic competition among them. As each, in the struggle to market the vastly increased output, strove against all the others, prices were reduced, and costs had to be cut. The hours of labor were progressively lengthened; the factories became more and more crowded with operatives; nothing could be spared for sanitation, nothing even for safeguarding the workers against accidents; the wages were reduced and again reduced, until only by the earnings of the whole family, man, wife, and children of tender age, could even a bare subsistence be obtained. Aggregated in hastily erected dwellings, in areas devoid of the means of healthy existence, the population of the districts of the factory and the mine sank even below the level of the mediæval village. The tragic process of this worsening of the conditions is described in every account of the Industrial Revolution. So far as Great Britain is concerned the account of what happened between 1760 and 1860 has during the present generation become a wearisome platitude of the history text-books. But those who realize what happened find it difficult to write about it without passion. Relays of young children destroyed in the cotton factories; men and women, boys and girls, weakened and brutalized by promiscuous toil in mines and ironworks; whole families degraded by indecent occupation of the tenement houses of the crowded slums; constantly recurrent periods of unemployment, and consequent hunger and starvation; food adulterated, air poisoned, water contaminated, the sights and sounds of day and night rendered hideous, these were the commonplace incidents of the industrial Britain of the beginning of the nineteenth century, discovered and rediscovered, in trade after trade, not by sentimental philanthropists and sensational newspaper reporters, but by government inspectors and legislative enquiries. Britain came first to this state, and perhaps went furthest in degradation. The condition of the people of the cotton-spinning centre of Bolton in Lancashire was described by Col. Perronet Thompson in 1842 in language that palpitates with anger. "Anything like the squalid misery, the slow, mouldering, putrefying death by which the weak

and feeble of the working classes are perishing here, it never be-
fell my eyes to behold nor my imagination to conceive. And the
creatures seem to have no idea of resisting, or even repining. They
sit down with Oriental submission, as if it was God and not the
landlord that was laying his hand upon them."

At the same time, the newly constituted Boards of Guardians
(the Poor Relief Authorities), throughout the whole of England
and Wales, were exacting useless toil from between forty and fifty
thousand adult able-bodied men in oakum-picking, stonebreaking,
and bonecrushing in the "Labour Yards" attached to the hated
workhouses, or "Bastilles of the poor," in return for pittances of
poor relief just sufficient to keep them and their families alive.
Of such workers as were fortunate enough to be still in wage-
earning employment, men, women, and children, "pent up in a
close dusty atmosphere from half past five or six o'clock in the
morning till seven or eight o'clock at night, from week to week,
without change, without intermission, it is not to be wondered
at," states a contemporary Government Report, "that they fly
to the spirit and beer shop and the dancing house on the Saturday
nights to seek those, to them, pleasures and comforts which their
now destitute and comfortless homes deny."

### III

Now THIS state of physical and mental degradation among the
wage-earners in the Machine Industry, and of widespread destitution and misery among "the common people," was not the "Act
of God." It was not the result of famine, pestilence, or flood,
or of any failure of nature to reward honest toil. On the contrary, it occurred in a country that was year by year extending its
dominion beyond the range of the world's greatest empires, without a rival in foreign markets, at a time when those in command
of the land and the machines, and of the commercial and financial
organization through which they were administered, grew rich
beyond the dreams of avarice. Nor was it due to any lack of
physical science, or to any backwardness in the inventiveness that
harnessed the newly discovered forces to industrial production as

fast as the capitalists could erect their mills, launch their ships, and construct their canals and railways. The hideous effects of the Capitalism of the first half of the nineteenth century in Great Britain were due, in the last analysis, to a state of mind; to the opinions generally held by the educated and enlightened governing class, and to the social organization, or lack of organization, which was the outcome of that state of mind. The destitution of the manual workers, and their consequent compulsion to become the docile slaves of the new machines, were, so Malthus taught in his "Law of Population," part of the necessary order of nature—the inevitable result of the pressure of population on the means of subsistence, which no effort of government or philanthropy could alter. It was inevitable, so the Political Economists declared in the Theory of the Wage Fund, that wages should oscillate closely around their "natural" rate, which could be no more than sufficed for the day to day subsistence of the manual worker's family. To the energetic capitalist employers, as to the comfortable class generally, this "natural law" seemed, not merely inevitable, but also actually advantageous and beneficial to the community, for was it not the necessary basis of all riches, all refinement, all learning, and civilization itself? "It seems to be a law of nature," wrote the Rev. Joseph Townsend, a popular clergyman in 1785, in a work which was repeatedly reprinted during the next thirty years, and quoted with approbation in contemporary government reports, "that the poor should be to a certain degree improvident, that there may always be some to fulfil the most servile, the most sordid and the most ignoble offices in the community. The stock of human happiness is thereby much increased whilst the more delicate are not only relieved from drudgery, and freed from those occasional employments which would make them miserable, but are left at liberty without interruption, to pursue those callings which are suited to their various dispositions, and most useful to the State. As for the lowest of the poor, by custom they are reconciled to the meanest occupations, to the most laborious works, and to the most hazardous pursuits. . . . There must be a degree of pressure, and that which is attended with the least violence will be the best. When hunger is either felt or feared, the desire of obtaining bread will quietly dispose the mind to undergo the greatest hardships, and will sweeten the severest labour."

"Without a large proportion of poverty," declared Dr. Patrick Colquhoun (the inventor of the modern Preventive Police force, to-day ubiquitous throughout Western civilization), "there could be no riches, since riches are the offspring of labour, while labour can exist only in a state of poverty. Poverty is that state and condition of society where the individual has no surplus labour in store; or, in other words, no property or means of subsistence but what is derived from the constant exercise of industry in the various occupations of life. Poverty is therefore a most necessary and indispensable ingredient of society, without which nations and communities could not exist in a state of civilization. It is the lot of man. It is the source of wealth, since without poverty there could be no labour; there would be no riches, no refinement or comfort, and no benefit to those who may be possessed of wealth, inasmuch as without a large proportion of poverty surplus labour could never be rendered productive in producing either the conveniences or luxuries of life." "Poverty," said the philanthropic Michael Thomas Sadler in 1828, "is the great weight which keeps the social machine going; remove that, and the gilded hands would not long be seen to move aloft, nor the melodious chimes be heard again."

The American reader, will, we think, recognize in these extracts from writers in a country debarred from negro slavery a close resemblance to the arguments used, between 1830 and 1860, by the Virginian and Carolinian defenders of the "peculiar institution" on which the civilization of the Southern States was in that generation based.

IV

THE first reaction from the realization of the condition of destitution and demoralization, into which the Industrial Revolution was hurrying the wage-earners subjected to it, came from certain farsighted philanthropists. What impressed Robert Owen, in the first quarter of the nineteenth century and Lord Shaftesbury in the second, was the imperative necessity of restraining, by the criminal law, the more heedless or the less scrupulous of the employers from making the conditions of employment in their factories and mines positively injurious to the health and vigor of the wage-earners, out of whose incessant labor so much wealth was being derived. In the successive Factory Acts of 1802, 1819, 1825, and 1833, and in the Mines Regulation Act of 1842, the foundation was laid of an altogether novel policy of systematically "blocking the downward way" in the competitive struggle. Without specific theory, merely as a means of preventing abuses, the Legislature extended the criminal law, so as to give to those who were shown to be oppressed the protection that they were unable to secure for themselves. In the course of the century this principle received an almost continuous extension. In the great industry of coal mining, which came to employ nearly one tenth of all the manual workers in the nation, successive statutes required more and more elaborate safeguards against accidents, prevented the piece-workers from being cheated in their earnings, ensured for them more sanitary conditions, limited the employment of women and boys, and more and more closely regulated, in the interests of the wage-earners, the technical processes of the industry. In the present century, this legal control of the industrial conditions of the mine was further extended, first to the limitation of the daily working hours of adult men, and secondly, by the enactment of a Legal Minimum of daily earnings. We see a similar evolution of legislation with regard to the great army of those who go down to the sea in ships. By the succession of Merchant Shipping Acts a constantly extending protection has been accorded to those engaged in the mercantile marine, with the object of securing them from accident, ill-usage, and oppression. The Regulation of Railway Acts of 1889 and 1893 empowered the Board of Trade to prevent excessive hours of labor among railway employees. By successive Trucks Acts, Factory and Workshop Acts, and Shop Hours Acts, practically all manufacturing industries and nearly all retail stores have been similarly brought under regulation and inspection, in order to prevent the wage-earners from being subjected to insanitary conditions, preventable

accidents, and excessive hours of labor.   The present century has
seen a similar protection against wages insufficient for subsistence.
In 1909 and 1918, by the Trade Boards Acts, which have been applied to industries employing nearly a million wage-earners, these
(men as well as women) have been given the security of a Legal
Minimum below which the law does not permit their wages to be
reduced.   This truly remarkable development of British industrial policy has not only received the endorsement alike of economists and of representative organizations of capitalist employers,
but has also been paid the compliment of imitation, in principle,
by nearly every other industrial community in the world.   The
nations naturally differ in the date, the nature, and the extent of
the successive adoption of what is now summed up as Factory
Legislation.   Similar prohibition of wrongdoing is embodied—
in Great Britain from 1848 onwards, and in all other industrialized
countries in the course of the nineteenth century—in the long
succession of laws relating to the Public Health, in all their ramifications, starting from the more serious infectious diseases which
injured the rich almost as much as they did the poor.   Whilst
Great Britain has on the whole led the way, yet at one or other
date, and with regard to one or other point, Switzerland or Russia,
Australia or Massachusetts, Sweden or France has from time to
time improved on the contemporary practice.   The International
Labour Office of the League of Nations now works persistently for
the improvement and the ubiquitous assimilation throughout the
world of this policy of "blocking the downward way."

v

So FAR, we have dealt only with the laws which prevented the
landowners and employers from using their freedom of competition in certain ways which had been proved to be demoralizing
and degrading to those who served them.   This principle of
"blocking the downward way" in the working of free competition may be said to constitute the foundation of a Framework of
Prevention.   A second, and more controversial, stage in that preventive framework was the provision, out of public funds, of

particular services and commodities for the use of all those, whether rich or poor, who were in need of them. The bulk of the work of the tens of thousands of local government authorities in all the countries of Western Civilization is done—as will be realized on reflection—on a communistic basis, that is, on the principle of "*to* each man according to his need, and *from* each man according to his ability." The earliest forms of this empirical communism may be seen in the paving, lighting, and sewering of the cities. Even more striking cases are the schools for the children and hospitals for the sick. The present generation has seen an enormous extension in range and in amount of this form of communal service. Germany led the way in the addition, by compulsory insurance, of Old Age Pensions for all men and women on reaching a certain age; and this provision, extended to widows and orphans, has been copied with various modifications by other nations. A corresponding, and equally costly system of compulsory thrift on the part of the hired persons, largely subsidized by contributions from their employers and from the taxpayers, now provides, in more than a score of States, at least partial maintenance when sick or unemployed, together with medical treatment and often the gratuitous services, in finding new employment, of a public system of Employment Exchanges. The Framework of Prevention thus includes, not merely an all-embracing code of protective legislation, and an extensive communal provision of public utilities for common use, but also communal payments to individual families, in Great Britain alone amounting in the aggregate to more than a hundred million pounds a year, at least two-thirds of it levied on the employers or the propertied class. It is paradoxical that there should be actually to-day in Great Britain much more "communism" in this economic sense than there is in Soviet Russia!

## VI

CONTEMPORANEOUSLY with the development of the governmental Framework of Prevention, in the legislative blocking of the downward way, and the public provision of necessary services for all who need them, there has grown up, from one end of Western civilization to the other, a different form of protection of the wage-earners against the worst abuses of the capitalist system. The new status of wage-earner had, it was discovered, the inherent economic drawback, in comparison with the position of the individual producer, that the capitalist employer in the Machine Industry had a position of vantage in the bargaining by which the terms of the wage-contract were settled. Not only could the employer easily afford to wait, whereas the day laborer could not; but even more serious, in the competition for engagement among men eager for subsistence, he could play off one wage-earner against another, so as to bring down the terms for the whole group to the level of the most necessitous and the most assiduous among them. In short, in the process of bargaining over wages, the employer was a combination in himself. It was inevitable that the wage-earners should seek by combination among themselves some way of regaining collectively at least a substitute for the independence that they had individually lost. Thus Trade Unionism arose to construct, by its collective agreements and regulations, essentially the same sort of shield against the worst offences of the Industrial Revolution as the Legislatures were devising in their Factory Legislation. In England, as in every other country, the resulting combinations of the unlettered workmen have made all sorts of mistakes, including everywhere a longer or a shorter period of violence and intimidation, marked, here and there, by the destruction of property, and even murder. But wherever Trade Unionism has progressed, it may be seen, in one country after another, settling down to the attainment of its ends by one or other of three methods or expedients, the Method of Mutual Insurance (preventing any member from being, by dire need, driven to accept anything that the employer offers); the Method of Collective Bargaining (preventing the common terms being brought down by competition of the most needy or the most eager); and the Method of Legal Enactment (securing minimum conditions by law, in so far as the Legislature will concede this). Trade Unionism, like Factory Legislation, was long objected to by the economists, and still longer resisted by the employers; but it has, in the best organized industries, in country after country, converted both the one and the other to the essential validity of its position; and with the gradual improvement in its methods—notably in the increasing substitution of negotiation for violence, and of the settlement of the terms of the wage-contract by public tribunals instead of by the wild arbitrament of the lock-out and the strike—it must be deemed to have definitely established itself throughout Europe and Australasia—we do not know how far the same can be said of the United States—as a feature of Western Civilization.

VII

It is interesting to notice that, at least in the European industrialized States, both Factory Legislation and Trade Unionism began as direct results of the Industrial Revolution, before the admission of the manual-working wage-earners to any share in government. Political democracy had, in fact, another origin. As an intellectual ferment, it dates, in Europe, from the Protestant Reformation of the sixteenth century, from which, however, it only gradually emerged. As a political movement in the course of the seventeenth and eighteenth centuries it was most dramatically manifested in the English Rebellion and Constitutional Revolution of 1640–89; the American Declaration of Independence and successful revolt of 1776–83; and the French Revolution of 1789–96. The British demonstration that monarchs could be made responsible to those whom they had regarded as their subjects; the emphatic American declaration of the inherent rights of all men to political freedom and social opportunity; and the inspiring gospel of Liberty, Equality, and Fraternity that France transmitted around the whole world, combined, throughout the nineteenth century, in re-moulding the thought and re-drafting the political constitutions of Western civilization, until, in the Great World War of 1914–18, not merely autocratic Kingship, but also aristocratic privilege expired. Though it took more than a hundred years, even in the most advanced countries, before the political franchise was granted to the whole adult population—and in some countries, such as Japan and Greece, and practically all those of Latin race in Europe as well as in South America, women are still excluded—yet we must notice that the successive extensions of the franchise were, practically everywhere, conceded by the governing classes to argument, and not wrested from them by force; a notable testimony to the slow but sure effect on public opinion of the resounding declarations of the preceding century. It is the separate nationalities that have had, in Europe, actually to fight for political self-determination, not the manual workers in each nation. Moreover, whilst we may ascribe to the general movement for Democracy the gradual, and pretty general, adoption of freedom of speech and freedom of association, it was especially to the intellectual influence of the theoretical Democrats of the United States and the Philosophic Radicals of Great Britain that we owe, along with universal voting, also universal schooling. The public educational systems of Western civilization, which to-day constitute (apart from the burden of debt and the cost of defence) in most countries the largest single item of public expenditure, are among the greatest of social achievements. It may, perhaps be regretted that the political philosophers, from whose teaching public opinion learnt Democracy, so far as elections were concerned, were seldom favorable to Factory Legislation, and not often even to the conception of a Framework of Prevention of working-class destitution—a fact which partly explains the lukewarm support given by the wage-earners for the greater part of the nineteenth century, to the merely political Democracy of "Liberal" thinkers. Not until the wage-earners, as a class, began to resort to political action on their own account, did the two streams join—in the present century, in Great Britain, to merge in the establishment of the Labour Party, the immediate result of which has been the greatly quickened rate at which, during the past twenty years, successive advances and developments of collective action for the prevention of destitution in the wage-earning class have been made by Parliament and generally accepted by public opinion.

DURING the past half century, in practically all the nations of Europe, the stream of Political Democracy has become transformed into that of Socialism. What was essentially a struggle for reorganization, on the lines of broader and more complete Democracy, of the political machinery of the State, has become a struggle for reorganization of the economic and industrial machinery of each community, so as to substitute public and collective for individual and private control of the main instruments of wealth production. What is commonly not appreciated is that there are, in the world-wide Socialist movement, two varieties, the one derived from Robert Owen and the Chartists of 1837–48, to which Great Britain and Australasia have been predominantly disposed; and the other, derived from Karl Marx, which captured the enthusiasm of the wage-earners (and received a great deal of support from the intellectuals) of continental Europe. The cleavage between the two schools is, however, historical and traditional, based rather on the methods of thought and political circumstances of the various countries than on any contrast of political programmes and immediate results. The special note of what may be called the British School of Socialism is that of the gradual and empirical application of collectivist doctrine in one field after another, relying more on the general acceptance, by all sections of the community, of particular changes, than on the conquest of power by the wage-earning class, leading to more spasmodic, though possibly less fragmentary, social transformations. The British Socialists, with those of Australia and New Zealand—perhaps also, we may say, in consonance with the practice of those of Belgium, Sweden, and Denmark—visualize the Socialist Movement as progressing smoothly and continuously, and resting always, at each stage of its advance, on general public assent, along the "Fourfold Path" of ever-increasing Collective Ownership, Collective Regulation, Collective Provision, and Collective Taxation. Many of the Socialists of the rest of Europe, on the other hand, together with many of those of America (who have not, as yet, had much experience of personal participation in government) contemplate an intensification and exacerbation of "The Class War," leading to a "Conquest of Power" by an advancing Proletariat—even to the forcible seizure of government by a Socialist Minority overpowering a rebellious Capitalist Minority, without the "Apathetic Mass" of public opinion necessarily expressing agreement with either the one or the other. Leaving aside the striking exception, in quite unique circumstances, of the decade of Bolshevist domination of Russia, with results on which it is as yet hard to form any confident judgment, and confining attention to the actual achievements of the Socialist Movement in the various other countries during the past half century—it is impossible not to recognize, throughout Western civilization, a large measure of similarity in what has actually been put in operation.

The observer will notice first, with the quickening of the completion of Political Democracy, to which we have already alluded, the rapid decay throughout all Europe, and often the practical disappearance, of the typically middle-class political parties and programmes, to which the world has commonly applied the term "Liberal." The electoral and governmental struggles have everywhere come increasingly to relate, not to enlarging the personal freedom of the individual to "do what he likes with his own," but to economic issues: to the enlargement of the social opportunities of the manual-working class, even at the expense of diminishing the almost unlimited opportunities of the property owner; and to the extension in range and magnitude of those collective services which promote the wellbeing of the whole community and make the special provisions required by its suffering members. Thus the whole range of Factory and Public Health legislation has been everywhere greatly extended; the collective prevention of disease and accident, and the collective provision for the infants, the sick and infirm, the aged and the involuntarily unemployed have gone ahead with a bound; gigantic systems of National Insurance have been adopted, usually by the opponents of Socialism as a means of staving off cruder and more dangerous reforms; the aggregate collective ownership of the instruments of production becomes every day greater, very largely through the growth of municipal and other forms of Local Government, mainly in such essentially public services as it seemed convenient to convert into legal monopolies, and in the public provision, not only of every kind of educational and humanitarian institution, but also of an ever-growing proportion of the dwellings in which the manual workers live. Who can measure the immensity of the improvement in the Standard of Life of the wage-earners of the world that has been wrought by these essentially Socialist developments of the past half-century?

## IX

VERY different has been the activity of that other derivative from Robert Owen, the essentially British movement of Consumers' Co-operation. This form of organization is characterized by its voluntary membership, in contrast with the State or Municipality, which are also Associations of Consumers, but of citizen-consumers, whose membership is obligatory. The Consumers' Co-operative Movement, which was for half a century unconscious of its own nature, may be said to have effectively started, after a couple of decades of abortive projects, in the establishment in 1844 by the 28 flannel-weavers, styled "the Rochdale Pioneers," of their little Co-operative Store in Toad Lane, Rochdale (Lancashire). From that humble venture, the Consumers' Co-operative Movement, on a predominantly working-class foundation—without, at the outset, any capital; without external aid; without government assistance; for a whole generation without countenance or approval from philanthropists or economists—has grown, in nearly all the countries of Western civilization, to a truly prodigious height. In Great Britain, for instance, it will, by the end of 1928, have nearly six million enrolled shareholding members, representing at least one third of all the families in the Kingdom. Its working capital, entirely accumulated from its own membership in the course of its own operations, exceeds one hundred million pounds sterling. Its annual turnover of commodities and services supplied to its members reaches two hundred million pounds sterling. Nor does it confine itself, as is often ignorantly supposed, to wholesale and retail distribution. It operates its own coal mine; its own arable, fruit, and dairy farms in Great Britain; its own tea plantations in India and Ceylon; its own wheat farms in Manitoba. It runs the largest flour mills and the most extensive boot factories in Europe; gigantic soap works, along with smaller cotton and woollen mills; extensive factories for all kinds of clothing; the making of jam, cocoa, confectionery, and all sorts of foodstuffs; bicycle and automobile works, furniture workshops, the production of every description of hardware; along with its own ships, its own building departments and its own printing works, its own departments of banking and insurance; its own depots and agencies in foreign ports serving its own organization for the importing or exporting of every kind of requisite to and from almost every country in the world. This vast industrial organization, almost entirely composed of wage-earners and employing two hundred thousand persons in the common service, is owned and directed upon the most democratic basis conceivable. Each of the six million members of either sex, however considerable the accumulation of savings or number of shares standing to his or her credit, has but one vote for the Board of Directors of his society. Each local Co-operative Society, as a constituent of the national federal organization, casts its vote for the supreme executives in exact proportion either to its enrolled membership or to the amount of its dealings with the federal body during the preceding year. Every executive reports to periodical open meetings of members, and is absolutely dependent for ratification of its proceedings, and for re-election for a further term, on the votes of these open meetings. Nor does Great Britain stand alone in this amazing and long continued progress of the Consumers' Co-operative Movement. In America, as in Australia and New Zealand, the wage-earners have, until recent years, found other channels for their aspirations and their energies, though there are now indications that the Consumers' Co-operative Movement is taking root. Throughout all Europe, however, and likewise in Japan—indeed in thirty different countries outside Britain, but mainly in Russia, Germany, Austria, Scandinavia, France, Belgium, and Switzerland—Consumers' Co-operation (now comprising, in the aggregate, at least twenty million families and everywhere enlarging its membership, increasing its annual turnover, extending its range of manufacturing as well as of distributing, and piling up the aggregate of its working capital and its reserves) is united in an International Cooperative Alliance working for the further development of a Movement very definitely distinctive of Western civilization as such, knowing no barrier of race, religion, or class, and visibly transcending all frontiers.

X

WE HAVE hitherto discussed the position and prospects of the wage-earning class in Western civilization almost entirely with reference to the advanced industrial communities of the Old World, in particular Great Britain, the country that we have taken as the oldest and still the foremost European exemplar of the results of the Industrial Revolution of the past two hundred years. How far can similar assertions be made, and like inferences be drawn, with regard to the country which is to-day pre-eminent in wealth production, the United States of America?

Difficult as it is to make general statements applicable to all the countries of Europe, not to mention also Australia, New Zealand, and Japan, it is even more difficult to do so with regard to the North American Continent. It can, at least, be noticed that the United States, on the one hand, and the Dominion of Canada on the other, started their own form of the Industrial Revolution in circumstances very different from those of the European nations, and that they have enjoyed exceptional advantages in its development. The United States in particular (leaving out of account the sparsely scattered aborigines) started with a population automatically selected for energy, adventurousness, and relative emancipation from the old ruts of custom and convention. For two centuries or more, the Pilgrim Fathers were followed by what was, on the whole, a stream of immigrants distinctly superior in mental and physical strength to those who were left behind. They had at their command a continent of enormous, and, as it seemed, unlimited natural resources. The mere growth of the population,

continuing for centuries at a rate unequalled at any time elsewhere, necessarily resulted in an ever-growing increase, not only in
urban land values, but also in the size and value of every kind of
business enterprise. By the individual appropriation of this per-
petually created "Unearned Increment," each generation of property owners and industrial employers for two hundred years has
had poured upon it continual showers of private riches, increasing in magnitude in every decade with every increase in population, and every successive conquest of natural resources, until,
within our own time, the profusion has reached a magnitude that
staggers imagination. And both the existence of so extensive a
population, and the production of so great an aggregate of wealth,
have been made possible by the ability of the American inventors
and the American employers, who have shown themselves not only
equal to their continually expanding opportunities, but also (in
assiduity, courage, and enterprise, and in openminded readiness
to apply new ideas and new processes) possessed of a peculiar
genius for industrial development that has left the Old World
amazed and admiring.

How, amid all this gigantic production of wealth, this perpetual heaping-up of unexampled riches, have fared the steadily
mounting proportion of "hired men," unforeseen by either Washington or Jefferson? The United States could not, it is clear,
wholly escape the evil consequences produced in Europe by the
Industrial Revolution and the growing predominance of Machinery and Mass Production. Boston and New York, Chicago
and San Francisco had, in due course, their patches of insanitary
and overcrowded slum tenements, as bad as anything that European
cities had to show; and occasionally their crowds of underfed and
diseased wage-earners, demoralized by unemployment and destitution; and their swarms of children without schooling, without industrial training, growing to manhood brutalized by their lives
and their surroundings. That the proportion of the total population falling below the "Poverty Line" has been at no time so
large as in the cities of Europe we may well believe. In America
the whole class of manual workers benefited at all times by the
opportunities open to the abler, stronger, and more adventurous

among their number—in the chance of taking up land in the West and all the prospects of freshly peopled settlements; in the exceptional mobility and almost frictionless passage from one vocation to another, and from grade to grade, in which America has so far excelled the Europe from which it sprang; in the conception of equality of social and political status, quickly translated into political democracy, which has so generally prevailed; and, finally, in the near approach to universal schooling for which the greater part of the population of the United States was early distinguished above even Prussia, Scotland, and Switzerland. In every generation, too—and notably in our own time—considerable sections of the wage-earners, in particular industries and in certain parts of the vast community, have shared, to an extent unknown in the Old World, by specially large earnings and exceptionally advantageous chances of rising into the higher industrial grades, in the golden showers of unearned increment enjoyed by the owners of urban land and business enterprises.

To cope with the destitution, disease, and demoralization, which formed, in the United States as in Europe, the dark shadow attendant on the development of the Machine Industry and Mass Production, the American people have relied mainly on private beneficence. Their public organization of Poor Relief, compared with that which England developed from 1536 onwards, has—perhaps fortunately—remained, in nearly all the States, extremely rudimentary. But in individual almsgiving, and still more in the unofficial organization of appropriate charitable aid to the indigent sick and infirm, widows and orphans, aged and unemployed, together with the victims of earthquake, fire, and flood, the United States has been, at least for the last three quarters of a century, unequalled by any other country. In the magnitude of their endowments of every kind, from Charity Organization Societies and hospitals up to universities and world-wide exploration and research, the American capitalists are as pre-eminent as in the magnitude of their wealth. In face of this boundless, and on the whole wisely directed philanthropy of the rich, it may seem ungracious to remark that—as American no less than European experience indicates—no amount of private charity, however skilfully organized, can succeed in preventing either destitution or disease, and the ever-spreading demoralization of urban slum life. In order to avoid flooding, the dyke that withstands the waters must be complete and coextensive with the danger. No efficiency of protection in some places, with neglected openings in others, will avert evil consequences, which cannot be confined to the immediate sufferers, but will inevitably spread, and exert their baleful influences on the community as a whole. Accordingly, America has not failed to provide the necessary dyke, by steadily increasing Federal, State, and Municipal action, which serves, to a greater extent than is commonly realized, as a Framework of Prevention comparable with that erected in Great Britain and the most advanced countries of continental Europe. Yet, as in these countries, the American Framework of Prevention seems to have its own incompleteness, and a special "patchiness," of which thoughtful Americans are themselves uneasily conscious.

With regard to the whole range of Public Health, from birth to death, there are American cities in which almost every branch of this important work—on the one hand the care of maternity and infancy, the provision for children below and during the school age, the medical treatment of the physically or mentally sick or disordered, the protection of the widow and the orphan, the infirm and the aged; and, on the other, the paving, lighting, and drainage, the water supply and the housing, the fire protection and the parks, the food inspection and the sanitary disposal of garbage—are, taken as a whole, not below the standard of the best governed cities of the Old World. In some branches of this work, indeed, many American cities are authoritatively reported to be superior to anything the Old World can show. Yet other cities, and the districts just outside even the best governed cities, will often be found to be, to the European eye, almost mediæval in their neglect of the most elementary requirements of Public Health. Perhaps the part of the Framework of Prevention in which the United States, taken as a whole, compares most favorably with nearly every other nation, is that of education. Yet even here there are large sections of the hundred and twenty millions of population which, in respect of the universality of common schooling, recall the conditions of the England of a century ago. The most striking instance of this characteristic "patchiness" of American civilization with regard to universal schooling is the practical exclusion from the common system of the not inconsiderable section of the young citizens who are Roman Catholics, clinging invincibly to the schools taught by teachers of their own faith, in a mental atmosphere of their own religion. That something approaching two million American children should be growing up in the "parochial schools"—uninspected, unsubsidized and, as a whole, inevitably far inferior in scholastic efficiency to the common standard—amounts to a gap in the national educational system which is of grave import for the future, all the more serious because, for various reasons, the Roman Catholics of all racial origins are the most rapidly increasing part of the population. European experience—some would say also Australian experience—indicates that there is no way of stopping this gap short of including in the national system, by appropriate administrative devices, denominational schools as such, for the minorities which insist on them. Another equally extensive and more commonly recognized gap is the serious inferiority of the educational provision for the children of color: a problem for which neither European nor Australian experience affords any solution. It is interesting to the Englishman to notice the beginning, here and there, of developments, corresponding with the remarkable extension of the British school system in the past twenty years, from the care of the child's mind to the care of the child's body. It is a feature of the great city of the twentieth century that there needs to be provision for the periodical medical inspection of the school child to discover incipient physical ailments and defects; for the "following up" by the School Nurse, or by the volunteer members of a Children's Care Committee, of children found to have "dirty heads," or to be in need of medical treatment or of such appliances as spectacles; for the actual provision of such treatment or appliances for those unable to buy them; even for the provision of meals or additional nourishment for children found to be suffering from hunger; and finally, on the one hand, for the transfer to special schools of the children found to be, in one or other respect, "subnormal" or abnormal; and, on the other hand, for the effective promotion to higher grades of schools, by means of maintenance scholarships, of the poorest children of superior capacity.

It seems to be one of the incidental drawbacks of the division into forty-eight autonomous States, all clinging to their "State Sovereignty," and protected by the rigidity of the Federal Constitution interpreted by a necessarily "conservative" Supreme Court, that almost insuperable difficulties stand in the way, in America, of any national system of employment exchanges that might minimize the time lost in shifting from job to job; and also in the way of any nation-wide provision against the not inconsiderable proportion of actual destitution that can hardly fail to accompany, in a community of hired wage-earners, sickness, accident, and premature infirmity, widowhood, and old age, and the prolonged involuntary unemployment due to fluctuations of trade.   It is not easy to foresee by what expedient American statesmanship will solve, as it certainly will, the problem of how to adapt to American political conditions some equivalent to the British and German national systems of universal insurance providing maintenance during those periods of life in which wage-earning is impossible.   In short, what American civilization seems most to lack—from the standpoint of the vast majority of the heads of families who are "hired men"—is economic security.   In spite of unparalleled private wealth, unusually effectively open to all, though necessarily attained only by a small minority—in spite too, of an average of earnings and of individual savings, throughout an unprecedented aggregate of wage-earners, higher than the world has ever seen—there remains the definite statistical probability that any given wage-earner will, in the United States, find himself at one or other time, ruthlessly "fired"; that he will at one or other period in his life go through at least one prolonged spell of involuntary unemployment; that he will be at various periods incapacitated by sickness or accident; that he will under one or other of these trials exhaust all the family savings; that his wife may be left a widow, and his offspring at a helpless age orphaned, without any adequate maintenance; that his children may grow up insufficiently protected against disease and very inadequately educated; and that, if they or their parents live the allotted span, the chances are that they will find their old age one of extreme penury, and possibly of dependence on charity. The statistician has to tell us that, however numerous may be the exceptions, these are the liabilities of the main body of wage-earners, the "common lump of men," in the United States as in the other nations of Western civilization, liabilities which, in no small fraction of the mass, are found to become actualities.

To what extent this statistical liability to penury and destitution is lessened by enforced abstinence from alcoholic drink, or minimized in practice by the exceptional economic prosperity and wide freedom of American life—in what degree, for instance, the ever-open opportunity for employment on the farms, or in the lumber camps, or in the mineral exploitations of the West, mitigates the successive industrial crises of involuntary unemployment—we are unable to estimate. But one suggestion we allow ourselves. If anything like similar conditions prevailed in Europe, experience indicates that the lack of economic security to which we have referred, accompanied, as it is in the United States by the customary expectation of a high Standard of Life among the wage-earners, would lead to a prevalence of lawlessness and violence, and to a degree of vagrancy and criminality, which northwestern Europe has not known for a couple of centuries. Whether the lack of economic security for the wage-earners in the United States to-day has anything to do with such features of American life only Americans can usefully judge.

## XI

WE SUGGESTED, at the beginning of this chapter, that what caused the evils attendant on the Industrial Revolution was, in the last analysis, not the substitution of the status of wage-earning for that of independent production, but the state of mind, alike of the contemporary philosophers and of the contemporary capitalists. What is the transformation of thought that has enabled those evils to be everywhere, in a greater or lesser degree, obviated and remedied by the Framework of Prevention erected during the past century?

In the first place, Western civilization has ceased to believe that widespread destitution and subjection, the "Poverty of the Poor," is the "Act of God," or otherwise inevitable. Neither in Europe nor in America are the nations' minds oppressed by the bleak horrors of the Malthusian "Law of Population," or by its economic recension in the "Theory of the Wage Fund," which were thought, a hundred years ago, to condemn the great mass of the people to eternal penury. Secondly, in America even more than in Europe, it is no longer believed that each man is morally entitled to "do what he likes with his own," or to find justification for his life in the amount of wealth that he can amass, regardless of the effect on his fellow-men or on the community in which he lives. The watchword for the business man as for the manual worker, for him who is wealthy by inheritance as for the creator of his own fortune, is, nowadays, "service." Nor is anyone prepared, in the twentieth century, to admit that the Legislature—the National Government or the Municipal Government—can safely and properly assume that if every man looks after his own interests, according to his own lights, the welfare of the community will necessarily be secured. No economist, throughout the wide world, to-day puts his faith in *laissez faire*. Instead of everything being complacently left to the arbitrament of the individual seeking his own advantage, it has become accepted that deliberate action needs to be taken, by governments and legislatures, or some collective agency for the promotion of the interests of the community as a whole, for the future as well as in the present. And here we recognize a wider meaning than at first sight appeared, in the statement that Western civilization is the outcome of science. Just as it is the discoveries of physical science that have created the Machine Industry, and made possible Mass Production, so it is principally on economic and political science that the world is dependent in the deliberate corporate action which is ever-increasingly typical of the present age. Individual decision may come from impulse and intuition; but what is done by Cabinets and Legislatures, Municipal Councils and Co-operative Committees has to be the outcome of deliberate concert, which, if it is to be successful, plainly needs to be informed, whether in Education or Public Health, Currency or Industrial organization, by all the science—physical or biological, economic or political, psychological or ethical—that each generation possesses.

Finally, it must be noted that the progressive development of corporate activity does not mean any lessening of personal obligation. It does not involve any transfer of responsibility from the individual to the community. On the contrary, the universal maintenance of a prescribed minimum of civilized life, which is to-day seen to be in the interest of the community, becomes the joint responsibility of an indissoluble partnership, in which the State and the citizen have each their several parts to play. It is an inevitable complement of the corporate responsibility and of the indissoluble partnership, which have come to form the intellectual basis of Western civilization, that new and enlarged obligations, unknown in a régime of *laissez faire,* are placed upon the individual citizen and enforced upon him by the community. The Bolton cotton-spinner of 1842, whom we mentioned at the beginning of this chapter, had no need to keep his children in health, or his house healthy; his wife could with impunity let the babies die; the parents could put their offspring to work at the earliest age; the whole household was free, in fact, to live practically as it chose, even if it infected and demoralized the neighborhood. Now, the cotton-spinner lives in a whole atmosphere of new obligations, such as the obligation to keep his family in health, and to send every child between five and fourteen daily to school, properly washed and dressed, and at an appointed hour; and the obligation not to infect his environment, and to submit when required to hospital treatment. While it becomes more and more imperative, in the public interest, to enforce the fulfilment of personal and parental and marital responsibility on every adult, it becomes more and more clear that no such responsibilities can be effectively enforced without at the same time ensuring to every adult the opportunity of fulfilling them. To secure the fulfilment of these obligations by the negligent and the recalcitrant, modern civilization has other expedients than the punishments of the criminal law. What happens is that the collective action of the community, by a series of deliberate experiments on volition, "weights the alternatives" that present themselves to the mind of the ordinary man. He retains as much freedom of choice as before, if not more than before. But he finds it made more easy, by the universal provision of schools, to get his children educated, and more disagreeable to neglect them. By the provision of public baths and cleansing stations, he finds it made more easy for him to keep his family free from vermin, and more disagreeable to let them remain neglected and dirty. By the public provision of hospitals and medical attendance, it is made more easy for parents to keep their dependants in health, and more disagreeable to let them die. The public organization of the labor market by means of labor exchanges makes it easier for the man out of work to find employment, and enables the State (as the Socialists and Trade Unionists are at one with the rest of the world in demanding) to make it more disagreeable for the "work-shy." In every direction, the individual finds himself, in the growing elaboration of organization of the twentieth century State, face to face with personal obligations unknown to his grandfather, which the development of collective action both enables and virtually compels him to fulfill. The claim is made that this new atmosphere of personal obligation results, paradoxically enough, in an actual increase, taking the population as a whole, in the enlargement of individual faculty, and in the opportunity for individual development. In short, in the transformation of Democracy from a merely political to an increasingly economic conception of the State, which has marked the past seventy-five years, law has been the mother of freedom.

## XII

CAN WE now define what, after a couple of centuries of travail, the Machine Industry and Mass Production have, in the most advanced countries of Western civilization, brought to their democracies of "hired men," in vast majority manual-working wage-earners, so far as their social condition may be measured in the means by which men live?

What is typical of Western civilization to-day, even after the catastrophe of four years of unparalleled warfare, in comparison with any previous age, is the relatively high Standard of Life enjoyed, especially in northwestern Europe, Australasia, and North America, by the wage-earning class. Any comparison of the conditions under which the wage-earners live to-day in the most advanced countries, with those enjoyed by the manual-working class throughout the Europe of the sixteenth or seventeenth centuries, makes it plain that the artisan or mechanic and his family, and to a lesser degree the unskilled laborer and his family, are to-day enjoying a definitely higher Standard of Life than the corresponding section of the population at any previous period in the world's history. As a result of medical science on the one hand, and of law and municipal administration on the other, the average workman's life is longer, the normal health at all ages is better, the periods of illness are fewer and notably shorter, the daily aches and pains and minor digestive troubles are less disturbing, and the chances of violent death or disabling injury are smaller than in any former age. The homes in which these wage-earners and their families live, even taking into account the shocking conditions still prevailing in many places, are more soundly constructed, more commodious and convenient, more abundantly and more comfortably furnished, with immeasurably better sanitation, and placed amid surroundings superior in respect of hygiene and amenity to anything usual in any previous century. These families, husband, wife, and children, are far better fed than their forbears of any previous generation. They have more leisure after work, and greater opportunity of making good use of their leisure. They are far better protected against violence, oppression, or tyranny. The reward which is the result of their work is, taking the manual-working class as a whole, greater than ever before; and what is now almost always a money wage commands a vastly widened range of commodities and services, effectively brought within their reach, according to their choice; and, in the aggregate, an increased amount of such commodities and services, in comparison with what fell to the lot of the manual workers when they were, for the most part, independent producers. Their boys and girls find open to them, even forced on them, common schooling superior to any their forefathers knew; opportunities for the more gifted to proceed to the heights of all the learning of the age; and greater freedom of access than ever before to the vocation of their choice. For the orphans, the sick, the mentally or physically disabled, the widows and the aged, there is more humane, more efficient and more universal provision than has been known in any previous century. Above all, there has been, for the manual-worker, throughout Western civilization, a most marked rise of status. He is no longer a slave, no longer a serf, no longer an illiterate incapable of understanding the civilization amid which he lives. For the first time in the world's history, he is a full citizen, legally and politically the equal of everyone with whom he comes in contact. How full of significance for the future is the fact that, within a single decade, in Great Britain and throughout Australasia, in all three Scandinavian nations, in Germany and Austria, and in other States of post-war Europe, governments have actually been placed in office composed of men of neither wealth nor social position, but of manual-working origin and Socialist opinions, definitely raised to power as the representatives of the wage-earners' own Parties, whilst for the whole decade all Russia has lain under what avowedly claims to be a "dictatorship of the proletariat."

What is there to be said on the other side? We have first to notice, throughout Western civilization, the wide gap between ideals and achievements. Even in the elementary conditions of human existence the National Minimum of Civilized Life, which every advanced community is now learning to prescribe, and is beginning to enforce, is far from being universally maintained. In every country of Western civilization there are extensive patches, even vast districts, in which this National Minimum is not reached. Everywhere there are large sections of the population for whom the necessary measures for the prevention of the evil consequences of the Machine Age have not yet been made effective. Yet it is actually a ground for hope that the most serious shortcoming, so far as the material condition of the people is concerned, is not any scantiness in each nation's resources, nor any weakness in its ideals, but the "gaps" still remaining in a Framework of Prevention of Destitution, which the world has learnt how to erect, and which every nation can, at its will, complete.

But material conditions are very far from being everything. We cannot here explore the manifold shortcomings of the manual-working class, or forecast its future in intellectual development, in artistic feeling, or in manners and morals, in all of which the actual progress of the manual workers, taken as a whole, during the past two centuries, has been, in every country, probably greater than during any previous period of the world's history. There is one point, however, on which a few closing words may be said. It is often alleged that, great as has been the workman's advance in material wellbeing and political status, and even in intellectual attainments, he has lost, by the coming of the Machine Age, his joy and freedom in production, and even his artistic capacity. The mediæval handicraftsman, who built the cathedrals of Europe, and both designed and wrought beautiful things in wood or metal, earthenware or stone, is contrasted with the brutalized laborer in a gigantic mass-production factory, condemned to endless repetitions of a single meaningless act, such as screwing on a nut, or dabbing on grease, as the moving band brings before him, from morning to night, a series of skeletons of an inchoate product in the design of which his mind has had no part, and which, in its finished form, he may never even see. Is this soulless Robot, we are asked, any advance on Giotto or Cellini? Needless to say, the contrast is illegitimate. The assumption that the manual workers of Egypt or Greece, Italy or England at any period whatsoever, were—apart from a numerically inconsiderable fraction of them—engaged on anything that could be described as artistic handicraft, is wholly unwarranted. In the heyday of the mediæval gild, there were always, even in the most artistic cities, far more manual workers outside the favored circle of masters, journeymen, and apprentices than within it. The manual-working population of the cities was, in fact, mainly composed of laborers who were lifelong hewers of wood and drawers of water, whilst that of the vast stretches of farmland and forest outside the cities was as devoid of art as of letters. And the proportion of merely mechanical work in the world's production has, taken as a whole, lessened, not increased. What a multitude of laborers quarried the stones, dragged and carried the stones and lifted the stones of the cathedral walls on which half a dozen skilled and artistic masons carved gargoyles? From the building of the Pyramids down to the present day, the proportion of the world's work of the nature of mere physical digging, pushing, carrying, lifting, and hammering, by the exertion of muscular force, has almost continuously diminished. From the cutting of the canal at Corinth to the cutting of that at Panama, the share of the thinker, the architect, the designer, the draftsman, the engineer, the toolmaker, the accountant, and the clerk, in every productive enterprise has become steadily larger; and the proportion of workers so engaged has grown accordingly. We may grant that there has been, to some undefined extent, a shift in development. The artistic handicraftsmen of Athens or Florence—small minority as they were—felt more than they could have expressed. In the machine industry the development among the superior minority takes what may be called an intellectual rather than an artistic form. Its product is exact thinking, calculation, adjusting, fitting. Yet is not this art? There is, for instance, one beauty of the architect, and another of the jeweller. And it must not be forgotten that, in Western civilization to-day, the actual numbers of men and women engaged in daily work of distinctly intellectual character, which is thus not necessarily devoid of art, are positively greater than at any previous time. There are, of course, many more such workers of superior education, artistic capacity, and interesting daily tasks in Henry Ford's factories at Detroit than there were in the whole city of Detroit fifty years ago! Alongside of these successors of the equally exceptional skilled handicraftsmen of the Middle Ages there has come to be a vast multitude of other workers with less interesting tasks, who could not otherwise have come into existence, and who represent the laborers of the cities and the semi-servile rural population of past times, and who certainly would not themselves dream of wishing to revert to the conditions of those times. It may be granted, that, in much of their daily tasks (as has always been the case) the workers of to-day can find no joy, and take the very minimum of interest. But there is one all important difference in their lot. Unlike their predecessors, these men spend only half their working hours at the task by which they gain their bread. In the other half of their day they are, for the first time in history, free (and, in great measure, able) to give themselves to other interests, which in an ever-increasing proportion of cases lead to an intellectual development heretofore unknown among the typical manual workers. It is, in fact, arguable that it is among the lower half of the manual workers of Western civilization rather than among the upper half, that there has been the greatest relative advance during the past couple of centuries. It is, indeed, to the so-called unskilled workers of London and Berlin and Paris, badly off in many respects as they still are—and notably to their wives and children—that the Machine Age has incidentally brought the greatest advance in freedom and in civilization.

## VI—LAW AND GOVERNMENT

### By HOWARD LEE McBAIN

I

THE countries of Western civilization are politically committed to what Disraeli characterized as "that fatal drollery called representative government." How long this commitment will run only the complacent or the visionary dares forecast. Its day is already rudely challenged by Bolshevists and Fascists.

Moreover, under the prevailing representative system, democracy in theory is not democracy in practice. The effective equality of voters is as far from the realities of life as that freedom and equality with which men in Jefferson's classic declaration are ushered into being, or the equality before the law which is the worthy though unachieved ambition of an aspiring jurisprudence. Popular sovereignty is an elusive concept; public opinion, save rarely, a will o' the wisp. The will of the majority is not nearly so practical a working formula of democracy as is the will of a minority, and for obvious reasons. On most of the complicated problems of modern government the majority have not and cannot have a will. It is usually the will of small minorities that prevails. Such a minority may be self-seeking, or self-righteous, or self-immolating. But it is nearly always cautious—at least in the more advanced democracies—and it is cautious because of democracy.

Among the rank and file of voters the franchise is not a prized possession. Large numbers ignore it and large numbers of those who vote are in fact indifferent. The "lower classes" may peacefully capture the government at will. Nowhere have they done so. On the contrary a very wide franchise, like a very narrow one, "appears to be most favorable to the conservative cause." Yet slumbering power is there, in the ballots of the masses; and those who govern must be wary not to arouse the heavy sleeper in respect of those relatively few matters political that are within his interest and his comprehension. In theory the rule of the people is the driving force of the ship of state. In usual practice it is far more comparable to a mildly retarding head wind. The driving force is a thing of great complexity and some mystery operating in the deep, dark bowels of the ship.

Such a realistic estimate of democracy can of course be pressed too far. On some political questions there is a public opinion, a will of the people. If opinion be widespread and positive it will in the end be realized in government. But it is exceptional that opinion is widespread and positive.

Democracy as a form of government was discernible long before the advent of the machine age. Down the centuries from Plato and Aristotle on it was discussed by philosophers. Occasionally it was approximately realized, though the classical democracies of Athens and Rome were in truth only fairly wide aristocracies superstructed upon slavery. It can scarcely be said that modern democracies were a product of the machine age, but certain it is that they grew into manhood as that age unfolded. Certain it is also that the massing of men, women, and children in factory, shop, and mine was ultimately a potent factor in most agitations for widening the suffrage. Still less can it be said that the machine age was produced by democracy. Democracy had little, if anything, to do with its coming. It is under democratic auspices nevertheless that the age has reached its present rich outpouring. Democracy neither hates nor hinders the machine. Quite the contrary. There never was any warrant for Sir Henry Maine's dogmatic certainty that universal suffrage would have prohibited the spinning jenny and the power loom and forbidden the threshing machine.

Whatever may be the connection between the advent of the machine and the rise of political democracy, it is certain that science and machinery have altered the operating conditions of democratic government. The point scarcely calls for illustration. If any be needed, we may take from among a thousand the power printing press and the telegraph. Their influence upon the accumulation and distribution of political knowledge, true and false, passes all calculation. When applied to propaganda, they can serve either dictatorships or democracy, but they work rather in favor of the latter. News and thought are not easily confined; they frequently escape the best of regulated censorships; they leak and creep far and wide through the agency of the press. Victims of propaganda turn upon their masters and laugh, if they do nothing more. The strongest government case is sure to be challenged in some quarters. What the radio and television will do to political campaigns can hardly be conjectured yet; beyond question the processes by which public opinion is formulated are being transformed by these new mechanical contrivances. If space permitted, it would be possible to trace innumerable ramifications of science throughout society affecting its political as well as its other habits, prejudices, and ideas.

II

A CENTURY and a half ago Edmund Burke made no apology for expounding eloquently the commonplace proposition that human society is a vast and complex thing. From his day to this day social and economic complexities have steadily increased in number and bewildering variety. The machine has been the chief if not the sole cause. The resulting burden upon society in its political organization is enormous. The capacity of democracy satisfactorily to cope with the internal and external problems of peoples is already taxed beyond its apparent limit. Candid and competent observers must admit that as to many of its larger tasks democracy is doing a poor, if admittedly a difficult, job.

In the last two decades of the nineteenth and the first decade of the twentieth century there were in Europe considerable extensions of communal enterprise. State railways, telephones and telegraphs were added to the earlier enterprise of the posts and state monopolies in a few manufactures were established. Municipal trading was extended to street railways, gas, water, and electric works, as well as to housing and other productive projects. Collectivism was given a chance to prove its efficiency. The experiment was not disastrous but it was frequently, perhaps generally, disappointing. Many state socialists were disillusioned. A decided reaction had set in when, in nearly every country, state socialism was given an immense upward thrust by the necessities of the war. Many thought this would be permanent. Mr. J. A. Hobson wrote with confidence in 1919 that any sudden lapse from the state socialism of war time "would spell disorder and disaster." An instinct of self-preservation would "impel the state to endeavor to retain after the war many of the emergency powers it has acquired during the war." "The war has advanced state socialism by half a century." He was not alone in believing this. But almost immediately events proved the error of such predictions. The cause of collectivism was, if anything, hurt by the war. There was sudden and sharp reaction from the war and all of its works. The "four pillars" of the programme of the English Labour Party support no actual structure. The socialization invited by some of the post-war continental constitutions has made slight progress. In Fascist Italy there has been an extensive denationalization of industries, although no return to former individualist production.

If state socialism is no longer widely accepted as a catholicon for political-economic ills it will not be wholly abandoned. The field of government ownership and operation will slowly widen. And each new enterprise will put additional strain upon the capacity of democracy. The points of this strain can only be hinted here. Democracies have not been model employers. Little, if any, democratic control has been introduced in public industries— not nearly so much as in occasional private industries. The government as employer faces the same labor problems as the private employer. It must cope with unionization and strikes. In the minds of many, however unwarranted the view, a strike of government employees smacks of rebellion. The fact is that a strike of the policemen of a large city would be not nearly so serious as the halting of all privately operated railways. Vigilantes can be more quickly trained than locomotive engineers, and food is more important to society than good order. It is not a question of public or private employment that matters. It is the relation of the service to the life of the community that is of importance.

Even in the United States, where government ownership has lagged far behind most European countries, about one in twelve of all who are gainfully employed are on government payrolls. A vast extension of government ownership would probably have serious political consequences for democracies. Government employees are also voters. Some of their organizations have been extremely active in promoting legislation for the advancement of their own interests. This has been true, however, chiefly of organized municipal employees; for commonly national employees, even though numerous, are residentially too scattered for effective political action relative to their strength. In any case a pressure group of public employees does not differ in kind from other pressure groups with which democracies are everywhere familiar. If the number of such groups were greatly multiplied, competitive interests and rivalries among them would doubtless prevent any cohering giant amalgamation. But the ultimate possible result on politics is problematical.

Apart from the political activity of public employees mention should be made of the benumbing effect of government bureaucracies on individual initiative. Sidney and Beatrice Webb have said of Great Britain that "the special skill in a civil servant which is most appreciated by his parliamentary chief and by his colleagues in the civil service is not initiative or statesmanship, and not even the capacity to plan and to explain the departmental projects, but either to avoid questions in the House, or, if these are asked, to furnish answers which allay without satisfying the curiosity of the inquirers." "The great mass of government today is the work of an able and honest but secretive bureaucracy." This is said of the most capable civil service yet developed in any democracy. Despite variations and many individual exceptions the bureaucracies of most democracies are not, generally speaking, able and are not always honest. Whatever the cause a spirit seems usually to pervade the civil service which argues for a maximum in security of tenure and a minimum of obligation to render service. There is no adequate substitute for the initiative that prevails in private industry. Public management, fettered by law and by custom, inculcating a spirit of the right to be employed rather than the right to be of use, results in poor and extravagant service. There seems to be almost a conspiracy of forces at work to keep public employment on a dead level of mediocrity.

State socialism is a direct product of the machine age. It is true that government ownership of a few enterprises antedated the era of whirling wheels. But these were relatively unimportant even in a relatively simple time. The dependence of the public upon monopolistic services made possible by steam and electricity and dissatisfaction with private control of such services led to government assumption. Dissatisfaction with private management of limited natural resources exploited by machines and with a chaotically individualistic system of power production and distribution pointed to further expansion of the economic functions of government. But dissatisfaction with government operation, to the extent that it obtained, as well as the opposition of powerful vested interests, gave and still gives pause. Meantime almost of necessity governments turned to a new kind of regulation—or, to be more exact, vastly extended a kind of regulation which, though of ancient origin, was exceptional rather than regular.

### III

THE regulation which antedated the machine age, which long survived, and which still prevails on a wide scale, was for the most part regulation by court-applied rules of law. The system was intensely individualistic. Every individual was guardian of his own rights under the rules. If he failed to assert these rights he suffered the consequences. Under a simple agrarian and handicraft economy the system tolerably sufficed. But with the expansion of industry entailing manifold social and economic complexities, it cracked at many points. It could not satisfy insistent social demands. The old law of private nuisance, for example, depending on suit by one aggrieved and proof of specific injury to him or his property, gave inadequate protection either to the individual or to the public. It had to be supplemented by the law of public nuisance. Merely to commit an act that might lead to or constitute this or that nuisance was made an offence. No proof of injury to anyone was necessary. Moreover, administrative agencies were set up to discover and abate nuisances, to issue orders both general and particular, and to prosecute. What had been a private wrong redressed by private action in law courts was made a public wrong; and the public through administrative action undertook to prevent and to punish.

In his relations with privately owned public services the individual was practically defenceless. There were, to be sure, a few elementary rules of law that he might theoretically assert in the courts. But there were overwhelming deterrents—ignorance of rights, cost of litigation, fear of retaliation—and the rules did not reach all the evils from which the consumer of services suffered. Statutes imposing additional restrictions were ineffective. They were either too inelastic or were unenforceable. Where they gave new legal rights to the consumer he was still helpless to vindicate these rights. Where they imposed penalties there was no sufficient machinery for detection and prosecution. Hence resort again to the agency of administration. Utilities were compelled to operate under rules and conditions prescribed and allowances granted by administrative officers. The discretion of their managers was subjected to curb. They were put under continuous and close official scrutiny.

This development of regulation by administration may be widely exampled. Buildings must be erected and even located under elaborate governmental supervision in the interest of safety and health. To the same ends factories, mines, and mercantile establishments are subjected to requirements and watched to insure performance. After long and bitter struggle the brutal common law doctrines of assumption of risk and of contributory and fellow-servant negligence were worsted, and industry was compelled to assume the burden of its toll of life and limb through systems of insurance administered by or under the eye of the state. The business of banking and insurance fell under varying degrees of state surveillance. By administrative agency governments also seek to discover and prevent the unfair practices of big business. And the end is not yet.

Twenty years ago a profound student of the law, Dean Roscoe Pound, declared: "Executive justice is an evil. It always has been and it always will be crude and as variable as the personalities of officials. No one who attempts to decide each case *pro re nata* will be able to show that '*constans et perpetua voluntas suum cuique tribuens*' which is justice. Nothing but rule and principle, steadfastly adhered to, can stand between the citizen and official incompetence, caprice, or corruption. Time has always imposed a legal yoke upon executive justice and incorporated its results into law. The only way to check the onward march of executive justice is to improve the output of judicial justice until the adjustment of human relations by our courts is brought into thorough accord with the moral sense of the public at large." Since that was written, however, executive justice—regulation by administration—has marched steadily onward.

Nor is there sign of its waning. Moreover, it is difficult to see how human intercourse in the tangled modern world can be guided into adjustment by lawmakers and courts alone. The law itself cannot be made sufficiently elaborate and sufficiently elastic to meet the endlessly varying facts of life. The individual is powerless to enforce even his stark legal rights against the stupendous organizations for production and distribution upon which he must depend. Primarily organized to settle controversies, the courts are ill-suited to afford general preventive relief to the many. Agencies of mixed powers—legislative, executive, judicial—seem indispensable. Investigator, lawmaker, prosecutor, judge, and jury are fused into a unit to reach desired ends which a division of governmental functions conspicuously failed to realize.

This is not to imply that these agencies are wholly free from judicial control. In America, where the courts enjoy power to declare laws unconstitutional, there is still uncertainty and confusion as to the extent to which such agencies have been or can be given final authority. The attempt to distinguish between law and facts and to permit administrative finality on facts though not on law has been far from successful partly, if not chiefly, because it is often impossible to determine where facts leave off and law begins.

But there are certain points of significance in the change from government by law to government by administration. First, while individuals initiate some of the "cases" before these agencies, the agencies themselves, on the basis of their own fact finding, initiate many others. Second, the persons or enterprises subject to control are put under the requirement to secure advance permission for many performances. Third, and most important, if litigation of rights ensues the parties to the controversy are, at least in theory, appropriate parties. It is not the suit of a Lilliputian against a giant; it is a controversy between a giant and an agency of government acting in behalf of a horde of Lilliputians.

There are those who argue earnestly for the necessity of subjecting administrative determination to judicial review, though no one has yet supplied a neat test of what should and should not be reviewable. To an extent the argument rests upon the general desirability of authorizing appeals as a check upon arbitrariness or incompetence. This is the basis of all appellate arrangements. But appeals may be and often are provided within the administrative hierarchy, just as they are provided within the judicial hierarchy. To urge that administrative agencies, because of their specialization, are less competent than are courts to formulate rules of law founded on broad considerations is to make assumptions that would be as easy to refute as to prove. If administrative agencies were uncontrolled by courts they would have power to determine their own competence under the law, but that, it may be answered, is a power which courts, uncontrolled by any other authority, also have. Nor is it probably true that these agencies in deciding a "case" or issuing an order are disregardful of precedents or unmindful that a rule applied may have wider consequences than the instant facts imply.

However that may be, government by administration, like government by direct operation, has its limitations. No one who has observed and studied it in action will be duped into adoration of its accomplishments or possibilities. Like all other democratic contrivances it merely lumbers and falters on. The goal of social justice is not attained—is indeed unattainable in a world of intricate and jealously competing interests and ideas. But it is probably more nearly approximated than it would be under an exclusive reign of court-applied law.

In one highly important field of economic relationships government by administration, as well as government by law, has signally failed. Too often controversies between organized capital and organized labor are still settled, when settled, by the savage methods of the jungle. Where the government touches these controversies, except in the role of a mediator abjuring power, its touch is frequently more hurtful than helpful. No doubt Mr. Justice Holmes properly diagnosed the difficulty when he said: "It cannot be helped, it is as it should be, that the law is behind the times. I told a labor leader once that what they asked for was favor, and if a decision went against them they called it wicked. The same might be said of their opponents. It means that the law is growing. As law embodies beliefs which have triumphed in the battle of ideas and then have translated themselves into action, while there still is doubt, while opposite convictions still occupy the battle front against each other, the time for law has not come; the notion destined to prevail is not yet entitled to the field." It may be that in the course of time relatively acceptable rules and principles for the settlement of industrial disputes can be formulated. But until that is done exertions of governmental power, whether by compulsory arbitration or through other use of force, will be largely abortive. Even attempts to preserve the public peace while the economic battle is being waged and to protect each of the combatants in his legal rights will be fraught with grave difficulty.

IV

GOVERNMENT by administration, extensive as it is, has by no means supplanted government by court-applied rules of law. It is still the obligation of the individual to press forward many of his legal rights, and these rights are increasingly determined by legislative enactments rather than by court-made rules. Even so, the modern civil codes of continental Europe, as well as British and American statutes, embody many rules, modified or unmodified, that were formulated and applied by the judges in the era of "free decisions."

It may be, as Woodrow Wilson once said, that changing a law by statute is "like mending a garment with a patch." But the problems of the machine age change swiftly, kaleidoscopically. A degree of stability and permanence is indeed indispensable to the law. Men must know what can be counted on tomorrow. But judge-made law often lags too far behind the times and, enveloped in its own impedimenta, the pace of its catching up is too slow. American judges, for instance, must know how absurd and how inconsistent are the rules that have "developed" to determine the liability of the various units of government in tort, but the skein of their unintended making will doubtless never be untangled by the courts. Statutes are the only conceivable remedy. Indeed changing the law by statute is at least occasionally less like mending with a patch than like weaving a new garment to replace a threadbare patchwork which the courts have been unable or unwilling to discard. Moreover situations may call for some attempt at solution or relief even before beliefs have triumphed in the battle of ideas. Statutes may be frankly experimental for they are as easily unmade as made. Judges dare not experiment too widely in rule-making for their rules once pronounced are too unyielding. The hand of the law, however aged or youthful, should be a living hand, not the hand of a ghost laid upon the quick. And statutes assist in making it so.

v

AT ANY rate the machine age is superlatively an age of statutes. Mass production is as characteristic of some legislative mills as it is of industrial factories. Sometimes it almost seems that law-making for its own sake has become a democratic obsession. This is especially true of the United States; it is less true of the countries of Europe where the whole process of law-making is centralized in and controlled by a ministry. Unquestionably some of this law product is silly, superfluous, ill-advised, and much of it is unskillfully wrought. But there is little use to rail about the multiplicity of laws. Directly or indirectly the machine is largely responsible. The motor vehicle, so to say, arrived only yesterday; yet it is difficult to list the branches of the law in which the motor car today figures—the law of crime, of traffic, of taxation, insurance, public utilities, tort, license, chattel mortgage. There is already a law of the air both for craft and radio. More important, however, is the fact that since the entire complicated industrial organization of modern society is so largely founded upon power production and transportation, and since the law attempts at innumerable points to control the framework and the operations of this organization, the machine is indirectly responsible for much more in law than superficially appears.

The onward press of statute law has not transmuted the judge into an automaton. In England and America statutes have by no means completely usurped the entire realm of judge-made common law. Moreover statutes regulating complex phenomena are themselves complex. Lawmakers are not only not omniscient; they are sometimes relatively ignorant; and they operate in a maelstrom of conflicting pressure currents. Nearly every law is a compromise; nearly every law has its vague spots. The thought of those who made it is not always crystal clear; and at best words are an imperfect tool of thought transmission. Statutes, therefore, must be construed. They must often be applied to facts that were beyond the contemplation of the legislators. Large leeway is in consequence left to the judge. Judge-made law has not disappeared. "By the decisions of the Paris Court of Cassation," says Eugene Ehrlich, "so many new ideas have been fused in the French civil law, statutes have been interpreted so frequently in a manner deviating widely from the intention of the legislature, that one may properly say: Whoever knows merely the statutory law of France has no conception of the law as it actually exists there." In varying degree this is true of all the countries of the western world.

However apparently natural its growth, the luxuriant flowering of the law under the joint and several husbandry of legislatures and courts has not been an untinged benefaction. From birth certificate to death certificate man is literally pursued by law. The man of business, otherwise lost in the labyrinth, must keep one hand constantly and firmly fitted into the hand of his lawyer. He must avoid the pitfalls that are set, not as traps it is true, but with like effect none the less. Of necessity the man of business learns some law. Of necessity the lawyer becomes a man of business. Not of necessity but of a certainty both cultivate and practise the fine art of law-evasion. More and more has the law become what Burke called it, "the lucrative business of mystery."

In the United States, more than elsewhere, the close tieup between business and law has resulted not only in a considerable domination of business by lawyers but also in the application of the standards and methods of business to the practice of the law. Law offices grow larger and larger; legal work becomes more and more specialized, parcelled, and unsupervised. Clients deal with a "firm," not with a personal lawyer—a firm which itself consists perhaps of a score or more of members and which employs an endless number of lesser lawyers, as well as bookkeepers, stenographers, messengers, and the like. Says a recent commentator, himself a lawyer of distinction, "legal work is ground out as if it were the standardized production of a factory." The legal profession is "no longer a learned profession but simply a business organization conducted by push buttons and call bells."

Despite their huge number, the cases in the courts represent an actually small part of the law's applications. They are in truth but occasional units that raise their heads for court inspection out of the ceaseless and resistless flow of a mighty stream of legal process. For in one thing at least the machine age is not standardized; it is capable of infinite variety and refinement of legal circumstances—to the never ending advantage of the ever enlarging and increasingly acquisitive legal profession.

By and large the spirit of the modern era is too urgent and its people are often too commonsensible to bother with dilatory courts. "Uncertainty, delay and expense," says Dean Pound, "and above all, the injustice of deciding cases upon points of practice, which are the mere etiquette of justice, direct results of the organization of our courts and the backwardness of our procedure, have created a deep-seated desire to keep out of court, right or wrong, on the part of every sensible business man in the community." Countless legal controversies are settled out of court by compromises. These range all the way from easily reached gentlemen's agreements to battles royal waged between hard-headed lawyers for tight-fisted clients across mahogany desks or deal-top tables. In these innumerable contests the court-applied rules of law, known or guessed, are often badly manhandled. The law that is in fact applied may not be the law at all. But it is frequently less costly and irksome to compromise even an unquestionable legal right than it is to sue. These non-court "cases" form the main body of the great on-moving stream of applied law. In a general way statutes and court-made rules serve as guide and compass. But the net result is not all cool and clean handed justice.

VI

ALMOST of necessity the lawmakers of the machine age have made some progress in fact finding and fact using. Neither *a priori* reasoning concerning human nature, nor "immutable and eternal principles of justice," nor a comparative study of foreign laws, furnish sufficient premises for law in the modern world. Facts must be found, statistics gathered, opinions heard. Innumerable investigations are undertaken by legislative committees and special commissions, as well as by permanent administrative agencies. Perhaps it is fair to say, moreover, with Mr. Graham Wallas, that this gathering of information tends to become more and more quantitative rather than qualitative. Yet the information that is assembled is sometimes bewildering, is often incomplete or one-sided, and is not always adequately studied. Moreover not every proposal for important legislation is preceded by an attempt to ascertain the facts.  In America the use of injunctions in labor disputes has been fiercely debated for years but no study of all the relevant facts has ever been made.  Nobody knows how many such injunctions have been issued nor in what industries, how many have been denied, how many temporary injunctions have been vacated and how many made permanent, what length of time temporary injunctions have been allowed to run before being vacated, how generally or successfully such injunctions are enforced, how many violations have been punished, what has been their effect upon industrial disputes.  There have been some strictly legal studies and much partisan special pleading, but the question whether the instrument of the injunction in industrial controversies is generally useful or abuseful is largely a matter of conjecture.  There is, however, no hesitancy in proposing to deal with the problem by legislation.

Even when in respect of this or that matter of legislation lawmakers do master an amplitude of facts, choice must be made of ends desired and of legal arrangements for the attainment of these ends.  It is upon the making of that choice involving nearly always a weighing of interfering interests that the forces of minorities furiously play.

However competent courts may be to discover the facts of particular cases before them, they are manifestly not instrumentalities that are properly organized and equipped for social fact finding.  There is an increasing tendency, however, to present to the courts, with or without their seeking, social and economic data that enable them better to envisage the social purpose of a statute under review or the social utility of a rule they are urged to apply.  In this general direction much remains to be done. The social and economic conditions out of which the law of the past arose have not been sufficiently understood or emphasized and the totality of actual social effects of the present-day application of many legal rules and doctrines is not fully known.  These conditions and effects need further and continuous study.  Busy lawyers have little time for such study and, regrettably enough, most of them have little interest in or capacity for it.

This social-utility approach toward the law has come to be

known as sociological jurisprudence. There is nothing essentially new about it. As Mr. Justice Stone has said: "It is the method which the wise and competent judge has used from time immemorial in rendering the dynamic decision which makes the law a living force. Holt, Hardwick, Mansfield, Marshall, and Shaw employed it long before the phrase sociological jurisprudence was thought of." True enough; but not all the rules of law have been made by wise and competent judges. Moreover it must be recognized that the great judges mentioned employed this method in a less complex era than that in which we now live. In simpler times social facts were more widely known to the casually well informed. John Marshall in 1819 probably needed no elaborate brief of counsel to assist him in apprehending the economic consequences of state insolvency laws. He knew how these laws operated alike to ameliorate the plight of the honest debtor caught in a snare and to further the chicanery of the dishonest. As Beveridge says: "All this John Marshall saw and experienced"; it "took place under his very eyes in Virginia." To a less degree certainly would the United States Supreme Court a hundred years later have been able to appreciate the economic and social questions involved in minimum wage legislation without the able factual briefs that were presented by Mr. Brandeis, Mr. Frankfurter, and Miss Josephine Goldmark. That the facts were flouted by the majority of the court does not weaken the point of contrast. In the machine age the law must grapple with innumerable relationships that do not unfold under the eyes of courts but are largely, if not wholly, beyond their observation or ken. The "experience" which Mr. Justice Holmes sagely says is the "life of the law" is not of course the experience of the judges themselves. Unfortunately for the law and for society it too often has been. Hence the increasing need in the modern world for so-called sociological jurisprudence.

If sociological jurisprudence is not wholly novel, even less so is the present-day demand for a "restatement" of the law. Time out of mind such demands have been recurrent and the result, if any, has usually been codification or revision of existing codes. But the genius of the common law of English-speaking countries is antipathetic to legislative codification, even though statutes more and more modify, embody, destroy, or otherwise encroach upon judge-made rules. The truth is that the legal profession as a whole is not greatly concerned with the lack of form and symmetry in the law, with its anachronisms, its inconsistencies, its outworn fictions, its occasional downright follies and injustices. The profession is however appalled at the growing volume and the rate of increase of legal literature—the materials with which lawyers must deal. In America the federal system of government with forty-eight separate state jurisdictions and a distinct national jurisdiction is in part responsible for this unwelcome surfeit. If, by some alchemical process, all of the dross—the useless rhetoric, the endless reiteration, the obiter dicta, the pomp and circumstance of legal learning—could be extracted from the law books that clutter the groaning shelves, the problem of simplifying the law of the past and present would not be so staggering, though obviously it would still be a mammoth task. If judges who are in fact not overly learned could be induced to forswear a vain show of learning, and if all judges, learned and otherwise, could be persuaded to greater brevity and more frequent silence, the future might not appear so loury. There are eminent lawyers and jurists who believe that English and American law can and must be simplified. The attempt is already under way. Its ultimate form and its measure of success remain to be revealed.

## VII

In humanitarianism the law of the machine age need not shun comparison with other ages. The number of acts for which penalties are imposed has unquestionably increased. Wholly outside of criminal codes modern statutes fairly bristle with penal sanctions. But in the course of only a hundred years or so many barbarous features of the law have been tempered. Women may no longer be whipped in public for petty crimes. Girls of ten years of age or less are no longer legally competent to consent to their own ruin. Pickpockets, horse thieves, shoplifters, and counterfeiters may no longer be hanged. Indeed the death penalty has

been completely abolished in a number of European countries
and in some American states. Grotesquely enough, suicide is
still a crime; but vengeful society no longer finds sadistic satisfaction in impaling the lifeless body of the victim; nor are his innocent heirs punished by the escheat of his property to the state.
On the Continent the accusatory method of criminal prosecution
is supplanting the less just and less reasonable inquisitorial method.

In the course of a mere half century the legal and political
status of women has undergone radical change. In most countries
a husband no longer has complete control of his wife's earnings
or the income from her property. Inheritance laws have been
revamped in her favor. No longer may a father deprive a mother
of access to or control over her own children nor oust her by
will from their guardianship after his death. Generally speaking,
divorce laws have been liberalized and, theoretically at least, have
been put within reach of the poor as well as the rich. But the
wide variations in the liberality of such laws (from the free divorce of Soviet Russia to the no divorce of South Carolina) offer
numerous comfortable choices to the incompatible well-to-do.
In a few places, as in New York, adultery is still regarded as the
only major sin against the matrimonial state, while in England,
until within a few years, an adulterous wife could be put away but
an adulterous husband could be discarded only if he were also a
brute or a deserter. With all its occasional pious appeal to magic,
the law cannot alter the fact that adultery in a man is socially con-
doned—not even by the foolish gesture of making adultery a crime,
as it is in some places. Hence under strict divorce laws collusion
is common. In England until recently it was only a little more
difficult and expensive, a little more humiliating for the woman,
and therefore a little more ridiculous than elsewhere. Gradually,
too, the learned professions have been opened to women; while
the war carried the ballot battle to victory in many countries
among the vanquished as well as the victorious.

Important as it is, little need be said of so-called social legislation; its ever lengthening chapters are too well known. Smug
and stupid oppositionists at length learned that much of this
legislation was of economic advantage to themselves. Since that

lesson was learned there has been less bigoted resistance to its progress, though resistance has by no means subsided. The machine age without such legislation would be unthinkable. Even in commonwealths with laws that are the most advanced in humaneness there is still an appalling amount of suffering and of unhappy circumstance of life for which the individual is not to be blamed. Law can and will no doubt in the course of time alleviate some of this. The history of the last century or more is not discouraging.

The struggle for political democracy was in most countries long and hard fought. Everywhere, however, its theoretical promise far outran its realizations, substantial as some of these have been. In consequence the instinct of self-preservation in democracy may not be so deep-struck as many serenely assume. Certainly the great experiment has not completely substantiated the Aristotelian conceit that man is by nature a political animal. Concerning the future of law and government in the Western world, as Richard Hooker said of God, no doubt the safest eloquence is silence.

## VII—WAR AND PEACE

### By Emil Ludwig

We punish an individual guilty of assault or murder, but the massacre of a people is considered a glorious deed.—SENECA.

I

STALWART in his war-chariot stands the handsome youth swinging his sword. In long glittering rows advance the men, half in armor, skins over their nakedness; as some bend forward laying arrows on their bow-strings, as others bend backward balancing spears in their right hands, as they battle with one another wielding clubs and axes, first in armor and finally unfettered with straining muscles, wounding and killing, then streams from every pore the strength of life, youth, and manhood, the will to action, the fire of victory—all fused in one grand ensemble just to present a hero to the observer.

For the hero does not tower thus before us in flesh and blood, but in marble and bronze, in dithyramb and rhapsody. In these forms, art has fashioned the hero's image and exalted it to the place of the gods. Were the deities more than heroic men? A little more, but what the man of antiquity loved and feared in them was the heroic attitude which he saw in his conquerors and transferred to his gods. In those days no photographer followed the soldier into the field and so the narratives of skeptics, who described warfare in the language of truth, could more easily be ignored and forgotten. Nor was this martial struggle conducted in the manner of the Centaur frieze at Pergamon or the metopes at Selinus; its form was the titanic duel of Homeric realism.

The antique world cherished strength and beauty of body more than sympathy and magnanimity; it was a segment of earth comprising many small countries which did not know, visit, or communicate with one another; which were all populated by more insular groups living in fear of the unfamiliar folk across the sea, or on the other side of the hills, and anxious to keep them at a distance; by men who were the sons and grandsons of superstitious, primitive men knowing only themselves, the sun, and the stars. It was natural therefore that these ancient peoples should need weapons when they ventured upon the road for a day or came into strange lands. From time immemorial, fighting and warfare had been necessities to them, were to be expected every day; and so they were venerated in word and picture and the hero was honored. Was it not true that, at a decisive moment, a single sturdy young man could rescue a whole city from slavery?

Those who were most powerful, having the support of friends or servants, expanded their might by means of threats or gifts, bread or offices, and so began very early to praise as heroic the service rendered by the masses whom they needed in their struggle with alien rivals and to glorify the sacrifice of other lives made in defense of their power. A man will risk all the advantages he possesses for the sake of money or property but he gambles with his life only when impelled by a romantic dream that promises immaterial goods—honor and love. He wishes to possess this woman, he would like to surpass that man, and therefore he throws his life into the balance. The hope of shining before thousands as the most courageous or being borne in triumph, the victor's fillet about his brow, through acclaiming multitudes, of returning home amidst splendid festivities—such a vision rises triumphant over his fear of death, for an immortal life is apparently offered only to those who hazard their mortal years on the throw of the dice.

It was, and still is even today, easy for clever kings or tribunes to induce men to surrender their lives by offering them visions of the victor's crown. It is easy to discover a few ideals. They are called nation, honor, or fatherland. What do these conceptions mean to us today?

## II

So long as kings entrusted their wars to hired and paid troops, there was nothing immoral or inappropriate in the procedure. Strong and dauntless men, adventurers who were tied down neither by religion nor work of any kind nor by a desire to lead an ordered or domestic existence, took up the profession of arms —when they did not go to sea. Although the Renaissance was their true golden age, until about a hundred years ago generals and soldiers fought, for the most part, on the side and in the interest of him who paid them best. The pretext and sham virtue of "higher purposes" had not yet been invented; if indeed the soldiers of the Middle Ages did not fight on the side of the Turks, they were restrained only by their common feelings as Christians— Europe was fighting against Asia.

Later on, during the Thirty Years' War, the disputed matters of religious belief, which were the basic causes of the struggle, prevented nobody from taking the side which happened to be profitable. At no other time has the cynicism born of the opportunity to gain, loot, and brawl flourished with more unbridled license than during the Wars of Religion, when both sides inscribed the name of God on their banners. Bravery was then an article of merchandise which was sold to the highest bidder. Tilly was a Belgian, Piccolomini was an Italian, and Wallenstein met his death at the hands of Scottish and Irish hirelings. When the battle of Rheinfeldern was fought, the Imperial German army was commanded by the French general, Meroy, and the French army by the German Duke Bernhard of Weimar.

So long as it was possible to enlist, or entice, slaves or poor men into military service by means of the sovereign's power or wealth, the blame could be laid only upon a social system which permitted slavery to exist, or upon a state of feeling which preferred brutality and anarchy to the right flowering of life. Thus was evolved the paradox that Christianity intensified rather than repressed the inclination to engage in warfare.

The man of antiquity had lived with, and subject to, gods who endowed him with strength, beauty, and the desire to excel others;

the Christian followed a God who forbade him all these things. The antique world had suppressed none of its natural instincts; Christianity enchained all instincts, threatened men with punishment in a life to come, and thus dammed the current of the natural desire for combat that in an earlier time had risen out of need— for which men had to train their sons in a practical manner.

Long before a universal civilization or the protection afforded by law had robbed force of its claim to a necessity, the Church had deprived the European, taught to love humanity and the particular group to which he belonged, of the legal opportunity to follow normally his natural instincts. Fighting and warfare alone remained. And if one could then proceed to commit murder in the name of God, the adventure acquired a two-fold charm. Those who took up arms in that era for the purpose of finding an outlet for their natural spirits were by no means the most debased in character. Faith and superstition co-operated in justifying the Christian wars. As mediæval man looked upon God as the source of law, the priest had only to formalize his interpretation of this law in order to gain credence for it. A legal trial in which recourse was taken to Divine testimony and judgment was an ideal easily made realistic to the people and in fact a defeat was held to be, in those times, a judgment of God. Only after reason had established itself more and more firmly in the place occupied by faith—during the seventeenth and eighteenth centuries—was the attempt to justify war on moral grounds destined to suffer. "Even though there were no God, the law of nature would nevertheless exist," wrote Hugo Grotius. During the nineteenth century, the state was everywhere accepted as the source of law; in the twentieth century its authority is being undermined by the association of classes and groups.

Indeed we of today are witnessing a conflict of ideas similar to that which took place five hundred years ago. Then the knight, who was losing his standing in society, took the law into his own hands and rushed from his castle to fall upon the merchant and rob him of his wares. This he did because he had once been rich and now was poor, because he once had been the lord and was now only an heir without a patrimony. The state was too weak to protect the merchant, although it had produced him. The emperor's authority had slipped from his grasp and the territorial prince was intent only upon the aggrandizement of his family.

Now the state, after an interim of strength, is once more too weak to furnish adequate protection for the merchant. So parliaments are warring against corporations, dictators against classes, and the habit of taking the law into one's own hands is gaining ground again. This time however it is not a decadent group which has recourse to self-help but new, striving groups eager to better their station. More and more the state is becoming a welfare institution.

### III

THE first argument advanced by contemporary friends of war is biological in character and may be stated in this way: Darwinism, the fighting instinct, healthful blood-letting, survival of the fittest are sanctioned by nature.

Although zo-ology gives many instances of animals extending mutual aid, we shall dispense with this help from science. We gladly make room for the fighting instinct innate in man, even give it praise, and declare that we should rebel out of sheer ennui against a tranquil world populated entirely by angels dressed in white—a world without a Mephisto, a society without struggle or sacrifice.

But in fact the constant battle of all against all, at least the struggle between classes, has assumed such proportions since the abolition of slavery that a new form of human destiny has become a competitor to the daily letting of blood. If in our time heathenish science provides for the preservation of human life better than did the Christian Middle Ages, the same science nevertheless, at the same time, works against its own eugenic practice by increasing and facilitating crimes and accidents in an equal measure. We hear of surplus population every day, and no war has noticeably reduced it anywhere. With each decade we hear less of living in too much comfort, less of sloth due to possessions, less of too much blood in the body politic; and no social physician has as yet established the necessity for a healthful letting of blood.

The second argument of the friends of war is expansion.

It is true that many of the wars of former centuries were started by rulers—or by their masculine and feminine counselors—because a certain district, about to be annexed to some other country through marriage or inheritance, was also claimed by some third party. Millions of men have been slaughtered because the House of Hapsburg or the House of Bourbon, the Spanish or the French Crown, demanded territories to which other kings advanced pretensions. Concerned about the power of their houses or perhaps about the security and wealth of their children and grandchildren, monarchs and nobles misused the name of God and the lives of their subjects, sacrificing both in order to gain a new province. The more a lord extended his realm, the taller his statue became. Sometimes culture and commerce profited by this extension of power, but nobody can determine whether the prize was worth the cost. At all events, none of these wars brought good fortune to the conquered districts. The people who had been subdued were counted, in grotesque fashion, as so many "souls." It would have been more accurate to speak of "bodies," for the souls remained unaffected after they had been conquered, and were, for the most part, quite indifferent to the prospect of being conquered again.

What did such a victory prove? Did it, after the fashion of earlier ages, demonstrate the greater health and vigor of a state? Or the superiority of intellect, the refinement of spirit, or even the affluence of available means? No, for the major portion, especially the greatest, of modern wars have been wars of coalition. The country which secured the best allies through making the most ample promises, resorting to the most clever diplomacy, or offering the most staggering rewards, almost invariably won out over weaker powers. Where exceptions to this rule occurred, the deeper cause of victory was fortunate geographical position, sometimes also the genius of a leader, but never the genuine and general superiority of a people. Nations without culture have vanquished more highly cultivated peoples in other times than

those of the Huns.   And the farther we remove ourselves from
the condition of brute force, the more paradoxical becomes the
effort of cultured peoples to attain the greatest possible crude
force.

The worship of might did not, of course, commence to diminish
only after Christianity had come into the world.   It has been on
the decrease since the time of Socrates, and even earlier; for the
primacy of the spirit has been developed independently of Jewish-
Christian principles, and sometimes in spite of them.   Whoever
values reason more highly than cannon and subjects the sword to
the spirit does not thereby enter upon the Christian conception of
life, far less accept it.   Such a man can die a pagan or a Chinaman.

IV

THE third argument of the friends of war is this: the progress of
industry in the victorious country.   This has been torn to tatters
during the last war, like a flag fluttering gaily in the bright parade
but rent asunder during the storm.   Everything that Norman
Angell had predicted, or calculated rather, some years previous has
been more than verified.   We have seen that a full-fledged victory
made the conqueror poorer and not richer—that even America,
which seemed destined to reap the largest profits, lost far more
during the years of war than it had gained during the years of
neutrality.   It is rich today in spite of its triumph.   Every European has experienced in his own person the cost of war to Europe.
Prior to the cataclysm of 1914, a Paris workingman paid (reckoning in gold) 18 francs for a month's rent and 30 centimes for a
kilo of bread.   After the victory he paid 72 francs and 125 centimes for the same lodging and the same bread.

Were all those leaders of industry in various countries, who
advocated war, simply fools?   On the contrary, they were too
shrewd.   We shall, they thought, manufacture cannon, shells
or battleships.   But they overlooked the fact that in our century
nobody can remain wealthy, in the long run, at the expense of
other people.   Precisely at the most dangerous point in Europe,
where the two "implacable foes" touch each other, precisely in

that district which had been most ruthlessly shaken, morally and physically, by four years of conflict, the leaders of industry met immediately after the war was over in order to come to an agreement as speedily as possible. Even before the war the manufacturers of arms so grotesquely managed their affairs that when the conflict came Turks fired upon French troops with French cannon, and Italians upon German soldiers with German cannon. But hardly had the struggle ended when the iron, coal, and potash interests of Germany and France combined for the purpose of working and profiting together—the same interests which during four years had sought to destroy each other through the instrumentality of bombs and gases.

What had become of the old hostility? Had men at length discerned the fact that coal deposits and potash fields extend under the earth regardless of boundary lines fixed by treaties and congresses, and that it is a mistake to fight those whose co-operation one needs in order to become more prosperous? Why did this realization come so late?

Because conditions are novel and because, even though thinkers had previously arrived at the same conclusion on paper, a great test had to be made by practical men in an experiment that led to negative results.

It was possible, in centuries gone by, to establish an approximate monopoly of money, coal, or petroleum through conquest. Today science has destroyed this possibility. In the first place, science always invents precisely that which humanity happens to need. If, for instance, all rubber were owned by a single nation, science would devise a substitute—as Edison is now, as a matter of fact, trying to do. Secondly, as we are taught by the example of coal rendered unnecessary through hydraulic power, science triumphs over the elements just in proportion as it returns to them. In the third place, it has transcended all boundaries and has intertwined the widely differentiated raw materials and industrial domains in such a manner that they can no more be readily defended indefinitely than a fortified city in the interior of a hostile country or even an island in mid-ocean.

Science has at the same time divested war of its divinity; made it devilish and ridiculous as a pursuit of man. Technique, above all, as a friend of the human race, has reduced to absurdity enmity between peoples, in that it surrendered at the same time to both warring parties and for that reason alone compelled both to unite.

The fourth argument, then, advanced by the friends of war—the splendour of heroic death—has, in the technical warfare of our time, become grotesque. During the cavalry attacks of Frederick the Great, yes even down to the battles of '70–'71, a trooper, galloping forward with bridle reins flung to the wind, could enjoy the voluptuous sensation of being a youth who risked his life in order to win personal renown. Today ambitions of this kind can spur only a few hundred aviators or sailors on a submarine. No battle of the World War was decided by a single man, like an occasional battle of old, or if there was such an incident, the fact remains unknown. Of course no one denies the part which the element of morale plays even today in the field and everybody knows that only an army resolved to hold out can gain advantage.

But the chance to win a battle by personal effort, through strategy or courage, which existed fifty years ago, has disappeared since war materials have become the determining factor, since the military machine has obtained control of everything, and since the soldier has been reduced to a servant of organization. Hand-to-hand fighting is still a reality, positions may be held by the resolution or the strength of a small force, but decisions are arrived at fifty miles behind the front, beside a telephone in a room, and are carried out twenty-five miles nearer the front in a dugout, by—let us say—a captain of artillery. Personal leadership in battle has given way to a remote, machine-like control, just as all other enterprises have. Now that it is possible to shoot over mountains at a target more than a hundred miles away, now that a commanding general need no longer push an army forward in order to capture a city in the heart of the enemy's territory but can destroy it with a gas attack carried out by aerial squadrons, war is no longer an affair between men, but a conflict between machines on the one hand, women and old men on the other.

Since physics usurps the rôle of the "human instrument of destiny"; since chemistry occupies the place of an attack, and statistics that of a call to arms; since the tension of high-voltage wires has replaced moral energy, and rigid discipline the spirit of voluntary sacrifice; since every military position has become a system of fortifications and whole countries a single citadel; since war, which was first a duel, then a knightly game, and then a profession, has become the fate of whole peoples, bringing destruction to millions remote from the battle area through bombs, gas or hunger: since all this has happened, the idea of heroic death has become a lie and every exhortation to win martial laurels a crime.

## v

THE fifth argument presented by the friends of war is this: the nation, the fatherland. How beautiful was the Roman Empire, extending from the Ebro to the Euphrates! How vast was the realm of the Caliphs! After the barbarians of the fifth century had overwhelmed the Roman might and partitioned it, the nations of Europe began to take shape. And yet during more than a thousand years afterwards every nationalistic antagonism disappeared so completely under the spell of a unifying faith that Dante could greet the German Emperor as a savior and Petrarch could summon another to Italy.

It was the Reformation that brought the first signs of patriotism to the surface in Germany; the Hussite wars were, perhaps, the first great nationalist movement. After England had developed a national consciousness during the Middle Ages, France, Spain, and other national powers came into being. Under Napoleon, who occasionally united several nations in one regiment, there existed momentarily something like a sentiment of a European fatherland. But after the nineteenth century had opened, Europe grew more and more divided. The Greek nation freed itself from the Turks, the Italians threw off the Austrian yoke, the Belgians parted from the Dutch, the Scandinavian peoples went their separate ways, and the Balkan nations discovered themselves. National states organized themselves everywhere and most of them became permanent. But Ireland and Poland remained in bondage to what they considered foreign domination, and two great imperial states—the Hapsburg monarchy and Turkey—united many peoples under their sway.

These powers discovered and nurtured their nationalist sentiment partly after, partly before, their actual establishment as independent states. They began to find it a source of pride. So long as a race or family is oppressed, one understands that it should vaunt its strength. But once a family is free, any member of it who continues loudly to praise his stock will hardly be understood by anyone. In the case of peoples however the game seems to be permitted, with the result that what is a private bad habit is transformed into a public virtue. And when the leaders of a young nation require patriotic sentiment, they easily find professors who prove that it exists. Thus Bulgarian savants found 1,100,000 Bulgars and only 700 Serbs in Macedonia, while Serbian authorities found 57,000 Bulgars and 2,000,000 Serbs in the same country. The Greeks meanwhile had been unable to discover a single Serb.

In similar fashion a great stock-taking of races started in the department-store called Europe, with a view to giving all races the justice they desired according to the demands of nationalities. No one knew (or if someone did, he concealed the fact) that after two thousand years of blending there were no more pure races in Europe, and that the only population of relatively undiluted blood dwells on the isle of Iceland, far out to sea, where the self-same Scandinavian immigrants have lived for a thousand years. But though only amalgamations of peoples, desirable for political reasons, existed—and no pure races or providentially appointed nations were discovered—nationalistic sentiment was nevertheless nourished everywhere. A few scattered customs and songs were so skilfully grouped that even the eight mutually inimical nations of Austria-Hungary and the forty-eight nations of Russia which were perfect strangers to one another managed to produce both an Austrian and a Russian national feeling.

To both groups, the sixth argument of the lovers of war—the hope of restoring the common tongue by a military victory—bristled with significant difficulties. Why was German spoken in the Baltic provinces of Russia, and Polish in German Masuria? Why do Basques and Bretons speak a French less pure than that used by the Canadian in English Quebec? How does it happen that, in spite of conquests and reconquests, the inhabitants of border provinces cannot make up their minds to speak any one pure language, and cling tenaciously to a jargon like the Alsatian dialect? And, on the other hand, how is it possible that a couple of dozen peoples, mingling in the United States, agree to use a single language so quickly that the sons of Italian or Polish immigrants are unable to understand the speech of their mothers? Where languages are forbidden they are preserved, but the emigrant forgets them speedily. It would seem therefore that the language of a country is dependent upon circumstances and not upon any national sentiment and that this last is developed among voluntary and even unwilling emigrants when they adopt one tongue, as is in the case in America. Apparently the community of land, language, and interests creates certain associative feelings but this implies not common enmity to those living elsewhere but common friendship for those who are neighbors. When deserters from various countries found themselves banded together in Switzerland during the World War for forced labor, they lived peaceably together, although their brothers at the front massacred one another on behalf of national sentiment.

Admittedly, sentiment of this character animates many individuals and those not of the worst sort.

"Italy is a religion," exclaimed Mazzini, and in vain did Bakunin object that Italy was composed of five nations—the clerical caste, the grande and petite bourgeoisie, the workers, and the farmers. A little earlier it was said in England that "God first revealed Himself to Englishmen"; and William II was honestly convinced that God "has in mind a very especial destiny for His Germans." Before and after the War, poets and scholars arose on all hands to cry out that theirs was the chosen people; and then when men ultimately began, amidst the thunder of assembled cannon, to call upon the German, English, French, or Russian God, every people believed, at first, in its own righteousness. Gustav Hervé believed in it, although a year previous he had led in establishing as a

dogma the negation of patriotism, and had courteously declared
that none of the existing nations was worth even a single drop of
a workingman's blood. All, or nearly all, speedily fell victims to
suggestion. The great powers especially were convinced of the
presence of God with them, although many spoke a little cynically
of the Bulgarian, Portuguese, or Montenegrin Deity. As if the
God of Christians were not always with the weak!

One of the romantic subsidiary motives of the nationalists,
which we will not stress overmuch, is the wish to see the "individuality of a people" conserved, and the belief that it would perish
under the influence of international union. The dances, songs,
and costumes of the olden time would otherwise, it is said, disappear completely. But when one bears in mind that today the
same collar is worn by Catholics, Mohammedans, and Confucians
in three continents, that the same business letter is despatched
from Honolulu and cities in Alaska, and that the same jams are
eaten by white men and negroes, one marvels at these lovers of
"individuality," who still seem to believe that Europe is a costume
ball, and that the preservation of a few racial customs associated
with church-going or shooting festivals are more important than
the preservation of thousands of human lives.

A final objection that arises to confute those who are concerned
over individualities of race and speech is the fact that we are today
experiencing not a horizontal but a vertical migration of peoples.
The diagram of the century results not from the longitudinal cuts
which divide Europe into nations, but from those cross-cuts which
split it up into classes. If one desires to understand the puzzle, one
must look diagonally from the bottom upward, not simply straight
from the top down.

## VI

THE seventh argument advanced by the friends of war is "national
honor." It is the most dangerous and most unreasonable of all;
wherefore it comes home to everyone. It leads directly to the
problem of the fatherland. Lessing said that "Love for one's
country is at best an heroic weakness"; but Goethe went still

farther when he wrote: "Patriotism as well as knightly conduct are now as much out of date as chivalry and priestcraft." These bold German opinions were balanced by French views. "The world is our country, men are our brothers," Paine had written; and in the National Assembly of 1790 Mirabeau declared: "I propose to you that the ministers or agents who have undertaken a war of aggression be pursued as criminals. The time will undoubtedly come when all Europe will be a single family. Weakness alone calls for war!" At the same time, General George Washington said: "My sincerest wish is to behold war, the shame of mankind, banished from this earth."

National honor—sometimes called prestige—is the corollary of heroic death. Both have been invented in order to arouse quiet, reasonable men to that fury which is indispensable to any attempt to storm an enemy position. Since no one is any longer stirred to martial ardor by the thought of defending the Cross or of fighting in behalf of the right interpretation of the Gospel, because all now permit others to believe what they think right, since the nation state has superseded the theocratic state, the "honor of the country" has been revised.

Though the concept of what constitutes this kind of honor has undergone many changes during recent centuries, one fact has remained: there is no such thing as the honor of a collective body. When the knight, festooned with flowers and wreaths, rode out to joust for his dame, determined to win or to fall, when a contemptuous glance from a neighboring loge—an offence against honor—was sufficient to doom one of two men to death, at that time, no nobleman went without a sword, and the history of the world was fashioned by aristocrats or the clergy. In such an age knightly conduct was a genuine thing, and the legends of mankind would be poorer without the scenes, anecdotes, and epigrams which grew up round about it.

Meanwhile, however, the world has discovered that lawyers and journalists, trade-unionists, teachers, and artisans guide the fortunes of peoples, that the nobility have lost their privileges, and that only the priests have conserved their ancient influence. The rapier is now found only in museums, at the opera, and in the castles of old families. Even in Germany dueling is restricted to very especial cases of mortal insult. Its place has been taken by assassination—a less knightly, a more cowardly and cynical, way of destroying an opponent.

And now, in the face of this transformation of the concept of honor, in an era when adultery is calmly discussed, forgiven or merged in divorce, and avenged by a bullet only in old-fashioned novels, at a time when one even goes to an unknown and official judge in order to obtain, through the state, revenge in the shape of money for an insult (thereby, incidentally, rendering oneself, the author of the injury, and the state ridiculous)—at such a moment in the world's history we are expected to believe that the honor of a nation can be violated, as even the newest treaties of 1928 do declare. In all truth, the spirit of no nation has ever been conscious of an injury to its honor. The fact is, rather, that a dozen ministers and popular orators, or a few hundred newspapers, have asserted that the nation has been insulted and must be avenged. In so far as such declarations have been masks behind which some group sought to conceal an attack, they have been means of overpowering through suggestion and excitement a few million tranquil citizens, most of whom had not, as they read the account of the injury, been so deeply stirred as to strike the table with their fists.

Collective honor is as unthinkable as collective love. These two most subtle manifestations of the human heart have always been experienced only by individuals. They are like stars which shine only in the lonely darkness and fade in the light of the omnipresent sun.

How weak must be the self-possession of a nation which permits itself to be changed by the threatening speeches of a neighboring statesman, by the incivility of a king making a vacation tour, by an article in an official journal or by the note of a minister of foreign affairs! If what we label patriotism really existed in the hearts of men, if the matter were not rather a natural affection for one's family, countryside, and state, there would exist no conscription. This is just as unethical as the so-called "matrimonial duty," which even the most modern codes of law still impose upon women. The existence of conscription would in itself suffice to prove that the kings who invented patriotism a hundred years ago were just as little certain of finding it in their subjects as legislators have been with respect to the existence of love in marriage relations. For this reason kings forced citizens to defend a country which nobody had attacked for any natural motive, and which therefore needed no defense.

"Standing armies," wrote Immanuel Kant, "should in time cease to be, for they constitute a perennial threat of war to other states. . . . The condition of peace is not a state of nature, which is rather constantly at war; but it must be established. . . . The civil constitution of every state ought to be republican. . . . International law should be based upon a federation of free states. . . . The idea of a world civil law is a necessary complement to general social rights and so to lasting peace, as are civil and common law." Simultaneously with the enunciation of these granite truths was heard the melodious voice of Voltaire, *"Dans tous les guerres il ne s'agit que de voler,"* and the declaration of his disciple, Frederick II, that wars are "the fever-fits of mankind." In 1820 Jefferson wrote a letter proposing that the earth be divided into two halves: one Europe, the land of martial heroes and belching cannon; the other America, home of peace and freedom.

Fifty years later Victor Hugo said: "Obliterate boundaries, get rid of border and customs officials, send the soldiers home: in other words, be free! Peace will then follow!" And Lamartine writes in his manifesto to the Europe of 1848: "The world and ourselves, we would advance toward brotherliness and peace . . . not the fatherland but the free man incurs the greatest danger in war time."

But long before the exuberances of these poets and thinkers, a few statesmen attempted to use practical measures in preparing a way which, in our time, only a few venture to take. In all ages the crowd has ridiculed as utopian ideas which it feared for one reason or another, chiefly habit. The first man who sought to establish an international tribunal with executive power in Europe was a Czech who had come into prominence first as a politician and governor, then as an elected king. He was George von

Podiebrad who in 1462—nearly five hundred years before the time of Wilson—sought to unify the Christian nations into one parliament and to create an international militia as a means of defense against any disturber of peace. But the Pope laid a ban on him, and the age passed him by. A century later, Henri IV conceived a similar plan in Paris.

Every era of great wars enkindles anew the will to peace. It seems as if, in this respect, men remain all their lives like children who abstain from sugar only when and as long as they suffer from stomach-ache as a result of too much nibbling. In times of peace the desire for unison among peoples grows steadily weaker; and it would be entirely forgotten if a few thinkers, here and there, did not repeat their warnings over and over again.

Living in the seventeenth century, under the deep impression which the longest of all wars had made upon him, the Dutch scholar, Hugo Grotius, fought against the notion of a chosen people. The Frenchman Emeric de Lacroix proposed a permanent international congress having its seat in Venice, and the Englishman William Penn suggested a congress of states. Then the whole spirit of later times was dominated by the work of the Abbé St. Pierre, who in his turn demanded a permanent congress of states, the reduction of armed forces in every country to 6,000 men, and punitive expeditions against every recalcitrant member. This plan was first formulated in France by Turgot and the Encyclopædists, in Germany by Leibnitz, and in England by Bentham.

The year 1815 was a great year for the peace movement. Twenty years of war had once again stirred the consciences of Europeans. This time, however, a new part of the world was in evidence for the first time, making its appearance in a characteristic way. During the same month that witnessed the meeting in Paris of the three most powerful sovereigns of Europe, for the purpose of establishing, with mighty words and petty reservations, with pomp and falsehoods, "eternal peace" through the medium of the so-called "Holy Alliance," there assembled, in a New York cottage, a few dozen Quakers to form, without pomp and circumstance, the first society for the promotion of peace recorded in history. The Holy Alliance devised by kings in armor was soon undermined and wormeaten by the flagrant family interests of their dynasties, but the modest club formed by those humble liberty-loving American citizens multiplied within ten years into fifty such associations scattered throughout the United States. Other Quakers made a similar beginning in England, a year after the American society came into being, and a little later "Friends of Peace," the first periodical of its kind in the world, appeared in London.

Not until 1830 did the Continent follow this example by founding the first European society for peace in Genoa. In 1843 the first Peace Conference met in London. The leading spirits of many nations—Cobden, Peel, Disraeli, Hugo, Garibaldi, and also Napoleon III—were captivated by the new idea. During the nineties, Germans took the lead; Alfred Fried and Berta von Suttner offered themselves to ridicule in an Empire prospering in a coat of mail; a Peace Bureau was established in Berne; Nobel, Carnegie, and other manufacturers of war materials, dying, bequeathed millions to rid the world of war; and mankind even witnessed the spectacle of the Czar of all the Russias, formerly commander-in-chief of the largest army in the world, summoning a congress to The Hague, for the purpose of founding an international tribunal. So great was the fear of war in the hearts of those engaged in preparing it!

The tragi-comic history of this Conference closed the nineteenth century and its era, grown so drunk with old thoughts of power that it could be awakened only by the noise of a vast catastrophe. The whole nineteenth century had been marked by reaction against the peaceful solution of international problems because it had witnessed the rise of nationalist states and, under the influence of nationalist concepts and the interests of so-called *Realpolitik*, concern for both moral and economic considerations had been trampled in the earth. The World War, which was on the verge of breaking out in the very first years of the opening century, is the great liquidation of debts created in the previous era and we desire and demand that it be associated with the nineteenth century. The second Hague Conference of 1907 was only a farce. During the weeks for which the third meeting was set in the summer of 1915, oratory could no longer be heard in The Hague for nearby thundered the canon of Europe.

The cost of armament during the years from 1910 to 1914 amounted to 1.8 billions of dollars for Austria and Germany together and 2.4 billions for France and Russia. The total was more than four billions. Yet these were small sums compared with those piled up by the War. On land and sea or in the air, 12,-990,570 soldiers were killed in the World War. The War cost the combined combatants 250,000,000 billions of dollars, half their total national wealth.

Thus, within four years, for no reason and without any essential consequences, Europe had sent up in smoke half of all it had gathered together during centuries. How should we characterize an act of this kind on the part of a large bank or a powerful family?

In so far as the victorious powers are concerned, France was a creditor nation to the extent of 30 billions before the war and a debtor to the extent of 31 billions afterward. During the struggle, the national wealth of Franch decreased by one third; that of England by one fourth. Even the United States Government had to expend during two years more than it had previously laid out in the course of a century; and if in spite of this fact it remains today the creditor of the world, the reason is not participation in the second half of the war but rather abstention during the first half. The small countries which remained neutral are in a relatively better position than any of the imperialist states.

With the exception of America, all the warring countries lost millions of men and billions of money; and any territory gained in the process at the expense of the conquered peoples is of intrinsic worth only in the case of the new free states established at the end. During the past ten years Germany, though beaten and stripped of considerable territory, has recuperated more rapidly than enlarged and victorious France—a new proof that neither vastness of domain, number of "souls," the fortune of arms, nor the rôle assumed at the signing of peace determines the strength of a nation but, rather, a series of biological factors. Even the single positive result of the World War—the destruction of four

realms anachronistically ruled by emperors, and the creation of
eleven republics—was therefore purchased at a price which, in civil
life, only an insane person would pay.

VII

THE primitive negro who first beholds a white man shrinks back
from the stranger in religious fear.　A long time passes before he
discovers that this demigod dies of thirst without water, is hungry
if there be no game to eat; that red blood flows from his wounds,
which are painful to him also; and that his children are born and
suckled in the family pickaninny manner.　The fact that certain people wear bear skins, eat blubber, and live in snow-huts
keeps them worlds apart from the Hindu who chews almonds and
washes himself and his breech-cloth daily in the stream.　And
yet the mysterious mechanism of their bodies, so much more wisely
and complexly constructed than all houses and machines, functions in both in the same manner and living energy radiates in the
same waves through both organisms.

The great thinkers, teachers of wisdom to mankind, knew this
well because their thoughts went back to the fundamentals of our
existence and did not rest content with the particular customs
and beliefs of their own peoples.　Confucius and Buddha, Socrates
and Jesus, Francis of Assisi, Spinoza, Voltaire, addressed their
words to a being who must breathe, eat, drink, and die; who can
feel, dream, think, and invent; who desires, suffers, and enjoys;
and who is at home everywhere on this round earth which we shall
soon encircle with ships that ride the air.　Here we have the word
which, more than all the wisdom of philosophers, will girdle all
the earth, building one common society in which men like unto
one another will dwell:—the word *velocitas*, which means speed, is
the word to which our century hearkens.

The wars of our time had their genesis in the minds of a few;
they could be brought into being, however, only through the aid
of propaganda, which averred that those who live "over there" are
different from ourselves and are therefore evil, having what we do
not possess and longing to possess what we have.　These people,

who wear wooden shoes and blue mantles instead of leathern boots and jackets, who eat sausages and drink beer instead of mutton and red wine, who take the chalice at the Lord's Supper rather than the Host alone—these are not worthy to own that beautiful district. And vice versa. The chauvinists have always flattered their own folk, and defamed foreign peoples.

Therefore we are told again and again, in the self-satisfied manner of those who have no vision, that war must be as long as there are men. For the most part, persons who talk in this strain are beyond the age of military service. But why should those who will be sent into the fray not pause to consider how this ignominy may be overcome?

The robber barons, who sat in their "romantic" castles enjoying a clear view of the commercial highways on which they took their plunder, would also have smiled if someone had told them that before one or two centuries passed armor and long swords would have gone out of style. "But how shall order be maintained, how shall people realize that I am a nobleman, if I carry no death-dealing weapon?" they might have asked.

What would these gentlemen say if they could behold cities erected without walls to afford protection against their forays, fortresses which have been levelled, castle moats converted into flower-gardens, their own grandsons going about with a gilded foil, and their great-grandsons carrying nothing more destructive than a cane!

It was possible after all for a world comprised of law-abiding citizens to develop out of a state of affairs in which every house was its own fortress and every head of a family carried a weapon to defend his nest and his rights, as soon as communities decided to live peaceably inside the common walls and to allow judges to settle grievances. It was possible, furthermore, for a time to come when the walls of cities could fall and the diverse portions of a continent could be linked with one another openly by means of iron rails stretching from city to city, promoting tranquillity and labor in common. Are we now to believe it impossible that these same rails, which in reality pass beyond all barriers created by tariffs and newspapers, which are of the same gauge throughout a great portion of the earth, which carry the same cars everywhere, and which are indifferent to hateful words about the bad neighbor who boils his chicken instead of roasting it, shall not overcome these words out of sheer practical necessity?

Are they not carrying similar things through the wide world? The bananas offered for sale by the street vendors of Paris and Berlin grew on neighboring trees in the primeval African forest. Was this admirable English white bread baked of American or Russian flour? Is not the coffee percolator in a San Francisco drug store the same as that in the *Espresso* in Rome? A Russian farmer who has saved a little money rides in a Ford car to a field which he plows with a German tractor; in China people carry German parasols and wear American snowshoes; the same types of manufactured articles turn up in all countries, because the pictures displayed in trade magazines are wafted round the world. The machine impresses its identical forms upon the brain of all mankind. The gesture of a Korean manipulating the throttle of his motor is international in character, and he thinks the same thoughts regarding the refusal of his automobile to budge as does the handsome gentleman tourist on the broadest highway in Sussex. The roads of the whole world are similar, for autos are destined to go everywhere; the clothes of the whole world repeat one another and all autoists must wear auto coats or mechanics' trousers. Even the air, in which the traveller could once perceive real differences, is becoming homogeneous. Wherever men are, there also is the smell of machine oil.

The joys of men are coming to resemble one another. The phonograph records played in Uganda in front of the kraal of the chieftain are the same as those whirled off in a Parisian dance hall. And possibly the old negro recognizes something African, coming to him in a roundabout way, in the jazz rhythms. The film tragedies manufactured in Hollywood are reeled off in Tokio and Melbourne at the same time.

In the place of things, which once had a differentiating effect upon men, impelling them to discern that which was strange, not that which was common, in the simple affairs of life, have now come machines which bring people together more quickly than could the conferences of their statesmen—conferences at tables which are green, like the congress tables in centuries gone by. Machines and merchandise, railroads and newspapers, technical effort and science, are all compelling us toward peace. When viewed from an elevated standpoint, war is now seen to have become as mediæval as a tourney.

### VIII

When the festive parade that honored the occasion of Queen Victoria's jubilee came into view, a beggar made the following comment: "I own Australia, Canada, New Zealand, and India, but I am starving nevertheless, because I have no bread. I am a citizen of the greatest world power, and everybody should bow before me. But when I asked a negro for alms yesterday, he gave me a kick instead."

The fact that the propertied man in this anecdote was a negro and also a British subject renders this tragi-comic story doubly true. For while we Europeans have reintroduced slavery among ourselves in the form of conscription, the Africans have occasionally been emancipated from slavery through the same conscription and enabled to demand their rights in accordance with Mr. Wilson's programme. Though this century may not witness the end of war, it will certainly experience the end of colonization. Therewith there will fall into the discard the last argument which once seemed to offer a recommendation of war. If our century does not see the peaceful unification of Europe, it will behold militant unification should the colored races join against the white world. "If the inhabitants of Mars were to invade our midst, we should have a world nation tomorrow," said Zangwill.

### IX

If they would preserve themselves, civilized states must achieve some kind of unity. For internationalism is not the antithesis to nationhood, but verily rather a synthesis of nations. "No people," said Lord Grey, "can in the future consider itself victorious if it has sought security for itself alone and not, at the same time, for others."

This discernment is nowhere gainsaid, but the dullness of minds, the sloth of hearts, the force of habit all conspire to make most men conduct themselves in the fashion of thirty years ago, when President Krüger came to Europe an exile and was greeted by a French journal with these words: "Forgive Europe the circumstance that we were not in a position to do what we ought to have done and wished to do."

And yet all these millions of people, who look forward unmoved and inactive to an approaching war as if this were their fate, belong to various organizations which have long since broken through nationalistic bonds. All are Catholics or Protestants, Jews or Mohammedans, and so in agreement, inside their confessions, throughout the world. They are all either members of the capitalist class, doing business daily in foreign exchange, notes, papers, and bills of lading, or they are members of an international union of workers or of international congresses and institutes; if they can do nothing else, they mount railroad cars routed to foreign countries, or ships whose papers name foreign lands as their goal. If they belong, however, to the very small number who clamor for war—who sit in certain military headquarters or editorial offices in all countries—then they have nothing else to think about except the foreign countries which they intend to conquer and destroy.

The League of Nations is the first institution which has begun to carry into effect the plans of the Czech king and the Dutch scholar whom we have named, and to express in terms of reality the idea which meant so much to Kant and Leibnitz, Goethe and Lessing, St. Pierre, Lamartine and Hugo. Conceived in Europe, advocated in America, it has now been established, with many imperfections, on the banks of a Swiss lake. But however little one may venture to compare dream and reality in this instance, it is certain that the marble tablet on the quay at the Lake of Geneva quite properly bears the name of Woodrow Wilson. As the letters of that name, inscribed in gold, face the summit of Mont Blanc, the man whom they recall seems, in all his earthbound limitations, to summon forth the giant whose godlike head is there only occasionally revealed through a drifting of clouds.

*La vérité est en marche.* In all countries, particularly in England and America, societies founded for the unification of lovers of peace now number millions rather than thousands. But it is obvious that the chief leaders are not those who thus instruct and dedicate themselves to the cause, that our hope must lie rather with the young who are now growing into maturity and will believe what they are taught. If we give our boys tin soldiers, take them to gaze upon the monuments erected to victorious kings, teach them the names of battles, the songs of tramping men, the renown of generals, the splendor of armies marching to the field, the glory of a uniform, the charm of decorations, the prestige of the state, the superiority of the fatherland, the pride of conquest, they will accept it all. And when they arrive at maturity, they will seek to attain the goal that has been pointed out to them as the ideal.

But reveal to them the fleeting honors of martial success as compared with the enduring victories of the spirit, contrast for them the achievements of triumphant captains and the work of thinkers and inventors, compare generals sending men to death with doctors devoted to saving lives. Teach them to realize the faults of their own countries and to appreciate the virtues of others. Show them their close kinship to children who speak an alien tongue. Emphasize the fact that they have in common mountains and streams, that national boundary lines do not mark vital differences between the people on both sides, that customs and clothing, faith and superstition, present similarities throughout the world, that literatures supplement one another, and that great foreign cities are friendly neighbors which can now be reached by aeroplane in a few hours. Do this and they will believe and be governed accordingly throughout their lives. Above all, teach them what a battle really is, show them photographs—terribly true—of life in the zone of battle where human bodies are mangled beyond recognition and beautiful lives are snuffed out in smoke and flame. Teach them the mathematical terms in which a victor nation must reckon its success when war is over. Let them learn modern languages so that they can go about everywhere. And while you educate your sons to seek an outlet for their ambitions and energies in tasks that will bring success to them, give your daughters to understand that they, the natural guardians of life and hearth, must likewise realize their solidarity with one another so that, in case another "fever-fit," as Frederick termed it, attacks humanity, they may arise and extinguish it before it bursts into war. For theirs are those weaponless hands which, since primeval times, have been superior to hands bearing arms.

## VIII—HEALTH

### By C.-E. A. Winslow

THE question which has been asked of the contributors to this volume reminds one a little of an episode in Wells' "Food of the Gods." The "Children of the Food" have become giants eight times the stature of mankind with an equivalent intellectual and spiritual development. One of them wanders into London and astounded at the mass of busy, crawling humanity he asks: "What are you all for, you little people? What are you all for, anyway?"

Professor Beard has put this question to our modern scientific civilization. It is a sound question and a pertinent one; but it takes a little answering. It involves consideration of what has been accomplished, of the values and the costs of the results attained, of future probable tendencies and of the underlying philosophy which, however unconsciously, animates our civilization as a whole. It is a challenge which we, who believe in evolution and in the fruits of evolution, should be proud to take up as best we may.

In the field covered by the present chapter, that of health, the first question noted above, as to what has actually been accomplished, is relatively easy to answer. There may be differences of opinion as to whether man is more or less pugnacious, more or less philosophical than he was. That he is more healthy can be demonstrated beyond the shadow of a doubt.

As the simplest and most obvious measure of achievement we can take the life span to which the average man may look forward at birth. In the eighteenth century, acccording to the few estimates which can be made, this expectation of life in civilized English and American communities (Carlisle, England, Massachusetts and New Hampshire) was between 35 and 40 years. In some cities (Northhampton, England and Philadelphia) it was under 30 years. From 1838 on, we have full data for England and Wales which may be cited in round figures to the nearest full year as follows:

| | |
|---|---|
| 1838—1854 | 40 years |
| 1871—1880 | 41 years |
| 1881—1890 | 44 years |
| 1891—1900 | 44 years |
| 1901—1910 | 48 years |
| 1910—1912 | 51 years |
| 1920—1922 | 56 years |

During the last half of the nineteenth century there was a gain of only four years in the average expectation of life; during the first quarter of the twentieth century there has been a gain of twelve years. For the United States, the same thing has occurred, an increase in expectation of life from forty-eight years in 1901 to fifty-eight years in 1925.

Whether this remarkable increase in the length of life is due to chance or to vague and uncertain biological and social tendencies or whether it is the direct result of purposeful public health efforts, we can judge by an analysis of the specific causes of death which have chiefly contributed to the total result. For this purpose I may cite, as entirely typical, the statistics for my own city of New Haven which have recently been analyzed in detail for the past half century.

For 1877–1881 the death rate from all causes in New Haven was 1820 per 100,000—that is out of every 100,000 persons in the population 1820 died each year. In 1922–1926 the corresponding rate was 1250. Comparing these two periods, the rate for pulmonary tuberculosis dropped from 282 to 41; for diphtheria, from 124 to 5; for typhoid fever, from 47 to 5; for scarlet fever, from 40 to 2; for infant diarrhea, from 105 to 19. These five causes alone account for an aggregate decrease of 526

per 100,000 or 92 per cent of the total net decrease in the death
rate from all causes, If we can reasonably account for the decrease
in these five diseases we shall have gone far to explain the major
changes in expectation of life during the past half century.

We shall return later on to those factors in the death rate which
have shown an increase. It suffices for the present to note
that the major decreases have occurred in the five diseases listed;
and how these decreases have been accomplished, we can say with
considerable definiteness. Typhoid fever has been controlled
chiefly by the purification of water supplies, the pasteurization of
milk, and the use of vaccine; diphtheria, by the use of antitoxin,
and more recently by toxin-antitoxin immunization; scarlet fever
by isolation and very recently by serum treatment; diarrhea, by
pasteurization of milk and breast feeding of infants. In the case
of tuberculosis, the causal relationships are less well established.
Discussion of the reasons for the decreasing death rate from this disease offer a happy hunting ground for the mystics who from time
to time seek to substitute vague cosmic tendencies for more obviously apparent causes. The statement that the fall in the tuberculosis rate has been a continuous process irrespective of public
health activities is, however, simply untrue. The sharp and sudden
decrease began about 1890 when the anti-tuberculosis campaign began and not before; it has taken place in countries where there
has been an organized anti-tuberculosis campaign and not in other
countries. Some part of the decrease is without doubt due to
improved economic status since everything which affects physical
well-being affects this disease. There was, however, improvement
in economic status before 1890 but it was accompanied by no such
spectacular results as have since accrued from a combination of
improved economic status and organized public health work. If
the same rate of decrease which has occurred since 1890 had existed
prior to that date we must assume that all the deaths which occurred from all causes in 1840 were due to this disease.

Furthermore, for the purpose of our present argument, it is of
no moment whether tuberculosis has been conquered by sanatoria
and dispensaries and public health education or by higher standards of living. It is the whole impact of modern science upon

human life with which we are concerned; and the outstanding material prosperity of the common man is the fruit of science as truly as is the improvement in the special field of public health.

We may summarize then by saying that during the past half century a phenomenal thing has happened—a fundamental and startling revolution in the conditions of human life. Over one third of the total burden of disease and early death which weighed upon the human race fifty years ago has been lifted from its shoulders; and this is the result of modern science, chiefly of medical science, applied directly to the problem of public health, and in part of chemical and physical and mechanical and industrial science which have operated indirectly by raising the general standard of living throughout the civilized world.

## II

It might seem superfluous to argue as to the values to mankind of the results above. If we could say to a given individual on his deathbed, "You can have twelve years more of life," the boon would generally be accepted with satisfaction—and that is exactly what the advance of public health science has said to the average man of today. Yet there are those who question the social value of a reduced death rate on two different grounds with sufficient persistence to warrant a consideration of their arguments.

The first of these criticisms is based on the assumption that a total increase in human population is in itself a menace, tending to lower standards of living and to aggravate international rivalries. It is to this view that the late Professor W. T. Sedgwick referred in his suggestive address on "The Reappearance of the Ghost of Malthus." The fear, in theory, perhaps seems a just one for there would be little gain in replacing pestilence by its grim sisters, war and famine. Fortunately for mankind, however, the theory does not actually work out in that way.

We may take the statistics of New Haven once more as an example although the same general facts would appear from an analysis of vital statistics from any other community in the civilized world. We have seen that the death rate from all causes de-

creased from 1820 per 100,000 in 1877–1881 to 1250 per 100,-
000 in 1922–1926; but during the same period, the birth rate
decreased from 3120 per 100,000 to 2150.  In other words, the
net excess of births fell from 1300 to 900 per 100,000.

This is, in greater or less degree, a world-wide phenomenon; and
it is a phenomenon of great significance.  Malthus was right in
diagnosing an unrestricted increase in population as a menace to
the human race; but his remedies of famine, plague, and war were
crude and primitive ones.  Nature (if we may use a good old
abstract term which has its usefulness) has a better medicine and
uses it.  It does not seem entirely certain to the writer that the
phenomena observed are wholly due to voluntary birth control for
there may also be subtler physiological forces at work.  The fact,
however, is clear that all over the civilized world the birth rate is
falling at a rate so rapid that the decreasing death rate barely, or
scarcely, keeps pace with it.

The diminishing death rate is then clear gain from a purely
quantitative standpoint.  If the birth rate would have decreased
in any event, the fall in mortality has checked the human race
on the road to extinction.  If the falling birth rate is a concomitant
of the falling death rate the combination remains still an unmixed
good; for there is no social profit in the bearing of children doomed
to die before they reach maturity.

A second school of skeptics challenges the values of the modern
public health campaign on qualitative rather than quantitative
grounds.  They claim that sanitary science interferes with natural
selection and preserves the unfit; they paint for us a doleful picture of a world full of degenerate cripples as the contribution of
medical science.

This fallacious line of argument depends on two fundamental
errors—errors which have dogged the steps of naïve Darwinians
in many another field.  The first of these is an exaggerated view
of the scope of selection; and the second is the assumption that
"fitness" is a single simple factor and not (as Darwin himself well
understood) a collective noun.  In the first place the toll taken of
mankind by epidemic disease was in large measure not selective at
all.  The babies who died of infant diarrhea were condemned, not

by inherent weakness but by the pure chance that they were fed on decayed milk. The people of a town which suffered from a devastating epidemic of typhoid fever or cholera were no feebler than those of a town which escaped. They were merely unfortunate in the character of their public water supply.

To say so much, however, is after all only to say that natural selection is a wasteful process. A second point, which is more important, concerns the specificity of "fitness." Let us grant that if a group of infants be fed with the same bad milk, a group of adults with the same polluted water, some will perish, and some will survive as a result of differences in innate powers of resistance. It does not at all follow that the survivors will be fitter than the victims in any other respect whatever—mentally, morally, or physically. In many instances there is no reason to think that their inherent vigor in regard to any other disease will be greater than that of those who had perished, for resistance is in a large measure a definite and specific condition due to the structural character of a given tissue or to the presence in the blood of a specific chemical compound. In certain other cases it is true that survival may depend on the strength of some vital organ such as the heart; but even here it can scarcely be doubted that death at fifty from organic heart disease represents a clear gain as compared with death at twenty from typhoid fever.

Furthermore, there is another side to this problem which is of far greater practical importance. A death from diarrhea or diphtheria, from scarlet fever or tuberculosis, represents ten or twenty other cases which did not terminate fatally. These ten or twenty survivors, whatever their inherent vigor, have suffered a severe strain upon their vital forces. They have been wounded if not killed; and it very frequently happens that their wounds never wholly heal. It is among such survivors as these that we find weak hearts and kidneys, with increased susceptibility to disorders of all sorts. It is these lamed individuals, far more than the unselected, who constitute a source of true racial weakness. And the proportion of these crippled beings in the population is decreased in direct measure with the decreasing death rate from preventable disease; for it is prevention of infection, not cure of acquired disease, that has played the major part in the sanitary progress of the past half century.

We may conclude from the evidence available that the conquest of communicable disease has, through its interference with natural selection, tended in negligible degree to increase the proportion of weaklings in the population since the action of epidemic disease is mainly non-selective and since such selective action as it does exert is chiefly specific and unrelated to general health. On the other hand it has exerted a very real tendency to increase the vigor of the race by eliminating the widespread crippling which obtains among those who have survived an attack of such diseases. There is a net gain in quality as well as in quantity.

It is this intimate connection between mortality and disability which is indeed the heart of the whole problem. The two are inseparable and whatever affects one also affects the other. The fact that infants are rationally fed does not merely protect them from intestinal disorders. It also makes them bigger and stronger. We can not by taking thought add a cubit to our own stature; but we can, and we have, added inches to the stature of our offspring, as statistics show. It would be a poor triumph to prolong the average length of life by twelve years if it meant merely the accumulation of a horde of doddering cripples. But it does not mean this. It is, I believe, impossible to prolong the average length of life by ten years without tending at the same time to make the man of seventy equivalent in vigor to the man of sixty of an earlier period. The individual who dies from a given cause is but one member of a group suffering from crippling wounds due to the same factor. If we remove the cause we save that whole group from their disabilities.

The object of the modern public campaign is, then, health, not merely survival. Its ideal is set forth in that picture drawn by William James in his glorious phrase, "Simply to live, and breathe should be a delight." Nor is physical life and physical soundness to be thought of by the man of this modern scientific age as separable from the life and the soundness of the mind and the spirit. We are recapturing the Greek ideal of a whole man. We know that a Darwin or a Stevenson may accomplish wonders under heavy physical handicaps; but we look to the sound mind in the sound body as our goal.

III

IF public health, as a modern scientific social movement, has yielded certain results and if those results seem inherently valuable, the next question which concerns us is the cost involved. As the late Dr. Hermann M. Biggs taught us, "Public health is purchasable. Within natural limitations a community can determine its own death rate;" but is the investment a good one? Even if the fruits are sweet, are we paying too much for them? Do they involve the sacrifice of other goods, material or spiritual, in unreasonable proportion to the gains which are won?

From a purely material standpoint the question is easily answered in the negative. The cost of a standard community health programme as it is understood at the present day is between two and three dollars per person per year. This includes ordinary health department service, complete public health nursing service, clinic services for tuberculosis and venereal disease, and prenatal and infant and school hygiene. Even if we assume that this sum may be doubled in the future to permit of certain possible expansions to be discussed in a succeeding paragraph we have only the equivalent of one day's wages for the average American working man. Double this again, to allow for such complete preventive medical supervision as is now given to the student in our leading colleges or to the worker in certain favored industries, and we have still only ten dollars per person per year as compared with at least four times that sum which would be a highly conservative estimate of the burden of largely preventable illness at the present day, as measured in the loss of one week's working time per person each year plus the cost of physicians and nurses and hospitals and medicines. Financially, preventive medicine is a sound investment.

The question whether public health involves sacrifices of a non-material nature is also worthy of consideration. Indeed the most important problem to be dealt with in this volume is here concerned. It is quite certain that in our scientific age material prosperity has been accompanied, in some respects at least, by losses of spiritual values. We must ask ourselves seriously whether the connection is an accidental one or whether it represents a temporary phase of adjustment to a new condition or whether it is a price which we must agree to pay for the results attained.

The first criticism which is commonly leveled at the twentieth century by those who yearn for the thirteenth is that it tends to materialism, and the second is that it involves the crushing of the potentialities of the individual beneath the load of a deadly uniformity. They are serious charges and if they were justified we might well have reason to pause and consider. In the field of public health they are not justified.

First, as to materialism. To those who are in the least familiar with the tendencies of preventive medicine it must be obvious that materialism is not one of its fruits. It is the sick man who is obsessed by his body, not the well man. Health sets us free for higher things; and it is health, positive health, not negative freedom from disease, which is the watchword of this movement. The driver of a car who has his carburetor cleaned and his engine overhauled is not dominated by hypochondriac fears but by the desire to glory in a perfect smooth-running machine. He is far more likely to be able to enjoy the beauties of the countryside than his fellow driver who stalls by the roadside. His car in the long run takes far less of his time and attention than does the sickly machine driven by the more careless.

Nor does the modern public health movement involve subjection to a soul-destroying type of social control; quite the contrary. From the sacred books of Persia onwards the life of primitive people has been shadowed by taboos of a mixed medical and religious origin. Irksome quarantines and brutal treatment of the leper and the mental case darkened the life of the Middle Ages. The modern public health movement itself began in large measure as an exercise of police power. Regulations enforced by the strong arm of the law and dealing with the sanitation of the physical environment dominated this movement from its inception in 1840 almost to the end of the last century. The isolation of communicable disease and the protection of the public against smallpox by vaccination were accomplished by compulsion.

Today, however, all this is changing. The problems of modern public health are subtler and more difficult of accomplishment; and we recognize that they can be attained only by enlisting the voluntary and intelligent co-operation of the individual. Education replaces compulsion. The public health nurse supplants the sanitary policeman; and with the most fortunate results. The marvelous success obtained by immunization against diphtheria with toxin-antitoxin has been achieved without a single law interfering with personal liberty. When one case of smallpox occurred in the city of New Haven last spring (with three others in surrounding towns) 102,000 persons were vaccinated within a week in a city of 185,000 population, with no legal compulsion whatsoever.

I think I voice the sentiments of all progressive health officers when I say that we would agree to the removal from the statute-books of every health law whatsoever of a mandatory nature—provided that we be given in exchange adequate funds for a full health programme of education and of services along clinic and nursing lines.

The modern public health movement is not, then, based on autocratic dictatorship but on democratic education of a free and intelligent people by the force of expert leadership.

## IV

THE scientific age is still in its infancy; and public health is no exception to the general rule. It will be well to consider briefly some of its potentialities for the future.

The modern public health movement began in England in 1842 with the report of Edwin Chadwick on the Sanitary Condition of the Laboring Population of Great Britain. It was at first essentially a movement for environmental sanitation in the strictest sense. It was based on more or less crude and incomplete theories of disease, for Pasteur's epoch-making researches were still in the future. Yet there was enough truth in Chadwick's conceptions of the relation between filth and disease to make them work—which is all we can demand of any scientific theory. As water supplies were improved and age-long accumulations of filth were cleared away, the major plagues and pestilences of earlier days, cholera, typhus, gradually disappeared.

In the eighties, following on the fundamental discoveries of Pasteur, came the golden age of bacteriology. The germs of disease were discovered and we learned how to detect cases and carriers and to replace blind "gunshot quarantine" by intelligent selective isolation of individuals. The principles of vaccine prophylaxis and serum therapy were discovered and diphtheria, typhoid, meningitis and, most recently, scarlet fever were added to the list of maladies which need no longer take their toll of the children of mankind. Of the entire group of acute communicable infections only pneumonia and influenza now remain as still beyond the scope of effective control. Our basic knowledge in regard to these diseases is still incomplete; but that their turn will come in the future we can scarcely doubt.

At the beginning of the present century a third line of attack was initiated which today dominates the public health campaign —the development of an organized programme of popular education in the principles of personal hygiene. By 1900, environmental sanitation and the bacteriological control of the acute contact-borne infections had already begun to bear fruit; and with the impending disappearance of typhoid fever, scarlet fever, and diphtheria, the health administrator began to look for new worlds to conquer. Tuberculosis was the outstanding health problem of that day; and this disease could not be attacked along the lines of sanitation or of serum therapy but only by education in personal hygiene. With the organization of the National Tuberculosis Association in 1904, there was launched the first of the great modern movements for health education and for mobilizing the whole public in a volunteer community warfare against disease. The movement succeeded and was quickly followed by a similar programme for the control of infant mortality; and by others designed to deal with venereal disease, with mental disease, with heart disease, and with cancer.

It is this type of programme which dominates the public health movement of the present day: It involves two essential elements —education of the public and the development of a new relationship between the physician and his patient. Each of these problems requires novel social machinery of first-rate significance.

In the first place it must be noted that the type of education required involves something more than mass propaganda. Bulletins, newspaper articles, cinemas, radio talks, exhibits help to prepare the soil but the seed must be planted in the home itself. "The Kingdom of God is within you" and the kingdom of health in the last analysis is an individual matter. It is not merely vague generalities about food, fresh air, exercise, and the rest which are needed. They must be applied to John and to Susan, with John's and Susan's specific potentialities and limitations. We needed an individual teacher to carry the message to Garcia in the individual household. For this purpose we turned to the visiting nurse and she was transformed into the public health nurse, not merely a minister of healing but a messenger of health, carrying the gospel of hygiene to the worker in the factory and to the mother in the tenement. The nurse, as teacher, is the central figure in the public health movement of the present day.

If, however, the nurse was to teach personal hygiene as applied to the individual something else was needed. She must know just what health teaching the individual required, and such knowledge could only be based on a medical diagnosis. From this situation was born the conception of a new relationship between the medical profession and the public. In the past the physician was a repair man, called in only when suffering became so acute as to call for relief; and in such circumstances only relief and not cure or prevention can generally be anticipated. The true use of medical science as a preventive of disease has only dawned upon us during the past quarter of a century.

The new conception has worked itself out empirically in response to specific demands. Tuberculosis clinics were organized for the diagnosis of this disease in its curable stage. Medical examination of school children was introduced. Infant welfare stations were developed, not to care for sick babies but to keep well babies in good health. Prenatal clinics followed. Here and there heart clinics were established, and cancer clinics. The campaign for annual health examinations was launched. We glimpse today a far-reaching and comprehensive change in the whole organization of the medical profession and in the basis of payment for medical service as possibly necessary if really preventive medical service is to be made available for all the people, rich and poor and of median economic status, in city and in country, and at a cost and on terms which the people can be persuaded individually or collectively to pay.

The problems involved are by no means simple ones. They should be solved without sacrifice of the splendid traditions of individualistic medicine and they can be solved wisely only with the active co-operation of the medical profession itself. That they must somehow be solved is, however, clear. The old artificial line between prevention as a function of the state and cure as that of the private physician can no longer be maintained. Disease is a process. The physician cures (so far as possible) the damage already done and prevents that damage from going further. He, and not the engineer or the bacteriologist, must be the central figure in the public health programme of the future. He must be given whatever new form of social organization can be devised which will make his work most effective.

The importance of this new type of public health—social in its conception, individual in its application—is made clear by a consideration of the actual nature of the objective of the campaign of today. Fifty years ago the chief causes of death were tuberculosis, diphtheria, typhoid fever, and diarrhea. All of these except tuberculosis have practically disappeared and even tuberculosis has fallen to fifth or sixth place among the items in the death roll. Today we are dying of heart disease and apoplexy and nephritis and cancer and pneumonia; and it is toward the control of these conditions that our programme must be directed.

The first four of these causes of death have shown not only a relative but an absolute increase during the past half century in the United States. This is in part of course due to the fact that they are chiefly old-age diseases and if people do not die of diphtheria and tuberculosis in youth they are likely to die of heart disease or cancer in later life. Even at a given age, however, cancer mortality has progressively risen, whether as a result of some real increase in prevalence or, more probably, as a result of better diagnosis. The same thing happened with heart disease and its related conditions, apoplexy and nephritis, for the first part of the period under consideration; but it is encouraging and significant to note that for the last two decades the mortality from this group of conditions has begun to decrease at all ages under seventy.

It is unnecessary here to enter into an analysis of the complex factors of age and race which have affected the earlier and the later decrease. It will suffice to point out that there is real encouragement in the figures as they stand. "The rising tide of heart disease" has been checked and is on the ebb again. Yet heart disease, apoplexy, nephritis, and cancer remain the outstanding causes of death. They can be controlled only by the application of organized preventive medicine, by early diagnosis and prompt medical or surgical or hygienic treatment. They challenge us to develop machinery for this purpose as the major task of public health in the immediate future.

Finally, behind all this public health programme of the past and the present, there opens up a new field of almost unlisted potentiality. This is the field of mental hygiene.

Mental diseases and defects do not play a large part in the death rate in comparison with such conditions as those which have been discussed above. If, on the other hand, we consider the problem of disability and the burden placed upon society by such disability, it is probable that disorders of the central nervous system outweigh in significance disorders and disabilities of all other organs of the body taken together.

We know that the provision of institutional facilities for the care of mental disease and defect, even today, is approximately equal to the total of hospital beds required for all other diseases; and we know that such facilities are grossly inadequate to meet existing needs. Dr. Frankwood Williams tells us that in the schools of the United States today there are one million children who are looking forward to becoming business men or housewives or clerks or industrial workers but who will end their days as inmates of institutions for mental disease if present ratios hold. It is the testimony of nurses and social workers that, in the average family throughout the land, the burden due to mental disease and defect is fully equal in magnitude to that imposed by the total burden resulting from all other types of disease and disability.

Here, then, is a new field of social activity, equivalent in its scope to the whole field of public health as we have known it in the past. We must build up in the case of mental disease the same sort of machinery used with such success in connection with infant hygiene and tuberculosis. We must educate the public to understand that mental disease, like tuberculosis, is a disability not a disgrace; and that, again like tuberculosis, it is often curable and preventable. "Insane asylums" must be fully transformed into hospitals for mental disease. They must be supplemented by psychopathic wards in general hospitals to furnish "first aid to the mentally injured." The viewpoints of the psychiatrist must dominate more fully the procedure of our penal institutions—perhaps even to the point visualized by Governor Smith of New York in his suggestion that judges and juries should merely pass on the physical facts of a crime, leaving diagnosis and treatment to a commission of experts.

We must build up a chain of mental hygiene clinics where the first symptom of mental disease can be detected and alleviated and where mental defect can be determined and provision made, either for the safeguarding of the defective in the normal life which a high-grade defective can often lead, or for institutional segregation, in the extreme case whose hereditary defects it is essential to eliminate from the stream of human inheritance.

Nor must we limit our consideration solely to the more obvious deviations from mental normality. The cases of mental disease and defect so pronounced as to require, or to threaten to require, institutional care are serious enough. Yet I believe, if we could really measure all the effects involved, that the burden laid upon society by such acute conditions is less than that created by the innumerable minor mental maladjustments which hamper all of us in the conduct of our daily lives. The thousand petty fears and jealousies and prejudices and inhibitions which keep us hour by hour from perfect internal harmony and perfect adaptation to the persons and the conditions which surround us—here is the supreme problem of mental hygiene.

It is in mental hygiene thus widely interpreted that the basis of a new industrial order must be found. There are few disputes between capital and labor which could survive a discussion about the same table by employers and employees both free from inferiority complexes and defense reactions. In international affairs the same thing holds true. We have overstressed economics and ignored psychology as the cause of class struggles and of wars between nations. It is a supreme value of the League of Nations that it constitutes a great experiment in mental hygiene. Geneva is no super-state; it is an *atmosphere* in which straight and honest thinking about international relationships by men who stand face to face with each other in the public eye is easier than such thinking has ever been before.

I know that these things of which I write are still in the future. I know that psychiatry is still a young science—that its really competent votaries are few—that the quack and the charlatan are abroad in the land. I know that extreme Behaviorism and extravagant Freudianism may do more harm than good. Yet I know, too, that there is a technique involved which promises to give man, who has so largely conquered the material universe, an ultimate mastery over his own mind and spirit.

The first fruits of a new science are apt to be disquieting. When we discover a new force we misuse it, as a child makes a noise with a drum or breaks windows with a bow and arrow. I am inclined to interpret many of the disturbing influences of our present civilization as similar results of a novel instrument with which mankind is half unconsciously and rashly toying. It is significant that the dominant figures in American life today are the advertisers, that the great fortunes of the moment, political and industrial, are built on exploitation of mass psychology rather than on service. Razor-blade and chewing-gum kings form a less inspiring aristocracy than the railroad builders and steel men of fifty years ago. Our visitors from the East are quite right in considering the native susceptibility of America to mass suggestion a menace to America and to the world. All these things are manifestations of unconscious attempts to apply half-perceived principles of mental hygiene for selfish and individual ends. Yet I am confident that this is a transitory stage. Science is always born of magic, as Lynn Thorndike has shown us. Astronomy began as astrology, chemistry as alchemy. We are in the magic stage of control of the human mind; but this stage will surely pass.

As we learn more of the new powers which a knowledge of the laws of mind will yield it seems possible that we shall even begin to bridge that gap which yawns between the mind and the spirit. There have always been the two types of men, those in whom reason was dominant and those who were stirred chiefly by emotion, which is indeed the "moving" force. Science and the machine have always appealed to the rational man and repelled the artist. May we not hope, as science goes more deeply into the foundations of human motive, that it may itself learn to be psychological and may learn how to interpret logic to the emotions—that we may gain a common ground for progress toward a society which shall include beauty as well as order in its essential makeup?

### v

WE may perhaps contribute to such an ultimate understanding by granting as scientists that the life of the spirit is after all the ultimate goal at which we all must aim. If prolonged life and increased vitality were bought at the cost of shorter vision and decreased joy in living they would be too costly. It behooves us, who believe in the modern world, to make our statement of faith in its hidden and fundamental values for it is such values alone which are of permanent significance. Chardonne makes the hero of his latest novel say, "Toute civilization a paru décrépitude et folie à ses contemporains. Les patriotes reprochaient à Péricles de dilapider le trésor de guerre pour bâtir des temples . . .

J'espère que nous construisons des choses que nous ne voyons pas."

First of all, then, the man of science is a man of faith. He need not, and does not, entertain the conception that the universe is a simple physical machine whose attributes can be described in the largely obsolete terms of mass and motion. But he does believe in a universe of order and causation, a universe which we can trust, insofar as we understand the language in which it speaks. He is not, he cannot, be blind to the conflict between certain laws of this universe and others (for instance the law that men should desire life and the law that men must die); yet on the whole he believes that the universe as it stands is worth living and dying for. He thinks that in the progress up from the slime in the rock pools to the mind of Shakespeare and of Darwin there is ground for a reasonable hope. He finds the twentieth century on the whole finer in its possibilities than the tenth or the thirteenth. He holds the game worth the candle.

Perhaps this attitude of mind is determined by purely physiological conditions in the individual. Like Chu-Yin in "Marco Polo," when the Khan asks if his prayer is true and wise, we can only answer, "It is *thy* truth. It is *thy* wisdom." Perhaps the once-born is a man with a constant excess of some vital hormone, the twice-born a man with an intermittent supply, the confirmed doubter a man with a permanent deficiency. Perhaps hope and courage will some day be controllable by chemical or psychiatric means. Hitherto, in any case, there have always been religious men who felt that life on the whole had a meaning and a value and irreligious men who did not. In this sense applied science is a religion; for it involves this primary act of faith.

In more concrete terms our attitude toward life is illuminated by the conviction that man through science can arrive at power. In other days one could take the world as he found it or he could turn from this world to fix his gaze on a life to come. Today we have a third choice. We believe that we can take this universe about us in our hands and within limits make it safer and freer and happier. There are limits (though just where they lie no one can yet say). The game has its rules. But our part in it is a dynamic one; and from age to age it seems that mankind is win-

ning.  We refuse to be Babbitts on the one hand or Menckens on
the other.  We neither submit to the universe nor defy it.  We
purpose by comprehension and courage to remould it nearer to the
heart's desire.

There is a third element no less important, I believe, than faith
and hope in the creed of science; and this third element is charity.
We do not improve on the formulas of the old religions but merely
reinterpret them.  Charity, love, liberalism, all mean the same
thing.  It is as the Scriptures tell us the greatest of the three and
the most difficult of attainment.  It is just because of the lack of
this element that our modern scientific civilization (like all earlier
ones) is most open to criticism.

It is impossible not to recognize that mass-production wars
against beauty, that concentration on material success threatens
idealism, that autocracy crushes out personality.  Immediate efficiency may be purchased at too high a price, by Lenin in Moscow,
by Mussolini in Rome, by a democracy instinct with Calvinistic
materialism in the United States.  This is our danger and it is a
real one.

Yet it is no new danger.  Nor is it, I believe, a danger created
by the scientific spirit.  It is, on the contrary, a limitation imposed on this, as on every previous civilization, by the indolence
and impatience of man, aggravated by the new powers with which
he finds himself endowed.  Since our ancestors lived in the caves
of the Dordogne, it has been easier for men to imitate than to
create, to eat than to think, to follow than to lead.  This vast
inertia is the stuff we work in.  From it, civilization emerges like
a Rodin head, still half imprisoned in dead marble.

Science did not forge these chains.  Rather it is the Perseus
which shall at last unloose them.  Science, real science, knows
full well the significance of the individual, the essential value of
freedom.  Is not every scientific discovery a revolution, made by
an individual man, through the study of individual facts?  Is
not an adventurous freedom the very condition of scientific progress?

The scientific investigator is indeed the modern protagonist of
the King of Ithaca who, in his old age cries out that

All experience is an arch wherethro'
Gleams that untravelled world whose margin fades
Forever and forever when I move;

and tells how his "grey spirit" is

yearning in desire
To follow knowledge like a sinking star,
Beyond the utmost bound of human thought.
The lights begin to twinkle from the rocks;
The long day wanes; the slow moon climbs; the deep
Moans round with many voices. Come, my friends,
'Tis not too late to seek a newer world.
Push off, and sitting well in order smite
The sounding furrows; for my purpose holds
To sail beyond the sunset, and the baths
Of all the western stars, until I die.

The old enemy is subtle. The half understood truths of science, like the half understood truths of religion, are used to replace the shackles upon mankind. But true science and true religion, true art and true philosophy are converging roads of attack upon a common citadel of truth. Dogmatism is a barrier along every road and between each of these roads and the others.

Yet the way opens always. It seems to some of us as though the barriers were less high and forbidding than was once the case. Whitehead's philosophy, which teaches us, so far as laymen can grasp its meaning, that reality consists, not in matter or in energy, but in relationship, is a reconciling gospel. It embodies in the broadest form the dynamic science of today as Descartes generalized the mechanistic science of his century. It permits us to glimpse through the underbrush even the converging paths of art and of religion. As scientists we know that the properties of salt will always emerge when sodium and chlorine combine under the right conditions. Yet we also know that those properties are new properties which did not exist in either constituent. Something has been created; and in this conception lies the germ of a philosophy which can include the highest things we know.

There is in truth no longer any inherent antagonism between science and religion, between science and philosophy, between science and beauty. There is antagonism, deep and fundamental, between all of these pathways to reality and the dark and tangled forest of ignorance and doubt, of confusion and ugliness by which they are surrounded, the "old chaos" of the poet. That full mastery has not been secured need not trouble us. That as we attack ever greater problems the difficulties increase, need not dishearten. A wise old bishop when taunted with the "failure" of Christianity, replied, "Christianity has not failed. It has never been tried." We may say the same of science.

## IX—THE FAMILY

### By Havelock Ellis

I

MANY believe that the family is today in a perilous position. The ever-increasing approach to social and industrial equality of the sexes, the steady rise and extension of the divorce movement, the changed conceptions of the morality of sexual relationships, and the spread of contraception—these new influences, it is supposed, must destroy marriage and undermine the family as it has hitherto been known in our Western civilization.

It has to be admitted that all these influences are real, probably permanent, and that they have never been found at work before in combination, seldom even separately. Not one of them, however, when examined with care, bears within it any necessary seeds of destruction. On the contrary, they may purify and fortify, rather than weaken, the institution of the family; enable it to work more vigorously and effectively rather than impair its functions as what has been termed "the unit of civilization." It is true that the younger women of today are often dissatisfied with marriage, but that attitude is a belated recognition that they are entitled to satisfaction, and we may accept it as wholesome. The greater economic independence of women assists them in the task of sexual selection, and is found to be conducive to marriage, though it is also favorable to divorce when marriage is disrupted.[1]

[1] These points are discussed, as regards Germany today, in the *Zeitschrift für Sexualwissenschaft*, Nov. 1927, p. 312.

The greater facility of divorce aids the formation of the most satisfactory unions. A greater freedom between the sexes before marriage, even if it has sometimes led to license, is not only itself beneficial but the proper method of preparing for a more intimate permanent union. And the exercise of contraceptive control is the indispensable method of selecting the best possibilities of offspring and of excluding from the world those who ought never to be born. As a matter of fact, marriage, so far from dying out, tends in various countries of the West to increase in frequency; thus in England, in 1921, out of every 1000 women over fifteen years of age 520 were married, though ten years earlier (1911) only 506 were married. While as regards the production of children through the agency of the family, the danger that faces Western civilization today is not of a deficient production but of an enormous excess. So that, whatever changes of form it may undergo, we clearly have to reckon with the persistence of the family, whether that is a prospect which causes our hearts to sink or whether it fills us with satisfaction.

We might reach the same conclusion even without any close examination of the sociological data of today. It is enough to survey the fundamental biological facts on which all human or other societies must rest, or to glance at the history of marriage and the family in mankind from the earliest period at which our knowledge begins. This has been done in recent years by two scholars, Westermarck and Briffault. They differ on important points in the early history of marriage. Westermarck regards the family as having proceeded uniformly, though with endless minor variations, from the anthropoid ancestors of man on to civilization, in a predominantly monogamic (though occasionally polygamic) form, in which the father always had a recognized and important place. Briffault emphasizes the significance of a stage in human history, of which we but vaguely discern the traces, where the father's place was small and subordinate, and the family was organized on a mainly maternal basis, so that when, in the progress towards civilization, the matriarchal system gave way to the patriarchal system, with new economic conceptions and the development of the idea of personal property, an almost revolutionary change took place in human history. These differences of opinion are of interest, though they may be harmonized if we suppose that each writer has passed over too lightly some aspects of the subject that the other has unduly emphasized. Westermarck perhaps unduly emphasizes the frequency with which the husband or the wife has only one conjugal partner, and Briffault unduly emphasizes the frequency with which husband or wife has more than one conjugal partner. From the point of view of the family it makes little difference, save that in the one condition the father, in the other the mother, becomes the predominant parent. But all that it concerns us here to observe is that even if we adopt the view that the family was primitively a mainly matriarchal institution we are still constrained to admit that, under whatever changes of form, it has always persisted, so that its existence may even be said to be woven into the texture of the species.

## II

THERE is indeed one important aspect in which our Western civilization is changing the relationship of the family to society. Hitherto the question of the family has been mainly, if not even altogether, the question of marriage. To a large extent it must continue to be so. But it is a distinguishing characteristic of our Western civilization, in all the countries it has touched, that this is no longer the case in fact. In the history of mankind in general marriage has meant a family, and when no children appeared the marriage has often been dissolved, sometimes almost automatically. With us, not only is the absence of children considered no adequate ground for the dissolution of the marriage, but the marriage may at the outset be planned to avoid procreation, whether temporarily or permanently. That is becoming a characteristic of our marriage system, and it is of immense significance in relation to the family. Not that it can affect the existence of the family, since that rests on a biological foundation which cannot be destroyed. But it furnishes an altogether new control over the forms the family may assume, and it renders the family adjustable, in a way that has never before been possible, to the developing direction of our general social organization.

This is notably conspicuous in relation to the changing economic position of women.  In the phase of civilization out of which we are growing, a phase which persisted unimpaired until the Industrial Revolution at the end of the eighteenth century, the economic position of woman was as wife and mother at the head of the home.  That was no small position to occupy, and it required most diverse gifts, since the home was a centre of industrial activity for a large part of its own needs.  But woman today occupies a totally different position.  She has lost her industrial activities in the home, but has regained them in the wider world, and added to them the freedom to adopt, if she so chooses, most of the activities formerly reserved to men.  At the same time she tends more and more to accept, at all events as an ideal, the principle of complete economic independence, even in the exercise of her functions as wife and mother, since she no longer considers that as wife and mother she becomes the servant of a man and entitled to wages as such, but holds that she is gratifying her own desires.  That principle, however, though it may be reasonable, leads to a grave conflict if pushed to its logical extreme in practice.  If a woman, when she becomes a wife, is to follow the example of the woman of the old world and spend her time and strength in bearing perhaps a dozen children, of whom not half may survive, she cannot possibly be economically dependent on her own exertions.  She must remain unmarried or renounce her independence in becoming wife and mother.  The difficulty is always real, but it has now become, in some measure at all events, adjustable.  It has become clear, that is to say, that the number of children and the times when they are to be borne may be arranged according to the circumstances in which the two parents are situated, and it is also seen to be reasonable that, since the mother must necessarily devote a larger share of time and care to the child, the father may be called upon to take a larger financial share, without the economic equality of the two parents being thereby impaired.

### III

THE desirability of controlling the appearance of children in the family brings us to the question of contraception.  That is a question around which in the immediate past much controversy raged.  It cannot even yet be said that it has ceased to rage.  And since in some countries of the West there are yet legal disabilities to be removed in order to bring the law into harmony with custom and opinion, propaganda is artificially stimulated.  There is, however, no longer the shadow of doubt that both the principle and the practice of birth control are now firmly established in all civilized lands, and gradually becoming accepted by every class of the community, so that before long the only matter of dispute will be concerning the best method by which it can be carried out.  It is estimated that at the present rate birth control will become practically universal in our civilization within from twenty-five to fifty years, and it is probable that, with better conditions of sexual initiation and the cultivation of self-control, mechanical methods of contraception will become less necessary.[2]

There are three main lines along which this development has proceeded.  In the first place there has been the insistence of women that they will no longer be mere breeding machines, destroying alike themselves and their excessive progeny.  In the second place the economic conditions of life for all social classes in the modern world tend to render caution and foresight necessary in family life, and there are now but few parents who can afford to disregard so completely these conditions, and the responsibilities of bringing up children in the world of today, as to have an unlimited family.  In the third place scientific demographers and statisticians are now, with ever greater decision, pointing out that the enormous increase in the earth's population, which up to about a century ago was practically stationary, cannot be much longer continued, since even another century may suffice to reach the limit of possible expansion.  Each of these lines of argument is legitimate.  When combined, they are of irresistible force.[3]

[2] In Russia, where the birth-rate rises and the infantile death-rate is falling, the need of contraception is recognized, but not yet fully established.  Abortion is legalized and conducted with due precaution, but this is a poor substitute for contraception.

[3] It is sometimes supposed that the Catholic Church is opposed to contraception

## IV

ANOTHER modern condition which has an important bearing on the family in our Western civilization is constituted by the increase of divorce and the ever greater legal facilities for securing it. Speaking generally (there are always exceptions), it may be said that in savage societies, as probably in the primitive world, matings, provided they are formed with members of the group with which mating is permitted, are easily formed and rather easily ended. In more advanced barbarous societies, in which property becomes a chief factor in society, masculine influence is more predominant than before over feminine influence; the marriage bond grows more rigid and is specially rigid in favor of the husband. In the latest civilized social states, this rigidity is relaxed, divorce becomes easier and more frequent, and the rights of the sexes tend to be equalized. We may see that process in classic Rome. Beginning, it may well be, in a social state of more or less matriarchal constitution, when the Roman social order became patriarchal marriage in some of its forms was almost indissoluble, and divorce, so far as it existed, was usually a privilege confined to the husband, except in a "free" marriage, where the wife did not fall under the *manus* of her husband. But in the later developments the privileges of free marriage were extended to *manus* marriages, and Roman law became equally liberal to husbands and wives in the matter of divorce. That represents

and that Catholics refuse to practise it. Both these suppositions involve some misapprehension. It is certain that some Catholics practise contraception. France, a largely Catholic country, has been the leader in the movement, and in Germany the Catholic birth-rate is falling; in the United States it is found at Mrs. Margaret Sanger's clinic in New York that the proportion of Catholic women who apply for advice is about 32 per cent, that is to say, nearly as large as the proportion of Protestant women, which is 33 per cent. In some countries, it is true, statistics show a higher birth-rate among the Catholics than among the Protestants, but in those countries the Catholics usually belong to a lower and less educated social class which would inevitably show a higher birth-rate whatever religion they professed. Dignitaries of the Catholic Church have sometimes distinguished themselves by denunciation of contraceptive measures. But they speak for themselves. It is hardly possible for a Church which venerates chastity and maintains the celibacy of the clergy to be opposed to contraception, since without contraception chastity and celibacy can hardly exist. The only dispute possible is with regard to methods of contraception, and that is a comparatively trivial matter. There would appear to be no dogma of the Church incompatible with contraception.

approximately the stage that we have today reached in Western civilization.

The frequency of divorce has much increased since the Great War, but it was steadily though more slowly increasing long before, though in France the frequency of divorce increased up to 1921 and since then has somewhat decreased. The post-war so-called "epidemic of marriage" was naturally followed by an "epidemic of divorce," which is now subsiding, although we may still expect the rate to rise slowly as the impediments are removed. In Japan, it may be remarked, which comes next to the United States in frequency of divorce, there was no post-war rise. The United States holds the record; in 1923 there were 360 divorces to 100,000 of married population (or 149 to 100,000 of the whole population). And in some States this means one or more divorces to every five marriages. In Europe, Austria and Switzerland stand high, and England (1922) very low with only 6.8 divorces to 100,000 of population, though that is four times as many as ten years earlier. In Russia divorce may be obtained at the wish of either party (and at the wish of both it may be arranged before the Registrar, without recourse to the Courts), yet divorce is far less frequent than in the United States, and the younger generation cultivate ideals of self-discipline and self-control. Such differences represent differences of social opinion and of religion, as well as discrepant facilities for obtaining divorce. The general advance of divorce corresponds to the normal condition of advanced civilization and represents a necessary and healthy adjustment to the complex social conditions. Divorce by mutual consent (and even on the demand of either party) seems to be the goal towards which we are moving, and it has already been reached in some countries. It is reasonable that a contract formed by mutual consent should be dissolvable by mutual consent, and so far from divorce being destructive to the family, we may agree with Westermarck that it is a necessary means of preserving the dignity of marriage by ending such marriages as have ceased to be worthy of the name.[4]

[4] Westermarck, "History of Human Marriage," Vol. III, ch. 33; Burgdörfer, "Statistik der Ehe" in Max Marcuse's "Die Ehe," 1927; art. "Marriage" (by various hands) in Hastings' "Dictionary of Ethics and Religion."

The tendency to diminish the rigidity of marriage ties is being carried further, it may be added, than an increased legal facility for divorce can carry it. There is undoubtedly a tendency in our Western civilization to recognize the existence of sexual relationships outside marriage altogether, always provided that such relationships are not for the procreation of children. It may be said that such extra-marital manifestations of the sexual life are no novelty. Prostitution has flourished in secret, and even been defended in public, while what is called "seduction" has everywhere been taking place. But the novelty lies in the fact that both prostitution and seduction are diminishing. Prostitution is becoming less attractive and seduction less possible. The palmy days of prostitution (which seems to have begun as a religious rite) were before syphilis entered civilization, and its prestige has been gradually falling ever since. Seduction in the legitimate sense of the word (as "seduced" is often merely the expression used by women of low social class to describe their first act of sexual intercourse) is only possible when the woman is unduly ignorant of the nature of sexual relations, and in proportion as the task of what is called "social hygiene" is fulfilled, such ignorance becomes unusual. But when prostitution and seduction are, so far as may be possible, eliminated, the objections to the formation of sexual relationships—in the absence of higher ethical or religious considerations and provided offspring are not contemplated—largely fall away. There can be no doubt that this new condition is becoming appreciated by the younger generation. Young people of both sexes are now in a position to view a larger proportion of the facts involved than were open to the generations preceding them, and they are acquiring the courage to act in accordance with the facts. That means that many mistakes are being made, for the deepest facts of the sex life can only be learnt by experience, and experience can only come slowly. But it is perhaps better to make the mistakes of facing life than to make the mistakes of running away from life. For those mistakes may enrich and enlighten, while these are apt to prove futile. The paths of the sex life are beset by difficulties; but so is the whole of life. If we are to live in any true sense at all, we are compelled to live dangerously.

A large number of the men and women of today form sexual relationships outside marriage—whether or not they ultimately lead to marriage—which they conceal, or seek to conceal, from the world. The prevalence of such relationships, and the new attitude taken towards them, has led to the conception of the "companionate marriage," that is, an openly acknowledged and recognizable relationship less binding than ordinary marriage, though liable to become ordinary marriage should children be born. This conception has not been put forward as a method of relaxing morals, but rather of supporting them, on the theory that the open recognition of a kind of relationship which already exists secretly on a large scale cannot but be a steadying and ennobling influence.[5]

The preceding considerations represent conditions which are modifying marriage in our Western civilization. But they are far from overthrowing marriage or threatening the life of the family. On the contrary, they help to strengthen them. It is the rigid institution that is broken; the institution that cannot change is dying. By its flexibility and its adaptation to changing conditions an institution reveals its stability and its power of growth.

v

So WE still have, notwithstanding all the modifications that we can regard as within the limits of probability, the family persisting, essentially, in its primitive form: father, mother, offspring. The impulses that make these three units a trinity are all primordial: the desire of the parents for each other, the desire of each for the child, and the dependence of the child on its parents, righty considered on both its parents, for even where there is no material need of a father there is yet a spiritual need.

It is true that, in the supposed interests of the child, the idea

[5] M. Knight, "The Companionate and the Family," *Journal of Social Hygiene,* May, 1924. Judge Ben Lindsey, with his wide experience of social conditions, has powerfully advocated this conception in his "Companionate Marriage," 1927.

has been put forward (first of all by Plato in the famous fifth book of his "Republic") that the infant should be removed from its natural parents and placed in the hands of nurses skilfully trained in all the science and art of modern hygiene in general and puericulture in particular. Certainly it is possible to find innumerable parents who are completely and lamentably ignorant of this science and this art. But to be content to leave the mothers in ignorance and to train up in the knowledge of the duties of maternity a body of women who are not intended to be mothers, except for other women's children, seems a perverted attempt to escape the difficulty. It is not calculated to benefit, and still less to render happy, the real mothers, the artificial mothers, or the children. It is scarcely surprising that we find little indication that this method is likely to be followed on any large scale, if at all. It seems only in place when we are concerned with motherless waifs and strays. The legitimate method of approaching the problem—as is constantly becoming more widely recognized—lies in training the real mothers, and, so far as possible, before they have begun to be mothers. In our world motherhood has ceased to be an inevitable fate of every woman who enters marriage and many who remain outside it. It may be said to have become a vocation. It is true that nearly every woman, at some period in her life, desires to become a mother, and that most men desire to become fathers, sometimes indeed without clearly realizing that fatherhood implies motherhood and that it is a vastly more difficult task to be a mother than to be a father. But this is a vocation which not all who feel called to it ought to follow. Only those who are fitted by nature, and also by training, should attempt to follow it. In various countries now, and on an ever larger scale, efforts are being made to provide this training. The establishment of Schools for Mothers, in some countries facilitated by law, constituted a notable step along this path.[6]

[6] Dr. Miele of Ghent has sometimes been credited with initiating this step, which, however, naturally grew out of the insistence on puericulture by Budin and Pinard in France. An early pioneer in the establishment of Schools for Mothers seems to have been Dr. E. S. Goodhue, of California and Hawaii, who is still active in this field.

## VI

SO FAR we have been viewing the family as a domestic institution. It is that in the supreme degree, being the central and essential core of all human and even animal life, the primal institution. In the most primitive conditions, before any wide social bonds were formed, or any compact community existed, we must postulate the family, for we cannot conceive how any creature with the prolonged helpless infancy of human beings could otherwise survive in this dangerous world. But with the formation of communities, with the multiplication of social ties, the family ceases to be a merely domestic institution, and it is possible, and even probable, that the family became more complex in its relationship, even at a fairly early period of human prehistory. It is certainly complex today among those peoples whom we are pleased to regard as "primitive." [7]

With the development of civilization the form assumed by the family becomes again more simple and independent in appearance, but the family remains in an intimate relationship with the community to which it is constantly furnishing new members. Beyond its elementary domestic functions, the family thus necessarily enters into reciprocal functions of responsibility with the community. The community undertakes duties—which may vary to a wide extent—towards the family, and the family, in return, is called upon to contribute, to the best of its abilities, to the community. There are wide variations in the conception of the duties on either side, and this leads today to a frequent conflict in opinion and practice. On the one hand, there is the tendency to diminish the duties of the family and of the state towards each other to a minimum; on the other hand the tendency to increase them to a maximum. The former tendency is commonly called Individualism, the latter Socialism. It is common for those who associate themselves with one of these tendencies to sneer at the other or denounce it as dangerous. From the

[7] See, for instance, the fascinating books, based on intimate knowledge, of Professor Malinowski concerning the social and sexual life of the Trobriand Islanders of New Guinea.

social point of view, however, as is fairly obvious to an impartial observer, both tendencies are necessary. A society without socialistic impulses could not cohere; a society without individualistic impulses could not survive. But with regard to the limits to be set to each group of impulses opinions are bound to vary. We may believe that with regard to many elementary requirements, of which all have an equal and common need—such as provision of open spaces in cities, a pure water supply, and a sanitary system—the collective activity of the community is rightly invoked; and that in regard to religion, to opinion in general, and to the higher branches of education a large scope must be left to the individual. But there are many spheres in which arguments clash. In this special question of the family, for instance, we may ask, how far children are reared for the parents of the family and how far for the community. And if, as we are bound to hold, children have a value as future members of the community, should the community, in addition to other services, contribute financially to the upbringing of the children? In this way we have the question of mothers' pensions.

It appears that the idea of "Family Endowment" was first put forward by Thomas Paine, that great fertilising genius whose suggestions on so many subjects, Utopian when he formed them, are now becoming embodied in our Western civilization; and he was followed by Condorcet, who was also the pioneer in publicly advocating the use of contraceptive measures, for there is no opposition between birth control and family endowment. On the contrary, it may be said that the prevention of unwanted children and the proper care of wanted children (whether or not that should be aided by the State) are closely related measures.

There is still dispute as to whether children should be subsidised by the State, and although the principle is becoming widely transformed into practice, the implications of Mothers' Pensions (for it is generally held that the payment should go direct to the mother) are not yet always fully understood or realized. In France such assistance is given partially, especially to the families of state employees, in various ways, from anxiety to increase the growth of population (which, however, it fails to do), on militaristic and

Catholic grounds, and with no regard to the quality of the children who may thus be produced; nearly half of the wage-earners of France, it is said, now benefit in some way or other by these measures. In Germany, modifications of the same methods, on a more socialistic basis, have been put into action, but do not seem to flourish. In Russia, with the idealistic hope to make a Paradise for children, mothers receive state aid and special funds. In Australia, the problem of family endowment has been approached in a logical and systematic manner, and a Government Commission was set up to investigate its feasibility. Every political party is said to favor it, but the cost of a thorough-going scheme is so vast that no Australian State has yet ventured to set it up, except (1927), on a comprehensive but modest basis, New South Wales. New Zealand had previously adopted the plan on a small scale.

There are, however, many convinced opponents to any scheme of this kind. They hold, on the one hand, that there is not the slightest need to assist maternity since the population is nearly everywhere increasing already at too rapid a rate, and, even if there appeared to be such need, maternity is not a suitable function for state endowment, since it is not essential to a woman's life to become a mother, and there are ample recompenses in maternity itself. Even among those who are not opposed to a State subsidy there is severe criticism of the motives and methods of the schemes usually adopted or proposed. Nationalistic and militaristic motives are here out of place, nor can they often appeal to the mothers it is proposed to assist. On the other hand, the real interests of the community demand a discriminate selection of population, and for the State to offer to assist the procreation not merely of the highest and best—who scarcely need such assistance —but of the lowest and worst is to stultify itself and to work for its own decadence. A wiser and more reasoned scheme than has yet been devised is needed, if the present tendency to maternal endowment is to prove of substantial benefit to the community.[8]

[8] The Cause of Family Endowment is ably and persuasively stated, and the present position of such schemes in various countries set forth in detail, by Miss Eleanor Rathbone in her "Disinherited Family" and "Ethics and Economics of Family Endowment" (1927). She fails to insist adequately on the need of birth control and eugenical safeguards, but argues that to help the mother is to aid "orderly and

When the question of mothers' pensions arises, and the function of the community in supplying financial aid towards the production of children, we are faced by a problem which is often ignored when this measure is adopted or advocated. That is the problem of how far the community really needs its production of children to be subsidised, and how far it is desirable to afford that subsidy aid without regard to the probable quality of the children produced. The measures adopted or advocated for maintaining or increasing the population of a State have so far been confused, unintelligent, and even maleficent. The old feverish anxiety to increase the population at all costs has ceased to be reasonable. The growth of the world's population has become during the past century so enormously rapid, being doubled every hundred years, that we are approaching a period when the strongest country will be that which increases most slowly or not at all.[9] Even among the nations concerned in the Great War, Russia, with the largest population and the highest birth-rate, was almost the first to succumb, for the size of a population is not the measure of its strength. The two countries of the Old World which today display the greatest anxiety to stimulate their own growth in population, France and Italy, both illustrate the methods which should not be adopted. In France the growth of the population is small but the country has reaped many benefits from that slow growth, which is not, however, due to a low birth-rate but to a high rate of infantile mortality. Yet the official policy of France

self-respecting living which is the best cure for indiscriminate and dysgenic breeding." She remarks that family aid in France has done nothing to increase the birth-rate, though introduced for that purpose, and points out that grants may be limited to the early children of the family and refused altogether where the heredity is bad. An argument on which she forcibly insists is that equal payment to men and women for equal work is not practicable unless in association with family endowment.

[9] The whole question of the rapid growth of population in modern times and its bearing on the future of the world is discussed in a masterly manner by Professor E. M. East, "Mankind at the Crossroads," 1924. For a more recent discussion of fundamental population problems from various points of view, by leading scientific authorities of Europe and America, see *Proceedings of the World Population Conference*, 1927, edited by Margaret Sanger. And for a clear and authoritative statement, in a concise form, see Sir George Kimball, "The Fundamental Elements of the Problems of Population and Migration," "*Eugenics Review*, Jan. 1928; he concludes that the great problem before Man now is "how best to *control the rate at which he multiplies*."

is directed much less to the task of better caring for the children
born than to the encouragement by all sorts of small benefits of
still more births, without any regard for the quality of the children thus to be born. In Italy, where the rate of population
growth is already high, the energetic encouragement to further
increase, for which the Fascist government is responsible, can only
lead to internal suffering and discontent or to external trouble,
due to difficulties with other countries refusing to accept immigrants and to the resulting temptation to risk war, which from of
old has been the method for arresting internal rebellion and reducing superfluous populations. A wiser course is being pursued
in the New World. The United States, in view of the growing
perfection of technical processes and the increasing tendency to
unemployment, realises that the desirable limits of population are
being reached, and is slackening its own rate of growth (it once
doubled its population in twenty-three years), excluding all but
a small proportion of foreign immigrant peoples, whose rates of
increase are usually higher than its own. To the United States
thus belongs the honor of being first, among great nations, to
assert, virtually, the international importance of Birth Control.
In Australia, also, though in a less definitely formulated manner,
the same attitude prevails, and while internal expansion has not
yet reached its limits, although at the present rate of increase
it is rapidly drawing near them, the tendency is now towards
hostility to immigration.

## VII

WE thus approach the problem of the desirable size of the family.
It is a problem which has only in recent years become practical.
In old days children were "given by God," and God who gave them
often took them back again with extreme rapidity. The population was practically stationary and yet families were frequently of
enormous size. Many were called into the world but few were
chosen to live. In old family records we see two or even three
brothers of the same name. "John" was christened and "John"
died, so the name was available for a later "John," and, if he too
died, for a third. Nowadays the progress of medicine and hygiene

has rendered life safer; when a child is born there is a reasonable probability that he will live, and we can afford to be more economical in child production. The old methods, indeed, become impracticable; they would produce too large an excess of population. If we desire to retain that almost stationary population which has, on the whole, been normal for mankind, we can no longer effect it by the method of large gross production and small net results.

The optimum number of children in a family has often been exaggerated, especially by those who have not realised how greatly in modern times the conditions of life have changed in the direction of diminishing wastage. Thus Grotjahn in Germany has stated that an average of 3.8 children is required per marriage in order to maintain the population in equilibrium. But this is, as a general rule, certainly too high. In England, it is calculated, an average of about 2.5 children per marriage now amply suffices to do more than maintain a stationary population, by ensuring a considerable increase. The optimum size of the family now therefore oscillates between two and three. To many marriages we find more children, and to many we find fewer or none.

VIII

WE cannot yet attempt to calculate all the benefits arising for the community from the diminution in the size of the family which has now become possible owing to new hygienic and medical conquests in the economy of life. There is far more in it than the simple ascent to a higher level of well-being inevitably resulting from a diminution of our excessive procreation, our excessive diseases, and our excessive deaths. The family may be the unit of civilization. But in any developed civilization it must become much more than that. In so far as the family is merely an isolated unit, civilization still remains primitive. It is by its capacity for interpenetrating contacts with the community that family and community are alike enabled to develop a finer civilization. It is largely because the family has been so much a self-centred unit, absorbed in the constant stress and strain of self-reproduction that our civilization is still, on the whole, so crude. An important factor in this development is the liberation of women who are mothers from an undue absorption in maternal functions. It is estimated that a healthy woman in a healthy environment, when left to nature, produces on an average fifteen children. Apart from the fact that the world nowadays has no use for such women, it is obvious that a woman whose life was thus occupied had little time or strength left over for the wider functions of social life. She could not exercise a profession and she could not bring her knowledge and experience to bear on the life of the world outside her own home. Moreover her knowledge and experience were so limited from lack of contact with that larger world that, unless when rarely gifted, she was not fitted even to conduct her small domestic life wisely. The affairs of the world, so far as women are concerned, were left to the unmarried, often by the limitation of their experience narrow and prejudiced, and to a few fine exceptional women who, when the period of sexual activity was over, still had the strength and ability for wider activities. These conditions are responsible for the severe criticisms which have often been mistakenly directed against the activities of women in the life of the community, mistakenly because it is not women, but a special and untypical class of women, whose activities arouse this criticism.

The proper fulfilment of all that maternity means involves, even for the average 2.5 children, the devotion of a large slice of a woman's life. But it is very far from demanding the whole of it, and by a due apportionment of her time and energy between her family and the world a woman may enrich both to an extent in previous times impossible. In Russia, where the social equality of women is legally established in accordance with the original intention of Lenin, who declared that "every kitchen maid must learn to rule the State," [10] it is found practicable for women to work and even to occupy high posts without prohibiting mater-

[10] This was not an empty boast, surprising as it may seem to those who only knew Russia in the days of Czardom. Today women in Russia form a larger proportion of the ruling class than in any other country of Western civilization, and are, it is claimed, proving worthy of their opportunities. See, for instance, Dr. Helene Stöcker, "Zum Vierten Male in Russland," *Neue Generation*, March, 1928.

nity, the woman being released from work and provided for by the State for two months before and two months after her confinement, assisted in her maternal duties by communal nurseries and kindergartens, and not mulcted in salary for the time spent in suckling her infant. The obstacles that in many countries are only slowly being overcome are due less to any inherent difficulty in combining work and motherhood than to effete traditions and blind prejudices.

This is well illustrated in the special and important case of teachers. A large proportion of teachers are today women, often not only for children of their own sex but for boys. There cannot be the smallest doubt that women who have had sex experience of their own and children of their own are incomparably better fitted to deal with the special difficulties of children than those who have not. A few gifted women may be found who can make up for personal inexperience by insight and artificially acquired knowledge, but they are rare exceptions. This is a fact that should be fairly obvious even to one who knows nothing about schools and education. But it becomes conspicuous when we observe the actual conditions that prevail. The teacher who has had children of her own is seen to possess an almost instinctive comprehension of children which is seldom present in her unmarried colleagues. The scholastic attainments of the latter may be of the highest, and yet they may be unable to meet even the simplest emergencies of child life, themselves little more than children, and sometimes—indeed often—more ignorant of the facts of human life, and more afraid of them, than are their pupils, whom they are supposed to be competent to "educate." Children today are apt to be acute critics of the abilities of their teachers, and if children had a voice in the selection of teachers the level of education would certainly soon be raised. At present a large majority of elementary teachers (in England nearly 80 per cent), and a considerable proportion in secondary schools, are women. Yet how many of them are encouraged by the official authorities, or even allowed, to acquire the essential experiences of motherhood? In spite of the recent progress of science, the depths of human imbecility have not yet been plumbed.

## IX

BUT the family is not only a domestic question; not only a social question as the almost tragic failure to recognize it in the great function of education brings home to us. It is, finally, a racial question. The well-being of the individual in the home, his due equipment in the community, and, ultimately, his fate in the species, must rest on the sound organization of the family. The increasing recognition of this fact on a scientific foundation is one of the most notable features of our Western civilization.

In an almost instinctive and unconscious manner it has been recognized and acted on ever since human society became organized. Equally among savages and among the founders of the classic cultures of Greece and Rome, from whom we inherit so much, it was recognized, without question and without discussion, that the population must sometimes be restricted and that only the best children should be allowed to live. The method of infanticide has everywhere been the most usual method of attaining this end.[11] Then a new ideal, supported by Christianity and emphasizing the value of every human being as a soul, began to be developed, and finally to be carried out in an extreme form, owing to the modern advances in medicine and hygiene. That movement has meant much for the growth of human sympathy and solidarity. But it was unbalanced, for it failed to perceive the precious elements that had been lost in the decay of the earlier ideal. Our civilization today is marked by an increased perception of both the fundamental conditions of racial well-being. We have gained the ability and the will to cherish every human creature, however feeble, that is brought into the world. But we also see the cruelty of bringing into the world human creatures that are maimed, physically or spiritually, merely that we may prolong or alleviate their sufferings. And we realize how heavy is the burden that we thus place on the race, not only of today

[11] The various methods which Man throughout his history has practised in order to reach the ends now possible through birth control and eugenics are fully set forth by Prof. Carr-Saunders in his elaborate work, "The Population Problem."

but of tomorrow, by thus cherishing the feeblest specimens of humanity and enabling them to increase and multiply. We further realize—and that is our main discovery—that it is unnecessary. The advance in medicine and hygiene which enables us to preserve the defective members of our kind also enables us to prevent, in large measure, their production, by methods which, unlike those practised in the early world, are humane.[12]

There are two lines along which these measures for the eugenic good of the race are being embodied in our general life: by legislation and by education. The first has often been resorted to, because for the ordinary mind it is the easiest. But it is futile without the second. Many eugenical laws have been passed, especially in the United States, merely to be evaded or become a dead letter because they are not in accordance with the general sentiment of the community. On the other hand, when a line of action is spontaneously carried out by the community without penal sanction, legislation became unnecessary, save ultimately in order to whip into line a small recalcitrant minority. It is only by the growth of scientific knowledge, by the spread of education, and by an increased sense of personal responsibility— all now slowly permeating civilized communities—that we can expect any sound advance in the eugenic field. By a reasonable regard for the probabilities of heredity, and a well-directed attention to personal fitness or unfitness for paternity or maternity, we are moving, even though at present slowly, in the right direction. Certificates of fitness for marriage—more accurately for fatherhood and motherhood—are now actively advocated or projected in various countries. But they cannot be effectively introduced by legislation; they must first become the imperative demand of each individual for himself and herself, and his or her partner. When they become that, all is effected that we need trouble about, and legislation becomes a matter of comparative indifference, except to set the seal on a social custom of the first importance for the purification of the race.

[12] For the history of contraception, see M. C. Stopes, "Contraception: its Theory and Practise," 2nd. ed., London, 1928; and for discussion of all its aspects—medical, eugenic, religious, moral, and international,—see Proceedings of *The Sixth International Neo-Malthusian & Birth Control Conference*, edited by Margaret Sanger, New York, 1926.

It used sometimes to be asked: What has posterity done for me that I should do anything for posterity? The question was wrongly put. "Posterity" is only another name for Mankind, and when we pose the question rightly there can be no dispute about the answer. If we put aside the part that belongs to Nature or to God, we owe everything to Mankind. All that we are, and all that we possess in civilization, we owe to the everlasting aspiration and struggle of Mankind before us, and to the slow accumulation of knowledge and art on the topmost level of which we now stand. Our immense debt to Mankind in the past can only be repaid to Mankind in the future. It is our privilege, if we do not regard it as our duty, to pass on, in ever finer shapes, the great traditions which have been handed to us.

## X—RACE AND CIVILIZATION

### By GEORGE A. DORSEY

RACE is the garment we are born in and is set in our biologic or blood inheritance; civilization—or culture, to use a more comprehensive term—is the garment we learn to wear and depends on physical and social environment: time, place, parents, teachers, society. The author of this chapter holds, in common with his fellow-anthropologists, that no necessary or innate connection between race and civilization has yet been proved, and that while such connection is conceivable it is highly improbable. He holds further that there is no warrant for the assumption that certain races are "higher" than others, or that there are any "pure" races, or that race mixtures or "hybrid races" are biologically (or culturally) inferior; or even that any existing classification of mankind according to biologic or heritable features and psychologic or cultural traits has any permanent scientific merit or furnishes any real clue as to how peoples and cultures are genetically related.

I

AND yet a group of writers, not inappropriately termed "heredity mongers," not only make such assumptions but assert that race and civilization are innately related, and use their assumptions and assertions as arguments for political legislation and social reform. In fact, the amount of false biology, infantile logic, and bad faith that these heredity mongers bring to bear on our enormously complicated and complex racial and cultural problems is unbelievable. Wittingly or unwittingly, they juggle biologic, psychologic, and cultural factors to suit their convenience, and pour forth flimsy arguments based on dogmatic and unfounded assumptions as scientific facts to gratify their race phobia. They demand attention solely because of their prominence or academic standing, or because as "best sellers" they attempt to mould American civilization in ways biologically unwarranted and socially false and misleading.

Race phobia is as old as human nature and springs from the same primitive impulse: *We* are the People. Race phobia in its modern form [1] began (in 1854) with Count Arthur de Gobineau's "Essay on the Inequality of the Races of Man," which undertook to prove that the decisive factor in civilization was race, or physical structure; that national development depended on keeping the race pure; and that the "Aryan" race only had founded a really great civilization. Max Müller, in his work on Aryan tongues, indirectly and unwittingly helped establish the idea of an Aryan race; and in spite of the fact that Aryan tongues are spoken by peoples of India and of diverse racial type, "Aryan" came to be synonymous with Blumenbach's European or Caucasian race, and especially with the blond peoples of North Europe —the Teutons or "Nordic" race.

The World War produced a recrudescence of race phobia that has not yet run its course or possibly yet reached the height of its virulence. But the original "Aryan" race has been resolved into three "races" represented by the blond Teuton, the heavy Slav, and the darker Italian—or, the Nordic, Alpine, and Mediterranean. Due to the flood of emotion which swept this country during the war, the "Teutonic" race quite gave way to a Nordic obsession or an Anglo-Saxon myth. This virtual abandonment of the Aryan for a Nordic idea was largely due to the "Foundations of the Nineteenth Century" by the Scotsman, Houston Stewart Chamberlain, who deserted his country for Germany. Schultz's "Race or Mongrel" (1908) definitely brought the Nordic idea to America.

With Madison Grant's "The Passing of the Great Race" (1916)

[1] The complete history of this movement is beautifully told in Part I of Professor F. H. Hankins' "The Racial Basis of Civilization: A Critique of the Nordic Doctrine."

the doctrine of a specific Nordic race was definitely let loose on the public. That doctrine has already been put to work in America in keeping the Nordic stock "pure" by restricting immigration of "inferior" races, and is now being invoked by the eugenics cult to make it purer by encouraging "superior" people to out-breed their "inferiors" and by discouraging inferior people from breeding at all. Nonsense of course; but potentially so dangerous that a critical examination of the doctrine and its inferences is properly a part of this discussion of race and civilization.

Grant's book alone, in spite of its formidable display of "authorities" (especially prepared by a Columbia student as window dressing for a later edition), could not have reached its vogue without the endorsement of a great name—Professor Henry Fairfield Osborn. He wrote a preface to two editions.

How ruthlessly Professor Osborn argues and how well he knows "facts" (quite unknown to anthropologists) is best revealed by the following extracts from his letter to the *New York Times*, April 8, 1924:

"The Northern races, as is well known to anthropologists, include all those peoples which originally occupied the western plateau of Asia and traversed Northern Europe, certainly as early as 12,000 B. C. In the country which they occupied the conditions of life were hard, the struggle for existence severe, and this gave rise to their principal virtues, as well as to their faults, to their fighting qualities and to their love of strong drink. . . . They invaded the countries to the South, not only as conquerors but as contributors of strong moral and intellectual elements to more or less decadent civilizations. Through the Nordic tide which flowed into Italy came the ancestors of Raphael, Leonardo da Vinci, Galileo, Titian; also according to Günther, of Giotto, Donatello, Botticelli, Andrea del Sarto, Petrarch and Tasso. . . . Columbus from his portraits and from busts, authentic or not, was clearly of Nordic ancestry. Kossuth was a Calvinist and of noble family, and there is a presumption in favor of his being a Nordic; Kosciusko and Pulaski were members of a Polish nobility which at that time was largely Nordic. Coligny, Colbert, Richelieu, Lafayette, and Rochambeau, beyond all question were of French (Norman) Nordic nobility, and in modern France we observe that two of the leaders in the recent great struggle, Joffre and Foch, are both Nordic, while Clemenceau and Poincaré are of

Alpine blood. France includes among her great artists Rodin, of Nordic origin; among her leading literary men, Lamartine, Racine, Anatole France, all Nordics. The intellectual influence of the Northern race is also apparent in Spain where it appears in her greatest man of letters, Cervantes; also in Portugal in the poet-hero Camoëns, whose ancestors were Gothic. Of the fighting stock of Italy, Napoleon, although born in Corsica, was descended from the old Lombard nobility, of Nordic origin, and it is probable that Garibaldi with his Teutonic name was largely of Northern stock. . . .

*"Columbus from his portraits and from busts, authentic or not, was clearly of Nordic ancestry."* This sentence seems worth requoting—even italicizing; comment would be superfluous.

In the first preface to Grant's book, Professor Osborn asserts that race plays a larger part than language or nationality in moulding human destiny: "Race implies heredity and heredity implies all the moral, social, and intellectual characteristics and traits which are the springs of politics and government. . . . Thus the racial history of Europe . . . might be paraphrased as the heredity history of Europe." He then speaks of "the gradual dying out among our people of those hereditary traits through which the principles of our religious, political, and social foundations were laid down and their insidious replacement by traits of less noble character."

By the time of the writing of the preface to the second edition, the United States had entered the World War. Professor Osborn found that it was the "Anglo-Saxon branch of the Nordic race" that was "again showing itself to be that upon which the nation must chiefly depend for leadership, for courage, for loyalty, for unity and harmony of action, for self-sacrifice and devotion to an ideal. . . . In the new world that we are working and fighting for, the world of liberty, of justice, and of humanity, we shall save democracy only when democracy discovers its own aristocracy as in the days when our Republic was founded." Professor Osborn is plainly in the grip of race phobia.

With Professor Osborn so baselessly dogmatic we need not be surprised if Grant asserts anything he wants as *evidence*, but when he claims that "modern anthropology has demonstrated that racial lines are not only absolutely independent of both national and linguistic groupings, but that in many cases these racial lines cut through them at sharp angles and correspond closely with the divisions of social cleavage," he claims something that no living anthropologist admits as demonstrated.

Equally unfounded in observable fact is his claim that "the great lesson of the science of race is the immutability of somatological or bodily characters, with which is closely associated the immutability of psychical predispositions and impulses. This continuity of inheritance has a most important bearing on the theory of democracy and still more upon that of socialism, for it naturally tends to reduce the relative importance of environment."

Does Grant know what a "race" is? Or the result of hybridization? Or whether there are "higher" races? Let this quotation answer: "Whether we like to admit it or not, the result of the mixture of two races, in the long run, gives us a race reverting to the more ancient, generalized, and lower type. The cross between a white man and an Indian is an Indian; the cross between a white man and a Negro is a Negro; the cross between a white man and a Hindu is a Hindu; and the cross between any of the three European races and a Jew is a Jew."

But "mix" they will, especially "women of the better classes." In fact, man's "perverse predisposition to mismate" is one of the greatest difficulties in classifying man!

Yet in spite of these "difficulties"—and he has not named half of them—Grant "easily and surely" finds a Nordic, Alpine, and Mediterranean race. With equal ease he finds racial "aptitudes." His three European races "vary intellectually and morally just as they do physically. Moral, intellectual and spiritual attributes are as persistent as physical characters and are transmitted substantially unchanged from generation to generation. . . . Each race differs in the relative proportion of what we may term good and bad strains, just as nations do."

Thus the Alpine race, although "submissive to authority both political and religious, being usually Roman Catholics in western Europe, tends toward democracy." But the Nordics are "a race of soldiers, sailors, adventurers, and explorers, but above all, of rulers, organizers, and aristocrats in sharp contrast to the essentially peasant and democratic character of the Alpines . . . domineering, individualistic, self-reliant and jealous of their personal freedom both in political and religious systems and as a result they are usually Protestants. Chivalry and knighthood and their still surviving but greatly impaired counterparts are peculiarly Nordic traits, and feudalism, class distinctions, and race pride among Europeans are traceable for the most part to the north."

No Brahman of Benares, London, or Boston ever looked down upon a pariah from a dizzier height than that from which Grant looks down upon the whole non-Nordic race of human outcasts. And what is the point of this false science?    To serve as a basis for the ethics of a Gorilla, to warn us that "we Americans must realize that the altruistic ideals which have controlled our social development during the past century and the maudlin sentimentalism that has made America 'an asylum for the oppressed,' are sweeping the nation toward a racial abyss. If the Melting Pot is allowed to boil without control and we continue to follow our national motto and deliberately blind ourselves to all 'distinctions of race, creed, or color,' the type of native American of Colonial descent will become as extinct as the Athenian of the age of Pericles, and the Viking of the days of Rollo."

One is reminded in this connection of a remark of John Langdon-Davies in his "The New Age of Faith":    "If America had set out to attract Dantes and Benedetto Croces she would have had no alien problem at all, but the fact is she set out to attract cheap labor and as a result she has got Chicago."

Professor William McDougall's "Is America Safe for Democracy?" might be ignored except for the fact that it is based on lectures entitled "Anthropology and History, or the Influence of Anthropologic Constitution on the Destinies of Nations," given at the Lowell Institute when he was Professor of Psychology in Harvard University; that he cites "evidence" that our "social stratification" is "positively correlated with a corresponding stratification of innate moral and intellectual quality"; and that "the upper social strata as compared with the lower contain a larger proportion of persons of superior natural endowments." "Every human being, every community of human beings, every populace, inherits from its ancestry a stock of innate qualities which enable it to enjoy, to sustain, to promote, a civilization of a certain degree of complexity."

From the following we may learn Professor McDougall's idea of "evidence": "The colored men of the Northern States showed distinct superiority to those of the South, in respect of their performance in the army intelligence-tests. Have they not a larger proportion of white blood? I do not know, but I suspect it. . . . We have pretty good evidence that capacity for intellectual growth is inborn in different degrees, that it is hereditary, and also that it is closely correlated with social status." Also that "just as that peculiarity which enables a man to become a great mathematician (or a great musician) is certainly innate and hereditary, so also the development of the highest moral character only proceeds upon the basis of a hitherto undefined innate and hereditary peculiarity."

After an "it seems," Professor McDougall finds "good reason" to add to his "hypothesis" an "assumption," namely, that the "herd instinct" is relatively stronger in the Mediterranean than in the Nordic peoples, and that the "Nordic race" is more curious and less sociable!

Alfred Edward Wiggam, in his "The New Decalogue of Science" and "The Fruit of the Family Tree," has broadcasted more false views about race and civilization than any other one man. He is *the* spokesman of the Nordic faction, the silver-tongued champion of the eugenics cult, the popularizer of genetics *par excellence*. He even ventures the assumption that had Jesus been among us he "would have been President of the First Eugenics Congress"! And he would re-write the Golden Rule: "Do unto the born and the unborn as you would have the born and the unborn do unto you." That, by the way, is the "biologist's conception of the brotherhood of man" and "the final reconciliation of science and the Bible."

Mr. Wiggam, it need hardly be added, has no doubt about his "biology" when he speaks of the "integrity of the racial blood." Unless we keep the blood currents of our race "rich, regnant, and alive," there can be "no ethics, religion, art, democracy, idealism, philosophy," nor can "any other dream of man long succeed."

Mr. Wiggam's biologic "evidence"?  Certain Darwinian gener-
alizations, a microscope, sweet peas, guinea-pigs, human stud
books, fruit flies, biometric calculations; but he "cannot present
the highly technical proof."  Why should he, when "every biologist knows that intelligence is inherited, energy is inherited, insanity is inherited, emotional possibilities are inherited, a man's inner character is inherited"?  And if what "every biologist knows"
is not proof enough, the curious are invited to examine Woods'
"Royal Families of Europe," Thorndike's twins, and the conduct
of our Pilgrim forefathers!

Why pile up "evidence"?  Because in the past two decades we
have admitted to America "at least two million oppressed peoples
of other lands, of lower intellectual ability than our ten million
or more Negroes already on hand."  Because Brigham's interpretation of army intelligence tests "gives ample evidence that especially the Nordic elements of our population are being forced out
by other races whose representatives in this country are of distinctly lower average mental alertness and of less social coherence
and political capacity."  (Wiggam, by the way, nowhere alludes
to the fact that these same tests showed that New York State
Negroes had a higher intelligence rating than the Nordics of Alabama.)  "This (Nordic race) has contributed a vast share of all
political wisdom and scientific discovery to the modern world."

Lothrop Stoddard's "The Rising Tide of Color" is appropriately
introduced by Madison Grant, who presents the great Nordic
race and Stoddard as its prophet.  Certainly no fair-skinned man
can read that introduction and not be proud of his Nordic ancestors.  They and they alone saved civilization on four separate
occasions, and, if that great race ever passes, civilization passes with
it!  Then what?  "An unstable and bastardized population,
where worth and merit would have no inherent right to leadership and among which a new and darker age would blot out our
racial inheritance."  But that catastrophe cannot happen if the
Nordic race will get together, shake off the shackles of its inveter-
ate altruism, discard the vain phantom of internationalism, and
reassert the pride of race and the right of merit to rule!  "Demo-

cratic ideals among an homogeneous population of Nordic blood, as in England or America, is one thing, but it is quite another for the white man to share his blood with, or intrust his ideals to, brown, yellow, black, or red men."

Dr. Ellsworth Huntington assumes to be an authority on race and civilization problems, and, while he solves them in terms of climatic changes, he is also a confirmed Nordic propagandist. Were he not connected with Yale University, and did he not pretend to set forth "fundamental facts, principles and relationships" fit for use in "classes in human geography, sociology, oriental and biblical history, and the philosophy of history," we might pass by his "The Pulse of Progress." While climate in a way, according to Dr. Huntington, is intimately related to civilization, civilization and race are innately related. For example, "would any amount of training ever make the *average* Chinese as good a boatman as the *average* Eskimo, or could the average Eskimo by any possibility be as careful and patient a farmer as the Chinese?" After posing other questions equally absurd, a "thoughtful answer," we are led to infer, would be that there is "such thing as innate mental differences between one race and another"; at any rate "the vast majority of people believe in biological differences in the mentality of different races"—as though such belief were in itself of any weight in any court of science.

But Dr. Huntington knows that anthropologists do not believe in such differences. How get rid of them? By a trick worthy of a shifty lawyer: "The people who chiefly question this (innate mental differences) are a relatively small group of scientific men, *especially those who belong to races that are not dominant,* and a rather large group of persons with strong philanthropic and religious tendencies." (Italics mine.) He is referring, of course, especially to Professor Franz Boas, whose "Mind of Primitive Man," although a classic in anthropological literature for seventeen years, has never, so far as I know, been mentioned by Osborn, Grant, McDougall, Wiggam, or Huntington. That "relatively small group" presumably also includes three other leading American anthropologists of international reputation, Robert H. Lowie, Alfred L. Kroeber, and A. A. Goldenweiser. Imagine a

Nordic physicist thumbing his nose at the hypothesis of relativity because propounded by a man who belongs to a race that is not dominant! And yet Dr. Huntington knows so little of the history of the Jews that he speaks of them as a "pure" stock, and accounts for their being the most religious nation by "a long eugenic process which began with the patriarchs and culminated in Jesus."

Edwin M. East is a professor in Harvard University, and by profession one of those geneticists who, in the words of his preface to his "Mankind at the Crossroads," as a result of their labors "with fruit flies and guinea-pigs, with sweet peas and corn, with thousands of animals and plants, have made heredity no longer a mystery but an exact science to be ranked close behind physics and chemistry in definiteness of conception"! Professor East talks much of genes and chromosomes, and has no doubt of the laws of inheritance—at least in sweet peas. There is nothing mysterious about the *how* of inheritance, he tells us; in fact "a superficial acquaintance with Mendelism is expected today of every schoolboy . . . but what the scientists appear to have neglected to tell the general public is how these facts [which every schoolboy should know] affect the human race directly and personally." He will tell us.

Not only are "mental attributes inherited" but "great gaps separate the races. There are huge series of hereditary units possessed exclusively by each. Thus the white race has developed intellectual qualities superior to the black race, *though the black race can resist malaria much better than the white.*" (Italics mine.)

Professor East quotes McDougall with approval, and finds Stoddard one of the ablest writers on the "doctrine"—that world supremacy is imperilled and that there is a very real danger of the colored races supplanting the white race. Therein lie the crossroads. The finest families are hardly replacing themselves—the incompetents are taking their place. What is the answer? Not restriction of immigration but eugenics—"parentage must not be haphazard."

Not content with his crossroads puzzle, Professor East returns to the fight to save the world for the elect in his "Heredity and

Human Affairs." "Thoughtful members of society" can get one version of biological determinism from "newspaper men and professors of journalism, from certain retired lawyers and bartenders, from preachers and social workers, who write out of the fullness of their hearts"; or "another version from the works of Morgan, of Bateson, of Conklin, of Guyer, who write out of a fullness of critical experience which has made genetics a science." Why no mention of Pearl or Jennings—lack of critical experience? But he does quote Wiggam approvingly.

Between writing his "Crossroads" and his "Heredity" Professor East evidently heard of Professor Boas, for "Heredity" has a chapter on an analysis of Boas' investigations on changes in head shape in the children of certain immigrants. But still no overt mention of "The Mind of Primitive Man"; only this: "Today the Jews retaliate by proclaiming the Nordic race a myth."

Professor East's logic in establishing a point is typical of the heredity mongers. Thus, speaking of Alain Locke's "The New Negro," his "wide experience in making genetic judgments" forces him to conclude that "the developed germ-plasm causing the making of this book is nine-tenths white at least." Or, paraphrasing Professor Osborn, whether Locke's skin color is authentic or not, his germ-plasm must be at least nine-tenths Nordic!

Professor East not only knows how heredity works but what is inherited. "The physical differences between races are extraordinary . . . the mental differences are just as great. We cannot suppose that nature has produced the red man, the brown man, the white man, the black man, the pigmy and the giant, and has stopped there. No matter what value one may assign to precept and example in moulding the mind of man, his mentality is due fundamentally to his hereditary endowment, to his inborn traits"!

And yet Professor East would dismiss with contempt anyone still unconvinced that genetics can solve any problem in heredity—all is "crystal clear" except to fools and knaves. For Christianity, which he characterizes as "a little geocentric universe created as a kind of preserve for the *Hominidæ*," he would substitute "something infinitely more grand and glorious," science—the science of genetics, whose proved facts are so simple and obvious

that "there is no difficulty whatever in accounting for the emer-
gent individuals like Carlyle and Lincoln in otherwise undistin-
guished families." With genetics elevated to the rank of religion,
we can dispense with obstetrical societies, aseptic surgery, prenatal clinics, certified milk stations, public hospitals, higher wages,
slum renovation, and all such social amenities—they favor the
survival of the poor, are "unsound biologically," and nullify the
"natural elimination of the unfit." Nature eliminated the unfit
—why shouldn't we? Down with civilization, back to the jungle,
and long live the new religion, genetics!

The chief difference between these heredity mongers and the
Ku Klux Klan is the difference between kid gloves and a night-
gown—they have the same ethics. There is no problem of race
and civilization; they know. Their only problem is salvage: how
may the Great race, the Anglo-Saxon branch of the Nordic race,
be saved and perpetuated in all its "purity," with all its "genius for
democracy" and other inherent virtues.

In fact, between the religious prejudice of a Bryan's ignorance
and the class prejudice of a McDougall, Grant, East, or Osborn,
there is little to choose and less to excuse. Bryan had Genesis to
support him, Grant has Osborn, both have McDougall, all three
are endorsed by Wiggam, who is endorsed by East. All of them,
by stooping to loose reasoning, easily find what they want. To
build hypotheses on assumptions and use them as facts from which
they can, by faulty logic, draw as much proof as they need to
support a dogma is bad enough, but to put on blinders and deny
observed facts is to prostitute science and put scientists in the fundamentalist boat.

If these words seem harsh, let us isolate one more passage as
typical of the "science" of the whole Nordic group. Professor
Osborn in his preface to the second edition of "The Passing of
the Great Race" says: "It should be remembered also that many
of the dark-haired, dark-eyed youths of Plattsburg and other volunteer training camps are often three-fourths or seven-eighths Nordic, *because it only requires a single dark-eyed ancestor to lend the
dark hair and eye color to an otherwise pure Nordic strain.*"
(Italics mine.) Professor Osborn in effect says that if I, a pure

"Anglo-Saxon of the Nordic race," marry a female of the "Mediterranean race," my son may have dark eyes and hair, but he will have the courage, loyalty, self-sacrifice and idealism of my branch of the Nordic race! I need hardly say that neither Davenport himself, nor Castle, nor Walter, nor Morgan, nor any geneticist who prefers his science to his infantile beliefs, would agree to such a conclusion or ever pretended to find any evidence for such a principle of inheritance.

Or, turn to Professor Osborn's well known "Men of the Old Stone Age" for further light on his idea of heredity and his reasoning when he is forced to solve a problem in heredity. In trying to account for the great change in the Cro-Magnon "race" between the Aurignacian and Magdalenian periods, he says: "It is probable that in the genial climate of the Riviera these men (Cro-Magnon race) obtained their finest development; the country was admirably protected from the cold winds of the north, refuges were abandoned, and game by no means scarce, to judge by the quantity of animal bones found in the caves. Under such conditions of life the race enjoyed a fine physical development and dispersed widely"; in fact, became "one of the finest the world has ever seen."

But by the Magdalenian period this superb race had become something else, and Professor Osborn accounts for it by change in physical environment—"very severe climatic conditions." But if mere environment change can account for a difference in cranial capacity as great as that between *Pithecanthropus erectus* and a modern Nordic, and a difference in stature as great as that between a Pygmy and a modern Frenchman, what becomes of *heredity*, and what becomes of the doctrine of racial purity and the theory of the germ-plasm? And yet these Nordic "fans" accuse anthropologists of over-emphasizing environment, or sneer them out of court with a gesture of contempt.

## II

GENETICISTS give one version of heredity, says Professor East; bartenders, preachers, journalists, etc., another. I offer still others.

And turn first to the biological laboratory of Johns Hopkins University, directed by Professor H. S. Jennings, specialist in genetics, authority on heredity.

Professor Jennings says that heredity is neither an entity nor a force which does anything, and that we would be better off without the concept. As for "unit characters" about which East is so certain, "there is no such thing. . . . At least fifty genes must work together to produce a single feature such as red eye" in the humble fruit fly. That is, there are fifty or more separate ways in which an insect's eye character can be altered. Predicable characters are extremely few. No pair of parents can be certain of the character of their prospective offspring. Nor is it true that a given set of genes must produce just one set of characters and no other. In other words, inheritance is not foreordained. "Characters are not inherited at all; certain material which will produce a particular character under certain conditions is inherited."

Knowledge of the natural history of the oyster is useless in predicting the behavior and social organization of ants; the natural history of neither enables us to predict man's behavior—"only knowledge of the biology of man himself is relevant." Thus, as Jennings points out, the difference in stature between Jones and Smith may be due to heredity; that between the same Jones and Brown, to environment.

Well, if there are no inferior races, how about the eugenic programme to wipe out defective germ-plasm, which in some unexplained manner seems to have become so prevalent even inside the Nordic race itself? Professor Jennings thinks that possibly some cases of insanity belong to the small group in which the known number of single gene defects is so serious as to justify measures to stop their propagation. But the defects of such individuals, along with those with thyroid deficiency, etc., are "mingled with similar defects that are due primarily to environmental conditions, operating on special gene-combinations, so that it is difficult to know whether the stoppage of propagation in these classes gets rid of the main cause of the defects."

As for mental characteristics, "the rules for their inheritance are little known." Are they innate? They "are the organism's reaction to the varying environment, differing under different environments." From which an outsider might infer that at least one outstanding geneticist knows little of the inheritance of so-called mental characters and thinks they are due primarily to environment.

Raymond Pearl, Professor of Biology and Director of the Biologic Institute of Johns Hopkins University, is also a geneticist, and not without honor in his own country. He maintains (in "The Biology of Superiority," *American Mercury,* November, 1927) that the science of genetics has not yet produced a superior pod of beans or flock of hens. He characterizes eugenics literature as "a mingled mass of ill-grounded and uncritical sociology, economics, anthropology, and politics, full of emotional appeals to class and race prejudices, solemnly put forth as science, and unfortunately accepted as such by the public." Eugenics has fallen into disrepute "because of the ill-advised zeal with which some of its more ardent devotees have assigned such complex and heterogeneous phenomena as poverty, insanity, crime, prostitution, cancer, etc., to the operation of either single genes or to other simple and utterly hypothetical Mendelian mechanisms."

There is "no support to the view that the somatic (physical) characters of the offspring can be predicted from a knowledge of the somatic characters of the parents." The eugenists' claim that "like produces like" and that "superior people will have superior children" is contrary to the established facts of genetics and in the long run does the cause harm. He asks eugenics to clean house, and throw away the "old-fashioned rubbish which has accumulated in the attic."

"The epoch-making achievement of genetics during the last quarter of a century," he declares, "is the complete, comprehensive and general demonstration that heredity does *not* mean that like produces like." And yet the public teaching, legislative enactments, and moral fervor of the eugenists are "plainly based upon a pre-Mendelian genetics, as outworn and useless as the rind of yesterday's melon."

In his "Differential Fertility," in the *Quarterly Review of Biology*, Professor Pearl emphasizes still further his disagreement with "the eugenic condemnation of whole social or economic classes," directly or by inference; such condemnation is "unwarranted by anything now known. It has yet to be demonstrated that either poverty or lack of membership in a social aristocracy are biologically inherited traits."

And, finally, the dean of geneticists—certainly qualified to express an opinion on the relations of genetics and human affairs—Professor Thomas Hunt Morgan, in his "Evolution and Genetics," is "inclined to think" that considerable individual differences are "probably" genetic. But, he insists, there is:

. . . no real scientific evidence of the kind that we are familiar with in other animals and in plants. I will even venture to go so far as to suppose that the average of the human race might be improved by eliminating a few of the extreme disorders, however they may have arisen. In fact, this is attempted at present on a somewhat extensive scale by the segregation into asylums of the insane and feeble-minded. I should hesitate to recommend the incarceration of all their relatives if the character is suspected of being recessive, or of their children if a dominant. . . . Least of all should we feel any assurance in deciding genetic superiority or inferiority as applied to whole races, by which is meant not races in a biological sense but social or political groups bound together by physical conditions, by religious sentiments, or by political organizations. . . . If it is unjust "to condemn a whole *people*" . . . how much more hazardous is it, as some sensational writers have not hesitated to do, to pass judgment as to the relative inferiority or superiority of different *races*.

If within each human social group the geneticist finds it impossible to discover, with any reasonable certainty, the genetic basis of behavior, the problems must seem extraordinarily difficult when groups are contrasted with each other where the differences are obviously connected not only with material advantages and disadvantages resulting from location, climate, soil, and mineral wealth, but with traditions, customs, religions, taboos, conventions, and prejudices. A little goodwill might seem more fitting in treating these complicated questions than the attitude adopted by some of the modern race-propagandists.

I offer still another version of genetics, from the physiological laboratory of the University of Chicago, directed by Professor A. J. Carlson. In his address at the Third Race Betterment Conference, Professor Carlson was skeptical even of the fatter hogs and faster horses that have been produced by selection and controlled breeding: "Have we thereby secured a better hog and a better horse? We know many factors that injure the individual, and a few that injure the race, but in our almost complete ignorance of the mechanisms of race improvement, we seem impotent on the positive side." But even if we knew how to improve the "race," we are still far from agreement as to the goal: "Is the super model of *homo sapiens* to be constructed on the line of a Mussolini, a Gandhi, an Einstein, a Dempsey, a Darwin, or a Henry Ford? Is he to be 'wet' or 'dry'? Should he be white, black, yellow, brown, pink, or gray? Should he be six or sixty feet tall? Should he be a more rational or a more emotional machine? Is he to be a pacifist or a man fitted to wage bigger and better wars? Are we to aim at a better co-ordinated society of masters and slaves or a democracy?"

As Professor Carlson points out, man has reached his present state of development almost without any conscious direction whatsoever based on accumulated experience. We do not know what our forebears ate and drank and how much, nor how they worked, rested, and loved, and without that knowledge we are hardly entitled to label our way of living or our artificial environment "favorable" or "unfavorable." What is known today of the influence of diet, work, behavior, environment, etc., on physiological processes tends merely to limit or permit full development of individual growth and functions, and hence is not significant in relation to race betterment. "The only clear instances we have · of rapid modification of the germ plasm by experimental (drugs) or environmental means seem to be injurious or destructive. Man today is like a curious and clumsy and very ignorant child tinkering with the watch; will he tomorrow contrive a superior mechanism? The lesson for the present seems clear: *The germ plasm can be injured; some phases of the present man-made environment seem to enhance such injury.* Are the ablest, the strongest, the wisest men merely grave-diggers in disguise?"

I offer still another version of genetics, this time from an insane asylum. Professor A. Myerson, neurologist and psychiatrist, author of "The Psychology of Mental Disorders," has especially investigated the question of heredity in relation to mental diseases and feeble-mindedness. Is feeble-mindedness inherited—or "intelligence"? And how about the Jukes, etc., of whom so many thousand pages have been written?

The Jukes, Kilikaks, etc., are bad enough, Myerson says, but "it has not been proved that they are really feeble-minded; nor even if they are feeble-minded has it been proved that they are typical of the bulk of cases of feeble-mindedness." While psychoses such as dementia præcox and manic depressive *may* run in families, even such diseases "appear as isolated characteristics of one individual and cannot be linked up with mental disease of the family, or appear without any hereditary linking up which is worthy of the name. . . A few cases of three-generation disease are recorded, only one or two where four generations were mentally sick. It appears that mental disease, like physical disease, either destroys the stock which it attacks, or there is final recovery." But even if a father has a psychosis and his son or daughter is feeble-minded, "there is no known hereditary bond between the two states."

After paying his respects to the "surprisingly omniscient way" certain people pass judgment on the dead as well as the quick, Dr. Myerson admits that he finds it hard to "evaluate individuals after a close study and after a long acquaintance with mental and physical disease. . . Much of feeble-mindedness is environmental in origin, much is hereditary, but the most is of unknown origin, and may represent the inexplainable downward movement of intelligence, just as genius represents its inexplainable upward movement." Eugenics "needs research more than legislation. . . It does not yet need publicity so much as it needs scientists and scientific work. . . We are still far away from real understanding of the bulk of mental diseases and of feeble-mindedness, and no amount of statistical evaluation of improper data will bring us light."

## III

WELL, how about the far-famed "intelligence tests" made on millions of army recruits and since on millions of school children of various "races"? Do they not prove innate connection between race and intelligence, do they not definitely prove that the Great race is greatest in innate ability? These tests have been a mighty arsenal of ammunition for the heredity mongers, cited again and again as proof that races differ in innate mental capacity.

But what do the tests test—"intelligence"? What is intelligence? Whatever it is, the outstanding fact brought out in the tests is that it is astoundingly scarce. Why this is so is well put by Dr. Myerson. Few people, comparatively speaking, are really interested in matters beyond their immediate concerns, or have any intellectual interest at all. Most people lead a parochial existence, absorbed in their own problems of livelihood, sex, and pleasure. They read little beyond the innately interesting things, and avoid real mental exertion. They forget readily the fragments of culture which reached them in school and which bob up now and then in newspaper and magazine. And yet, while the average adult may rank lower in "intelligence" than a bright child, he "ranks much higher in qualities that tests cannot evaluate—experience in life, sober judgment, special efficiency, etc."

And that is just what the tests do not test—ability to learn from experience.

The tests may furnish samples of knowledge, but there is no way whereby inborn capacity for intelligent behavior can be directly measured. At best they can only give a measure of behavior. Any test, to serve as measure of innate capacity, must be made on individuals who have been subjected to the same social environment. The really significant thing brought out in the army tests was the enormous variation in the same "racial" strains and amongst individuals of practically the same environment. What they have not shown is that there is anything in the anatomical make-up, physiological processes, or chromosomes of a son of the chief of the *Mano Nera* of Catania which will predispose him, on the East Side of New York or the West Side of Chicago, to follow in the footsteps of his illustrious parent. That such a youth at the age of twenty, reared in a New York or Chicago Little Italy atmosphere, should not rate highly in an examination paper prepared by a one hundred per cent American school-teacher, is to be expected. Whatever the tests showed, they did not measure capacity to learn, and they are therefore, so far as criteria of innate "racial" capacity are concerned, worthless.

IV

THE last version of genetics—the problem of innate relation of race and civilization—I shall offer, is that of the anthropologists, of those whose life business it is to study mankind in the making, man's genetic history, his cultural achievements. Are these two necessarily related?

Professor A. C. Haddon of Cambridge University, in "The Races of Man," says: "A classification based on culture may be of interest to the sociologist, but it is obviously one which can have no prime importance in regard to genetic relationship, though it may indicate the influence of peoples upon one another. There is no such thing as racial culture. The culture of any given people is primarily dependent upon their mode of life, which is in itself largely an expression of geographical conditions."

With that dictum, I need hardly add, I am in complete agreement—as are, I believe, practically all living anthropologists. Professor Haddon is not of the, or a, non-dominant "race"; he belongs to the "Anglo-Saxon branch of the Nordic Race"!

Professor Franz Boas, in the chapter on Race Problems in the United States in his "Mind of Primitive Man," specifically raises the question as to how far the undesirable traits that are today found in our Negro population are innate, and how far they are due to social surroundings for which we are responsible. In answer to that question he emphasizes the fact, known to every ethnologist, that the culture of the African Negroes is that of a healthy primitive people with much personal initiative, talent for organization, and with imaginative power, technical skill, and thrift. "Neither is a warlike spirit absent in the race, as is proved by the mighty conquerors who overthrew states and founded new empires, and by the courage of the armies that follow the bidding of their leaders. There is nothing to prove that licentiousness, shiftless laziness, lack of initiative, are fundamental characteristics of the race. Everything points out that these qualities are the result of social conditions rather than of hereditary traits."

Boas thinks, however, that there may be differences in the mental make-up of the Negro and other races. But there is "no evidence whatever that would stigmatize the Negro as of weaker build, or as subject to inclinations and powers that are opposed to our social organization. An unbiassed estimate of the anthropological evidence so far brought forward does not permit us to countenance the belief in a racial inferiority which would unfit an individual of the Negro race to take his part in modern civilization. . . In short, there is every reason to believe that the Negro, when given facility and opportunity, will be perfectly able to fulfil the duties of citizenship as well as his white neighbor."

In an article on "The Question of Racial Purity" in the *American Mercury*, Professor Boas insists even more strongly that "nobody has ever given satisfactory proof of an inherent inequality of races."

Professor Robert E. Lowie states his opinion as to the existence of innate racial capacity thus: "As to the existence of superior races, I am an agnostic open to conviction. All evolutionists admit that at some point an organic change of fundamental significance occurred. It is *conceivable* that the Bushmen and Negritos, Pygmies and Negroes are organically below the remainder of living human types, and that differences of one sort or another even divide more closely related stocks."

Between Boas' "nobody has ever given satisfactory proof," or Lowie's "it is *conceivable*," and the flat-footed assertions of those who assume to know races as such and to classify them according to innate virtues or traits, there is not the difference between Tweedledum and Tweedledee but a gulf. That gulf is so wide that, it may confidently be asserted, no one yet has definitely and conclusively associated, either for individual or for race, any innate connection between physical structure and cultural trait or "mental faculty."

Physical features are, within certain limits, heritable traits, and something is known of the laws which govern their transmission. Such innate factors are rooted in biology, the same for man as for other species of animals. To classify mankind by the way they look, or by their physical features or anatomical traits, is one thing; to classify men by what they do is an entirely different thing. As the behavior of an individual depends, certainly in some measure, upon the training he receives at the hands of parents, playmates, teachers, and social environment in general, so the cultural behavior of families, groups, tribes, and nations is dependent upon historic and psychological factors never in any way proved to be heritable traits.

Indeed there is no evidence that man's capacity to learn human behavior has increased in the slightest since he definitely left the trees and became man. During that long period, variously reckoned from 50,000 to 250,000 years, due to factors little understood as yet, fairly distinct physical types have come to be formed in different parts of the world, physical types marked by varying proportions of anatomical features, character of hair, pigmentation of skin and eye, etc. Human culture has varied from one generation to another. Just as every normal newborn "Nordic," Jew, or Negro born in New York City in 1928 inherits in general the features of his near ancestors, so he is heir to a culture environment or stage of civilization unlike anything the world has seen before. What that youngster will be twenty, forty, or sixty years hence, no one can possibly predict, because no one can possibly predict the social and conditioning factors which will play upon him and to which he will learn to respond, not because of his physical inheritance but because of his common human inheritance of a capacity to learn any human language or culture.

The outstanding fact about human beings is individual variation of physical type. Equally striking is the capacity of every normal newborn to learn or acquire human behavior. Why one individual of a family, or why one family in a group of families more or less closely related by blood, achieves different results culturally, is a problem that is yet far from solution, but the primary factors in that problem seem to be psychologic rather than biologic. That is to say, so far as we know at the present time, the factors which make for, say, a given state of culture among the aborigines of Australia at any given time are the incidence of geographic and physical environment and the antecedent historic and psychologic factors which made that culture what it is. What any individual, family, or physical type could or would do under different geographic and social environmental conditions is something which no one at present is warranted in asserting dogmatically. *Conceivably*, the Australian, or the Bushman, Negrito, or Pygmy, for any evidence we have to the contrary, could learn to behave like a Nordic if he were reared in a Nordic environment. What is too often left out of account is that the Nordic social environment makes it difficult, if not impossible, for the alleged inferior to develop to the fullest his innate capacity.

v

THERE is no such thing as racial culture or Nordic civilization. Is there such a thing as race or Nordic race? Obviously, Nordic, Alpine, Caucasian, Mongolian, etc., are merely abstract terms, convenient, as Haddon says, only to the extent that they help us appreciate broad facts. "A race type exists mainly in our own minds." What are the "broad facts"?

Of the dozens of attempted classifications of man by anatomical traits, no two agree. Presumably never will agree, because there are no outstanding, sharply defined physical traits by which groups of mankind can be partitioned off from one another. To classify human beings by shape of head is one thing, by stature another, by pigmentation of skin or eyes another, by color and character of hair still another. Any classification made on any one of these traits is to classify mankind by such a trait and by no other. But there is always overlapping. When the attempt is made to classify man by a combination of two or more of these traits, hopeless confusion results. When the attempt is made to combine as many as five physical traits, the proportion of "pure" types becomes, as Ripley says, almost infinitesimal. "We are thus reduced to the extremity in which my friend, Dr. Ammon of Baden, found himself, when I wrote asking for photographs of a pure Alpine type from the Black Forest. He has measured thousands of heads, and yet he answered that he really had not been able to find a perfect specimen in all details. All his round-headed men were either blond, or tall, or narrow-nosed, or something else that they ought not to be."

Possibly the difficulty in finding a satisfactory classification of man on the basis of heritable traits is because the influence of environment on innate structure is not yet known. We do not yet know why men vary in stature, in amount of pigmentation, in head form, etc., nor how permanent are such variations. No anthropologist has succeeded in isolating a pure race or type, presumably because there is no such thing. Hence the probability that races in a strict sense of the term do not exist, or if they did once, cannot be distinguished because of inter-breeding.

But there are pronounced differences between, for example, the tall blond of Northern Europe and the diminutive Pygmy of Africa, or between the European in general and the native of Australia. Why they differ, or the extent to which these differences would persist under changed environment, is not known; nor, I repeat, is any inherent connection between these physical differences and psychologic or cultural abilities known.

Only in a very limited sense, then, can we say that "racial inheritance" has any significance. Traits common to every individual of a race, and which set him off from every individual of other races, may be spoken of as hereditary racial traits. Thus we may speak of the black skin and kinky hair of the African Negro as hereditary racial traits. All Negroes have these traits. But shape of head and size of brain cannot be spoken of as traits which set off Negroes from Whites, because there is great overlapping amongst the two groups in these respects. Such overlapping of types found everywhere today is presumably due to intermixture, but we are not, as Boas points out, on that account entitled to assume that extreme physical types represent pure races. Thus the classification of Europeans into Northern or Nordic, Central or Alpine, and Southern or Mediterranean, in no sense represents *races* but merely extreme forms of three physical characters: stature, skin color, and head form. The extremes of these forms are not typical of a "race," much less of a pure race; they are only the extremes in an unbroken series from the North to the South of Europe. Anyone not content with three European races can have thirty-three, or in fact as many as he wants.

The argument put forth by our racial purity propagandists falls to the ground. There is no evidence for pure races, no evidence that the extreme forms of any type represent the purest, nor any evidence for the assumption that inter-breeding of different types in any respect lowers their capacity for culture or civilization. Nowhere does the ethnologist find evidence of correlation of racial achievement and supposed race purity; nor is there any substantial proof of inherent lack of mentality or capacity for intelligence in any race or racial type. On the contrary, all that we know of human history makes the claim for racial inferiority seem improbable.

Race and civilization, then, are not interchangeable terms. No classification of mankind by blood will coincide with classification by language or culture. No one language or culture belongs to any distinct physical type. Hence every attempt to classify mankind from a combined physical and cultural or linguistic point of view has failed, and must inevitably fail.

Perhaps the best known attempt to combine blood and culture is the classification of F. Müller, who, basing his classification on hair, discovered two great races (woolly-haired and straight-haired), and within these, minor divisions based on linguistics. But as the laws governing the inheritance of language and culture are based on psychologic and historic factors, and the laws which govern physical inheritance are biologic, his classification has only historic interest.

Early classifications of mankind were geographical—a race to a continent. Thus Linnæus found four varieties of man: European White, Asiatic Yellow, American Red, and African Black.

Blumenbach (1775) added a fifth: the Oceanic or Brown. That was the classification which I learned in school, and is still embodied in our Federal laws as Caucasian, Mongolian, Ethiopian, American, Malayan. Cuvier (1800) hung his three "races" on the sons of Noah: Shem, Ham, and Japheth.

Thereafter it was a perpetual open season for race hunting, with widely varying results. Haeckel could only find twelve races in 1873, but a few years later succeeded in finding thirty-four. Topinard found sixteen in 1878, and a few years later discovered three more. Deniker also had difficulty with his count, but in 1900 decided there were six "grand divisions," seventeen "divisions," and twenty-nine "races." Why these differences? Because, as Blumenbach had observed, "the innumerable varieties of mankind run into one another by insensible degrees"; because, as Pritchard in his "Natural History of Man" said, "the different races of man are not distinguishable from each other by strongly marked and permanent distinctions. All the diversities which exist are variable, and pass into each other by insensible gradations."

Races do not exist; classifications of mankind do. And Kroeber's, in his "Anthropology," or Haddon's, in his "The Races of Man," are as good as any, and have the merit of being up to date.

Personally, the simple scheme proposed by Boas many years ago is the classification I like best. It is easily remembered and requires no stretch of the imagination. Boas finds two great forms or groups of the human species in which skin color, shape of hair, form of face and nose, and body proportions, are characteristically distinct. The Negroid, represented geographically as the Indian Ocean, is contrasted with the Mongoloid, or Pacific Ocean group. The Negroid form is dark-skinned, frizzly-haired, flat-nosed, as opposed to the light-skinned, straight-haired, high-nosed Mongoloid division. Boas does not pretend, of course, that these two groups represent pronounced and sharply contrasted forms of humanity, or that there are not individuals in one group that in certain respects differ more from their own group than from some of those in the opposite group. The Mongoloid group is found in both Americas, Asia, and Europe; the Negroid in Africa, and presumably once in the whole of Southern Asia and the islands on the West side of the Indian Ocean.

Outside of these two great divisions of mankind are certain pronounced physical types, such as the North Europeans, the Australians, and the Pygmies, but how they are genetically related to one or the other of the two main groups of mankind is not known. Europeans differ in pigmentation from the Negroid more than from the Mongoloid type, but in form of hair, proportions of body, and form of eye and cheeks, are not so different from the Negroid as from the Mongoloid. The Australian natives in certain respects are rather sharply set off from the rest of mankind, and possibly represent a type differentiated early in the history of the human race. The Pygmy people are found irregularly distributed in many parts of Africa, the Andaman Islands, Malay Peninsula, the Philippines, and New Guinea, and in early times were possibly more widely distributed. They form in themselves a distinct, definite, and wholly unsolved problem in the genesis of the human species.

Europeans presumably came into their physical characteristics in Europe or nearby Asia. But the difference between the skin color of the European and the Mongoloid group is neither so pronounced as is commonly supposed nor so common as to make it a distinguishing mark of race. Many Asiatics have a skin quite as white as the average European. Boas has even found among the Haida Indians of British Columbia, white skins, brownish red hair, and light brown eyes. The Indian tribes of the Upper Mississippi had also a very light complexion, yet the Yuma Indians of Southern California are often as dark in skin color as the lighter skinned Negroes. Thus the most we can say is that the very light-skinned European represents an extreme variant of pigment deficiency, in itself characteristic of the whole Mongoloid group. While blond hair is not found among the Mongoloids, yet reddish brown hair is common. The European nose varies among Europeans, and in line with similar variants in the Mongoloid group. From these and other considerations Boas believes the European type to represent nothing more than a recent specialization of the Mongoloid group.

If no definite innate connection between physical type and cultural capacity can be discovered, and if there is no agreement as to the genetic relationship of the varying physical types of mankind, it seems hardly worth while to inquire whether some races or types are, anatomically speaking, lower than others; yet inasmuch as it is a favorite diversion of certain geneticists to arrange races according to the supposed distance from their animal ancestor, let us see what basis there is in observed fact for the existence of "higher" and "lower" races.

The real point brought out by all such graded series is that the gap between man in general and his anthropoid progenitor is wide, but qualitative rather than quantitative. The Negro, to be sure, has a broad and flat nose and a protruding jaw, which seems to bring him nearer the anthropoid than the European. But while the European and the Mongoloid have the largest brains, the European shares with the native Australian the doubtful honor of remaining the hairiest of the human race, a peculiarly animal-like trait. The red lip, one of our most human characteristics, is most strongly developed in the Negro. Again, in proportion of limbs the Negro is most human—that is, has diverged most from ape-like forms.

In other words, divergence from animal ancestor has developed in varying directions in varying types. Such differences are at best purely anatomical. We have no reason to infer that they have anything to do with "mental faculty." We have been misled by associating features that seem to us brutish, with brutality. Karl Pearson, after extended inquiry into the whole subject, expressed his conviction that there is little relation between physical and psychical characters in man. Nor could Manouvrier, the great French anatomist, discover any direct connection between anatomical characteristics and mental ability.

How about size of brain? True, whatever difference there is between Europeans and Mongoloids or Negroids favors in general the Europeans, but this difference in itself is no proof of increase in ability. If the majority of eminent men have had large brains, so too have the majority of murderers. Some of the most eminent men of Europe have had very small brains. Dr. Franklin Mall, who specially investigated brain weights, concluded that, because of the great variability of individuals of each race, racial differences, if they exist, are exceedingly difficult to discover. But even if we could assume that ability is inherent in brain capacity, the most we could say is that the European is likely to produce more men of commanding genius than the African. As a matter of fact, there is no distinct gap between European and Negro brains. They distinctly overlap in size; only in Europe there are a few who reach a size not found in Africa. We have neither anatomical nor psychological evidence that the European or so-called white race is physically the highest type of man.

As for the three alleged European races—Nordic, Alpine, and Mediterranean—they simply do not exist other than as abstract conveniences. The Alpine type, for example, includes such diverse languages and cultures as French, German, Italian, and Slav. There is good reason to believe that these peoples are related in blood and sprang from common ancestors; today they are far apart in language and culture.

How, then, can we account for the fact that the European has developed a civilization which has encompassed the globe and which makes all other civilizations appear fundamental or in a state of arrested development? And if the culture of the European is superior to all others, why is it not because of innate capacity?

The ethnologist, familiar through long personal contact with so-called savages, and accustomed to view his own civilization objectively and hence more or less unemotionally, has no difficulty in seeing the fallacy implicit in such questions as I have just posed. And is grateful when a philosopher comes to his aid, as does Professor John Dewey, in saying that "the present civilized mind is virtually taken as a standard and the savage mind is measured off on this fixed scale. It is no wonder that the outcome is negative: that primitive mind is described in terms of 'lack,' 'absence'; its traits are incapacities." Then there was the visitor to a savage tribe who wrote of its Manners and Customs: "Customs, beastly; Manners, none."

The fallacy I spoke of above is in the "lack," "absence." I may lack a dress suit: that does not necessarily mean I cannot afford one or cannot learn to wear one; it may only mean that I, as King of the Cannibal Islands, have no need or desire for a dress suit—or having seen one, devoutly hope Customs and Manners will never force me or my kind into one.

The answer to the *why* of present white supremacy must be sought in a historic review of human achivement. We cannot assign dates to the beginnings of human culture. Even in the remote past there were certain fundamental inventions and beginnings of culture known to all peoples.

Only a few thousand years ago we find types of culture approximating civilization beginning to develop on an extensive scale in Asia. In the course of time these higher types of culture—or civilization—fluctuated, moved about from one people to another. Civilization seemed to ebb and flow, now here, now there. At the dawn of recorded history the contrast between so-called civilized peoples and savage peoples was about as sharp as it is today. But throughout this vast land area there was constant conflict, civilized peoples often being vanquished only to have their culture taken up and carried on by their conquerors, as was the case with the Mongol Manchu conquerors of China. Centres of civilization shifted from one part of Asia to another. Meanwhile, the ancestors of modern Europeans possessed culture in no wise superior to that of primitive man, or of savage man today who has not yet come in contact with modern civilization.

What was the origin of this ancient Asiatic civilization? Does it indicate a special kind of genius or any special innate capacity? Seemingly not. The peoples of Asia were fortunate in their social environment. Asiatic civilization was the product of the genius of no one people; each contributed something toward general progress and the general fund. The more we know of the history of this civilization, the more abundant become the proofs that culture was disseminated from one people to another whenever and wherever tribes or nations came in contact, neither race nor language nor distance limiting the diffusion of culture. Hamitic, Semitic, Aryan, and Mongol alike made invaluable contributions, each offering of its genius.

Meanwhile, on the more isolated continent of America, in at

least three centres, a high culture developed. In the highlands of Peru and Mexico, and in the Ohio Valley, we find highly developed political organizations and elaborate divisions of labor and an intricate organization. Huge public works requiring the co-operation of master minds and swarms of people were undertaken and successfully carried through. Many animals and plants extremely valuable to man were domesticated; the art of writing was invented.

As Professor A. C. Tozzer, in his "Social Origins and Social Continuities," says: "The Maya calendar functioned without the loss of a day for 2000 years, until it was broken up by Spanish priests. Marginal corrections were applied to take care of the variation in the year and the true solar year—a means more accurate than our method of leap year. It was not until 1582 that the Julian day was invented, which corresponds to the Maya day count—2000 years after the same principle had been adopted by the Mayas."

The ancient civilization of the New is not the ancient civilization of the Old World, but its general status was almost as high. There were differences, but the nature of these differences is essentially the same as that between the ancient Asiatic and the ancient European culture—simply a difference in time. One reached a certain stage a few hundred or a few thousand years in advance of the other. Natural causes, in which we may include the vast land area and a more abundant natural supply of animals, especially the horse, cow, elephant, and dromedary, and plants suitable for domestication—these seem to have been the chief factors which predetermined that the development of human culture was to make more rapid progress in the Old than in the New World. There is nothing strange in the course of such a race for cultural supremacy. Europe alone in the last two thousand years furnishes innumerable parallels, not only in one people arriving at a destination sooner than another, but in the phenomenon so often presented in Asia two or three thousand years ago, of the van of progress being assumed now by one people, now by another. Thus the lead in civilization has been held by Greece, Rome, Byzantine, Bulgaria, the Moors, Portugal, Spain, France, and Holland, to go no further.  Of two children born at the same time, the difference in their progress by the age of fifty is likely to be much greater than the difference between them at the age of ten; and in each case it is possible generally to evaluate the factors which accelerate or retard their development, rather than to account for them by hereditary or innate inferior or superior capacity.

Applying this argument to human history, we are justified in concluding that, considering the vast age of the human species, a difference of a few centuries in becoming what we call "civilized" is to be accounted for on purely historical grounds, and not on any real or fancied innate capacity.

But, it may be argued, when we contrast modern European civilization with that of the primitive peoples of Africa and the peoples of other areas equally backward, we find a difference more fundamental than can be accounted for by the mere element of time.   I can find no valid ground on which to base this argument. Modern competition—that is, the clash between the European, who has objectified and perfected his methods of warfare and transportation, and primitive peoples—is along unfair lines; primitive man cannot compete with the power of the white man's machine. Further, primitive tribes in certain parts of the world, as in America and Siberia, have been swamped by the crowds of alien white immigrants they have had no time to assimilate.   The average American Indian had no more chance of holding his own against the Europeans than had the Chinese armies a few years ago, equipped with bow and arrows, against the bullets of the British.

In short, a peculiar sequence of historical causes has had infinitely more to do in furthering the rapid growth of civilization amongst some people than amongst others; and this growth is due to these historical causes rather than to innate faculty.

Even granting as we must the actual cultural superiority of the Whites or Europeans, the weakness of the argument for correlation of race faculty and civilization becomes apparent when we try to evaluate the relative parts played in culture history by the several divisions of the European or Caucasian race.   Thus Kroeber would award the palm to the Mediterranean branch for its long-continued lead in productivity and having reared the largest portion of the structure of existing civilization:

To it belonged the Egyptians; the Cretans and other Ægeans; the Semitic strain in the Babylonians; the Phœnicians and Hebrews; and a large element in the populations of classic Greece and Italy, as well as the originators of Mohammedanism. With the Hindus added as probably nearly related, the dark whites have a clear lead.

The next largest share civilization would owe to the Alpine-Armenoid broad-headed Caucasian branch. This may have included the Sumerians, if they were not Mediterranean; comprised the Hittites; and contributed important strains to the other peoples of Western Asia and Greece and Italy.

By comparison, the Nordic branch looms insignificant. Up to a thousand years ago the Nordic peoples had indeed contributed ferment and unsettling, but scarcely a single new culture element, certainly not a new element of importance and permanence. For centuries after that, the centre of European civilization remained in Mediterranean Italy or Alpine France. It is only after A. D. 1500 that any claim for a shift of this centre to the Nordic populations could be alleged. In fact, most of the national and cultural supremacy of the Nordic peoples, so far as it is real, falls within the last two hundred years. Against this, the Mediterraneans and Alpines have a record of leading in civilizational creativeness for at least six thousand years.

I am in entire accord with Tozzer's conclusions that:

There is no present evidence, physical, psychological, or cultural, to prove that contemporaneous savages are fundamentally different in mind, body, or estate from the sophisticated human product of civilization. The savage is "bone of our bone and flesh of our flesh." He is, in short, a "poor relation, but our own." . . .

Savages the world over have come to possess in some form every basic institution of civilized society. There is no reason to believe that they owe such social institutions to precept, example, or imitation of the so-called "Higher Cultures." On the contrary, these "Higher Cultures" owe much to the institutions from which they have been derived. . . .

The evolution of institutions may, like physical life, have had many mutations. . . . They are characterized by many spontaneous growths, individual creations of life-forms (the product of the workings of the mind). . . . Similarity of nomenclature does not always mean either identity of structure or a common history.

The savage in his customs and social organization manifests a genius for diversification, a skill in practical adaptation, and a willingness and often a surprising ability to modify and to improve which make it unsafe to assume that primitive man is either stagnant or degenerate. Any modern group of savages with health and unmolested by the grosser benefits of civilization may have the potentiality to work out for itself an abundant spiritual and material enrichment.

All of the defects behind the so-called irrational follies of the savage, evidenced in superstition, credulity, suspicion, and vanity, are the common inheritance of all mankind. The same psychological principles are behind the same psychological weaknesses both in savage and in civilized life. They are actively functioning among the ignorant of the civilized peoples and are by no means atrophied in those human groups which have been most constantly exposed to education. . . .

If we compare the relation between opportunity and achievement of the savage and of his more cultured brother, we soon realize that, from this point of view, our superiority is very doubtful. The complexity of institutions is not a measure of their validity, nor is the multiplication of inventive devices a true criterion of progress.

The savage is a rational being, morally sound, and in every respect worthy of a place in the "Universal Brotherhood of Man."

For "savages" read Hottentots, Chinese, Japanese, Russians, Sicilians, Mexicans, Greeks, Jews, Choctaws, and I am still in complete accord.

In conclusion, then, we may say that judgments of cultural capacity—or, specifically, the capacity to enter into American civilization—based on the known contribution of this or that race to civilization, or judgments of races through sampling of individuals in so-called intelligence tests, are inconclusive and for practical purposes worthless. Nor have we any reason to believe that further mixture with our present sub-stratum by immigrants from any part of Europe or Asia will destroy the integrity of our race, hybridize it, or in any way lower it. Such racial mixtures as we have in America today are in no essential different from race mixtures which have been going on for thousands of years in Europe and Asia, and which we have no reason to believe have ever resulted in inferior races or in breaking up civilization.

Our problems, then, are not those of race and civilization, but of too little understanding and too much prejudice. Result: too many aliens in our midst socially unadjusted. Answer: less race phobia, more intelligent understanding of the nature of civilization. Like human behavior, civilization is made and not born. Like life itself, it must be nourished day by day, ceaselessly, with new energy and new materials, or it sickens and dies.

## XI—RELIGION

### By JAMES HARVEY ROBINSON

#### I

VARIOUS notable attempts have been made during the past two thousand years and more to understand and explain man's religious life; but these have been rare and inconspicuous compared with the heated polemics of convinced factions, engaged in attacks and defense. When I was a boy, among the protagonists were Matthew Arnold, Huxley, Tyndall, Ingersoll, Gladstone, Bradlaugh, Beecher, Horace Bushnell—each after his kind. There was Emerson, and some recollection of Theodore Parker. All these did their part in keeping religious issues alive and in shifting them somewhat from their old moorings. Lecky's "History of Rationalism" and his "History of Morals" furnished hitherto neglected material for a reconsideration of the actual record of Christian leaders. Henry C. Lea had issued his story of priestly celibacy to be followed by many stately volumes which amounted to an arraignment of the Mediæval Church based on a terrific accumulation of first-hand information. But all these seem now far-off echoes of a remote past, if one happens to be reading the newer books on religion.

The intellectual climate in which religious beliefs and practices must hold their own underwent a sharp and surprising alteration in the early twentieth century. New, or previously over-looked, information about man, his origin and proclivities, his ancient ways and his observable habits in various stages of culture, promised to explain, or at least recast, the whole estimate of religious phenomena. Considerations which could not have occurred to

Arnold, Huxley, Lecky, and Lea have now become fundamental. It is to this astonishing revolution wrought by science rather than by theological controversy, that we propose to turn our attention. But first some general reflections on the current use of the words "religion" and "religious" are called for.

Almost everyone takes his own religion for granted, and only in rather exceptional circumstances does he bother much about its contrasts with other forms of belief. But to affirm that one has no religion would not only seem shocking but downright unintelligible to most of our fellow citizens. It is a common, but by no means novel, feature of our times for those who have lost faith in the older tenets to construct a new religion "to put in its place." Their inventors and converts bereaved of their former comforts take to themselves a younger and fairer spouse. Marxism has become a religion for many who have no slightest patience with the older foundations of faith. This has been most interestingly and acutely shown by Max Eastman. C. E. Ayres even suspects that Science is being taken for a new religion, although a false Messiah in the way of betraying the multitudes with baseless hopes.

Books on reconstruction of religion flow in an even stream from the presses. The newer varieties usually turn on how much can be retrieved from the desolation wrought in old convictions by increasing knowledge. They ask what can an intelligent person continue to cling to in the way of comforting purposefulness in this universe of ours. I have on my desk a tiny volume called "Troasm," written by a Middlesex schoolmaster, who for prudential reasons would not have his name revealed. I will quote his opening sentences as pertinent to this discussion:

"There is an ancient anecdote, almost threadbare with service, of a disputant who closed his argument with the aphorism that all sensible men professed the same religion; adding, when asked what that religion might be, that no sensible man would ever tell." This has been the attitude of a good many thoughtful people in earlier times. The writer continues: "There can have been few periods in the world's history when the need for a religion that would stabilize and comfort mankind was felt more deeply or more universally than now. Organized creeds seem, to the majority of men, to have had their trial, with almost everything in their favor for so long a time that their failure to influence even the surface of the conduct of mankind places them out of court as possible foundations for the religion of the future."

The writer finds no churches in Great Britain whose honest and orthodox adherents number more than "an entirely negligible percentage of the population, and it is possible to assert in almost any company, without fear of contradiction, that heresy is now a social duty." The writer of "Troasm" holds that "there must be a religion in the world—that, indeed, if civilization is not to fall to pieces, there must henceforth be religion infinitely more intense and universal than any the world has yet known." I have quoted these passages as a sort of text. So far as the United States is concerned I suspect there is still a far wider acceptance of the older religious beliefs than the writer finds in England, but certainly to judge from the church notices in the newspapers, "partisans of all the churches are even now shouting from the house tops that the supreme want of the world is religion."

New religions perpetuate many old mystic assumptions and a good deal of respect for tradition—witness one of the most conspicuous, Christian Science. In the case of "The Creator Spirit, a Survey of Christian Doctrine in the light of Biology, Psychology and Mysticism," by Canon Raven, we may find, according to *The Churchman*, that "the frankest and fullest knowledge revealed by modern science is only an aid to the deeper reliance upon the spirit of God." Certainly the wonders of the universe are becoming every day more numerous and impressive, so that, if one is sure that God made it, the more startling instances that can be unearthed of his skill, the surer one is that one is right. This is however no new enterprise. The old Bridgewater treatises of nearly a century ago proposed to illustrate and confirm by the scientific knowledge of the time "the power, wisdom and goodness of God, as manifested in his creation." One of these volumes boldly explains "The adaptation of Nature to the Moral and Intellectual Constitution of Man."

So it seems agreed that a religion is something fundamentally essential to human welfare. But what *is* religion?

II

THE word religion is perhaps the vaguest of all the important nouns in our language. Innumerable pathetic efforts have been made to define the most indefinite of terms. Benjamin Kidd in his "Social Evolution" busied himself by collecting definitions of religion, from Seneca to Dr. Martineau. Kant says that religion consists in our recognizing all our duties as Divine commands; while Ruskin declares: "Our national religion is the performance of Church ceremonies, and preaching of soporific truths (or untruths) to keep the mob quietly at work while we amuse ourselves." Huxley and John Stuart Mill, not reckoning any more with God, still liked the word Religion and found it to be reverence and love for ideal conduct and our efforts to pursue it during our life. Alexander Bain, following a new trail, says that "The religious sentiment is constituted by the Tender Emotion, together with Fear, and the Sentiment of the Sublime." Solomon Reinach, reaching far back into primitive religious practices, defines religion as *Un ensemble de scrupules qui font obstacle au libre exercice de nos facultés*—which, as a critic remarked, would describe a university board of trustees just as well.

All these definitions are about as individual and personal as the portraits of the men who forged them. So far as Europe and the United States are concerned all religious people, and most irreligious ones, would concur fundamentally in Dr. Martineau's view that "Religion is a belief in an everlasting God; that is, a Divine mind and will, ruling the Universe, and holding moral relations with mankind." God is to be feared, praised, worshipped, beseeched and obeyed. We do his will when we attend the ceremonies prescribed by the particular church to which we belong. Certain forms of sacrifice, fasting, and penitence are deemed pleasing to God and essential to the soul's welfare. It is the duty of Christians to follow the straight and narrow way of salvation described in the New Testament, through belief in their Saviour. They are commanded to love their neighbors as themselves—and neighbors are those who hold the true faith. All these things would be commonly accepted as salient features of religion in Christian lands.

So much for the attempts to define religion. Would it not be better in the interest of clarity to regard religion, not as a mystic and essential entity, but as a label which we attach to one division of our beliefs, emotions, and deeds? We have many moods, fears, hopes, aspirations, scruples, loves, and abhorrences. Some of these we are wont to call religious, but not so very many. We take various and varying action every day of our life; we make decisions and pass judgments. A part of our decisions and judgments affecting ourselves, and especially others, we classify as religious, and a much smaller part of our overt behavior. Secular affairs may well engage us from Monday morning to Saturday night while on the great day of the Sun a goodly portion of our population goes to church and remains there for an hour mayhap. This is deemed a religious performance. If one goes to his office on Tuesday and writes out a cheque to the order of the Charity Organization Society, is that a religious performance? If so, would it be a religious act to write a cheque to replenish the funds of Paterson strikers? Pure religion and undefiled before our God and Father has been described as visiting the fatherless and widows in their affliction, but does this include the widows and children of labor agitators? So even if we give up trying to define religion we are beset with difficulties when we try to distinguish between what we are inclined to call "religious" as over against things of this world where such adjectives as holy and sinful seem inapplicable.

The word religion represents something that practically all those who have turned their thoughts on the matter regard as an essential to social and individual welfare; as the great and only barrier against moral corruption and intolerable anarchy. Nevertheless they come to no agreement on what religion is, or even what things are religious. They agree only in thinking that those who differ from them have a false religion. St. Paul was sure that

St. Peter was wrong; Luther denounced Erasmus; Calvin, Serve-
tus; Kant could not stand for Voltaire's God; Huxley was certain
that the Archbishop of Canterbury harbored fantastic super-
stitions.  The author of "Troasm" sees no hope unless we give up
the most fundamental elements of older religions and substitute
recently revealed scientific discoveries in regard to human motives
and their purposeful modification in the cause of righteousness.

What about false religion?  It seems to abound, according to
all accounts.  Does its noxious falsity offset its precious religious-
ness?  Writers often give the impression that they think religion
in general essential and yet condemn pretty much everything
that passes for religious among their fellow creatures throughout
the world.  The Roman emperors are applauded by Gibbon for
cherishing religions that suited the tastes and traditions of the
various peoples of the Empire on the ground that they were all
good and useful so long as they did not, like that of the Christians,
refuse due respect for the imperial government and the goddess
Roma.  This seems a consistent recognition of the value of religion and the need of gracious toleration.  It has not been the
view promoted by Christians; yet something of the attitude of
the Roman government seems to lurk in religious discussion today.  It is urged, for instance, that religion is good for "the
Masses," even if their beliefs seem a quite absurd set of notions
to the person who advances the argument.

In this welter of confused thinking its seems some gain to give
up the idea that there is an entity or supernatural agency, religion, which can be discovered and defined.  The case is at least
somewhat simplified by resolving religion into thoughts, beliefs,
moods, revelations, scruples, judgments and acts which take place
under auspices which would be generally pronounced religious
by participants or on-lookers.  We cannot hope for any very
precise agreement even on the basis of the older conceptions of
religion, much less if one takes account of the newer developments to be mentioned in due time.

What may be called religious phenomena, that is, what has gone
on and goes on under religious auspices, seem to fall into two rather
easily distinguishable classes.  Santayana, who defines religion as

poetry mistaking itself for science, distinguishes between *primary* and *secondary* religion.   The first takes the form of convincing personal experiences and peace and comfort, lifting of intolerable burdens, sense of security, relief from perplexity, active fighting for God and his righteousness and ultimately a fine sense of merging into the eternal.   Then there is a mere acquiescence, an unquestioning pursuit of sanctified routine—going to church, singing the appointed hymns, listening to the lessons or sermons, repeating the creed or litany, following the prayers and greeting one's neighbors when the service is over.   In Catholic churches there is more warmth and symbolism in the ancient ceremonies—the Mass, the resonant Latin, the ringing of bells, the swinging of smoking censers, and the richly garbed officient.   And it should not be forgotten that over two thirds of the Christians of the world are either Roman Catholics or belong to the Greek Orthodox Church.   In the United States the Catholics claim about a fifth of the population.

Each one can come to terms in his own mind as to how much of his religion is primary, how much obedience to habit; in what respects he feels strongly, in how much he merely accedes and obeys.   The range of varieties of religious experience, as William James names his book, are tremendous, from the light-hearted choir boy cheerfully chanting the recessional and looking forward to a Sunday dinner, to Saint John of the Cross in his cell, who sought to mortify joy, hope, fear, and grief, to deprive himself of every natural satisfaction and to imitate Jesus, as he thought, in repudiating everything agreeable.

### III

WE come now to the main purport of this chapter.   What kind of new knowledge has placed the matter of religion in a setting so different from that in which it was conceived fifty years ago?

In the first place a great deal more is known by European and American scholars of wide-ranging religious phenomena than was possible a half a century ago.   Herbert of Cherbury, as early as the days of Charles I, denounced bitterly the provinciality of Christian controversies.   He maintained that the belief in God, in man's responsibility to him, and in a future life of rewards and punishments, had existed among men everywhere and always— although fearfully disguised was this natural religion by priestly imposture. Spinoza analyzed rather coldly the religion of his remote ancestors and his writings charmed Matthew Arnold. But with the mastering of Sanscrit, of Pali, of Chinese, of Egyptian hieroglyphics and Mesopotamian cuneiform, and of Pahlavi, an incredible addition was made to the scanty stock of information upon which previous estimates of religion had been formed. Christianity took its place for the first time in a large group of still more ancient forms of belief, each with its venerable wisdom and teachings in regard to man's duties and fate.

During the period in which the comparative study of highly developed religions was progressing, travellers and missionaries were busy reporting the religious practices of wholly illiterate tribes in Africa, the Americas, Australasia and the isles of the sea. These reports contained suggestions respecting the assumptions and myths upon which the more sophisticated religions had been built. This invited attempts to surprise primitive survivals in the early portions of the Old Testament, in the Vedas and the Homeric poems. And such attempts have proved highly successful; if sometimes painfully disconcerting to the old type of believer.

A second and rather unexpected contribution to the understanding of religious scruples, emotions and aspirations has come with the recognition of the overwhelming importance of childhood; not merely the so-called childhood of races, but the childhood of each and every man and woman. It has been shown that a great part of the general impressions which remain with us through life are gained in childhood and are never very seriously modified. As Mr. Trotter has pointed out, it is just those beliefs which were inculcated or absorbed in childhood which retain the most inescapable hold on us and which it seems perverse and unholy to question. This fact was not formerly recognized in dealing with religion. It is now eagerly grasped by many as the golden key for unlocking previously mysterious doors and seeing within them the forgotten survivals of earlier days.

The third and far more distasteful suspicion is that many extreme perturbations of human emotions, which have been deemed divine and holy manifestations of saintliness, suggest common enough dislocations and exaggerations which, if not cloaked with religion, would land one in an insane asylum.

In addition to the newer types of criticism suggested by the (1) comparison and interplay of other religions than our own; (2) the recognition of highly primitive elements in all religions; (3) the reckoning with the survival of childish impressions; and (4) with the possibly pathological nature of mystic experiences, we should take note of two more novel factors in our efforts to assess religious matters today.   There is (5) an historic trend toward secularization, that is, the reduction of the number of the thoughts and deeds of mankind which display themselves under religious guise; (6) the weakening of the old belief that religion is essential to right conduct in a worldly sense, for this seems to decline *pari passu* with the shrinking of the dominions of religion.   Here we have six fairly new and at present very conspicuous considerations in handling those aspects of experience which are commonly called religious.   These will be taken up in turn.

IV

It is obvious that, whether one is engaged rather dully in routine religious practices or is filled with religious fervor, he consciously or unconsciously refers his acts and feelings to a remote past. That is, without a substantial historic background he could neither act nor feel as he does.   As it was in the beginning, is now, and ever shall be, lurks behind religious security.   Accordingly the recently developed study of comparative and especially of primitive religious phenomena is bound to make far clearer than ever before the heavy traditional element which is to be discovered in even the most novel formulations of religious beliefs.   Veneration for the remote past, for the long accepted assumptions, for the incomparable wisdom to be found in the sayings of ancient seers and in venerable books, are in all the more advanced religions— in India, China as well as in the Western World—primary in establishing religious faith.

Syncretism is the name given by historians of religion to the re-combinations and blendings and modification of traditional elements which enter into all seemingly new religions. And, as Hatch, Reville, Legge, Harnack, Glover, Conybeare and many others have shown, Christianity is in no way an exception. It is explicitly founded on the ancient religious beliefs of the Hebrews, but many tributaries which did not have their origin in the hills of Palestine augmented its stream during its development under the Roman Empire. The religious beliefs of the Hebrews had already been deeply affected by Mesopotamian and even Egyptian influences. Christmas and Easter, for example, far antedate, as festivals, their adoption by the Christian churches.

It is assumed by most Christians, ignorant of history, that the teachings of Jesus were highly novel and that the prevailing of Christianity was so startling an event as alone to prove its divine character. Neither of these beliefs can be held by one familiar with scholarly books on these matters. There is a gap between the latest books contained in the Old Testament and the earliest writings in the New. This "period of silence" has been narrowed down to somewhat less than two centuries, by the recognition that Daniel, for instance, and certain of the Psalms were written in the second century before Christ. "But recent research," according to one of the chief scholars in this field, R. H. Charles, "has shown that no such period of silence ever existed. In fact, we are now in a position to prove that these two centuries were in many respects centuries of greater spiritual progress than any two that had preceded them in Israel." A number of the religious works of this intermediate period still survive, "written probably for the most part in Galilee, the home of the religious seer and mystic. Not only was the development of a religious but also of an ethical character. In both these respects the way was prepared by this literature for the advent of Christianity, while a study of the New Testament makes it clear that its writers had been brought up in the atmosphere created by these books and were themselves directly acquainted with many of them." Jesus it seems was a son of his time so far as his views and admonitions are reported to us. Many of them can be readily duplicated or paralleled in the contemporaneous religious literature of Judea. The fatherhood of God and the kingdom not of this world had been already proclaimed. This discovery, be it observed, *in no way diminishes the value or importance* of the gospels; it merely serves to reduce the miraculous and revelationary element in their origin, hitherto claimed for them.

As for the spread of Christianity it was gradual, and turbid with the controversies between innumerable sects, calling themselves the only true followers of Christ. Harnack, one of the greatest certainly of contemporaneous church historians, shows how the revised beliefs spread to Jewish communities scattered over the Roman Empire. It will be remembered that Jesus addressed a terrible rebuke to the clergy of his time, reported in the twenty-third chapter of Matthew. Among his many accusations was that "Ye compass sea and land to make one proselyte; and when he is become so, ye make him twofold more a son of hell than yourselves." This prejudice was shared by gentiles throughout the Roman Empire. The Jews had far more missionary ardor than used to be supposed. If, as it would now appear, the teachings of Jesus were in accord with the advanced religious and ethical ideals of his people, his disciples, who accepted him as the long-expected Jewish Messiah, could find ready converts among the many Jewish communities throughout the Roman Empire. Towards three hundred years elapsed however between the death of Jesus and the effective acceptance of the new religion by Constantine. This was no prompt or surprising victory compared with that of the religion of Mohammed, which spread with really miraculous speed and exeeds in its adherents today all the Protestant Christians in the world.

v

BUT Christianity is itself a recent religion compared with all in the way of religious beliefs and practices which preceded it. The seven sacraments of the Roman Catholic Church were first formulated clearly by Peter Lombard in his famous textbook, the

*Sentences,* less than eight centuries ago. Two or three of these are accepted by the Protestants. Even the Old Testament, which in its earlier portions contains many primitive ideas, is recent compared with man's history. The belief in a soul, in the gods and their propitiation, in a life to come, are all so very much more ancient! The thoughtful Greeks and Romans were quite as "monotheistic" as the Christians through the Middle Ages. The Stoics often talked of "God." It is true they used "the gods" too, which was equivalent to our "heavenly powers." Catholics accept a great number of beings which the Romans would have called gods, Christ, the Virgin, angels, archangels, and the saints, to whom they appeal, as well as Satan and various other wicked spirits. The Protestants say less of the devil and his minions nowadays, but cling to the persons of the Trinity, and deny not the angels, who surely are supernatural and god-like beings, as the classical peoples would have estimated them.

Vestiges of what modern archæologists are impelled to class as religious observances are indicated in prehistoric remains and are reported from every known tribe of illiterate people whether in Melanesia, Polynesia, or the Americas. As George Foot Moore says, it is the prevailing opinion of anthropologists that "existing races on a lower plane of culture have religions whose present state implies long antecedents, and that among the remains of palæolithic culture in some regions objects are preserved which, if they were modern, would unhesitatingly be interpreted as religious." It would clearly be out of place to go into details in recalling the various classes of precautions which primitive peoples have been wont to take in dealing with the mysterious "powers" or virtues of things which they believed endangered or promised to benefit them. It was an old idea to derive religion from fear, and Dr. Moore deriving it from "the common impulse of self-preservation" is expressing a similar view. The self-preservation would of course include precautions of all kinds, veneration for the totem, and a strict observance of taboos. Later anthropologists tend to see a period of "mana" or realization of the various powers of things preceding the birth of animism, which came with

the assumption of a sort of spirit or soul, with its human-like desires and purposes.    Such a spirit could be lodged in animals and
plants, stars and rocks.

All this however touches human nature so congenially that it
needs hardly such lengthy disquisitions as are devoted to it.    Solomon Reinach reports that, as a child, he had a blue shell which
seemed to be a faithful protector.    William James says that when
the earthquake happened in California in 1906 it shook his bed-
room as a terrier would shake a rat.    "It was to my mind absolutely an entity that had been waiting all this time holding back its
activity, but at last saying 'Now go it,' and it was impossible not
to conceive it as animated by a will, so vicious was the temper
displayed."    Reinach's shell was an up-to-date fetich, and William James enjoyed the animistic dismay of a savage.

Totemism, the reverence for ancestral animals, sometimes plants,
to which groups in a tribe ascribe their origin is, as Reinach expresses it, "the hypertrophy of the social instinct."    We still have
our mascots and animal emblems, such as the American eagle
and the two-headed, now extinct, Austrian bird.    On any British
consulate one can see the lion and the unicorn.    These things are altogether too contemporaneous to seem very strange when we
reflect that apprehensions and current precautions are not unlike
in us all, and have been since culture began.    We can detect
tendencies to fetichism, totemism, animism and the observance of
taboos, with not a little lust for magic, in our feelings and sometimes in our behavior.

All these primitive elements continue to find religious sanction
in one form or another although they tend to take a symbolic
form.    For example, savages are commonly fearful of the dead.
They take elaborate precautions to prevent their return.    The relatives may paint themselves black, and cautiously close all entrances to the hut so that the spirit may not recognize them or
penetrate into the house.    Lewis Browne finds here the traditional
background of deep mourning and of closing the shutters of a
house in which a dead person lies.    The modern woman does
not have the origin of her crape in mind; she sees in it a symbol of
grief and thereby publicly proclaims herself a stricken being.

The closing of the shutters seems a decent exclusion of the sunshine of life during a period of sadness. Today the scattering of rice on bride and groom is no longer a symbol of the blessing of fertility and has degenerated into a conventional jest, which only gives the porter of the sleeping car cause of murmuring.

It is from primitive beginnings, ignorant and squalid though some may seem to us now, that modern anthropologists believe that the higher and nobler conceptions of the immortal soul, of one supreme God, maker of heaven and earth, of salvation, heaven and hell, all must inevitably have originated. The visions of the night have played a great part in the creation of ancestor worship, which is of profound religious significance in India, China and Japan, though singularly enough it has no such significance in the West. But in dreams one not only saw and talked to the dead, he might himself leave the body and wander forth and so realize that he had a double or spirit far freer in its movements than his heavy body. As he viewed the dead he could see that their spirits had departed.

As these discoveries, which have come with the study of religions of today and yesterday, are more and more widely known, in spite of the ignorance and expostulations of those who see in them a very real menace to the perpetuation of their particular beliefs, they will inevitably influence both the older and newer religious ideas. To the earlier defenders of existing religious systems the discovery that "Religion" was a universal characteristic of the human race came as a comfortable and efficient weapon to be used against supposed "atheists." They did not suspect that the new knowledge might influence their own particular faith far more potently than the talk of any atheist.

VI

ALONG with the examination of the religious beliefs and practices of primitive and ancient peoples has appeared another approach to the subject of religion. This has to do with childhood, when religious ideas and scruples are implanted. Once it was supposed that religion was the product of the mature and inspired thought of highly exceptional religious experts. Whatever contributions these may have made, they are slight compared with the childish impressions derived from father and mother and such religious instruction as reached us when children. Bryan exhibited through his life no more knowledge of religious matters than he could easily have acquired at ten years of age. Sermons of the commoner sort contain only what both preacher and audience accepted before they were grown up. Religion does not tend to mature in most cases. It is what we learned at our mother's knee. In later life we are preoccupied with business and amusement, and there is no time to keep up with the course of religious investigation, even if we had the slightest disposition to do so. Billy Sunday talks as a big husky boy to other boys and girls. Even distinguished scientific men solemnly discuss the relation of Religion to Science, when, if they but stopped to think, they would find they were assuming that they know all about Religion, without having given it much thought since childhood, although they will readily admit that after a lifetime's work they know very little about Science. Paul says confidently that "When I was a child, I spake as a child, I felt as a child, I thought as a child: now that I am become a man, I have put away childish things." Alas; this does not take place with many of us. The majority of men and women do not heartily revise many of their earlier impressions after thirteen or fourteen years of age. Only exceptional ones learn enough more to criticize and recast thoroughly and continuously, as the years go on, what they were given in childhood. This is rather specially true of religious beliefs, which are matters of simple faith and not supposed to be subject to individual modification, rectification or rejection.

The very language of the Christian religion is that of the family. We are all God's children. There is the Heavenly Father and, among the Catholics, the pure and devoted Mother, whose arms are open to those who call upon her; Christ is the son and elder brother. The saints form a single family, whether they be quick or dead, "though now divided by the stream—the narrow stream of death," "part hath crossed the flood and part is crossing now."

The divine shepherd tends his flock, repels the wolves of sin, seeks
the wandering sheep when it goes astray.

> *Saviour, who thy flock art feeding,*
> *With the shepherd's kindest care,*
> *All the feeble gently leading,*
> *While the lambs thy bosom share.*
>
> *Never from Thy pasture roving,*
> *Let them be the lion's prey;*
> *Let thy tenderness, so loving,*
> *Keep them through life's dangerous way.*

To all the timid and sensitive as well as to the downright "sick
souls," life is beset with menace, self-reproach, perplexity, disap-
pointment, bereavement, the sense of ill-usage, and sometimes
with the keenest and most poignant suffering. We hunger for a
defender and protector and one who will right our wrongs. We
thirst for assured tenderness and love in a hard and fickle world.
We long to rest in someone's loving arms, to return to our mother's bosom and have our tears wiped away. We become children
and fall back on the child's hopes of comfort and reassurance.

> *Discouraged in the work of life,*
> *Disheartened by its load,*
> *Shamed by its failures or its fears,*
> *I sink beside the road;*
> *But only let me think of Thee,*
> *And then new heart springs up in me.*
>
> (Samuel Longfellow)

It would not mend matters to cite Lucretius at this point—that
we are but a negligible and fortuitous concourse of atoms, dissi-
pated at death; that we have always been grousing, and that even
if a longer life were granted us we should go on sulking; that no
matter how long we live it will make no difference in the eternity
we shall be dead. It would be like interrupting a Christmas party
to read an article from Hastings' "Encyclopædia of Religion and
Ethics" to prove the unauthenticity of the accepted date of

Jesus' birth, or reading Kempf's "Psychopathology" to the love-intoxicated St. Theresa, or "The Golden Bough" to an adorant of the Mass.

But the solaces of religion are not confined to moods of apathy and suffering; it meets our requirements for ultimate glory and victory, for successful conflict and the utter undoing of those who have refused to open their eyes to the light vouchsafed to us and ours.

> *With Thy favored sheep O place me;*
> *Nor among the goats abase me;*
> *But to thy right hand up-raise me.*
>
> *While the wicked are confounded,*
> *Doomed to flames of woe unbounded,*
> *Call me, with Thy saints surrounded.*
> (Thomas of Celano, XIII Century)

And the faithful can join the divine cohorts, and be participants in final conquest of evildoers, and reign forever. What heart so torpid, whether of believer or unbeliever, can, without heightened beat, read:

> *The Son of God goes forth to war,*
> *A kingly crown to gain:*
> *His blood-red banner streams afar:*
> *Who follows in his train?*
>
> *Who best can drink his cup of woe,*
> *Triumphant over pain,*
> *Who patient bears his cross below,*
> *He follows in His train.*[1]

[1] A very interesting article on "The Psychology of Hymns" by Kimball Young, was published in the journal of Abnormal Psychology, Vol. XX, pp. 391 ff. The writer finds that well over half the popular hymns suggest infantile regression or the hope of final reward. "Simple, obvious themes, childlike expressions, much repetition; these, coupled with the emotional arousal from musical accompaniment, are the outstanding characteristics of hymns. The hymns have one dominant motif as a rule—a central point which expresses the infantile feelings in the socially acceptable, that is, symbolic, form." Whatever the merits of this contention it illustrates the novel way of looking at "praising the Lord."

## VII

RELIGIOUS moods in rare cases take on an intense, obsessive form, in which mystic intimacies with God or the Saviour occur. There may be ecstasies which the subject does not think of as religious; but there are scattered through the history of Christianity (as well as the history of primitive and highly sophisticated religions) instances of absorbing interest in which the saint finds himself ineffably one with the divine. Special works are devoted to mysticism, of which William James' "The Varieties of Religious Experience" is one of the altogether most remarkable. More recent works are cited in Leuba's "The Psychology of Religious Mysticism," which excellently presents and discusses many mystics not alluded to by James.

It is impossible to take up these unusual instances of saintliness. One unfamiliar with the literature will be shocked and repelled by many of the experiences reported. Modern psychiatrists will readily resort to hysteria and sex-repression to dispose of some of them. They are to be found at almost every level of culture and are connected with artificial intoxication of various kinds, fastings, stimulants, narcotics, excessive exertion, macerations—but by no means always. In solemn ecclesiastical conclaves mystics have been canonized and beatified long after their death. We may leave this phase of religious phenomena with the observation of Professor Leuba: "There are those who are satisfied when they have described these states as divine possession or union. But nothing is thereby explained, . . . for, the term 'divine' in itself throws no light upon these facts. It is the reverse: *'divine' gets whatever significance it may possess from the experiences to which it is applied.*" In short it may be that the ideas of the "divine" were derived from what the "possessed" person did or said, as in the case of the Pythian priestess of Delphi, who wrought herself into a frenzy before she delivered her oracles. One's assessment of mysticism will always depend fundamentally on whether he is looking for divine revelations or is not. I take it Professor Leuba is not, whereas Marguerite Marie Alacoque, born in 1647, *knew* that Christ had told her most simply and directly, "I have chosen you for my bride."

I infer that a good many persons have some kind of mystic experience during their lives. Dreams often seem revelations. There are in almost all cases intimations in usual human experience of those things that appear in more grandiose fashion among the mystics. James' analysis of asceticism is very ingenious, but more recent psychopathological studies have gravely altered the analysis and evaluation of mystic phenomena. In general the Protestant sects are much less hospitable to reports of saintliness than the Catholics. They seem to feel that God reveals himself in less spectacular fashion.

## VIII

THERE is a persistent claim, often finding expression even today, that idealism, morality, decency, and fairness depend upon and are re-enforced by religious beliefs. No one thinks that the godly are always good, but only that the godless have thrown off the restraints which hold them back from a life of heartless self-indulgence and wicked disregard for the rights of others. The relation of religion to ethics is a far more obscure and intricate question than would appear at first sight. That at least may be safely said. There has been much of a religious nature in the past which had to do merely with prudential measures in making terms with gods, who were themselves no better than they should be, and with fighting off devils. Then the Christian theologians have disputed much over "good works"; and Calvin taught the Presbyterians to hold that every man and woman was predestinated before the foundation of the world to heaven or hell, without any reckoning with his earthly conduct. The number of the saved and damned is, according to the Presbyterian confession of faith, "so certain and definite that it cannot be either increased or diminished." Yet Presbyterians are not conspicuous either as saints or sinners in spite of their theory of the hopeless irrelevancy of daily behavior to salvation.

There is space here available for only a few observations on the modern phases of religious faith and works. They would seem to be drifting apart. Careful observers, such as Reinach and Professor Shotwell, detect an unmistakable tendency toward the secularization of human affairs. That is to say, less and less goes on under religious guise. So rich and varied and ever-changing are human preoccupations today that it is impossible to bring them within the ancient religious categories. The percentage that seems in accord with God's behests, or in violation of them, tends to decrease.

A few instances may be given: modern physicians do not assume that the devil is at the bottom of disease; they do not resort to prayers and exorcisms but to serums and the knife. The provisions of the "Rituale Romanum" for dissipating an approaching storm raised by evil spirits would seem futile to most of our countrymen. Treaties between nations are no longer concluded in the name of the Holy Trinity as they were a hundred years ago. No one would longer justify negro slavery, as did the Southern clergy before the Civil War, on the ground that Noah had cursed Ham and his offspring for making light of the old man's drunken relaxation. These examples might be multiplied indefinitely. So it is clear that not only have modern business corporations failed to assume the religious tinge of the mediæval guilds; and telephones and motor cars to ask for religious sanction; but many previously heavily sanctified affairs of life have become secularized. It is this worldly tendency that has created suspicions with regard to the older claims that the supernatural directs and controls human improvement.

## IX

A BROOKLYN clergyman, Richard Storrs, whose learning and eloquence would overwhelm the most wary, wrote a large book over fifty years ago on "The Divine Origin of Christianity Indicated by Its Historical Effects." Further increase of knowledge and less eloquence have produced reservations in the minds of historical students. But such reservations are easily countered if one ac-

cepts the Rev. Storrs' warning that Christianity like the sun may
be hidden at times behind thick clouds. "It may seem grotesquely
or hideously tinted, by steaming vapors rising to intercept it from
forges and factories, from chemical laboratories, or from the
noisome reek of slums. But these pass away, and the sunshine
continues: the same today, when we untwist its strand into the
crimson, gold, and blue, as when it fell on the earliest bowers
and blooms of the earth."

Warming with his argument and the unfailing abundance of
incontrovertible evidence as he comes down through the ages, Dr.
Storrs closes triumphantly: "Whatever may be our just criticism
of modern society—or whatever on the other hand, may be our
confidence in ethics, legislations, improved industries, widened
commerce, the general distribution of letters and knowledge—it
seems almost impossible to doubt that the religion of Jesus is at
this hour the commanding factor in whatever is best in the character and the progress of persons and states. It has not merely
rectified particular abuses, removed special evils, exerted a benign
and salutary influence on local institutions. It has formed and
instructed a general Christian consciousness in the world, which
is practically ubiquitous and commanding in Christendom: to
which institutions, tendencies, persons, are more and more distinctly amenable; which judges all by an ideal standard; to which
flattering concessions to wealth, to power, to genius or culture,
are inherently offensive."

It was perhaps easier to write these lines in the early eighties
than it would be now. The crimson, gold and blue have been
notably obscured in the years that followed. But flattering concessions to genius and culture have at least grown no more servile
in the twentieth century than in the nineteenth. This seems the
only striking instance of the constancy of Christian influence.

To claim however that the disappearance of witchcraft and
slavery, and the introduction of religious toleration were the effects of Christian teachings seems not to stand inspection. The
leaders of the various churches have most rarely raised their voices
against what seem to us now ancient and happily extinct atrocities.
They were not the ones who did away with them. On the con-

trary they very generally supported religious intolerance, accepted slavery, blessed war, and cursed those who suspected the gloomy deceptions of witchcraft. So much for the arguments of the Reverend Dr. Storrs.

The clergy have not been ethical innovators. Leo XIII in 1891 summed up what until very lately has been the theory of the Protestant churches, not alone of the Catholic. Labor is the painful expiation of sin; the rich and the poor are ordained by nature to maintain the equilibrium of the body politic:

" 'Cursed be the earth in thy work; in thy labor thou shalt eat of it all the days of thy life.' In like manner, the other pains and hardships of life shall have no end or cessation on earth; for the consequences of sin are bitter and hard to bear; and they must be with man as long as life lasts. To suffer and endure, therefore, is the lot of humanity; let men try as they may, no strength and no artifice will ever succeed in banishing from human life the ills and troubles which beset it."

In preventing strife between rich and poor and making it impossible, "the efficacy of Christianity is marvelous and manifold. First of all there is nothing more powerful than religion (of which the Church is the interpreter and guardian) in drawing the rich and poor together, by reminding each class of its duties to the other, and especially the duties of justice."

One sees slight evidence in the account of contemporaneous labor disputes that issues and adjustments turn often on the marvelous and manifold efficacy of Christianity. Nor have they in the past. When the German peasants in Luther's time drew up their twelve godly articles based on evangelical fairness, Luther sided not with them but with the possessing class, and urged the latter to use all bloody measures necessary to put down the rebels on the ground that "they deserved death of body and soul many times over."

When we come to daily observations we cannot distinguish between the believer and the unbeliever by his conduct, by his honesty, generosity, and other homely virtues. Bradstreet does not reckon with religion in establishing one's credit. The custom house official would not pass unexamined the luggage of one professing the Athanasian creed or submitting a certificate of good standing in the Brick Church. The rain continues to fall on the just and unjust alike; and, as Jesus reminds us, in a passage almost universally neglected by his followers: think ye that they were offenders above all men in Jerusalem on whom the tower in Siloam fell? As late as 1897 the horrible fire in a Paris charity bazaar was attributed by a French priest to God's vengeance on those who rejected the teachings of the Catholic Church. But in general this primitive notion is on the decline. It was not widely urged when San Francisco and Yokohama were desolated by earthquakes. These horrors were generally accepted as the result of geological episodes, not as "acts of God." Scientific knowledge has spread far enough to discredit the older cosmology. As Samuel Butler says, it was not hard in his boyhood for the ordinary English clergyman to think of God's moulding Adam in the rectory garden, and retiring to the greenhouse to form Eve. Those who cling to a heavily anthropocentric universe have now to alter their lines of arguments. Henry Drummond set this example late in the nineteenth century.

It has become apparent that there have been many, many elaborate systems of religious belief, of which the various Christian churches and sects afford modern instances. It is not the aim of this chapter to appraise these as to the truth and value of their claims. It is possible to have hopes and aspirations to which none of them has assigned a prominent place—for example, the increase of human knowledge and imagination as over against ancient dogma. The effort to engineer life in the light of already existing intelligence would in itself be perhaps as holy a task as any hitherto essayed by saint or martyr. Contrasting St. Anthony's fierce struggles against temptation in the Egyptian sands and the ideal community described by Rabelais, where desire merged into prompt fruition, Havelock Ellis wisely closes his "Dance of Life" with the suggestion of "how vast a field lies open for human activity between the Thebaid on one side and Thelema on the other."

## XII—THE ARTS

*By* LEWIS MUMFORD

I

DURING a great part of history, the arts were an indivisible part of the life of a community. It is difficult, as Karl Buecher pointed out, to say where work leaves off and art begins: drama is in origin the significant rehearsal of the "thing done," the planting of seed and the gathering of harvest; song and dance rhythmically recapture the ecstasy of courtship or martial triumph; painting and sculpture visualize divinity, or realize, in more perfect composure, the forms of men and landscapes; to live is to experience art. Among all the occupations known to men and practised by them down to modern times, the only one that was degraded, to the exclusion of art, in the process of conducting the work or shaping the materials or sharing in civic life, was that of the miner. From the miserable slaves that worked the silver mines of Athens to the serfs that remained in the mines of Great Britain up to the nineteenth century, the miner alone was condemned—along with the public executioner—to exist without benefit of the arts.

The industrial period begins with a reversal of this condition. The miner develops the steam engine and invents the railroad; for a while, the steam engine, the railroad, and a great array of mechanical contrivances occupy the centre of men's activities; and the one art that throughout human history had been a symbol of degradation dominates the scene, displacing human desires and human standards, and erecting, as an Iron Calf for the multitude to worship, the notions of mechanical efficiency and merely pecuniary wealth. Every art feels the shock of this change: living becomes subordinate to working, and working is no longer enriched by the whole personality. The new working class, as it is called, can alas! neither produce art nor respond to it; the intricate folk dances disappear; the folk songs lose both in fun and in depth; the manufactured furniture, rugs, curtains, and dress materials that take the place of the old products of handicraft lose all æsthetic value; by the middle of the nineteenth century the age of non-art has, apparently, begun.

Was the displacement of art that marked the introduction of machinery a permanent or a temporary process? It was impossible to answer this question in John Ruskin's time; but by now I think we may say confidently that the process was only a temporary one. While those who value the traditional arts are chiefly conscious of the loss—and as I shall show the loss was vast and widespread—we are now also conscious of the fact that industrialism has produced new arts, associated with the application of precise methods and machine tools. Will these new industrial arts altogether replace the traditional ones? Will the traditional arts recover some of their lost ground? Has the machine age developed a new æsthetic, or is its bias essentially anti-æsthetic? Will the expression of the human personality through the arts regain its ancient place and will art once more accompany all human activity? These are some of the questions we must ask. Let us take stock of the whole environment before we attempt to answer them.

## II

WHAT was the effect of modern methods of production and intercourse upon the cities and countrysides of the Western World? The primary result, without doubt, was the wholesale defacement of the landscape and the reckless misuse and perversion of almost every natural resource; above all, the stark misuse of the workers themselves.

The coal that was brought to the surface to run the engines in the new factories resulted in the horrid debris of the pithead;

carried by railways into the new towns, it created the smokepall which shut out sunlight, reduced the aerial colors to foggy grey, and, falling in a sooty film which effaced every gradation of color in street and building, it sank into the lungs and the pores of the industrial denizen. In certain industries, the escaping gases or finely divided particles destroyed the surrounding vegetation; while in others the refuse dumped into the streams killed the animal life and made the water unfit to drink or to swim in. The dissolution of solid forms in the later paintings of Turner and in those of Whistler in the next generation was partly a witness of the early coal régime. Without the soft obliteration of fog, the landscape was hideous: the sole beauty that remained was that of atmosphere.

The new towns of the nineteenth century suffered as miserably as the countryside. One has only to compare the old town of Oxford with its new industrial additions to be aware of a contrast that holds throughout Western civilization. The industrial towns themselves were built entirely without art: the new parts were laid out in rectangles designed solely for convenience in sale, and the parts most necessary for purposes of recreation, namely, the waterfronts, were completely dedicated to manufacture and commerce. The town grew within the interstices formed by vast railway yards that pushed into its heart; and as a centre of culture and art the city survived with difficulty, if at all; the new civic centre was the stock exchange, and the only functions that prospered were those of sale, exchange, monetary appreciation. When the directors of the London and Northwestern rejected Watts' offer to paint appropriate frescoes on the walls of Euston Station, gratis, they merely expressed the deep contempt of the successful philistine for a purpose so foreign to early industrial enterprise as art.

In this environment architecture totally collapsed, except so far as it was still carried forward by the momentum acquired in an earlier age. There was a period in England during the eighteenth century when it seemed as if the architect would effect a reasonable transition from the stylicism of the classical revivals to a modern vernacular which would be adapted to every new purpose; some of the buildings of the time oddly anticipate the designs of modern European architects like Le Corbusier. But these forms did not survive the anti-art bias of the industrialist: useful buildings, with occasional exceptions, grew more ugly, and in natural reaction against this ugliness the architect sought by picturesque touches derived from the past to give back to the individual building the order and beauty that had once pervaded the city.

If architecture fared badly in the mass, it did even worse in the more intimate forms of decoration and furniture. In these departments a practised handicraft was eliminated by the steady introduction of labor-saving machinery—the lathe, the scroll-saw, the planing machine, the power loom; and this process was accompanied by a positive loss in design. It is hardly an exaggeration to say that from 1830 to 1890, the period when the traditional methods in all the industries were supplanted or at least modified by machine production, there is not a book, a piece of furniture, a pattern in textiles, a cup or saucer of new design which deserves a place, except as an historical curiosity, in a museum of art. While in America the rural housewife produced rugs and bedspreads of brilliant design, and while an occasional rebel against the machine system, such as William de Morgan or William Morris or John LaFarge executed wall-papers and ceramics and furniture that had warmth and beauty, the early products of the machine were for the most part destitute of any value, except as raw material—defaced.

On every hand, this period brought disruption to the traditional arts; they survived, if at all, by isolation and "backwardness," as peasant pottery survived in Brittany and Mexico, as hand-weaving persisted in Scotland and Ireland, as wood-carving continued at a low level of traditional design in the Tyrol. The reason for this is fairly plain. Under the method of handicraft, the knowledge necessary for the conduct of the arts is empirical or rule-of-thumb; it consists of rules, saws, formulæ, workshop receipts, which are handed down from craftsman to craftsman with such slow additions and improvements as experience and skill may make. The introduction of the experimental method of science, with the quickening of invention and the elaboration of new processes and methods broke up this limited but living tradition and destroyed the body of taste, the sense of proportion, fitness, fine design, which was part and parcel of the handicraft worker's knowledge. Henceforward, during the period of transition, knowledge and taste occupied different departments: the industrialist was one person, the æsthete was another; the operative was one person, the designer was another. This divorce had begun to take place, under the influence of aristocratic patronage, during the Renaissance; it was widened with the breakup of the guilds, which were the main repository of tradition; and it was carried to completion during the nineteenth century.

The quarrel between the romanticist and the utilitarian was the natural outcome of this process; and, now that we can view the spectacle at a distance, we can see that both were right. The utilitarian was right when he insisted upon living in his own age and taking advantage of the instruments this age had produced; the romanticist was right when he declared that the human personality could not be split up, and that a philosophy which arbitrarily limits our practical functions and divorces them from questions of taste and beauty is an instrument of degradation.

### III

THERE are two exceptions to this general story of depletion and decay—music and painting—for they survive and sometimes flourish in the cloister, even when the avenues of popular achievement are closed to them.

Up to the eighteenth century music was largely, but not entirely, a personal performance and an accompaniment to the other arts. It embroidered the ritual of the church; it set the figures and movements of the dance; it lightened the labors of the sailor hauling ropes or the weaver at the loom or the blacksmith at the forge, quickening the work with an appropriate rhythm, moving whole bodies of men in grand synergy. In industry, the orchestration of work by music was replaced by the impersonal processes of factory organization, in an environment whose clank and whirr and din denied all opportunities for musical accompaniment. With this divorce from labor and ritual, music ceased to pervade human life and entered upon a period of emotionally intense, but socially restricted, activity.

In a sense, music repeated on the plane of the spirit the general development of science and industry. The symphony orchestra comes into existence as a contemporary of the modern factory: with the development of machine-technique, many of the traditional instruments were remodelled during the nineteenth century, for the purpose of achieving greater accuracy and range; new ones, like the saxophone, were invented by one of the foremost manufacturers; and the technical possibility of projecting lights and colors of uniform tone and intensity led Scriabine, the composer, to attempt the orchestration of light and sound—from which it was only a step, albeit hemmed with technical difficulties, to the modern color-organ.

In the symphony orchestra, the individual performer concentrates his personal skill, but has his chief significance as a subordinate member of the whole group. The relation of the composer to the orchestra is not unlike that of the industrial engineer or designer—but there is no need to push the parallel into absurdity. The fact is that, in a period when industrialism had undermined most of the traditional arts and depleted their vitality, music flourished: from Bach to Moussorgsky one is aware of a grand succession of composers who, to all appearances, are not crippled by the experience of their generation, and who, unlike the great Victorian men of letters, do not lose a good part of their energies in bitter but ineffectual revolt. If their sonatas and symphonies are not heard on the street, if popular music becomes banal to a degree that makes the Elizabethan song or the mediæval ballad seem the work of impossibly gifted people, fine music becomes almost a religion; and the concert hall is its church.

While this fact is all to the good, and must ameliorate the general picture of the arts during the first hundred and fifty years of industrialism, one must not overlook the possibility that it bears a less favorable interpretation. It may be that music during this period has been in the same position that typography occupied during the transition from script to machine-printing. During the sixteenth and seventeenth centuries, there was a great outburst of beautiful typography; the work of the Venetian and Florentine printers was worthy, in its own way, of the great schools of painting; in their originality, the masters of type-design seemed inexhaustible. But the period of new types waned in the eighteenth century. And why? The answer is, I think, that the great types were the result of long practice in handicraft lettering; and as the tradition of manuscript writing dwindled away, the type-designer lost the basis for his art: his efforts to create original types became weaker and poorer. The new types of the nineteenth century were as bad as the new architecture; one of the last fine types, Bodoni, has an element of uncouthness and rococo exaggeration.

It may be that a similar situation exists in music. Bach used the existing church music as a basis for his own work; and in one degree or another every composer had drawn upon the singing voice and the traditional melodies of the dance and the worksong and the lullaby and the ballad. With the lapse of the singing voice, with the reduction of the musical amateur to the mere listener, one cannot be too sure that the soil out of which music grows as a personal, organic experience may not be impoverished. The perfection of mechanical transmission, which we now have in the phonograph and the radio, may result in the final rigor of death; the spread of music by mechanics may presage extinction of music as a direct spiritual experience. Let us not be deceived. The modern maker of mosaics, for instance, has almost literally a thousand colors to work with, whereas the creators of the Ravenna mosaics had only a child's palette; but our skill in design has not increased commensurately with our skill in manufacture; quite the contrary. If the process of mechanization is unfriendly to the human spirit, it will be inimical to music; and in the long run, the spirit must either assert itself or commit suicide. If the second happen, who will listen to music? If the first happen, who will bother if the factories and the sales departments find themselves glutted with unmarketable instruments of reproduction?

THE ART of painting took a somewhat different course from music. During the nineteenth century painting survived by a complete retreat from the hurly-burly and by a willingness to forego active contemporary patronage. The artists of distinction were either, like Cézanne, men with a small "independent" income who could afford, in the economic sense, to be amateurs; or, like Meryon and Van Gogh and a hundred others, they lived for long periods at the point of starvation.

The practical environment for the painter was perhaps never so unfavorable as it was during this progressive century; for the stuffy bourgeois home, filled with the bric-a-brac and claptrap of the auction room or curio shop, was not the sort of background against which a Turner, a Delacroix, or a Redon could be seen with advantage; whilst the art-museum, the form under which the treasures of the country house became available to the industrial population, harbored only the most paltry art of its time, and resolutely turned its back upon contemporary æsthetic masters. Occasionally, in France, the country where painting survived most happily during the nineteenth century, the artist was fortunate enough to have a public destination for his work, as Puvis de Chavannes had in the lecture theatre at the Sorbonne; but, for the most part, the great artists were out of touch with the bourgeois patrons and contemptuous of their demands.

It is important, perhaps, to realize that this withdrawal was not due to the painter's inability to take contemporary life and thought as materials for his art; it was rather due to the indifference of the new financial and industrial masters to any scheme of life or thought which did not in some way reinforce the dominant ideology—the belief in money-making and material comforts as the supreme end of existence. For the fact is that the great intellectual interests of the time were more completely mirrored in painting than in any other art: Turner reveals the contemporary interest in Nature; and the Pre-Raphaelites, under the influence of Ruskin, carry this so far that their work, which ranks low as art, might nevertheless have earned for them a place in the natural history museum. Corot, in a more idyllic vein, carried on this same interest in nature, treating it religiously, as an object of wonder and love; while Monet, following the lead of Constable and Delacroix—who had studied Chevreul's researches on color—carried his palette into the open air, and in his pure colors and luminous skies proclaimed the healthy joy of stirring about in the open and blinking, like an animal, at the sun—a joy which brought him close to the same source that created men of science, such as Darwin, Haeckel, Candolle.

The bourgeois patron, who wanted his wife, his mistress, or his dog represented with unctuous sentiment, looked upon the retreat of the artists with sour repugnance; the artists that pleased him, the Landseers, the Leightons, the Bouguereaux, the Delaroches, did not mock at his charities as Daumier did, or feel greater sympathy with the poor peasant than with the elegant wife of the manufacturer, as Millet did. So the patron denied the significance of the new art, and accepted it, if he accepted it at all, only after he had starved the artist himself into the grave and had found the price of the despised pictures rising steadily, like a good speculation on the stock exchange. In the new industrial society, art was still alive, but patronage was dead. By his withdrawal, the painter gained intensity; but he lost the opportunity of expressing triumphantly the interests of the collectivity, as the painters of Giotto's time expressed the universal religious interests of the community.

v

IN WHAT way did science or technology affect the situation? There were both direct and indirect relations between science and painting; and neither was altogether unimportant.

As to the actual process of using pigments, it was necessary for the painter to recover by laborious experiment a great body of data which the Renaissance painters had empirically arrived at. This involved the order of building up colors on the canvas, the testing of new colors, and the discovery of the most favorable combinations of colors for the working palette. Moreover, scientific researches into the physics of light and color established certain definite relations between the nominal color of an object and its actual color under specific conditions of light, atmosphere, reflection; Seurat, likewise, discovered in the method of pointillism a means of placing pure colors in juxtaposition to obtain a third color of purer quality than could be mixed directly on the palette; in both these departments, the effect of experimental science was a tangible one.

The indirect relations with science were perhaps equally important; for both the scientist and the artist brought to light and exhibited certain aspects of life to which the European had long been insensitive: landscape painting developed again with the advance of botany and geology: Barye, the sculptor, was a true contemporary of Geoffroy St. Hilaire, the naturalist; while Courbet's reason for not painting angels—"he had never seen any"—would have satisfied Huxley, if anyone had demanded why the constitution of angels was not investigated in the South Kensington Laboratories. In our own day, the researches of the cubists in abstract representation, and the attempt of Duchamp and Picasso and Brancusi, at a certain stage of their art, to abandon static forms and to portray the passage of solids through time or space was a response to the impulses that were becoming dominant in mathematics and physics. Do not misunderstand me: the artist does not illustrate science; the point is that as a living, thinking being he frequently responds to the same interests that a scientist does, and expresses by a visual synthesis what the scientist converts into analytical formulæ or experimental demonstrations.

There is still a third way in which science has reacted upon art. By transforming technology, the physical sciences have created new forms and patterns, in instruments of precision, in machines and grain elevators and warehouses and bridges; and the artist has seized upon these forms as fresh materials for his art. A subway station, for instance, with its regular piers, its monotonous surfaces, its sudden crystallization of color in red and green signal lights, presents an æsthetic experience. The hardness, the abstraction, the absence of surface variations, which characterize machine work, the intricate relation of parts, the lack of subtle modulations in color, the uniform illumination of electricity—all these things belong particularly to the modern world and have not, in this precise form, existed before. To these new products of exact technology the modern artist has become sensitive. Dismissed as mere utilitarian ugliness in one generation, they come back to us, through the purer experience of the artist, as things of beauty: Duchamp-Villon models a machine with the same zeal that he would model a human figure, or, seeing the world as an expression of machinery, he sees the living form itself in a mechanical aspect and creates the mechanized plastic equivalent of a horse.

As with every new idea, the discovery of the æsthetic value of machine forms has been attended by exaggeration and grotesque overemphasis: just as the impressionists, for a while, disclosed a world dissolved in color, and in the act of doing so weakened line and almost obliterated the architectonic qualities of painting, so the simpler cubists, coming upon the hard solids and voids of machinery, have forgotten that man is not a robot but an organic being, with desires, lusts, and ideals that are not represented by mechanical forms: he reacts to the sunset as well as to the dynamo, to mountains as well as to skyscrapers, to the ripple of muscles or the fresh sensuality of the body, which Renoir delighted in, as well as to the precise plunge of pistons or the uniform whirr of dynamos, to fog and mystery no less than artificial light and mathematical theorems.

The innovators, who conquer a new realm in art, often have the illusion that they have achieved possession of, or displaced, the old realms as well; but it is fairly plain that the æsthetic revolution of the world as a system of mechanics is only one of the movements of the human spirit. This does not lessen the merits of the artists who have made us sensitive to these new forms; on the contrary, they have not merely given us pictures, like those of Bracque and Duchamp in France; of Baylinson and Benton and Lozowick in America; sculptures like those of Archipenko, Brancusi, and Duchamps-Villon; and photographs like those of Stieglitz and Strand which are excellent in their own right: they have also helped to acclimate us to the world in which we live—a world in which machinery exists not only to perform useful services but to be, as far as possible, enjoyed.

Here one becomes conscious of the reciprocal functions of the arts of use and the arts of contemplation; for although they are different in origin and intention, they are forever crossing back and forward across the line that divides them. On one hand, the arts of contemplation, feeding primarily upon the religious, philosophic, and æsthetic ideas of a period or a tradition, create an independent reality. But the picture or the statue so created becomes a stimulus: he who enjoys Michelangelo is more conscious of the architecture of the human body; he who enjoys Albert Pinkham Ryder responds more intensely to the green twilight of moon over an open sea, he who enjoys Stieglitz awakens anew to the meaning of the sky. On the other hand, the arts of use, when they are perfected, produce forms which are themselves subjects for contemplation: barns, ships, grain elevators, constructed without direct æsthetic aim, become objects of happy contemplation and suggest new themes to the artists.

In periods of active culture, the inner and the outer, the contemplative and the useful, recur in the ordinary rhythm of life; and, as in science the dilemmas of the shipbuilders were an incentive to Lord Kelvin and those of the wine-growers to Pasteur, so the pure artist is none the worse for being confronted from time to time with some contemporary actuality.

One of the great difficulties of the artist's retreat during the nineteenth century was that this vital and organic relationship in the arts was almost impossible to secure; and though an isolated man of great talent, like the Englishman, Alfred Stevens, might both create the Wellington Monument and design steelware for Sheffield cutlery, it has not been until the present generation, with the application of Picasso to stage design, of Dufy to the design of cretonnes, of numerous French, Dutch, and German artists to architecture, that any such intercourse has taken place. Nevertheless, it is quite plain that the divorce of design from the act of craftsmanship, under machine production, has made the pure artist an indispensable collaborator in many departments of production: his relation to design is like that of the pure scientist to technological method. And just as technology can advance only to the extent that there is free play of hypothesis and experiment, without any subordination to immediate industrial needs, so the application of the pure arts to industrial design, in house-building, furniture making, linoleum stamping, and so forth can exist only after the contemplative arts are practised and valued for their own sake—when we prize art solely for what it gives us in immediate emotional realization or intuition.

The arts which are least fettered to material conditions, except those which they establish for their own purpose—painting and music for example—owe the smallest amount to the accidental limitations of their environment and most to their heritage and to the needs of the human personality. In the nature of things, the heritage as a whole in the arts and the human personality itself are a relatively stable thing: that which any generation contributes, either through new activities or through technical achievements, is little in comparison with what art and life have deposited in the past. It is this freedom from the contemporary and the contiguous that gives the arts their great part in the economy of the personality: for the artist not merely bears the stamp of his environment; he also has a means of reacting upon it and giving it, in one degree or another, a different stamp. A man who loves the human body, as Rodin did, or who seizes obscure moments of mystic insight, as Redon and Ryder did, has an even more essential part to play in a machine age than the artist who responds solely to the mechanical aspects of our environment; for he gives freedom to the expression of the personality as a whole, whereas the dominant routine may curb such expression and dehumanize the personality. In so far as our age has been prostrated and paralyzed by the machine—and in many important respects this is true—the need for a superficially unrelated art, an art, that is, more deeply related to life and personality, has become greater. In literature, a Shakespeare or a Melville may be more important for us than a Shaw; in philosophy, Mr. Santayana may become more significant than William James, precisely because the remoter writers stand outside the conventions that we so helplessly conform to. The same thing holds true in the arts. A worshipper of nature, like John Marin, is no less essential to the expression of our time than an experimenter in machine forms like Marcel Duchamp. Society, as Okakura Kakuzo said, speaking out of the experience of an older culture, is the sphere of the conventions; art is the sphere of freedom. If we are to maintain our freedom we must be ready to foster, even in adverse circumstances, expression in the pure arts. These arts are not the product of any particular state of economic life; they began their existence under the province of another race of men than our own, in the Aurignacian caves, and why should we think they will cease to exist because we now sink mine-shafts and subways?

## VI

WHEN we turn from the traditional arts to the new arts that arose with the machine economy the picture becomes somewhat different. Engineering as an exact art came into existence during the Renaissance and entered upon a period of astonishing growth in the eighteenth century, the century that saw the perfected steam engine, the power loom, and the iron bridge. Even in its primitive applications, in the art of fortification in the seventeenth century, engineering showed results which placed it, at times, on the level of architecture.

With the development of mathematics and physics, the art of engineering flourished. By exact measurements, by tested formulæ, by fine calibrations, a new technique in handling materials came into existence whose success was measured, not by its incorporation of the human touch and the human personality, but by its total elimination of these characteristics. Engineering deals in known quantities: it seeks to achieve calculable results; and its highest products have been in those departments where the unknown or uncertain factors could be reduced to a minimum. By making cast-iron and steel available as a common material of art throughout Western Europe and America, metallurgy placed at our disposal a substance more pliable than stone or wood, and much more hard and tough and strong in its various possible mixtures than copper and its alloys; while in the lathe, the drill, and later the planing machine, the art of adapting this metal to the finest mechanical adjustments was made possible. The specialized machine itself is a derivative product: it is the machine-tool that is the source of our triumphs in the exact arts.

Without steel, our machine-tools might have produced instruments of exquisite accuracy, but they would have been few in number; without machine-tools, our plentiful supply of iron would have had little formal effect upon design, for this material would still have been subjected to the characteristic modifications of handicraft. Both these possibilities were explored in the early development of technology; for up to the eighteenth century the exact arts had produced as their crowning achievements only small instruments like clocks and watches, while as soon as iron came into general use, the early designer succumbed to the temptation to treat it in the fashion of handicraft stuff, with modelled and cast embellishments in the form of flowers and birds and fruit—decorations which appear equally on the barrels of cannons, on the girders of bridges, and on the vacant parts of the earliest typewriters.

In spite of numerous sorties down these blind alleys, engineering by the middle of the nineteenth century, when the Crystal Palace was built in London, had begun to find its legitimate task and its proper canons of workmanship. The first complete demonstration of its power to produce great works of art came in the construction of the Brooklyn Bridge in New York. Without doubt, the Brooklyn Bridge is one of the great masterpieces of nineteenth century engineering, and, considered by the standards of æsthetics, it is perhaps the most complete work of architecture on a large scale that the century can show—a perfect expression, in line and mass, of all that the structure demands from the engineering elements, and of all that the eye requires in their disposition.

That engineering demands imaginative design, and is not the less an art because all the æsthetic conditions must be achieved within a narrow set of material limitations, is likewise established by the large number of badly designed engineering structures that we have produced: against a Brooklyn Bridge one may pit the uncouth design of the Williamsburgh Bridge, against the Army Supply Base in South Brooklyn one might put a score of unrhythmical, boxlike factories; and in general, for every example of strong imaginative engineering one might put a dozen examples of feeble work to prove that, while the impersonal arts are as capable of beauty as the humane arts, the mere employment of mathematical formulæ or the close adherence to machine patterns is no guarantee whatever of æsthetic success.

During the last thirty years we have become more conscious of the æsthetic possibilities of the exact arts; and it is no accident that our newest instruments, the automobile and the aeroplane, are not the weakest but the best of our machined products, a distinction which they share with American kitchen equipment and bathroom fixtures. Under our very eyes, an improvement in design has taken place, transforming the awkward mass and the broken lines of the primitive auto into the unified mass and the slick stream-lines of the modern car; or, by an even greater revolution in design, turning the imperfectly related planes of the push-power aeroplane into the more buoyant, gull-like tractor plane of today, with body and wing both gaining in beauty as they were adapted more carefully to the mechanical requirements of flight. So strong, so logical are these designs that they have inevitably a powerful imaginative effect; and one does not wonder at the impulse many European architects have succumbed to, to copy the forms of the aeroplane or the steamship even in buildings where their functions are foreign or irrelevant.

In appreciating the great achievements of modern engineering, as an art, we must not however forget their limitations. The fact is that all the indisputable triumphs of the exact arts have been in fields where the human element has been eliminated, or where the function of the machine itself expressed the only human desire involved—as the aeroplane expresses the ancient human desire for the powers of flight. The real test of our ability as artists and engineers will come when we attempt to carry the machine-technique into fields of activity where the personality as a whole must be considered, and where social adaptations and psychological stresses and strains are just as important factors as tensile strength, load, or mechanical efficiency in operation.

Up to the present our use of machine methods has been muddled by two different attitudes. One has been the pathetic error of using machine methods to achieve forms and qualities that are antagonistic to the nature of the machine: under this head comes the introduction of machine-carving in the manufacture of, say, Tudor chairs in order to simulate the ancient handicraft designs on a scale that will meet the vulgar mind. For anyone with an honest sense of design, the cheapest bent wood chair is superior to the faked replica of the machine. The contrary error is that of holding that the bent-wood machined chair is admirably suited to modern purposes because it is solely and entirely a product of the machine: this neglects the simple fact that it is totally unadapted in design to the contours of the human body in all but one or two brief stiff postures. To deny that the machine can produce art is a fallacy; to believe that everything the machine produces is excellent art is also a romantic fallacy. To curb the machine and limit art to handicraft is a denial of opportunity. To extend the machine into provinces where it has no function to perform is likewise a denial of opportunity.

If engineering shares with music the supremacy in the arts during the last hundred and fifty years—and after a careful appraisal of all its shortcomings I think that it does—this does not decrease the need of the opportunity for other modes of expression. When human functions become the norm, a good part of current machine work will inevitably drop out of existence. Our increased knowledge of physiology has cast into limbo the elaborate weights and counterweights and horses that the mechanical gymnastics of the nineteenth century laboriously developed, with perilous results to the human body. So our increased knowledge of education has shown the futility, for example, of highly specialized mechanical playground apparatus, such as see-saws fastened to fixed iron bases, when a simple plank and a saw-horse provide more varied forms of experimental play. Similar insight into human needs may turn many of our most triumphant advances in engineering into otiose rubbish—in spite of the utmost virtuosity they may exhibit as mechanical contrivances, or the financial profit their exploitation may bring. But engineering as an art will flourish all the more in its own right, when it ceases to claim recognition as a substitute for other arts; and in the long run it must profoundly modify our popular æsthetic.

VII

POLITICAL ECONOMY was written originally by professors of moral science and stockbrokers; and, in the light of their traditions, it is not altogether surprising that they conceived that the industrial revolution was primarily, if not indeed solely, a mechanical and financial one. As a matter of fact, the introduction of new foods into Western civilization, particularly the potato and maize, and the application of the experimental method to agriculture, with the overthrow of a backward, customary farming, was an equally powerful instrument of change.

In the mechanical transformation of the Western World, landscape architecture had a compensatory part to play. By a paradox, it came into existence in the very period that, in sinking mines, ruining forests, and extending slum areas, was blithely obliterating a good part of the natural landscape. This art is a classic example of the interrelation of science and ideology and the arts. On one side, landscape architecture acquired its æsthetic, its method of design, from the contemporary landscape painters, Ruysdael, Wilson, Claude, Constable; and on the other, in its acceptance of natural forms, and in its intention merely to modify, for more perfect enjoyment, the landscape as it exists in nature, it derived from Rousseau and Linnæus. The traditional art of the formal garden disappeared during this period—it lingered chiefly as an appanage of royalty; but the art of modifying the whole landscape came to life, beginning with the improvement of country estates, and reaching the cities in the form of the landscape park.

During the nineteenth century, this art became the chief communal art in cities that had otherwise lost almost every organ of a common life apart from industrial enterprise: Regent Park in London, Central Park in New York, and the great park system established for metropolitan Boston were perhaps the principal landmarks in this development. But in both Europe and America, the naturalistic interest went one step further: in Europe it led to the formation of walking trails through the high Alps, and in America it resulted in the conception of the "wild park," a park which would exhibit a minimum modification of the landscape by man; and in naturally picturesque places like the Colorado Canyon or the Yosemite Valley, vast areas were set aside for this end.

The deliberate culture of the whole landscape, for purposes not directly connected with the growth of food and timber, is one of the youngest of the arts; and it is only at the beginning of its influence. Parkways, riverways, state forests, town forests, mountain trails, dedicated to beauty and health and the renewal of the spirit—the development of these things modifies, it seems to me, our whole picture of the "machine age" and its future. If we left the desires and purposes that are so expressed out of account, we might easily believe that the great reservoirs of energy the machine-process is tapping would be expended in the future solely upon a more lavish mechanical equipment—two motor cars for every inhabitant, or a vacuum cleaner for every room, or some similar preposterous extravagance which a desperate salesmanship might invent. But there is also another possibility. We are now slowly learning to do as communities what rich individuals do occasionally as "country gentlemen"—revivify and restore the whole landscape, returning with love what we destroyed in our haste and our greedy, short-sighted financial exploitation. Regional planning and country planning are the current names for this process; and where the idea is taking root, the fact itself may presently break through the soil and shoot upward, on a far more extensive scale than we may now picture.

The arts of ordering the earth and improving its living forms— what Professor Patrick Geddes has called geotechnics and biotechnics—are as much indebted to the experimental methods of modern science as the purely mechanical departments of our life; it is a naïve habit of the paleotechnic period to identify science merely with the physical sciences, and to consider all the arts as subordinate to the machine. Our scientific knowledge of the earth and its organic forms is a later development than the physical sciences; but in the period that is now opening there is reason to believe that it may have an equally revolutionary effect upon the associated arts, whilst the machine itself advances from the muck and disorder and waste of the coal-and-iron-and-steam period to the finer and more conservative economy of electricity and the lighter metals.

VIII

It is not only in the arts that have been fructified by science that there has been a distinct gain. Once the disruption of the traditional arts was complete, it became possible to revive them on a modern basis; and since, roughly, 1880, there has gone on a revival in typography, textiles, furniture, in architecture and city planning which shows, I think, that science and technics, while they have altered the basis of these arts, have not done away with the possibilities of their proper growth and development. I shall concentrate on architecture and city design; for these are the master arts; and they flourish only to the extent that they can call freely on the accessory crafts.

Beginning first in America, among the group of original minds that began to design the warehouses and office buildings of Chicago during the eighties, a fresh impetus in architectural design has now spread throughout Western civilization. What is in back of it? Modern architecture differs from all the revivals that began with the Renaissance in that it springs out of a new logic of structure, instead of deriving from the last stage in architectural development—the ornament. This logic is founded on certain capital facts: first, that our habits of living have changed; second, that the functions of a building have been modified partly by the introduction of mechanical utilities for heat, drainage, equalization of temperature; finally, that modern technology has provided a whole range of new materials and methods—the steel cage and ferro-concrete construction for example—which have altered the essential problems of design.

As a result, the content and potential rhythm of a modern building has changed. Mr. Frank Lloyd Wright has altered the proportions of wall and window, making his ceilings low and his windows continuous; Mr. Erich Mendelssohn, in the Einstein Tower, has treated ferro-concrete as a completely plastic material; P. P. Oud in Holland and Messrs. Stein and Wright in America have designed dwelling-houses whose æsthetic value comes solely through the spacing and grouping of simple, standardized units; whilst the most original skyscraper architects, Messrs. Corbett, Kahn, Walker, Harmon, and Hood, have created vast structures which, by sheer mass and proportion and disposition of the parts, sometimes acquire the dignity of great building. There is nothing in European or American architecture since the seventeenth century to equal in originality of design and in positive conception the important buildings of the last thirty years, buildings like the Marshall Field Warehouse, the Monadnock Building, the Los Angeles Public Library, the Shelton Hotel, the Barclay-Vesey Building, the interior of the Hill Auditorium at Ann Arbor, the railroad station at Helsingfors, the Town Hall at Stockholm, the Bourse at Amsterdam, the concert-hall at Breslau—to mention only a handful of examples chosen at random. It is almost as impossible to characterize all the varied manifestations of this architecture, particularly during the last twenty years, as it is to characterize the Gothic; but, like the Gothic of the thirteenth century, it perhaps witnesses a common impulse towards synthesis throughout Western civilization.

Our achievements in architecture have been curbed by the fact that except in certain European cities the architect has lost his sense of the whole: the best buildings are not assured, by adequate city planning, of the best sites, or even of relatively important ones; so that, while in the actual order of development we have risen from good engineering to good architecture, and may eventually rise from good architecture to good city design, as numerous plans for city extensions and new communities already promise, it is only by reversing this process and securing control of the social situation that we shall be able to extend and perpetuate the advances we have made. What does this mean? It means modifying public taste through the creation of a new æsthetic; it means curbing extravagant ground rents and preventing the misuse of sites; in general, it means treating the community itself as a major element in design. Before architecture can produce more than isolated masterpieces, our social skill must be pushed at least as far as our engineering skill, defining the several functions of a city and controlling the use of land for the benefit of the whole community. Where this has been done by public authority in Holland, Germany, and England, architecture has profited.

IX

WE COME at last to city design. If one excepts the extravagant and socially dubious improvements made in Paris and Vienna during the nineteenth century, city design almost completely disappeared. With indisputable gains in mechanical efficiency, in the manufacture and transportation of certain products, there was a vast loss in the communal art of living. In the new cities the housing accommodation, not merely for the industrial workers but for a good part of the middle classes, was below decent hygienic standards; private gardens disappeared, and as the cities increased in area, population, and wealth the amount of sunlight, fresh air, open spaces relatively diminished.

There were many criticisms of this condition from Engels to Ruskin, from the physician who planned the imaginary town of Hygeia to the industrial magnates who attempted to improve conditions in Pullman, Port Sunlight, and Essen; but the first adequate conception of the problem was formulated by Sir Ebenezer Howard when he published his classic proposal for garden cities under the title, "To-morrow." Mr. Howard pointed out that the nineteenth century city had become amorphous: it had neither shape nor bounds: the only inter-relation of its parts was an inter-relation of mechanical utilities, sewers, water-mains, and transportation systems—and even these were designed at haphazard.

Adequate design, Mr. Howard saw, was not a matter merely of providing architectural approaches or "civic centres," nor was it a matter of elaborating further the physical utilities: it was essentially a sociological matter, and it must face every problem of the city's existence; any fine æsthetic result could only be the crown of a long series of efforts. Modern city design involved planning cities as units in relation to natural resources and recreation areas; it meant planning of house-sites and gardens and schools so that children could be bred under conditions that would further their physical survival and their culture: it called for the provision of factory-sites and the co-ordination of industries: and finally, it demanded as a condition of continuous growth the creation of new city-units, surrounded by rural areas, but with all the benefits of urban co-operation, schools, amusements, libraries, theatres, hospitals, and so forth. Modern city design meant the adequate resolution of all these problems—problems which actual city planning by engineers and architects not merely shirked but never even posed for themselves.

Mr. Howard's conception of city growth as growth by communities, related to their region and to its industrial life, challenged the existing methods and habits; for it shifted the whole emphasis from mechanical planning and patchwork, to comprehensive social planning. Although Mr. Howard's conceptions have actually been embodied in two English cities, Welwyn and Letchworth, and although they have deeply modified the current conceptions of city planning in Europe, and to a smaller extent in America, city planning is still the least progressive of the arts; and the new cities of the Western World are not organic centres but inefficient mechanical agglomerations. This state of affairs need not excite our wonder; for, compared with any single specialized industry, the co-ordinations and transformations required for modern city planning are infinitely more complicated, and the human variables are much more difficult to handle. Despite this tardiness in development, our city planning must eventually not merely reach the point that Messrs. Howard and Unwin had reached by 1904; it must even pass beyond it; for our new technological achievements in the automobile, the aeroplane, long-distance communications and giant power transmission have made our existing centres inefficient and obsolete.

Whatever the city of the future may be, we can now say with some confidence that it will not be the Leviathan of machinery, with manifold subways, multiple streets, windowless houses, and costly artificial substitutes for the natural elements that the vulgar imagination of today conjures up on the basis of an early Victorian ideology. The mechanical Leviathan, which cities like New York and Chicago now approximate and aspire toward, is a dead form: it is dead not merely because it burkes human functions and purposes; it is equally dead because it conflicts with the gains in modern technology. With our modern means of communication, the region is now the locus of activity, not the single unit of a city; and there is no more reason to cover the region over with continuous streets and houses in a day that knows the auto and the aeroplane, than there is to go back to the oxcart for transportation.

With the city planned for human functions and activities, the scale of our mechanical operations alters. When street areas are planned in relation to the capacity of buildings, and when sunlight and air are provided for every window, we do away with the necessity for such a costly engineering device as the double-decked street or artificial ventilation; when houses are grouped around parks and garden spaces, and designed for through ventilation and full sunlight for all rooms, the necessity for expensive substitutes like artificial sunlight is removed; when the telephone and the radio are employed, social intercourse is just as close in an open network of communities as in a congested metropolis; when giant power provides the power-line and our motor roads and airways the means of transportation our factories are no longer chained to the railroad siding or the terminal. In sum, modern community planning, when it plans in terms of human functions instead of speculation, ground rents, extravagant multiplication of utilities, and progressive chaos, will provide a new setting not merely for architecture but for all our social functions.

The role of city design in the future can hardly be over-emphasized. Our specialization in the arts is tolerable only when we re-unite them again in the city itself as part of the active functions of citizens—when music, painting, poetry, the dance, gymnastics have as essential a part in our daily life as subway rides and newspapers now have in the economy of the metropolitan worker. Today, the possibilities for such an integrated life are open only to a small, prosperous minority, a badly educated and largely futile leisure class; only an infinitesimal part of the industrial population, whether in the open country or in cities, live under conditions which are favorable to the complete humanization of man in society. In the main, their development is stunted and one-sided, a caricature of their complete heritage and potentiality, very largely because the communities in which they live are one-sided and partly developed whilst in the big metropolises, where a more complete development is possible, the routine of living—the depression produced by bad air, sunless streets, long suffocating hours wasted in the transportation of the human carcass, crowded housing quarters—vitiates the happy expression and fulfilment of life.

City design is the art of orchestrating human functions in the community. As, through the applications of the scientific method, our ability to forecast and control our purposes increases, regional planning must provide the framework for city design, architecture must avail itself more and more of community planning and engineering must give precedence to architecture—thus reversing the present condition under which there is a vast proliferation of misconceived and misapplied physical utilities and a perpetual scamping of human purpose and design. This is not an abstract conclusion; it emerges from the actual situation in the arts to-day. Once the framework for a humane life is prepared, the arts that arise naturally under these happy auspices will appear, not constrained, specialized, shrunken, often insignificant, as they are to-day, but in something like the original virility that characterized them throughout western Europe before the introduction of the machine.

x

IN SUM, we can now see, I believe, that the machine age is not a fixed monument in relation to which the arts must get their bearings. The machine age began with great discoveries in the physical sciences, with the application of experiment and invention to mechanical contraptions, and with the domination of engineering as the supreme art. Its early growth was marked by the dilapidation of all the traditional arts—except those which by their nature could retreat to the cloister. In the arts which arise out of personality and social needs, the machine age has developed slowly; but with the increasing application of biological knowledge to hygiene, agriculture, and medicine, of psychology to education, and of the social sciences to the actual problems of industry planning and city design and regional development, the one-sided emphasis on mechanical technique, which marked the early transition, should eventually give way to a more even-handed competence in dealing with every aspect of life. With the existence of greater opportunities for leisure, provided potentially by the machine economy but still far from actual achievement, the personal and contemplative arts, which were either isolated or reduced to frivolity in the early stages of industrialism, should flourish again.

There is, of course, no certainty that any of these things will happen. A disastrous series of wars might even throw us back into a pre-industrial era, or drive the spirit into a superstitious ideology in which compliance with inscrutable powers outside ourselves, powers working fear, disaster, death, would take the place of that active if unnameable faith which buoys up all those who now heartily pursue the arts and sciences. It is even possible that our financial organizations, taking advantage of sundry narrow psychological skills, may find a way of keeping the arts and sciences tethered to the market, and of emasculating them of every hypothesis that would upset the profit-making mechanism. Any or all of these perversions and miscarriages may come to pass; but none of them will arise out of the legitimate method of science, nor will they occur because tested and verifiable knowledge discourages the arts and annuls the function of the artist.

Science can not take the place of religion and philosophy; nor can engineering arrogate to itself the provinces of all the other arts. Our sciences, our ideologies, and our arts are, on the contrary, essential to humane living; and their expression in wholeness furthers and effectuates Life.

# XIII—PHILOSOPHY

## By John Dewey

NO QUESTION can be stated where everything is questioned. Ability to formulate a problem depends upon something which is admitted. Now what is taken for granted in the present inquiry is that men live in a world that is undergoing extensive and accelerated change, and that physical science and technological industry are the causes of this change. On the basis of this admission as to the character of contemporary civilization, the question is: What is implied for philosophy? Can philosophers stand aloof, indifferent and immune; or does this state of affairs say something to them, and say it so urgently that its voice must be hearkened to? It is proposed to answer the interrogation in the affirmative. The answer rests upon another premise which is taken to be admitted. It is taken for granted that philosophical problems and the theories suggested for their solution take their rise out of some social medium, past or present. The authentic subject-matter of philosophy is found in some state of culture, although all civilizations are sufficiently complex to provide quite diverse subject-matters to different thinkers. But a philosopher draws upon that element of culture which is most congenial—or most hostile—to his own temperament and desires, whether it be the contemporary scene, Greece, India, or mediæval Europe. Realistic content is derived positively from what is there; idealistic content is derived by way of recoil from the defects, perversions, and evils of the social medium.

The tendency of many philosophers to withdraw into the past and the remote—always easier to idealize—does not mark a private idiosyncrasy. The past furnishes an atmosphere in which imagination thrives and thought is less bound down; while the continuity of present civilization with that of the past necessitates this recourse. Ever since the time of the Greeks, European culture has been a borrowed one. The bases and chief values of life have been alien, not indigenous. Rome went in debt to Greece and the Orient; mediæval culture owed everything that was ordered and supremely prized to Greece, Rome, Judea, and Alexandria; the civilization we call modern has been a struggle to accommodate the outcome of these borrowings to new elements. Philosophers have oscillated between efforts to strike a balance, to repudiate the debts, to declare bankruptcy, and sometimes, though less often, to liquidate what is owed and establish the solvency of modern life. In a civilization largely built out of alien traditions, it is not surprising that thinkers have been more concerned about transmitted borrowings than about contemporary and novel factors. Bacon and Descartes set out with avowal of independence and originality, but even they conducted their intellectual enterprises on capital drawn from sources they nominally rejected.

Tension between old and new has, however, been sufficient to influence the course of philosophic thought since the sixteenth century. Curiously enough, the tension has been least felt in the New World, in the United States. The scene in which new factors have had the most unrestricted sway in fact, has been that in which thinkers, excepting a few outside of professional bounds, have lived most contentedly upon borrowed capital. The more, it would seem, actual life has been transformed by the application of natural science in industry and commerce, the more professional philosophers have ignored the contemporary situation and devoted themselves to manipulation of portions of the European tradition torn from its living context. The result is the thin meagreness of American contributions to the reflective thought of mankind. There is manifest neither the vitality that springs from acceptance of a living tradition that retains significance by struggle with forces which attack and would undermine it, nor that which might spring from appreciative concern with forces that actually dominate contemporary life.

Some European philosophies have been refuges framed for consolation and compensation. But these cities of emotional and moral refuge were at least sought out because of realization of imminent peril. Other philosophies have been deliberate protests against the inherited tradition; they have been revolutionary in intent. Others have given themselves to the task of reconciliation and mediation. In consequences, these European philosophies have been pregnant with meaning in their own social contexts. It is possible for a French historian to write a history of French philosophy with titles drawn from characteristic social movements. British philosophy until the nineteenth century was a deliberate attempt to supply a creed for liberalism and social reform, and its reliance upon German thought in the latter nineteenth century was an attempt to discover adequate means for counteracting disintegrative results of the earlier liberalism as that was carried into action. German thought, conventionally the most speculative and otherworldly of all European systems, has been either a social apologia elaborated by a highly technical apparatus, or a program of social revolution. As for Russia—there every social movement, conservative or radical, has openly, even flagrantly, linked its programme with some mode of philosophic doctrine. An American student is bewildered to find, for example, that Lenin considered it necessary as part of his practical movement to engage in heated polemic against every German philosophic doctrine, however innocently theoretical it looks in our perspective, that deviates from orthodox dialectical materialism.

In contrast with the vitality of European philosophies, American professional philosophy has taken with utmost seriousness intellectual formulations extracted from their actual setting. It has played with them in detachment. American philosophies were idealistic, realistic, or pragmatic of this or that shade, without leaving in their wake a ripple in American life. Santayana, the only American thinker who has systematically employed even reaction against the American scene as a factor in framing his philosophy, is of Spanish origin and no longer lives in the country. William James is the outstanding exception to what has been said, in that he used intellectually as much of the distinctively

American tradition as had in his day come to any consciousness of itself. But he probably had more influence abroad than at home and is here still criticized as uttering in effect a supine glorification of what is least worthy in American life. Otherwise, one has to go beyond philosophic bounds, to Emerson, Thoreau, Walt Whitman, to find a critical evaluation and report of the American scene.

The situation as described shows many signs of loosening, of breaking up. Such detachment cannot go on indefinitely. If the actual scene does not offer a sufficient challenge, that of the chorus of European critics does. The challenge is not one that should produce apologetic justification; much less petulant retort. It is a challenge to understanding. What *is* our materialism, our commercialism, our narrow practicality, our childish immaturity, our impatient preoccupation with hurry and movement? What *is* our alleged "practical idealism," our devotion to "social service," our curious combination of individualism with collectivistic standardization and conformity? What is the meaning of our union of ideals of peace and regard for the rights of self-determination of other people with an expansion that looks to the outsider remarkably like familiar economic imperialism? Whence and why our combination of complacency and restless discontent? Whence and why our multiplication of regulative laws conjoined with practical lawlessness? Why are our politics and our thinking so legalistic and our practice a matter of taking short-cuts across all legal boundaries? And so on indefinitely.

The challenge is the more peremptory because, if our European critics be correct, Europe, and probably the Orient, are themselves being "Americanized," so that what we are now the world in general is coming to be. For this fact (or prophecy—with whatever truth it may contain) recalls attention to the central fact that the force most active in contemporary life is growth of habits congruous with natural science and still more with the technological application of its discoveries. Practically every phase of our present technique of industry and commerce has its roots in some discovery made somewhere in some laboratory by some scientist engaged in physical or chemical research. Indeed, the connection is now so obvious to the "practical" man that a characteristic feature of our recent industrial life is the development within business itself of richly subsidized laboratories, the number of which is put at some five hundred, and the more important of which are engaged in "pure" research. We cannot discriminate, even if we should like to, the scientific phase of present civilization from its technological phase.

This intimate union of science and technology, realized in mechanical civilization, is a challenge to our most cherished philosophic tradition. For the outstanding feature of the classic tradition is the separateness of knowledge and practice, a separation in which adjectives of praise and honor are attached to the former and those of depreciation to the latter. European philosophy early in its career committed itself to a celebration of the contemplative life. The rise of natural science did not seriously disturb the tradition. Philosophers went on interpreting knowledge by means of the earlier concepts of its exclusively contemplative nature long after actual knowledge in its most authentic form had adopted experimental methods, in spite of the fact that experimentation depended upon the invention and use of physical tools and machines. The dependence of the worker in the factory upon mechanical devices is no greater than that of the worker in the laboratory. The latter consciously employs an elaborate apparatus of theory and theoretical calculations of which the factory worker is innocent. But the latter can ignore this auxiliary intellectual apparatus only because for him it is already physically incarnate in the machines he operates. The machine is the authentically embodied *Logos* of modern life, and the import of this fact is not diminished by any amount of dislike to it.

Philosophy has, however, been little affected by the transformation of the ways in which men actually pursue knowledge. It has remained, as far as possible, true to conceptions formulated more than two thousand years ago in Greece, when the experimental method was not dreamed of; when indeed the absence of mechanical appliances made the method impossible. Philosophy has paid deference to science; but its obeisances have been made rather to the conclusions of science than to its method. As far as the nature of the knowing operation and function is concerned, philosophers have disputed whether knowledge is a direct grasp and intuition of real things, or whether the only things directly known are impressions and ideas in the mind. They have disputed whether sensation or reason is the basic guarantee of knowledge. But the schools have retained the notion that in any case knowing is a matter of some contact or intercourse between mind on one side and things on the other, a contact and intercourse independent of the needs and instrumentalities of practical activity. At first sight this fact may seem of little importance save to professional philosophers. But in reality it involves two of the most significant problems of common humanity, and begs the question as to their solution. For there is contained in it an issue as to the nature of truth and as to the organ by which it is achieved. There is also included an assumption as to the nature of the "practical" that identifies it with the merely utilitarian or the commercial and the politic, to the neglect of any ideal content. The endeavor to pour the new wine of knowledge into old bottles of traditional notions as to the contemplative essence and function of knowing signifies in effect that ideas and intelligence inhabit a self-enclosed realm, and that vital human affairs are conducted by turning to personal and class account such conclusions of science as lend themselves to pecuniary gain and power over others.

Critics of our present social régime often assume that the evils of our industrial civilization are the exclusive products of the reign of mechanical technology. It seems to be inherent in human nature to want a deity to worship and a devil to abhor. Machinery has become the devil of a wide-spread cult. But the indictment overlooks the fact that our existing institutions and interests have their roots in the past, and that the use we make of mechanical instrumentalities is not due to these instruments alone but to their entanglement with a texture of beliefs and ideals that matured in a pre-industrial age. In such a condition there is more petulance than enlightenment in charging evils to machines and industry. The only thing certain is that, when men think and believe in one set of symbols and act in ways which are contrary to their professed and conscious ideas, confusion and insincerity are bound to result, and that in this chaos the unregenerated elements of man, lacking direction, avidly snatch at those immediate and nearby goods which present themselves as attainable. It would be absurd to hold philosophy responsible for the divided estate of civilization; it shows rather a reflection of the division in life itself. But unreconstructed philosophy gives an intellectual formulation of the division, and perpetuates it by the rational justification it thereby seems to provide. However slowly the ideas of thinkers filter into popular consciousness, the first move in straightening out, on the intellectual side, the tangle, in clarifying the confusion, lies with thinkers. They must set their own house in order before they can furnish any plans and specifications for a better integration of the activities of men. This fact seems to me to define the connection of philosophy in America with civilization.

Classic Greek philosophy and the mediæval synthesis at least reflected the conditions and aspirations of their own times in a coherent system of beliefs. Their ideas could be used to formulate a warrant and goal for their own conduct and institutions. The resultant religious-philosophic organization of beliefs permeated men's minds and was congruous with their deepest hopes and fears. It supplied the greatest need of man, that of an authority by which to live. The central point in this system of authority was the conviction that knowledge is obtained by direct contact of mind with reality, supplemented by revelation; that the knowledge so attained by reason and faith would bring about, when projected into the happier estate of life after death, a direct possession and enjoyment of the ultimate reality, God. That is, a theory of knowledge which isolated both its method and its outcome from practical action was the essence of the classic theory, and the theory had authority, since it laid down both the goal of life and the means of attaining the goal.

The traditional theory received a shock from the rise of new methods in physical science. Everyone is familiar with the struggle induced by the incompatibility of traditional astronomy, the "science" which underlay and justified commonly accepted beliefs about earth, heaven, and hell, with the astronomy of Copernicus and Galileo. We are familiar with a similar although less bitter conflict going on today in the realm of ideas about living creatures, plants and animals. The opposition to each other of fundamentalist and modernist is the latest expression of the results of a shock felt in the sixteenth century. Familiarity with these facts does not of itself, however, induce familiarity with a more important consideration. These special conflicts are but the outward and visible signs of an inner conflict that concerns the very nature of what is to be accepted as knowledge and truth, and the methods by which this knowledge and truth are to be attained. Since such truth—and the method of obtaining it—is the seat of ultimate authority, or affords the warrant of man's ultimate allegiances, the conflict reaches down to the depths of belief and to the patterns of conduct and institutions bound up with belief.

Hence it was practically inevitable that modern thought should make the problem of knowledge its central problem. It would require a long and technical discussion to prove the statement previously made that consideration of this problem has been dominated by retention of notions formed in a period in which experimental inquiry was non-existent. I can cite only an illustration or two. An illuminating instance is found in the formulation given to the problem. Is knowledge possible and if so how? What are its limits and extent? The answer to the latter question which the actual pursuit of knowledge would have suggested is: Knowledge is possible as far as we can develop instrumentalities of inquiry, measurement, symbolization, calculations, and testing. This is perhaps the one answer that has not been given. Solution of the question as to the legitimate extent of knowledge has been sought on the basis of inherited premises as to the nature of mind, of sensations, of concepts, and the relation, physical and epistemological, of mind to the nature of reality as pre-defined; that is, as thought of in a way that was independent of the results of inquiry.

There is something ironical in the very statement of the problem of the possibility of knowledge. At the time when science was advancing at an unprecedented rate, philosophers were asking whether knowledge was possible. And when the answer was in the affirmative, it was justified on the basis of notions about mind, sensation or reason. The straightforward course would seem to have been an examination of the procedures by which knowledge is obtained in actual practice. Men discover how it is possible to walk or talk or fly by examining how these things are actually done. What other way is there by which to find out how knowledge is possible? That this road represents the one road which was *not* taken may have some other explanation than that philosophers are so made that they naturally take the most back-handed approach to anything. The real explanation is that they have been primarily occupied with reconciling tradition with the new movement of science. From the standpoint of tradition, a report of how knowledge *is* obtained would so contradict inherited ideas of mind, in its isolation from the body and other agencies of practical action, as to constitute a serious and perplexing issue. Philosophers were not a unique class. They reflected the control which tradition, engrained in institutions as well as in beliefs, had over the minds of men even when their practice ventured into previously untried fields in ways incompatible with the tradition.

One further illustration may be drawn from an allied field. The deepest problem of modern ethical philosophy has been the reconciliation of human freedom with that phase of science which is called "the reign of law." All sorts of solutions have been propounded, from denial of the reality of freedom to the postulation of a realm above nature by entrance into which man's moral freedom is secured. Attention to the practical scene of contemporary human activity would have given an entirely different turn to the discussion. For every phase of technological civilization shows that an advance in knowledge of natural uniformities and necessary conditions increases man's working freedom, namely, control of nature, enabling him to harness natural energies to his own purposes. This operative power may not correspond to the traditional definition of freedom, for that originated in days when man was so enslaved to natural conditions that he could conceive of freedom only as escape from the bondage they imposed. But it is at least an appreciable part of what men actually want under the name of freedom. The freedom thus gained moreover is poorly thought of when it is conceived merely as increased liberty to realize desires already stirring in men. Its more considerable phase is the release of new desires, the creation and projection of previously unheard of purposes. It was the sense of this new kind of freedom, freedom to want and strive for all kinds of new possibilities, that expressed itself in the feeling of living in a new world lending itself to indefinite progress. This fact brings us to a consideration of that degradation of the idea of the "practical" which has been noted. As far as the traditional idea of the isolation of mind from natural conditions, and the superiority of mind to these conditions, persisted, the feeling assumed, of necessity, a romantic form. As far as actual practice was concerned, the new control was mainly used for personal material advantage.

Thus the traditionalist has a ready retort. He may claim that to offer *this* freedom, freedom to conceive and execute desires, as if it signified what man justly cherishes as true freedom, is only to exemplify the degradation of values and ideals which has been wrought by industrial civilization. For, according to traditional pigeon-holes, all desires that are capable of concrete realization fall within the strictly economic field, within the area of wants for material things and for material prosperity. What of spiritual freedom, of freedom in respect to things which are the dignities and ennoblements of human life; art, religious communion and adoration, the untethered flight of moral aspirations? What better proof can be found, it is asked, of the degeneration effected by industrial civilization than that liberation of economic wants by material means should be proposed as if it were relevant to significant human freedom?

The question reaches far. Before it is considered, it will be well to deal with another objection of a limited nature.

The position taken exemplifies, it may be urged, a complacent contentment with existing industrial conditions. Instead of extension of human control over purposes and their realization, machine-made and machine-bound civilization has deprived men of leisure and led to use of such leisure as they possess in mad search for amusement and foolish display. It has brought not freedom but enslavement to the machine. Work has been deprived of joy;

artistic feeling has been eliminated from its performance and its products. The masses have been condemned to become appendages to the machines they tend; and those released from this fate manifest their boasted freedom for the most part only in holding the activities of others in thrall. It is only heartless indifference which can behold in such a state of affairs a gain in human freedom.

The facts that underlie this indictment are undeniable. They are not to be wholly disposed of by setting against the indictment the deplorable state of the masses in all ages, or by pointing out that distance and ignorance effect an easy idealization of their estate in the past. It is more to the point to inquire how far the evils pointed to are solely chargeable to the machine and how far they are due to perpetuation of modes of desire, habits of thought, and institutions that developed in the delightful agrarian and feudal age. For the consciousness of the evil conditions under which masses live, the recognition of them as something humanly abhorrent, as something against which conscience and will should revolt, is itself a product of industrial civilization. One does not find the revolt in earlier civilizations; one does not find it in those parts of the earth which have as yet not come under the industrial blight. The peculiar thing is not the enslavement of masses of mankind to the necessities of making a hardly-won precarious livelihood; that has existed at all times and places. The distinctive thing is increased consciousness of this state of affairs and discontent with it; the belief that it is unjust and unnatural; the conviction that it is a monster to be extirpated. Such an attitude could not have risen until industrial civilization had sufficiently advanced to bring with it the perception of the possibility of a free life upon a higher level for all mankind; until command of natural energies by means of machinery had enabled imagination to conceive of leisure for all. The state of things which is now emphasized as the product of industrial civilization was through long ages taken for granted as part of the natural, the necessary, yes, the providential, order of things.

The modern democratic movement in its broad sense provides the background for our "humanitarian" aspirations. The machine age has resulted in a transference of the locus of the ideal of a larger and more evenly distributed happiness and leisure from heaven to earth. This is true even though the attainment of the ideal is as much beset with doubt in the earthly as in the other-worldly scheme. The facts represented in this transference are closely connected with the issue involved in the belief that industrial civilization inevitably degrades the higher interests of men, offering us at best greater liberty to procure material comfort and ease at the expense of the values which mark off the life of man from that of beasts. The trouble with this objection is that it proves—or assumes—too much. The possession of physical means for a higher degree of material security would not appear to be inherently hostile to creative effort and appreciative enjoyment in the higher arts and values of life. One would rather suppose that increase of security, even if not extending to possession of a large surplus of wealth, would release imagination and emotion to engage more generously in the pursuit of ideal interests.

I do not claim for a moment that this presumption is as a matter of fact realized in our present civilization. Only a blind man would deny that characteristic traits of present life are a mad scramble for material commodities, a devotion to attainment of external power, and an insensate love of foolish luxuries and idle display. But full acknowledgment of this fact settles nothing; it only sets a problem for inquiry. Why is this so? One possibility is that human nature is running true to form; that our industrial development supplies the means by which the ever dominant factors of human nature get a chance to express themselves: that men are so made that taken en masse they always devote themselves to material power and enjoyment rather than to religion, art, and disinterested science if they have the chance. But the adoption of this explanation indicates that the hold of higher values upon man was always accidental and compensatory. Such an explanation commits us to the idea that human nature is inherently so base that only the holy discipline of privation, sacrifice, and suffering can elevate man above himself. Even if this be so, it makes human nature, not industrial civilization, the cause of the evils complained of. The degradations of industrialism can only signify on this score that at last the natural man possesses the means for displaying himself; the evils of industrial civilization are an effect of the constitution of human nature.

Adoption of this alternative lands us in a desperate case. Those who remain loyal to the spiritual interest may repine, scold, or withdraw into seclusion. But by their own statement there is nothing which can be done about the perverse state of civilization. There is, however, another possibility. The present over-zeal for material goods and prosperity may be the fruit of long ages in which man has been starved and oppressed. It may be chiefly the product of the belauded former ages in which, it is asserted, higher values were held in esteem. In this case, the so-called lower desires of man, his demand for comfort, for enjoyment of material things, his foolish love of power over things and other persons for the mere sake of power, were held in restraint not by devotion to spiritual interests, but by force of surrounding external conditions. The pressure removed, these wants are released into action with an intensity proportionate to the pressure which had previously kept them in. In that case, the present situation is one of transitional unbalance, and it is not entirely utopian to look forward to recovery of a sane equilibrium after the so long inhibited appetites have glutted themselves. The prodigal may return to his father's house bringing with him a wisdom gathered in his own experience, not with mere reiteration of precepts forced upon him from without.

Explanation of some of the outstanding evils of industrialism by reference to an exaggerated rebound from a prior abnormal state raises doubts as to the quality of the values which form our inherited standards. These were directly shared only by a few; most persons had to take them on faith, vicariously and as postponed to a future world. And they could have had little depth of root, or the march of industrialism could not so easily have subverted men's allegiance to them.

The fact is that the standards by which we still conventionally judge not only values but also standards are so traditional, and the elements of that tradition are so far removed from the actualities of modern life, that we are almost wholly at a loss when we attempt to pass critical judgments upon what is now going on. Shall we employ standards that matured in an earlier day? If so, the conclusion is foregone. Since it is by the impact of industrial civilization that these standards have lost their vitality, when we measure industrial civilization by them of course it stands condemned. The condemnation, moreover, is not limited to evils that condemn themselves to any intelligent mind; it extends to industrial and scientific methods wholesale, since they are the causal factors. Shall we then employ standards congenial to, arising from, the new technological and scientific trend? But the difficulty is that they are as yet unavowed and unrevealed. We simply do not know what they are. Some of the ignorance is undoubtedly due to the newness and immaturity of industrial civilization itself. But this ignorance is intensified and complicated by the fact that philosophic thought has chiefly devoted itself to cultivating the older tradition instead of exploring the meaning of actual conditions and the possibilities that may inhere in them. In consequence, a nominal and formal intellectual allegiance to standards which have little relevancy to existing civilization is conjoined with practical surrender to forces we make so little effort to understand. The decline of the operative force of old standards and ideals is attended and confirmed by the withdrawal of philosophy from concern with actualities.

Thus we are brought back to the question of the relation of philosophy to existing civilization in its dominantly industrial character. Unless philosophies are to be Edens of compensatory refuge, reached through an exercise of dialectic ingenuity, they must face the situation which is there. It is their business to bring intellectual order out of the confusion of beliefs. For the confusion of which we have been speaking, due to lack of adjustment between ideas and ideals inherited from an older culture and the dominating interests and movements of present civilization, while not itself philosophical in origin, is both a datum and an opportunity for philosophy. "Acceptance" is an ambiguous word in relation to the office of philosophy. It may signify either acceptance of whatever is a fact *as* a fact, or acceptance of it as a value or even as a measure of value. Any philosophy which does not accept important facts is in that degree a philosophy of escape. This appellation holds, in my opinion, even with respect to those theories which would confine the legitimate business of philosophy to analysis of scientific premises or to synthesis of scientific conclusions, in isolation from the place and function of science in life. It is as an *operative* fact that philosophy has to accept the controlling role of technological industry in contemporary civilization. This acceptance is far from implying commitment to its characteristics as values, but it is precedent to any valid criticism of their value. Otherwise criticism is a complaint, an emotional cry, not an intellectual discrimination.

The discussion may be summarized in saying that industrial civilization presents philosophers with a double challenge. One of its tasks is to discover the full meaning of the experimental methods by which the advances of natural sciences have been made secure. In order to make this discovery, there is needed revision and even surrender of fixed prepossessions regarding the nature of mind, thought, and truth that are transmitted to us from a pre-experimental age. Ideas of these and allied subjects must be developed after the model and the pattern of what competent inquirers actually *do* in the attainment of knowledge of facts and principles. The accomplishment of this task is difficult. But it is of more than technical and professional significance. It signifies what is in effect a new logic in investigation and criticism of social institutions and customs. For this area, the one in which men concretely live, is hardly touched as yet by the experimental habit of mind. Philosophers of the seventeenth century did a great work in liberating physical knowledge from bondage, and in projecting the roads upon which it could move securely forward. There is now a similar opportunity and similar demand for the emancipation of knowledge of social affairs—legal, economic, political, religious. Until the implications of the experimental method are worked out in this field, the scientific revolution begun three centuries ago is incomplete and subject to warping and perversion—as it is now actually twisted and deflected when it reaches the popular consciousness and takes effect in action.

A second task may be suggested by saying that the relation

between instrumentalities and consequences, means and ends, must be reconsidered on the basis of the new tools and sources of power which come within human control because of applications of science. Upon the whole the record of the history of philosophy displays a division into things called ends-in-themselves and other things that are mere means, intrinsically indifferent to ends-in-themselves, the ulterior sources of value: into noumenal and phenomenal, physical and ideal, material and spiritual. All such separations root in the separation of ends and means from one another. The ideas of objects to which final worth is assigned are formed with little respect to existent conditions, to the realistic factor. Since the latter supplies the only means for the execution of ideas and the realization of desires and purposes, the outcome is that higher and more far-reaching ends become merely "idealistic"—that is, romantic, sentimental, compensatory. It is as if an engineer despised material and energies on the ground that they are merely material in nature. The issue affects equally the conception and the treatment of the "realistic" factor, things as they exist at a given time. Since they are viewed and used in isolation, they too become rigid and fixed. Regard for actual conditions is thought to imply mere accommodation and conformity. Since, however, desire and purpose, the setting up of aims or ends-in-view remains a constant function of human nature, this attitude signifies, in the outcome, that actual conditions *are* employed as means, but as means for ends that are near at hand, suggested by immediate circumstances, attainable by manipulation, and enjoyable on the existing level. Thus operative and controlling "ends" have little to do with professed and sentimentally worshipped ideals. They are then relatively trivial, and superficial; they consist in utilization of conditions as means to direct enjoyment and direct exercise of power over others. Here is the ultimate source of the confusion, insincerity, meaningless change, and unrest characteristic of so much of industrial civilization.

A philosophy of the relations of means and ends, of the materially existent and the ideally possible, based on the control of agencies and instrumentalities which the new technology has brought with itself, cannot terminate with, as it were, a mere *post mortem* dissection. It supplies impetus; its drive is to the future. It takes effect in restatement of the ideal or spiritual elements that have been contained in the religions, arts, literature, moralities, and polities of our traditional inheritance. They are revised so that they bear an operative relation to the state of affairs through which they are realizable. By the same movement of thought, existent conditions cease to be taken as fixed, changeable only by some external and accidental intrusion; they cease to be models and measures of conduct. It is worth while to recur to the analogy with the scientific situation of the seventeenth century. It produced an array of thinkers who clarified and organized the inchoate efforts of a small number of workers in the fields of astronomy, physics, and chemistry. These thinkers evolved an articulate system of ideas which provided subsequent workers with confidence and courage and gave direction and point to their activities.

In the succeeding century, in the period of the "enlightenment," philosophers turned their attention to man, to human nature and human interests. They saw in the methods and results of the new science the promise of complete control of human institutions and efforts by "reason." They predicted an era of liberation from all the oppressions of the past, since these had been conceived in ignorance and perpetuated in superstition. An era of indefinite progress and unlimited perfectibility was ushered in. The course of events gave the lie to their ardent aspiration. "Reason" did not assume a role of control and direction; it, and the new appliances of science, were seized as tools for the promotion of personal and class power over others and as means of new and frenetic display and enjoyment. It did not turn out bliss to be alive, but rather unregulated competition, conflict, and confusion. In consequence the philosophies of the nineteenth century, as far as we can view them with detachment in the present perspective, were infected with a reactionary spirit. Men looked backward rather than forward. The discovery of history considered as a record of the past was its great intellectual contribution.

"Evolution" is an idea which generalizes the discovery of history, and the idea of evolution was elaborated into an idea of cosmic forces which follow their own predestined course, and with respect to which the intervening inventive and directive intelligence of man is of slight account. The most systematic philosophic move-ment of the century, German idealism, fused this idea with ele-ments drawn from the classic religious and philosophic tradition of Europe so as to effect an intellectual rehabilitation of the latter. Many phases of this movement display nobility; all pos-sess pathos. But the movement was essentially apologetic; it jus-tified the existing state of institutions as a manifestation of some inner absolute Idea or Spirit engaged in the slow process of evolu-tionary expression. In effect, the philosophies contributed their support to acquiescence and impotence rather than to direction and re-creation, because they gave an inherent ideal value to what exists—inherent in the sense of independent of what deliberate action might make out of the existent.

A philosopher who would relate his thinking to present civiliza-tion, in its predominantly technological and industrial character, cannot ignore any of these movements any more than he can dis-pense with consideration of the underlying classic tradition formed in Greece and the Middle Ages. If he ignores traditions, his thoughts become thin and empty. But they are something to be employed, not just treated with respect or dressed out in a new vo-cabulary. Moreover, industrial civilization itself has now suffi-ciently developed to form its own tradition. If the United States is more advanced on the road of industrialized civilization than are Old World countries, the meaning of this tradition should be more legible here than elsewhere. It cannot be read, however, un-less it is observed and studied, and it cannot be effectively observed without a measure of intellectual sympathy. Such observation and reflection as discern its meaning—that is its possibilities—*is* philosophy, no matter by what name the discernment is called. If philosophy declines to observe and interpret the new and charac-teristic scene, it may achieve scholarship; it may erect a well equipped gymnasium wherein to engage in dialectical exercises;

it may clothe itself in fine literary art. But it will not afford illumination or direction to our confused civilization. These can proceed only from the spirit that is interested in realities and that faces them frankly and sympathetically.

## XIV—PLAY

### By STUART CHASE

IN A jungle clearing, a low brushwood fire is burning. About the fire a score of naked human beings are stretched upon the ground. Over the top of the black belt of encircling trees comes the full moon. Suddenly a man begins to sing, a deep, full-throated chant. The loungers leap to their feet and join the song. Singing, they begin to dance. It is a weird wild dance, involving every muscle of the body. They strike their thighs with their hands—in lieu of the musical instruments which they have never invented. The rhythm moves ever faster to a leaping climax. Each man is rapt, intense, dancing his own dance, yet there is a rough unity and form in the whole group. The climax reached, the dancers fall exhausted to the ground, panting, glistening with sweat, spent and satisfied.

This, according to the reporting anthropologist, is a favorite form of play among the Rock Veddahs of Ceylon—one of the most primitive of surviving nature peoples. The dance is connected with exorcism against wild beasts, but it is also a profound expression of personal impulse and desire. Muscles, voice, rhythm, senses are all involved. It is the vital principle of raw life at the full. If we would understand play, we must begin in some such jungle clearing. It is our base line.

From Ceylon we move to the most civilized city which ever the hands of man have built. Plato tells us of the philosophy of play in that city. "The mere athlete becomes too much of a savage, and the mere musician is melted and softened beyond what is good for him. . . . The two should therefore be blended in right proportions." The Athenian ideal of citizen was artist, athlete, soldier, statesman, and philosopher, all in one. A reasonably full order, but the Acropolis still stands to remind us of how well it was achieved. Nor must we forget that time in Hellas was measured in units of play; the four-year intervals between the Olympic games.

Athenian children were encouraged to play. Kindergartens were provided with a fairly complete equipment of toys, stilts, skipping ropes, kites, swings, marbles, see-saws, together with ball games and running games. Girls and boys shared these sports in their early years, but at seven or eight the girl was forgotten, while the boy went on to school where he read Homer, learned writing, arithmetic, singing, rhythm, and the use of the lyre and the flute. His free play was still encouraged, and to it were added dancing, wrestling, boxing, swimming, and discus and javelin throwing. At eighteen he entered the gymnasium and was introduced to the five-fold exercise, the pentathlon. And in the intervals of sport and study, he talked with philosophers and statesmen who foregathered there among the porticos.

The human body was reverenced for the beautiful thing it is— if given half a chance. The winner of the Olympic games was, for the time, the greatest man in Greece; his only prize an olive wreath. But Pindar inscribed an ode to him, and Myron fashioned his body in eternal marble. Such was the Golden Age. In the short century of its brilliance, a picked group of men fought and thought and played and lived as perhaps men will never do again upon this planet.

Tonight in the United States of America in the year 1928, thirty million people are in their homes listening to sounds coming out of a small polished box. Wrapt and motionless they sit. Anon someone turns a knob and the rhythm of the sound changes, but its eternal monotonousness never changes, save when it suddenly up-rushes into a voice like that of a very large and very startled crow. Then somebody turns another knob and the timeless chant goes on.

Once a singer sang a song. Conceivably he enjoyed it, and so his singing was play. That song was heard by an audience, who watched the singer; watched his lips, watched his movements, caught something of his spirit, and also conceivably enjoyed it—but at one remove; the audience did not itself sing. The song meanwhile, with the utmost scientific ingenuity, was inscribed upon a plate of composition material, and by running a sharp instrument over that material it could be reproduced, and still enjoyed—at two removes from reality. The plate and the sharp instrument are finally set down in front of a radio broadcaster. Not thirty million people, but a solid fraction of them, are, as they turn the knobs, listening to a song which one machine has caught from another machine, which was caught, lidless and blind, by the first machine from a more or less bored singer vocalizing into its dead and impersonal face. And those of us who hear this song, while we are indeed "playing" the radio, are not playing as the Rock Veddahs, and the Athenians, define the term. We are not playing ourselves; we are being played to—and at three removes from the original source.

Among Western peoples—particularly those which had adopted the Puritan way of life—play was not in high repute at the beginning of the machine age. In America with a stubborn continent to conquer, this was especially true. Unremitting labor was the price of survival. A Methodist school in 1872 voiced the prevailing conception in these words:

We prohibit play in the strongest terms . . . the students shall rise at 5 o'clock summer and winter. Their recreation shall be gardening, walking, riding and bathing without doors, and the carpenter's, jointer's, cabinet maker's or turner's business within doors. . . . The students shall be indulged with nothing which the world calls play. Let this rule be observed with the strictest necessity; for those who play when they are young, will play when they are old.

Meanwhile in Europe, a learned man proposed that "a young girl should never play; she should weep much and meditate upon her sins."

Against such imperatives Rousseau flamed. Presently Froebel came to his support with kindergartens for making play respect-

able again. In these dark days it is impossible to believe that
play for either child or adult was abandoned. But it was formally
ostracized, and, like prohibition-breaking today, more or less carried on behind closed doors. All of course within limited areas.
Most of the world in 1800 was playing openly and passionately,
as it had always done—in jungle clearings and out of them.

The Puritan ostracism died hard, indeed it is not yet altogether
dead, but from Rousseau to John Dewey, one champion after
another has come forward to insist upon the beauty, the necessity,
nay, even the utility of play, until now the battle is to all intents
and purposes won. In the great Cathedral of St. John the Divine in New York, there is a special altar for Sport. It is universally admitted that adults as well as children have a right to
play, and that on the whole it is good for them to play. Along
Broadway, a favorite comedy theme is the dancing grandmother,
a phenomenon heretofore unheard of.

What is play; is it an instinct to begin with? The latter is
still a matter for acrimonious debate between the behaviorists and
the more orthodox psychologists, and thus scientifically unanswer-
able. But there seems to be a pretty general consensus of opinion among those who have been concerned with the behavior of
mankind, that play is a vital principle in the growth of children,
and ranks as a major necessity, not far below hunger and mating, in the life of the adult. Furthermore with the coming of
the machine, and particularly in the United States of America,
the age-long biological balance is threatened by monotonies and
muscular repressions in work which give play an unprecedented
significance. Increasingly it becomes the flywheel of modern life.
"There is nothing in our inheritance which savors of factory,
treadmill, or office stool. We must acquire these priceless habits,
and often at the loss of our entire original inheritance which included freedom to fight or run, or everlastingly to fool around.
Life hates monotony but loves rhythm—in heart beat, in intestinal
contraction, in poetry, music, play." Which, from Mr. Dorsey,
brings us not so far from the clearing in the jungle.

The most rewarding forms of play, furthermore, are those in
which the player participates directly with his own muscles, his

own voice, his own rhythm. To exercise the faculty vicariously through the play of others, while frequently amusing enough, is far less helpful biologically. In brief, first hand is better than second hand.

If this distinction is a valid one, it follows that the value of play in a given culture may be roughly appraised by the volume of its participating as against its non-participating forms. A group given to doing is on the whole having more fun, and serving its nervous system better, than a group given to watching.

We have in the Western World a costly and stupendous organization of recreation and amusement. How much are we as citizens of that world getting out of it? Is it really providing us with fun, with release, with something of the satisfaction which the Rock Veddahs and the Greeks have known? No conclusive answer to this basic question will be found in this paper. An adequate appraisal would require months, nay years, of patient research. I can only sketch the barest introduction to the problem.

An initial step is obviously to secure some idea of the extent and of the specific forms of play now practised among Western peoples. The following table is an attempt to do this for the United States—the nation which is undoubtedly the outstanding exhibit of the machine age, and the type toward which other Western peoples, for good or for ill, are at present drifting. Nobody, so far as I can learn, has tried to construct a similar table, and accordingly it can only be regarded with the charity which a pioneering effort deserves.

### ESTIMATED ANNUAL COST OF PLAY

#### IN AMERICA

*Forms impossible without machinery*

| | |
|---|---:|
| Pleasure motoring (⅔ of total cost) . . . . . | $5,000,000,000 |
| Vacations and travel (Transportation element primarily) . . . . . . . . . . . . . . . . | 2,000,000,000 |
| Moving pictures . . . . . . . . . . . . . . . | 1,500,000,000 |
| Newspapers, tabloids, light fiction (in part) . . . | 1,000,000,000 |
| Radio . . . . . . . . . . . . . . . . . .. . | 750,000,000 |

| | |
|---|---|
| Phonographs, pianolas, etc. . . . . . . . . . . | 250,000,000 |
| Telephone—pleasure factor only . . . . . . . . | 100,000,000 |
| Flying, bicycling, etc.—pleasure factor . . . . . | 25,000,000 |

Total $10,635,000,000

*Forms conceivable without machinery*

| | |
|---|---|
| Entertaining, visiting, night clubs, road houses—(food and service factor) . . . . . . . . . . . . | 3,000,000,000 |
| Candy, chewing gum, hard and soft drinks—(in part only) . . . . . . . . . . . . . . . . . | 2,000,000,000 |
| Tobacco—(in part) . . . . . . . . . . . | 1,500,000,000 |
| Collections, hobbies, pets . . . . . . . . . . | 1,000,000,000 |
| Shows, theatres, concerts, religious revivals, lectures, etc. . . . . . . . . . . . . . . . . | 500,000,000 |
| Gifts (in part) . . . . . . . . . . . . . | 500,000,000 |
| Golf . . . . . . . . . . . . . . . . | 500,000,000 |
| Social clubs (upkeep factor only) . . . . . . | 250,000,000 |
| Children's toys . . . . . . . . . . . . | 250,000,000 |
| Indoor games—cards, billiards, pool, chess, etc. . . . | 100,000,000 |
| Playgrounds, camping, hiking . . . . . . . . | 100,000,000 |
| Dancing, jazz palaces, etc. . . . . . . . . . | 100,000,000 |
| Amusement parks . . . . . . . . . . . . | 100,000,000 |
| Processions, celebrations, pageants . . . . . . . | 50,000,000 |
| Swimming and bathing beaches . . . . . . . . | 50,000,000 |
| Musical instruments (non-automatic) . . . . . . | 50,000,000 |
| Hunting and fishing . . . . . . . . . . . | 50,000,000 |
| Gambling, including stock exchanges—(commission element only) . . . . . . . . . . . . . | 50,000,000 |
| Horse-racing . . . . . . . . . . . . . | 50,000,000 |
| Football . . . . . . . . . . . . . . | 50,000,000 |
| Baseball . . . . . . . . . . . . . . | 50,000,000 |
| Sport clothes . . . . . . . . . . . . . | 50,000,000 |
| Prize fighting . . . . . . . . . . . . . | 15,000,000 |
| Tennis and allied games . . . . . . . . . . | 15,000,000 |
| Yachting and boating . . . . . . . . . . . | 10,000,000 |
| Field sports . . . . . . . . . . . . . | 10,000,000 |
| Winter sports . . . . . . . . . . . . . | 10,000,000 |
| Indoor sports—gymnasiums, basketball, bowling, etc. | 10,000,000 |

Grand total, all forms $21,045,000,000

You wonder, perhaps, why I include the telephone. I include it—and only a portion of the total annual cost—for the simple reason that the Federation of Women's Clubs, in making a survey of recreation comprising eight million American families, so includes it. Among rural matrons, particularly on party lines, it is alleged to be a major indoor sport. There is, furthermore, a recognized telephone habit, allied to the ancient diversion of gossip.

Naked and undocumented as they stand, these figures cannot fail to tell us certain things which are both true and important. To begin with, the grand total of over twenty billion dollars— and I am convinced that this is a conservative estimate—indicates that not far from one quarter of the entire national income of America is expended for play and recreation, broadly interpreted. In the next place, perhaps half that sum is expended in forms of play new since the coming of the industrial revolution, and requiring more or less complicated machinery for their enjoyment. The outstanding exhibits are the motor car, travel, the movies and the radio. Finally, the table gives a fairly comprehensive list of the things which I have in mind when I use the word play, and so serves to define it. Incidentally, it has been calculated that the total mechanical horsepower of our automobiles is greater than all other forms of mechanical energy combined, in America. The most powerful thing we possess is thus a plaything. And, as we play with it, we kill 25,000 persons, and wound 600,000 more, every year—which must make the emperors of Rome stir enviously in their graves.

A similar table prepared for Western Europe would tell a somewhat different story. Not only would the relative amount devoted to recreation be less, but motoring, radio, moving pictures, and formal athletics would shrink in favor of entertaining, festivals, special foods and drinks, music, group games and dancing. But if we could watch these figures, year by current year, it is safe to assume that the traditional ways of playing—the fiestas and the community songs and dances—were slowly giving way to the forms which so triumphantly head the budget in America. There is a good deal of excited talk on the Continent about pre-

serving native forms of culture, but this talk is not reflected in
the statistics of either motor cars or Hollywood films imported
from the United States.   At the present time, nine out of every
ten films exhibited in foreign theatres are American made.

Another way to show the significance of play in figure form, is
to count noses rather than dollars.   Again the following figures
are for the United States only, and again they are mostly pioneering estimates.   The table is a rough attempt to find out what
proportion of the population goes in for non-participating, second-
hand amusement.

Newspapers and tabloids—35,000,000 readers a day.
Radio—30,000,000 listeners a night
Phonographs, player pianos—15,000,000 listeners a night.
Moving Pictures—50,000,000 admissions a week.
Theatres, concerts, shows, lectures, religious revivals—5,000,000 admis-
    sions a week.
The popular magazines—15,000,000 readers a month.
Baseball—40,000,000 admissions a year.
Horse-racing—10,000,000 admissions a year.
Football—10,000,000 admissions a year.
Prize fighting—10,000,000 admissions a year.
Golf, tennis, regattas, field sports—5,000,000 admissions a year.

Save for phonographs and radios—the air not having passed
into the category of private property as yet—all the above are
paid admissions.  The free watching of amateur sports—of
pageants and processions, of long-distance swimming events,
cornerstone laying, church and civic festivals, and championship
contests devoted to pie eating, coffee drinking, long-distance expec-
torating, the selection of bathing beauties, and the rest—would
make huge, but utterly incalculable increases in the total attendance figures.

Of these side-show championships, which are becoming increasingly prevalent, we might note a typical case. On September 13,
1926, Professor B. G. Burt of Jamestown, New York, broke the
piano-playing endurance record.  He ran the non-stop period
from 52 hours and 15 minutes up to 60 hours.  He did not cease
an instant for food, drink, or sleep.  He played over 5,000 selec-

tions from memory; his fingers hit the keys on an average of 72,-
000 times an hour, a total of 4,320,000 blows for the whole period
of the contest. He consumed 200 cigarettes and 50 cigars.
Meanwhile the contest was staged appropriately enough, in the
show window of a garage where the casual passerby might have an
opportunity to observe the devoted musician at his championship
labors.

Furthermore, many of our second-hand, and particularly third-
hand, thrills result not from the activity of the players—the line
and drive of their bodies in action—but from an entirely different motive; the money one is going to win or lose by betting on
the contest. Gambling is an ancient and universal form of play,
but its frequency and volume tends to be a barometer which
measures the success or failure of a given culture in providing
more direct and rewarding forms. Gambling is a revolt against
boredom. The greater the normal facilities for being bored, the
greater the volume of gambling. Second-hand play is thin por-
ridge, and we salt it with gambling.

A bookmaker at the races, who used to collect pennies for
a company operating slot machines, recently confessed his present profession as follows: "It's a good deal like collecting money
from slot machines except that, instead of getting it out of the
machines, I get it out of the boobs. It's a lot better too because
there are more boobs than slot machines, they are closer together,
they have more money in them, and they open easier."

It has been estimated that over a billion dollars changes hands
every year in poker playing. It is rapidly becoming a part of
golfing ritual—like silence when a shot is made—that a player
must back his prowess with a money wager. A foursome was
recently played for $10,000 a side, plus $1,000 a hole, plus a $5,-
000 Nassau, and before the match was finished $500 a stroke
was added. At the championship match at the Chicago Golf
Club, Mr. Hugh Fullerton estimates the total betting reached
$500,000. A match was recently played on Long Island for
$20,000 a side. "Try to get into a foursome and refuse to bet,"
asks Mr. Fullerton, "and see how often you will be asked to play
again."

There is a third and last exhibit to be spread upon the record. How do children play in the machine age? From many points of view this is the most important question of all. Fortunately there is a very careful statistical study available in this connection— though somewhat limited in area. Messrs. Lehman and Witty have tabulated the frequency of play forms among some 7,000 school children and young people, both urban and rural, in Kansas. They drew up a list of 200 common methods of play, and had each child grade frequencies on the list, and also note other forms not given on the list. (Altogether, over 800 forms of play were noted and tabulated.) The outstanding results of this inquiry, conducted at intervals in 1923, 1924, and 1926, may be summarized as follows:

### Most Frequent Play Forms

#### Boys and Young Men

[Numbered in order of frequency]

| | 8 Years Old | 12 Years Old | 15 Years Old | 18 Years Old |
|---|---|---|---|---|
| 1. | Funny papers | Funny papers | Funny papers | Reading newspapers |
| 2. | Reading | Reading | Reading | Funny papers |
| 3. | Playing catch | Playing catch | Playing catch | Automobiling |
| 4. | Drawing | Automobiling | Automobiling | Movies |
| 5. | Romping | Movies | Movies | Watching sports |
| 6. | Gathering flowers | Playing baseball | Baseball | Playing catch |
| 7. | Cutting with scissors | Playing football | Watching sports | Baseball |
| 8. | Listening to stories | Bicycling | Football | Reading books |
| 9. | Carpentry work | Wrestling | Radio | Football |
| 10. | Playing football | Carpentry | Basketball | Driving motor |
| 11. | Automobiling | Watching sports | Wrestling | Radio |
| 12. | Phonograph | Radio | Bicycling | Basketball |

*Girls and Young Women*

| 8 Years Old | 15 Years Old | 22 Years Old |
|---|---|---|
| 1. Funny papers | Funny papers | Reading newspapers |
| 2. Reading | Reading | Writing letters |
| 3. Skipping rope | Automobiling | Visiting |
| 4. Drawing | Playing piano | Going to shows |
| 5. Scissors work | Movies | Automobiling |
| 6. "Just singing" | Writing letters | Reading books and magazines |
| 7. Looking at pictures | Phonograph | Dancing |
| 8. Dolls | Visiting | Movies |
| 9. Playing house | Gathering flowers | Strolling |
| 10. Listening to stories | Singing | Phonograph |
| 11. Gathering flowers | Teasing somebody | Social clubs |
| 12. Playing piano | Looking at pictures | Playing piano |

The astonishing hold of the "funnies" needs no comment. One suspects that Kansas—primarily an agricultural state—is not unique in this regard. I can see no great evil in the funny papers; I can only see many other things which are conceivably more fun if the modern child had free access to them.

Indeed the children were asked in this same study to name what they would like best to play. For boys from 8 to 15, popularity ran to participating games—football, baseball, basketball, boxing, horseback riding. The funny papers came *eleventh* on the list. It would appear, accordingly, that Kansas children, at least, have not the space and equipment to play what they like the best. The newspapers, on the other hand, are always there. They constitute father's chief recreation as well. Furthermore, in this popularity grading, second-hand play forms—motors, movies, radio, watching sports, all tended to come *after* specific participating games. The boy seems to know his needs better than his world knows them.

Whatever else the patient researches of Messrs. Lehman and Witty show, they prove, beyond all peradventure, the hold of mechanized forms on the play of children, even as we have traced it in the recreation of adults.  The eight-year-olds were the freest both of machinery and commercial exploitation, but these forces tramped down upon them relentlessly as they aged.

The rebirth of play, since Rousseau, has grown year by year with the industrial revolution.  It has matured with steam turbines, turret lathes, and giant power.  Inevitably like every other factor of human life in the Western World, it has been profoundly influenced by these instruments.  The mark of the machine is all over the tables that we have been examining.  One can recognize a number of major ways in which the machine has affected play and which we will consider in order.

First, it has given us more playthings; more physical and mechanical apparatus with which to amuse ourselves.  Human beings are normally as curious as monkeys, and the opportunities to handle, explore, pull to pieces, boggle at, have been indefinitely expanded.  Unfortunately, however, many of these shining toys, such as motors and radio sets, are being made increasingly self-regulating and foolproof.  Not even the joy of tinkering with them is left to us.  We can no longer actively handle them, but only quietly submit to their perfect handling of us.  The output of all sorts of play implements has been enormously increased as a result of factory methods—skates, skis, balls, racquets, bats, stadia, golf sticks, what not.  The limiting factors of darkness, the weather, the seasons, have been set at naught by electric lights, heated swimming pools, artificial ice rinks, indoor tennis courts, innumerable mechanical devices for making play easier and more enduring.  There is even a machine which will register the number of yards you would have driven a golf ball—if the ball you hit had been a free agent, rather than tied by a string to the apparatus.

The machine age has given us more leisure in which to play.  The end of the struggle of the pioneer, the steady decrease in hours of labor, have markedly increased the number of hours in a day for which we have to find something to do.  The phrase "to kill time" is not without significance here.  One cannot kill time with genuine play; one can only improve it.  But with non-satisfying pseudo-play, time may be, and conceivably is, mutilated and murdered,

Thirdly, it has given us more income per family with which to buy the increase in the output of playthings. For the two-thirds of all American families below the income level of the budget of health and decency, this has not meant so much, but for the well-to-do and the wealthy it has meant a great deal. Palm Beach, Pinehurst, Long Island, the North Shore, Atlantic City have set standards for conspicuous consumption in play which take nearly all of the time, and a large fraction of the income, of the conscientious devotee. Indeed so far have matters gone, that the solemn trek in full regalia from one shrine of sport to the next has frequently been designated as a hard life. One can well believe it. With new millionaires being shot out of Pittsburgh, Oklahoma, Hollywood, Wall Street, at the rate of a dozen a week, the struggle not only to lead the band wagon but to keep one's place upon its slippery sides, is an exhausting affair. In a deeper sense this is not play at all, but exhibitionism. We note the same phenomenon on the Riviera.

The machine age has given us more congested cities where opportunities for free play are normally at a minimum. This bears hard on adults, but doubly hard on children. I have stood frozen with horror on East 42d Street, New York, watching a group of youngsters play ball under the wheels of trucks and taxicabs. They faced a terrible death a dozen times an hour. Every year some of them are killed; which furnishes eloquent and tragic tribute to the eternal biological demand for play. It has been said that the closing three decades of the last century, were the most malignant in their effect upon city children of any previous period which history has to record. Industry had created the choked city, the Puritan attitude towards play was still formidable, playgrounds were non-existent and parks at a minimum—indeed it hardly bears thinking upon, the life of millions of children in the dreadful eighties. With the present century, the change for the better has been marked. The Puritan has relaxed his grip on the Sabbath; and nearly every city in the land has its municipal playground and park areas, which have begun to bring play back into the life of children in the modern town. But my courageous friends on 42d Street attest that only a beginning has been made.

It is claimed that as ground rents rise and cities become increasingly congested, opportunities for real recreation decline, even as opportunities for second-hand play, duly capitalized, increase. What does the average adult city dweller do with his or her leisure? Here is a typical enough instance:

Goldie Cinnamon sold stockings in Bernheimer's department store. She had only Sundays and holidays to do the things she wanted and needed to do. She had planned this Sunday to wash her two pairs of crêpe-de-Chine teddies and her four pairs of silk hose. She wanted to make a pan of fudge, wash her hair, and sit on the fire escape while it dried, reading *True Confessions,* and smoking cigarettes. She hoped to go with her girl friend later in the day to the Criterion to see John Gilbert in "Passionate Perils."

For those who use the term "week-end," say one per cent of the urban population, there is plenty of real play to be had—in the event that they can keep sober (the week-ends of the prohibition era are becoming something of an endurance contest). But for the other ninety and nine, there are, in order: (1) The gross tonnage of the Sunday newspapers, particularly the funnies, the rotogravure section, and the succulent details of the last love nest murder; (2) an automobile ride in solemn procession, with a car five feet in front of the forward bumpers, and another five feet behind, and anywhere from a one-half to a three-hour wait at the ferries and other choked bottle-necks of the city's main arteries on a Sunday; (3) the moving pictures, happily held to the intelligence limit of the normal twelve-year-old child; (4) a rapid transit trip to an amusement park where, if one does not step on a broken pop bottle on the beach, he is reasonably sure of a banana peel; where owners of loop-the-loops commit suicide on rainy holidays; and where it is a very poor day indeed when fifty lost children are not entertained in the local police station

awaiting the entry of their frenzied parents; (5) a trip to one
of the city parks where there may be a patch of green not covered by a newspaper, but hardly a safe proposition to wager anything upon; and (6), a poker party at Joe's place.  Far, far down
in the list, comes that small, hardy, and courageous group who
brave hours of dreary transit to get out into the country and
really play, knapsacks on their backs.

In all fairness we should note that while the knapsack group is
small in numbers as compared with the total urban population,
its importance is steadily increasing.  Perhaps nowhere has the
out-of-doors movement made more headway than in Germany,
but America is rapidly organizing camping clubs, Boy Scouts,
Camp Fire Girls, Appalachian Trails.  Winter sports meanwhile
have achieved an unheard-of prominence in the last decade.
Against the encroachments of the modern city, the playground
and recreation forces make a valiant struggle—but a recent survey of Newark, New Jersey, showing two out of every three children with the streets as their chief playground, indicates how far
the movement has yet to go.  In the race between land values and
the right to play, the financial odds are with the former.

The machine age, as already noted, has given us more routine,
mechanized jobs.  These jobs demand a righting of an outraged
biological balance through some form of play.  In the automobile
industry today, the character of work has been summarized by
engineers, as follows:

|  | per cent of the total force |
|---|---|
| 1. Machine tenders | 40 |
| 2. Assemblers | 15 |
| 3. Skilled workers | 10 |
| 4. Inspectors | 5 |
| 5. Helpers for skilled workers | 15 |
| 6. Laborers, clean-up men | 15 |

Groups one and two combined constitute more than half of
the total, and these are the employees who can be taught in a day

or two the simple relentless operations on the machines, or "on the belt"; operations which kill every spark of interest in their daily work. Furthermore, these groups are steadily gaining in numbers against the other four. Nor is the situation in the automobile industry greatly different from other industries which have adopted mass production. As a result some millions of industrial employees are trying to work off the "unrelieved irritations of their psychic lives" in the thrills, excitement and intense stimulation of prize fights, ball games, race courses, roller coasters, tabloid murder stories, gambling, gin, and "torrid screen dramas of sexy souls." They take the only outlets they can find in a blind rush from the monotony of their appointed tasks. But the basic deficiency is not neutralized—as the curious visitor in Detroit can only too clearly establish. Even jazz dancing is but play in a Ford factory. Its pounding rhythm is as simple as tightening bolts. It gives very little scope for individual expression.

Nor is the revolt from the machine confined to manual workers. A strange and otherwise inexplicable phenomenon is appearing among business men, particularly of the medium salaried group. The unimaginative routines of their office work—standardized dictation, telephone calls, "conferences," recording, checking, submitting themselves to a given niche in a huge corporate structure—are forcing them in increasing numbers into the cap and bells of Mystic Shriners, Mooses, Rotary Clubs, Kiwanis, the cults of service, Ku Klux Klans—anything which promises color and life, humor and activity. The utter banality of where they land is in tragic contrast with the humanity of the urge to play which drives them forth. Not a few of the antics of advertising and the higher salesmanship should be written off to the same revolt. The consumer suffers, heaven knows, but the salesman at least secures some needed psychic relief.

Why did America enter the great war of which it intellectually disapproved, with such whoops and shouts of tumultuous joy? In part, I believe, because the war offered a substitute for that release in play which the piping times of peace did not provide.

Finally, the machine age has given us mass production in amusement, run according to up-to-date business methods. We have

been "sold" on play precisely as we have been sold on tooth
powder, bathtubs, snappy suits and electrical refrigerators. Motors, bicycles (presently aeroplanes), baseball, moving pictures,
Broadway, night clubs, college football, prize fights, Coney Islands,
radios, victrolas, lecture bureaus, tabloids, confession magazines,
best sellers, horse-racing, travel bureaus, plus fours, revival meetings, Boy Scouts, cigarettes, antique furniture—all have gone
into quantity production, following accepted formulæ of advertising, salesmanship, the limit of price the traffic will bear, and
all have proved soundly profitable, with wide margins of credit
from the banks, and as often as not a listing on the stock exchange.

At the first Dempsey-Tunney fight for the heavyweight boxing championship of the world, 135,000 spectators saw the match,
and they paid $2,000,000 for their seats—not counting what the
speculators made. Mr. Dempsey received $750,000 for 30 minutes
work, Mr. Tunney received $450,000, while the profits of Mr.
Tex Rickard, the promoter, were $437,000. Mr. Rickard's Madi-
son Square Garden voting trust certificates are listed on the New
York Curb Exchange. With such profits they should be in the
main tent, along with General Motors and the Radio Corporation
of America. In 1850, Tom Sayers, the English boxing champion,
was glad to fight 44 rounds for £5 a side. But perhaps he fought
for the fun of it.

In the eighteenth century prize fighting was a sport, beloved
of royalty and gentry. In the nineteenth century it became a
game, deserted by the élite and controlled by the underworld. In
the twentieth century it has passed into the category of big
business, financed by the banks, issuing securities, and licensed
by the state—like banking and insurance. In New York recently
a syndicate was organized by a certain Mr. Jimmy Johnson to buy
the contracts of champion boxers and leading contenders, and
so happily to effect a monopoly of the whole sport. "The boxing
industry (note the word industry) is reaching gigantic proportions and the time has arrived for big business methods. We propose to handle boxers in the same fashion that moving-picture

producers handle their star performers." Than which nothing could be more business-like.

Baseball has long since entered the ranks of big business with its 20,000,000 paid admissions to the two big leagues, its million dollar world series event, and its purchasing of the contracts of players to the extent of over $2,000,000 each year. It has been judiciously calculated furthermore that Mr. Babe Ruth, the home-run batter, is worth a cool $1,000,000 a year in extra admission fees to the American League.

Football has but recently broken into the admittedly professional ranks. A certain Mr. C. C. Pyle, popularly known as "Cold Cash" Pyle, induced the famous Mr. Red Grange to leave the lists of college football and act as cornerstone for a professional league. (This is the same Mr. Pyle who started tennis as big business with the purchase of Miss Suzanne Lenglen—for $200,-000.) On the day Red Grange left the amateur ranks, he cleared $375,000, with the promise of making a million before the winter was over. At the same time the use of his name was sold to a sweater manufacturer for $12,000, a shoe manufacturer for $5,-000, a cap maker for $2,500, and to a cigarette company for $1,-000—the latter bargain figure doubtless due to the fact that Red never smokes. A candy company sold six million "Red Grange Chocolate Bars" in thirty days, for a consideration not disclosed. During this period Red received 187 telephone calls, sixty telegrams, and thirty-nine personal visits from commercial firms eager to capitalize his name and fame.

Miss Gertrude Ederle, after swimming the English Channel, received over a million dollars worth of commercial offers, a gross even greater than Red's.

College football while amateur in name is professional in spirit, and constitutes what is known as a major industry. A good team is not only the chief claim to fame of a given college; it is also frequently its financial backbone. Its profits (running up as high as $500,000 a year in some cases) maintain all other college sports; while its success is a harbinger for endowments from rich and happy alumni. Speculators reap a magnificent re-

ward at every big game, selling $2 tickets to prosperous butter and
egg merchants for $100—more or less.    Meanwhile a retired col-
lege coach declares:    "I will guarantee any first-class high school
player that I can get him through any one of a half a dozen good
colleges with board and tuition paid and no one pressing him for
payment of his 'loans' afterward."    In these circumstances the
suggestion of Mr. Heywood Broun that college football turn
frankly professional, buying and selling its players as do the baseball leagues, seems eminently just.

The moving-picture industry turns out 150,000 miles of film
a year.    In 1895 it turned out 21,600 feet.    It is alleged that
68.2 per cent of the American population attend the movies fairly
regularly.    There are daily changes of programme in 14,000
theatres.    With such an enormous investment, is it any wonder
that the necessities of the art require a grade and volume of publicity in respect to the stars of the silver screen, that never for
an instant loses sight of the fact that sexual curiosity is perhaps
the chief interest of the modern world?

A concert singer has confessed how the exigencies of her
trade today require that she be "sold" like a circus.    She cannot
sing what she wants, but only what will pay, while her publicity
agent sees to it that she performs the requisite number of stunts
and somersaults.    In the theatre, profit has been standardized
under three heads, to wit: (1) tears, (2) laughs, (3) thrills—
standardized, say the Beards, with the rhythmic thump of a hydraulic pump.    Broadway's musical comedies are geared to the
spectator's emotions, as the belt in an automobile factory is geared
to the maximum endurance of those that seek it.    Sound box-
office stuff.

The editor of one of our confession magazines—with a circulation in the millions—tenders this advice to his authors:    "Here's a
man, see?    And his wife, see?    And another man.    Write about
that.    And let the shadow of the bed be on every page, but never
let the bed appear."    The resulting confection, duly browned to
formula, is served largely to the average woman in America, leading the common existence, only partially literate, with limited

financial resources; a drab, dull and often sordid life. From this drabness the confession magazine allows her a brief and heady escape. In this exhibit we probably find play at its lowest level. But immensely profitable financially.

The United States Santa Claus Company has recently been organized in Chicago. It undertakes to provide any home with a professional Santa at Christmas time, and thus relieve father of his time-honored role. It is guaranteed that the children's names will be remembered, that appropriate seasonal remarks will be delivered, and that no mistakes will be made in the distribution of gifts. Over one hundred orders were booked for Christmas, 1927. Thus goes another participating festival into the hands of standardized business enterprise.

A final corollary of the not altogether holy alliance of play and business is the over-competition that finds its way into so much of modern sport. It is dominated by a compulsion to win, rather than freely to enjoy. College football players are particularly under the domination of their non-participating alumni, and have repeatedly claimed that they hate the nervous pressure of the fall season. This is not play but work. One is adjured to make good in the paint and varnish business, and in the half back business. The terminology is identical; the saga of competitive success dominates both.

In its broadest outline the situation seems to be this: the industrial revolution has wrenched most of us away from those manual, handicraft tasks which gave us muscular activity and a margin of true play in making and fashioning things for our own use and amusement. With these tasks have gone the old community play forms, the roof raising, the barn dance, the Maypole, the harvest festival, the sugaring off. Such often flourished in the teeth of the Puritans. Our jobs today are less active, and even when we use a set of muscles in a factory, it is all too frequently the same set day in and day out. All-round development, such as the pioneer and the craftsman knew, is increasingly a thing of the past.

Meanwhile we have more time on our hands by virtue of shorter working hours. Children—with the abatement of the old-time chores—have far more time as well. Now to use this time, and to offset the non-active or over-specialized modern job, play is necessary. Furthermore, we have more income with which to finance this new demand. A culture which encouraged us to use that time and money by substituting valuable new forms of play for the forms which had been lost would be a wise culture. But the balance sheet of modern play that we have been examining is hardly a document of unalloyed wisdom. Not knowing where to turn we have turned into the clicking turnstile—at fifty cents a click.

A fraction of the extra time and money has been devoted to new participating forms of recreation, that do indeed release the human spirit, equate the biological balance, and return as much, or more, to life as ever was lost with the passing of the handicraft era. Particularly noteworthy in this respect is the out-of-doors movement, with its new parks, playgrounds, pools, beaches, trails and camping places. Also important is the growth in international sports, the Olympic games, the Davis Cup tennis matches and others, leading to friendly rivalry among nations. And perhaps even more important in the long run is the new conception of education through play which many schools are beginning to experiment with—though the relative number of children actually touched by this philosophy to date is very small.

But a far greater amount of money, and probably of time, is devoted to forms of play which at their best do not furnish an equivalent release, and at their worst compound the harm which flows from over-mechanized daily work. Motoring, movies, second-hand thrills in sports, in tabloid crimes, and in confession magazines, the funnies, the radio, even the remorseless rhythm of jazz dancing—all are burdened with elements against which the spirit of play beats its wings in vain.

As a male adult in reasonable health, the play forms which I really love to undertake are these: following mountain trails on foot in summer, on snow shoes in winter; following lonely reaches of lake and river in a canoe; swimming, sun bathing, and high diving; skating, hockey, tennis and squash. I like to sing

with a group. I like to improvise dances, to act charades, to
take part in amateur theatricals. None of these things I do particularly well, but all outrank any enjoyment I can suck from
motoring, moving pictures, gambling games, night clubs, or
watching other people play. And all of them without exception have no basic dependence upon a machine culture. I give
this personal exhibit only for what it may be worth, but I fancy
that the few of us who follow some such recreational bent have
more genuine fun than all the devotees at the twenty billion dollar shrine combined. Meanwhile the great majority of my fellow
citizens have had no opportunity to discover the joy, the beauty
and the cheapness of genuine play. Trapped in a great city,
their habit patterns are geared to more ugly and far more expensive relaxations, while the economic pressure to hold them to
that line is well-nigh relentless.

What the age of machinery has given us in time, it would
fain take away again by degrading the opportunities which that
time affords; by standardizing our recreations on a quantity
production basis, by making us watchers rather than doers, by exploiting our leisure for profit, by surfeiting us with endless mechanical things to monkey with—from gasoline cigar lighters to
million dollar cruising yachts, by forcing the pace of competition
in play until it turns into work, and above all by brutalizing
in recreation millions of human beings who are already brutalized
by the psychological imperatives of their daily labor. And it
will take more barn dances than Henry Ford can ever pay for,
to throw off the yoke of that brutality.

But who shall be the winner in another generation, only the
gods can tell.

## XV—EDUCATION

### By Everett Dean Martin

EVERYWHERE in Western civilization education is in a state of confusion. The present situation is inevitable and not necessarily alarming for the industrial age is new, and it should not surprise us to find that as Freud says, we are living "psychologically beyond our means." The Western nations did not wholly foresee or deliberately plan the industrial revolution. They drifted into it. They came into it with ideas, traditions, values, elaborated in an earlier civilization the economic structure of which had remained relatively the same throughout many centuries. The new ways of living necessitated important revaluations, new forms of social control, restatement of many of the aims of culture. There has been tragic blundering. New and hitherto inarticulate elements of the population—frequently people with but few civilized interests and almost no cultural tradition, or social responsibility—have risen to power. In the industrial struggle many priceless values, won out of a long past, have been temporarily lost. Others survive in antiquated form which often renders them irrelevant and sentimental in their modern application. In the general confusion, it is the habit of those with unsolved problems to offer education—usually the education of someone else—the masses—as the long sought solution.

I

YET in actual practice education is daily under fire of severe criticism. People demand of it all sorts of new things. At the same time they denounce it for its failure to meet the existing demands.

They forget that, in the scramble of the sudden transition into the industrial age, education also is bound to fall victim to the general cultural chaos.

The Western World has not as yet achieved a seriously considered philosophy of education. There is little agreement concerning what should be taught, or how, or to what end, or as to the value of learning anything at all. It is generally agreed however that what is taught is usually taught poorly. Attention has repeatedly been called to two outstanding facts. First it is a matter of common knowledge that the boards of trustees who exercise final authority over the system of education both in the public schools and in institutions of higher learning are made up largely of persons who do not know at all what education is about. It is not fair to say, as some critics do, that school and college trustees deliberately conspire to divert institutions of learning from their true aims to mere agencies for the conservation of the present industrial hierarchy, with its capitalist "ideology" and its special privileges. It is enough to say that for the most part they are sincere laymen, chosen to guide education not because of their own attainments in learning but because of political preferment or business success. It is natural that such persons should be more interested in success and in established convention than in scholarship. And who can blame them if they give little original thought to the question: What is an educated person?

Professional educators likewise give little thought to this question. Most of them are content to teach as well as they can the subject in which they have attained some proficiency. It is not their task, considering their place in the system, to concern themselves with the larger problems of education. Those who are concerned with these larger questions are usually administrators rather than teachers, and their interest is in problems of method, organization, discipline, and school politics, rather than in any such abstract matter as the ultimate aim of education. They are, or try to be, practical persons.

This leads to the mention of the second outstanding fact about modern education. The teaching profession does not offer to its members a career comparable in attractiveness with the opportunities of business or of some of the other professions.   It goes without saying that many high-grade men and women are in this profession out of devotion to scholarship and service to humanity. But such devotion calls for a degree of self-sacrifice which is not commonly expected of persons in other occupations.   Financial reward is small, advancement is slow and difficult, preferment depends largely upon the good will of superiors who are often administrators rather than scholars.   Popular prejudice is a hindrance to independence of judgment and freedom of expression.   Scholarly attainment is seldom appreciated, the public preferring to honor motion-picture actresses and baseball players.

Consequently the teaching profession—with notable exceptions —tends to be filled with deferential people, people who can be easily intimidated, who can trot in harness, conform to the system, take orders, and present controversial truths in an inoffensive manner.   Teaching becomes a kind of trade similar in a way to other trades, with an average quality of workmanship and standardized quantity production as its object.   People who all their professional lives must do just what they are told commonly lose the habit—if ever it was part of their nervous organization—of judging the ultimate significance of that which they are obliged to perform.   Hence it is futile to inquire of the educational system why it exists.   That responsibility would appear to be elsewhere. Education is here; that is all—a routine job to be done day by day.   Any account of its aim from this source must at best be largely conventional.

## II

MUCH of our present confusion, I think, is a result of historical accident, and of the state of the cultural tradition at the time the Western World entered the industrial era.   It is necessary to grasp the force of the position of education at the time the great transition took place.   It must be said that it was, on the whole, unprepared by its very traditions to interpret effectively the values of civilization in so unprecedented and unforeseen a situation.   Not only did the industrial revolution cast up as the actors upon the stage of modern life two classes, employers and employees, who were largely innocent of the educational traditions prevalent in the older ruling class—and for whom, in the new environment, many cultural standards must be revised—but the cultural tradition itself had at that time become so inadequate for the solving of vital human problems that the educator could do little more than insist upon a dead and irrelevant formalism. What was demanded of him was a return to the experimental spirit in which his tradition had its origin.

It is one of the ironies of history that, when the emergence of Western civilization duplicated in certain important aspects the psychological situation out of which the ancients won those cultural values that have been the ideals of educators ever since then, those very moderns who held most closely to the classical tradition were incapable of taking—when the times demanded it again—an experimental attitude similar to that of their great preceptors. The example and spirit of the ancient Greeks, in a situation in some respects similar to our own, ought to have given our educators courage. Unfortunately the ideas of men who like themselves were once compelled to meet a new situation in unprecedented ways had by the end of the eighteenth century become little more than an irrelevant intellectual orthodoxy. Otherwise it might have placed culture above "go-getting." As it was, it became a flight from reality that had nothing to do with the case.

With the ancients the pursuit of wisdom—a wisdom beyond mere immediate practicality—had everything to do with the case; it smashed tradition and placed before the human intellect the issue not of personal advantage but rather the function and necessity of wisdom in the common life of mankind. Education, as it was first given us by the ancients, was in no sense a genteel tradition aloof from contemporary reality. It was a quest for meaning and value in a world made new. It is my conviction that unless we understand the problem which the ancients tried to solve in the fifth and fourth centuries before Christianity, we can never get a proper perspective of our own problems. Otherwise the tradition of men who once grappled not wholly unsuccessfully with the task of making something more than a sordid economic struggle out of human relationships becomes a mere gesture in obeisance to a misunderstood past. One alternative is the casting off—as many do—of the accumulated wisdom of the ages. Modern man then becomes merely a creature of his own day and generation. But new as our age is I do not believe we can afford to ignore all that men in the past have struggled for in order to give living some meaning and scale of importance. We need the things that have marked the difference between men and beasts and between higher men and lower men.

I said that in one respect at least the educational task of the ancient Greek was like our own. He also found himself in a new world, responsible as master over a situation he had not foreseen. He realized that in the new situation his ancestral myths were no longer sufficient to guide his behavior. Education became a voyage of discovery, the search for knowledge and for an understanding of what constituted the good life. Old beliefs, presuppositions, popular opinions were examined by a dialectical method, the practice of which was at once education and philosophy.

Although designed for members of what we now should call a leisure class, this ancient education was not mere idle speculation or intellectual adornment. It was practical in the largest sense. The free man learned not merely how to employ his leisure time in polite conversation. He learned to take a critical attitude toward his prejudices. He discovered principles of reason with which he could free his mind from herd opinion, control his behavior and consider intelligently the welfare of the state. There was something courageous and ennobling in this early humanistic struggle of men to find by using their unaided intelligence, and without recourse to magic or miracle or divine revelation, meanings and values with which they might attain self-mastery. The tradition of liberal education in the Western World had its origin in the humanism of non-religious ancient Greece. At the beginning it was an adventure in "debunking."

But the humanism and spirit of inquiry did not always survive in the liberal education of subsequent ages. When Christian theologians in the Middle Ages rediscovered Aristotle, they naturally appropriated only so much of the Greek education and philosophy of life as could be assimilated with their religious culture based upon divine revelation. Dialectic was not now a voyage of discovery. It became a refined and subtle disputation designed to rationalize the mythus. The good life became the life of pious contemplation. The free man, the ancient man of leisure, was supplanted by one who found leisure through forsaking the world for the cloister. The full force of the meaning of the classical tradition was not felt by the scholastic mind.

It was the humanists of the Renaissance who for the first time in Christendom got some notion of what classical education was about. It was as if low-hung clouds had suddenly lifted and revealed—nearer their own humanity than men trained in mediæval-ism had as yet dared to imagine—the sunlit heights of spiritual value and cultural achievement to which men had once risen in supreme indifference to the entire system of beliefs and values of mediæval Christianity. The discovery was startling, disconcerting, revolutionary, and it immediately inspired a transvaluation of education. It was to the work of transforming education that men like Erasmus devoted their lives. Erasmus might still be nominally a Christian but he could write "Saint Socrates, pray for me," and it is to be noted that he raised an issue in every university he visited. People think of the Renaissance as an epoch in Italian painting and sculpture. From our point of view it was an educational movement, the aim of which was the recovery of the adventurous humanism which is the true spirit of the classical tradition.

III

THE educational aim of the Renaissance was bound to stir up a tremendous reaction. Men do not want an inquiring, sceptical, value-creating discipline which forces the mind to examine its beliefs, face reality, and stand on its own. They want to be told what to believe. They want the delusion of comfort and security. They ask of education not that it raise new questions but that it give a categorical answer to old ones. They expect it to train youth in the ways that the elders expect them to walk in. Education, instead of being free to do its work, is sidetracked. Its proper task is, as I have said in my "Meaning of a Liberal Education":

Something which will broaden the interests and sympathies of people regardless of their daily occupation—or along with it—to lift men's thought out of the monotony and drudgery which are the common lot, to free the mind from servitude and herd opinion, to train habits of judgment and of appreciation of value, to carry on the struggle for human excellence in our day and generation, to temper passion with wisdom, to dispel prejudice by better knowledge of self, to enlist all men, in the measure that they have capacity for it, in the achievement of civilization.

But education is always diverted from its true aim and made to serve ends which are irrelevant—the state, the church, popular notions of morality, efficiency, ambition, social security.

We cannot understand the anomalous position of education in the world today, unless we see clearly what happened to the classical tradition after the Renaissance. As should have been expected, both Protestant and Catholic turned against the humanizing influence of the Renaissance upon education. This fact should not astonish the psychologist. As I have shown elsewhere, after every intellectual awakening in history the masses have risen up in an effort to blot it out or repudiate its real meaning, and have made use of popular religious ideas as weapons in their struggle against a movement which at once demanded too much of men, made them feel inferior and robbed them of their traditional consolations. Both Protestant and Catholic turned against the humanism of the Renaissance. It was "Pagan," "worldly," "Anti-Christ."

It is interesting to note that both the Protestant Reformation and the Catholic counter Reformation—led by the Jesuits—did much the same thing with the classical tradition revived by the Renaissance. Both hastily established schools and colleges; both saw that the classical tradition in education was a challenge to pre-established beliefs and that "Humane Letters," once published, could not again be withdrawn from the curriculum. Some knowledge of them had become part of recognized education. Hence each, quite independently of the other, sought to capture for itself the classical knowledge.

Apparently they accepted the classical tradition, and then each denatured it, and made it serve its own theological ends. There was careful selection and expurgation. Emphasis was placed upon monotonous drill in learning Latin and Greek as dead languages—the more dead, the better—and all for "discipline" rather than for understanding of a great culture. And all was so taught—usually so badly taught—as to give the student only a superficial knowledge of the language and a disgust at the whole procedure, and almost no knowledge at all of the Pagan civilization and non-Christian values and ways of life that lay back of all this drill in grammar and vocabulary.

The teaching of the classics might have been the opening of a window on ways of life and thought different from our own, knowledge of which would have broadened the student's interest and sympathies and might have led him to take a critical and experimental attitude toward the problems of living similar to that of the ancients. All this however was carefully avoided. The scholastic spirit was revived in education. Students droned over dull lessons and translation, learned to adorn their speech with a few Latin and Greek quotations, passed examination and for the most part had no notion of what all the study of the classics was about—except that some proficiency in the dead languages was expected of a gentleman. It was a sign of refinement. The classical tradition had thus become the "genteel tradition" and it was with this meaningless baggage that the Western World entered the industrial age and expected that its education would lead it through the maze of machines and organizations and the brute struggle for power and advantage to the achievement of a bright and beautiful civilization. Such might have been realized had the classical tradition, which made up the greater part of the curriculum of school and college, been allowed to retain its vitality, its critical spirit, its humanism and discrimination of worth. But you cannot humanize a machine age with a dead language!

The ancient emphasis upon distinction of human worth, the

free spirit in its search for truth and beauty, the breadth of human understanding all embraced in the classical tradition—if it had not been so denatured—were the very things necessary for the humanization of the industrial age.

As it was, the dead language tradition remained an innocuous ground-work on which was superimposed a scientific and vocational training which by its very nature had to do with means rather than with ends. Real knowledge of science is possible only in graduate research institutions and thus accessible only to the few. The public, accepting the fruits of science and knowing little of its methods, marvels over its practical "wonders" and is afraid it will destroy its religion. Popular education becomes more and more vocational training, an instrumentality for gaining admittance to the white collar class. The dead language drill on which the "go-getter" animal-training is grafted is unable to give meanings to life that are relevant to our age or any other and hence there is much cleverness as to methods of achievement and little reflection on the question: What is worth doing?

Even in those religious circles which succeeded so admirably in capturing and emasculating the classical tradition in education, there is small leadership in the struggle of the modern world for value. Science is either repudiated or its meaning, like that of the humanities, evaded. The spirit of dogmatism has no educational relevancy in the modern world, and when dogmatism is thrust into the background there often emerges not so much a new intellectual spirit as a sentimentalism in which Christ and Rousseau and Mark Hanna are unintelligibly scrambled.

Education becoming secular has not found a philosophy that equips it for leadership in the new civilization. Everywhere the pillar of fiery cloud is replaced, if not by the ambulance, then by the technique of the efficiency expert whose interest in education seems to be that some marchers go faster than others and that the whole rate of marching be speeded up, but whither and to what ends neither dead language nor up-to-date animal-training is able to say. Is it to be wondered at that the two parties—the masters of dead languages and of the newer animal-training—should in our time fall afoul of each other, each party asserting that the other did not know where it was leading humanity? I said that everywhere in Western civilization, education is in a state of confusion.

IV

THE function of education in modern life is something which could not possibly have been foreseen by those who in the past fabricated the classical tradition. Nor is it comprehended by those moderns who seem to be content with specialization, vocational training, preparation for citizenship, new and easier psychological methods of habit formation, or that kind of social service according to which it is held that a university is fulfilling its proper end when it offers its students any sort of instruction that anyone may desire, all with little or no concern for the students' general mental development or orientation toward their world.

Western civilization, because of its industrial and mechanical basis, is like an artifact, a construct, an assemblage of parts, rather than like a process of organic growth. Its unity is not given like that of a living thing or like that of earlier societies. Its unity must be consciously thought out by someone and also consciously utilized and controlled. Successful adaptation to it by the individual requires something more than the assent which was sufficient in earlier civilizations—it requires understanding. It must, to a degree that earlier civilizations did not find necessary, depend for its survival and advancement upon deliberately constructed programmes of education. In agrarian civilizations continuity and integration were achieved largely by means of tradition and custom uncritically accepted. Education there was, but except in Ancient Greece (and perhaps China) legend was more important than reason. Society was relatively static. The past was more to be considered than the future. Distinctions of right and wrong were not subject to revision in the light of experience. They were definitely fixed by the wisdom of the fathers and by a supernatural will. Education was largely drill in the mores and in the established system of rationalization.

v

IN THE new age such an education is obviously fatal. At best it is
irrelevant, having nothing to do with the novel situations in which
behavior must take place. At worst it means stagnation and mal-
adjustment. Modern civilization is naturalistic, mechanistic, its
rhythm the tempo of machines, each one of which is a creature of
problem-solving intelligence. It is an unstable equilibrium of
forces, the shifting patterns of which require of mankind ever
more insight and calculation. To participate, otherwise than as an
automaton and helpless victim of circumstance, the modern man
must to some degree be initiated into the "mysteries" of his new
civilization. And these secrets are the discoveries of the laboratory, of scientific research, of exact measurement, and of mathematics. The formulæ of ancient wisdom may still be useful for
certain human valuations of the possibilities of modern life. But
they are not enough. The new order has no deep roots in the
past. The swiftly changing environment is a ceaseless challenge
to the educator. As new industrial processes emerge, together
with a succession of unpredictable inventions, and as devices of
all sorts of control of the forces of nature are placed in the hands
of the public at large, there must be continuous restatement of the
human issues at stake and ever better general understanding of the
methods of utilizing power for the achievement of value. With
rapidly moving machinery at their disposal men may not behave in
one world and think as if they were living in another. In the face
of every popular resistance—and resistance here is almost insurmountable—the educator must lead beneficiaries of the machine
age to face the realities of the world they are living in.

One such obvious fact, the import of which is not popularly
recognized—frequently not by educators themselves—is that industrialism is rapidly transforming society from an agrarian civilization to a new urban civilization. Yet many of the habits
and views of life on which school and college insist are those of
the country side, the small village, and rural parish of two or
three generations ago. Even in highly industrialized America our
prevailing culture has not yet passed the turning point where there

is general recognition of the situation as it exists. The very approach to such a turning point at which the urban and rural ways of life are arrayed in sharp contrast, raising some of the most significant issues of contemporary American life, still finds such issues officially suppressed both in practical politics and in the educational system. Popular moral sentiments are, as Mr. Mark Sullivan says, still those formerly inculcated by the McGuffy readers. Popular religious beliefs are still parochial, pre-Newtonian, ante-Darwinian. Political ideas are still largely Jacksonian. The Middle West is still thought of as "progressive." Americanism is still largely the inhospitality of the older agrarian immigration toward the newer immigration with its industrial urban population. Big cities are still "wicked"—though much of their superficial sophistication is universally imitated. It would seem that the intellectual urbanization of America is taking place with little guidance on the part of the educational system, a fact which may in part account for our tabloid newspaper mentality and other cultural vagaries.

The emergence of every urban civilization has brought with it, among other things, often of lasting gain for human progress, a period of cultural turmoil, intellectual ferment, and moral laxity. Our own promises to outdistance them all in these respects.

It is a question how effective the educator in the past may have been in directing the hot outflow of such volcanic eruptions into safe channels and in directions calculated to lay new and advantageous ground for human habitation and culture. I have not the historical knowledge to answer this question but I cannot believe that in the present transformation society may expect much guidance of those educators whose agrarian psychology makes them unable to think in terms of the problem with which they have to deal.

VI

THUS we find that education in Western civilization, confused as to its aims, and hesitant to recognize the full implication of the situation in which it is expected to lead, is at the same time a social necessity such as it has never been before. There is nothing new in the statement that without knowledge the people perish. But the statement is true in a new sense now.

Knowledge was never so imperative. And hitherto the chief task of education was the dissemination of knowledge. The knowledge to be disseminated was not far to seek. It was sure and easily obtainable. It was the wisdom inherent in the mores. To-day such wisdom must itself be revalued. The necessary knowledge must be continuously rediscovered and its principles revised and restated. And the people to whom it is to be given? They too are a problem such as the educator of no previous age had to meet. New situations must be met in new and still more new ways, yet always in such a way that those basic human interests for which men have always struggled be not lost, but in each readjustment augumented and made richer in objective.

The burden which Western civilization loads on the back of education can be borne neither by ignoring the present as do the classicists nor by ignoring the past as do many moderns. There must be a living union of the two—not a mere logical synthesis— such as has not appeared in education since the days of ancient Athens. Although in the machine age it is necessary that in the struggle for value men be enabled consciously to match and meet each change in the patterns of mechanical forces, nevertheless a living culture, like all organic behavior, is a continuity in which past and present are merged as one. It is the task of education in the machine age to achieve such a continuity.

Education is thus faced with two aspects of the same problem— that of practically orienting the individual to his world in the struggle for value. The practical problem of orientation cannot be divorced from the end of the struggle for value. To do so is to kill culture, turn the pursuit of value into futile sentimentality and the practical interest into a brute struggle equipped with means, but with no goal or meaning.

The dismemberment of education into an alleged "practical" and a "cultural" interest that seem to have little in common is not infrequently found among those who are engaged in the work of adult education. A vast majority of the two million or more persons in America who are enrolled as students in various classes and correspondence courses, which we speak of as adult education, are inspired by purely utilitarian motives. They are seeking a kind of training which will in the shortest time increase their economic efficiency and enable them to improve their material condition. This is a laudable aim. But I doubt if its prevalence should influence our philosophy of education. Yet this popular utilitarian spirit is often reflected in the thinking of the educators whose task it is to supply this widespread demand for practical information of a vocational nature. Not only is such specialized and elementary training considered education, but it is often taken for granted that this is the only adult education worthy of consideration and that "cultural" education, though not essential, may be embroidered around the periphery of the vocational—if one is inclined to such ornamentation. But in our industrial world it is considered an intellectual luxury—a sort of high-brow entertainment. I have reason to believe that such a view is not uncommon among those engaged in the work of formal education in school and university. One can understand such a notion when one remembers the lack of thoroughness and the aimlessness of much of the teaching of the humanities. But one wonders what Socrates or Abelard or Erasmus would have thought of the idea.

My point is, the educator's task is dual. He must equip the modern man with the insight and the intellectual tools which are necessary for adequate behavior in a world where natural science and modern industry are substituting mechanism for the older personal explanations and relationships. And he must at the same time go beyond means to ends. There is a possible education that will make men more than well ordered puppets in the passing show trained to make gestures, with no sense of the significance of the human drama and with no reflection beyond problems of material advantage.

The task of immediate adjustment is the simpler part of education. Although it is easier to dazzle the masses with the results of scientific research than it is to lead them to think scientifically —and the average man's belief in science must remain second-hand knowledge—a sort of *fides implicata*—still it is possible for the educator to block out innumerable vocational processes and to "sell" in the open market such expert information as will add to the efficiency of anyone from a paper hanger to a member of the diplomatic service.

VII

THE second part of the task—that which really makes it education and liberalizing—is that of leading men to reflect on the way they are going, to consider for themselves ends and values in the light of the experience and the serious thinking of all time, to break the bondage of narrow self-interest and of parochial prejudices with wider outlook and sympathies. If learning does not result in the ability to take a philosophical attitude toward experience, it is not liberal education.

The goal has been achieved all too infrequently even under the favorable conditions of a relatively simple and thus easily interpretable body of knowledge, a selected group of students, and leisure. Consider then the conditions under which the educator must labor in present-day civilization.

Saint Paul tried to be all things to all men. But this ambitious attempt was somewhat simplified by the fact that he had to assume these multitudinous rôles only in so far as the appearance was necessary to convert all sorts of people to belief in his creed— which was his specific purpose. Our civilization forces its educational system to try Saint Paul's ambitious experiment, yet with no such singleness of aim. Democracy and industrialism combine to load upon education a multitude of burdens under which it necessarily weakens. Try to do everything and you will do nothing well. The increased demands upon education are of two kinds. The range and variety of subjects to be taught are vastly extended. Second, our age insists upon giving (compulsory) educational opportunity to the whole population. We may for the present pass by the logical contradiction of the term, compulsory opportunity, and merely note in passing that no such demand was ever before made upon the educator. Could he have succeeded in re-orienting the nations, giving them a well considered knowledge of the elements of the good life, a criterion for the discrimination of worth, and habits of judgment which might have enabled men to deal with reality courageously and independently, the educator might have come into his own at last. He might have induced the population of the Western World to adopt a mentality which would have saved it from the comic vulgarities of democracy, the insincerities of our industrialism, and the menace of a future dictatorship. There is little doubt that such was the hope of early nineteenth century apostles of universal education. Those who held this visionary hope did not however take into account the psychological and social effects of the new economic system, the materialistic twist which was to be given to the motive of ambition, the will to self-flattery of the masses.

We have precedent and the force of the established order to protect our courts from the evils of personal greed and the passion of the mob. We know how often these protective devices fail. But we have literally thrown education to the mob and have subjected it to every sort of crowd influence. Discipline and prestige and precedent it has—often to its disadvantage—but as protective devices these are empty gestures. I have watched many local elections of members of boards of education and have noted the fact that commonly petty personal interests and crowd partisanship result in the choice of incompetent persons, whose influence upon public education everywhere is to make it not only susceptible to crowd prejudice but an actual fabricator of mob ideas. In 1917 I happened to be secretary of a citizens' committee in New York which strove to interpret an educational aim to the masses at a time when politicians made the so-called Gary School a campaign issue. I saw the school system of the metropolis of America trampled under foot by a hysterical mob which drove our speakers off the streets because, among other things, an ignorant candidate for mayor had promised to free the school system of experts who were conspiring to make "wage slaves" of the children.

We have all read with chagrin the attacks upon education in states like Tennessee and in the second city of the land, Chicago. These spasms are only exaggerations of a pressure which is all about public education all the time. Certain radicals have pointed out the menace of capitalist influence on education! It is a menace but a greater menace is the terrorism of the mob. There are few places in America where anything may be mentioned in the public school that is displeasing to Methodist preachers, the Catholic Irish, leading politicians, grocers, or any organized group.

## VIII

THERE is a growing tendency to look to education as the savior of the state—which means that it must inculcate the ideas of whatever group has succeeded through its organized lobby in controlling the legislature. Of course the school must teach obedience to law, no matter by what questionable methods the law was passed. The school must disseminate patriotic and moral sentiments. To this we all agree, but we should not forget the fact that many such prevailing sentiments are not only partisan but are disguises for material interests not always disclosed. The school, in teaching morals and patriotism, should be critical if it is not to be partisan. But the school is forced to become the agency of all sorts of propaganda—to such an extent indeed that most people "educated" in it are never afterward able to distinguish between education and propaganda. The idea that their education should enable them to examine all things is something that schooling never gave them. They think of the educator as one who tells them what to believe.

But if the school fails to develop critical faculties, at least it must serve the ends of personal ambition in the industrial world. It must make for efficiency of every kind. It is not so much as a guarantor of liberty as an agency of progress—prosperity—that democracy and industry support the school.

Evidence of the anomalous position of education in modern civilization is that, whereas people generally look to it for guidance, yet the gospel of "service" evolved jointly by business and by the temper of democracy tends commonly to place institutions of learning in the rear, not at the head of the procession. A recent critic of contemporary religious tendencies says that, whereas religion was once the pillar of fire and cloud that led humanity through the procession of the ages, it becomes in our times the ambulance which follows in the rear and takes care of the wounded and the broken. Something similar happens to education also.

The school or college, apologetic and fearful that its educational traditions may not be satisfactorily directed "toward life" and obliged, in our commercial society, continually to "sell" education if it is to hold its place in popular interest, desires to be of service to the community. The superintendent needs larger appropriations, the president larger gifts, for each feels an increasing pressure on the part of those who want to see results which are immediate and tangible. Is there a campaign to "put the town on the map," a city-wide religious revival, a "drive" in behalf of some approved community interest, a wave of warlike patriotism, a strong Fundamentalist or Ku Klux Klan sentiment, a fear of Bolshevism, a demand for better trained mechanics, an ambition on the part of persons seeking vocational training and opportunity, an imaginary need for the psychology of salesmanship? Forthwith the public school, loving our fellow man, surely as much as it loves pure learning, would see, like Abou ben Adhem, its name lead all the rest. But one may question whether this Abou ben Adhemism, making brotherly love the sole virtue often at expense of love of wisdom, is really conducive to that leadership which our civilization most needs, and should have from its educational institutions. And when college and university gather up their academic gowns and run after the band, offering academic standing to anything for which there is a popular demand, however narrowly ambitious, and are sensitive to every wave of "enthusiasm," one may well question how far leadership in the modern world is in the hands of educators.

Mr. Bryan, arch enemy of education during his latter years, did not mean to be cynical when he said that people who pay for education have the right to decide what shall be taught. He would have condemned this policy on the part of privately endowed universities but advocated it on the part of those publicly supported. He was merely describing a situation—that is the confusion of education in an age when everything is expected of it, while it is controlled for the greater part by the uneducated.

There are alleged realists who would say that all this is the normal course of events. They hold that economic tendencies must dominate education, as they do all else, and hence the idea of looking to education for leadership is a delusion. The school or university is merely a product of economic forces. It is but an agency for drilling the public in the ways of life required by the existing order. Its function is but to fabricate the ideology of the present system; it is a useful servant in the present-day industrial household, with little influence on the general trend of events.

If this theory is correct we should turn our attention away from education, give up the notion that it can in any way assist us in the present crisis of civilization, and base our hope entirely on the prophecies of those who are studying the balance of economic forces. It seems to me however that a theory such as I have suggested oversimplifies the situation. Among the elements which determine the destiny of any civilization there are many which are curiously inconsistent with dominant economic tendencies. Many of these tendencies are themselves the result of accident and of psychological factors quite independent of prevailing economic interests. Many are hangovers from earlier stages of culture and are evidences of the devilish inconsistency of human nature.

Hence the confusion about education is only made greater by the theory of economic determinism. Education becomes confused with propaganda. For instance, it is said that since prevailing education is nothing but capitalist "ideology," the new education must be the ideology of the rising proletariat—as if there could be a capitalist geometry and a working-class arithmetic; a capitalist geography and a working-class economics. This is nonsense. Things are either true or false and are so for all men. A man is either being educated or he is not. And if the pursuit of a disinterested wisdom may not pull our world out of its present muddle, upon what else may we depend? A blind struggle for power? In that case the confusion about education is universally accepted, and the notion that there is or can be any guidance of wisdom, at the very time the world needs it most, is a forlorn hope.

However, the gospel of service places education at the beck and call of every popular demand. The educator is like a manufacturer who, finding that his staple commodity is out of fashion, must turn his plant to the making of novelties of all sorts. Public school authorities, correspondence schools, and universities are forced to offer a bewildering array of courses of study in the up-to-date tricks of every human enterprise. Universities follow the high schools in this matter. Courses in Egyptian archæology, Aristotle's Ethics, Domestic Science, the sanitary laws of the State of North Carolina, Oral Hygiene, Soil Fertilization, Scenario Writing, Journalism, Engineering, High Power Salesmanship, Applied Psychology, Advanced Physics and Mathematics, Household Decoration, Personnel Management, Boxing and Poultry Raising all stand very much on a level. Are not credits for equal time allotted to all? Has not a president of a great university said that it makes little difference what one learns, since all learning is cultural? Hence the catalogue of a progressive institution of "higher learning" resembles nothing so much as a similar catalogue annually issued by Sears, Roebuck & Co.

One need not be astonished at the catholicity of modern education. It is to its credit and a sign of its broadmindedness that it tolerates anything beyond skill in the tricks of the trade. Modern life is chiefly concerned with results. Thinking is subordinated to doing. Much present-day educational psychology proceeds on the theory that we learn only by doing, and that learning is habit formation not essentially different from that habit formation which can be organized in animals by means of the conditioned reflex. It is possible in a laboratory to put an animal in a maze and to note on successive days, the diminishing period of time occupied by random movements which elapses before the animal is able to make the particular movement which leads to escape. It is held that the sucessful movement, being associated with escape and food, and being repeated daily, becomes "overdetermined." Hence while regarding the animal as a pure automaton, with no insight into the situation, the mechanics of the environment may be so arranged as to organize in the neurons certain tendencies to respond which we may predict and control. This process of neural organization, the requisite length of time for which may be written down as a curve such as scientists love, is education, the same for animals and human beings. Learning is habit formation, and why strive to learn or retain habits that are useless when so many are required by our everyday environment?

Recently an eminent psychologist was requested to make a study of the process of adult education. The substance of his preliminary report is somewhat as follows: The problem of adult education is the same as that of the facility in acquiring new habits. To ascertain the relative degrees of facility in this respect experiments were made upon several hundred subjects to find out at which age they could most speedily learn to write with the left hand and to speak Esperanto. Of course every scientific caution was resorted to in order to secure accuracy in such experiments. It was found that maximum speed in habit formation is most common between the years of 18 and 24. Before and after these learning years facility is about 75% and 80% that of the best period. Hence it is suggested that in view of the greater loss of time in acquiring habits in earlier years and also taking into account the loss of efficiency in forgetting, education should be so arranged that people may learn things only a short time before they are required to make use of habits so acquired. I understand that this advance in pedagogical science is to be corroborated by a series of experiments on rats of various ages, in order to learn at what period a conditioned reflex may be organized in these animals in the shortest period of time. Give a psychologist a rat and a graph and you will get about the last word on the subject of the philosophy of education in the machine age.

Those of us who have for many years been engaged in the work of adult education have sometimes stumbled upon certain criteria of the educational process which I think are pertinent to education in general. Long ago I became aware of a striking difference among the students of The People's Institute—a difference according to which I believe one may classify students in any educational institution beyond the primary grades. All alike were exposed to every cultural influence we could bring to bear on them. All were placed in an environment of investigation of ideas old and new. The best information at our disposal was given to all. A critical spirit was dominant and no one was requested to accept anything on the authority of the instructor. The aim was not to teach people what to think but how to think.

To such a stimulus we have always received two sharply contrasted types of response, one negative and one positive. The negative response was varied. Some came in the hope that in our lectures and classes they would find finality. They seemed to care little to what creed they were required to subscribe. But they wished to subscribe, not to think, or to be forced to ask questions. They are just natural believers and I have always told them that they had come to the wrong place: they should have gone to church.

Another negative type always puzzles the educator. We all find in our classes brilliant students who take our courses and yet never seem to learn a thing—they leave precisely as they came. From the beginning to the end they have been on the defensive. They have been so afraid that something might be said, some fact disclosed, some interpretation made, which might possibly result in a revision of the preconceived ideas with which they entered, that they carefully made their minds prophylactic to any educational influence. They throw off all that challenges the opinionated state of mind in which they entered. Yet many of these unteachable persons are very adept in acquiring habits of practical training.

The positive reaction of our students has not always been easy to check up. But there are students to whom something happens. Often they have entered a course as opinionated as anyone could be, and have at the beginning resisted everything that was said regarding every discovery and interpretation placed before them with profound suspicion. Slowly they changed. They formed habits of considering evidence and of respecting fact. They became critical of over-generalization and hasty conclusion. They learned to hold judgment in abeyance and to know what it is to have an open mind. They were forced to smile at themselves with their premature "know it all" attitude. It is at just this point that intellectual curiosity is stimulated, along with self-criticism and a love of truth for its own sake. Very often students come to me after one or two years of conflict: "Do you remember what a fool I used to make of myself? I thought that I knew it all and that you were trying to put something over on us. Now I begin to see what you mean by the disinterested pursuit of knowledge. I realize the fact that I have by no means as much knowledge as I thought I had when I came here, but I want to learn."

Here is something more than skill.

## X

WHEN this thing happens, a thing we look and wait for, we feel that education is going on and that a personality, a character, is emerging out of the impersonal forces of the machine world. In the environment of Western civilization this result is more difficult of achievement than was the end sought in those ages when education meant the drill necessary for conformity to an accepted ideal of civilization.

Education in ancient China—if I am correctly informed—consisted largely in training in manners, practical philosophy, and literature. That of the Hebrews—one of the most vital and persistent systems of education in all the world—was chiefly the study of the law and the prophets and the rabbinical commentators. The ancient Greeks, though, as we have seen, their education was aimed at independence of thought, were chiefly concerned with dialectic. The education of the Middle Ages was primarily concerned with theology, law, and the technique of disputation in the Latin language. That of the Renaissance was occupied with "humane letters."

Only a century ago, at the beginning of the Industrial Revolution, the task of the educator in the English-speaking world was relatively simple in contrast with that of our day. The aim was a rather aloof scholarship, the conventional training of the gentleman. In addition to language drill in Greek and Latin—the aim of which seems to have been chiefly to adorn the speech of members of the English Parliament—there was required a knowledge of the philosophy of such writers as Aristotle, Hobbes, Bacon, Locke, and Hume. Familiarity with the political ideas of these same writers and also of Burke, Blackstone, Montesquieu, and Rousseau was also considered a part of the equipment of an educated man. He must also have some acquaintance with modern languages other than his own, notably French or German, though this was not absolutely essential. But he must know the vernacular literature of his own nation.

On the whole higher education was class education. It was æsthetic and intellectual and its aim was training in the knowledge of general principles. It was believed that, once the student had mastered his few principles, their practical application could be left to his mature common sense. Education even at the dawn of the Industrial Revolution was thus essentially *theoretical* in contrast with the immediately practical interest which appears to dominate it in the age of machines.

This difference in the aim of higher education is reflected in the common school. The "schooling" given children in earlier times was not really considered "education." It was elementary training in acquiring the mastery of the simple tools of learning—not itself "learning."

Reading, writing, arithmetic were only the crude instruments of an education which was, if at all, to come later and after mastery. It was held that, once the student had mastered thoroughly these required elements of learning, he then possessed the key which could open for his mind—if he had opportunity and inclination— those chambers of ageless wisdom, entrance into which was the open door of education. No intelligent person in the eighteenth century would have thought a modern high school graduate in any sense an educated person.

From all this it is clear that the common school of a century ago was primarily a preparatory school. It was designed to point the way to a far-off scholarly attainment. Today the tendency is to abandon this scholarly aim—since only a minority of students can aspire to it or care for it—and to try to make the elementary school, in the short years of average attendance, a "preparation for life"—whatever that is. Consequently, in addition to drill in the elements of scholarship with the aim of thoroughness in these simple disciplines, I should say that, at the tragic expense of such thoroughness, children in common schools are bewildered by an ill-assorted curriculum designed to give them in these early years about all the knowledge they will ever systematically get of all the subjects that their elders think a mature person should know in this complex modern world. The notion that children can be prepared for life by giving them a superficial, censored, and child-like view of a hundred mature interests, while neglecting to give them a thorough grounding, when we have the opportunity, in the essentials, and such reading habits as will later enable them to acquire mature knowledge, is one of the infantilisms of modern democracy.

Little children must for instance be trained in the duties of citizenship. The State which supports the school requires this. Of course this is a future citizenship not to be exercised for many years. But it can easily be formulated—too easily—in terms of the child mind. But what can such training amount to? Good citizenship means that mature persons give careful and dispassionate consideration to the public good. Does infantile training in citizenship prepare children for such political duty? I do not think so. The common school can hardly do more than fix in their minds a hackneyed phraseology, a set of childish sentiments, a Santa Claus-like distortion of the history of their country, an uncritical hero worship. The total effect is to identify their infantile egoism with childlike symbols of the glory of their nation and to discourage independence of judgment in future years. I think the low political mentality displayed by the American electorate is directly chargeable to the public school. Politically conditioned in a child psychology, the average citizen never gives up but always retains an uncritical, infantile notion of citizenship in which the school drilled his mind. Now that there is also thrown on the school the burden of Americanizing millions of children of immigrants and of so interpreting our culture and history that children without our background of tradition can understand it and carry it with them all their lives, the unction and desire for quick result add to our national infantilism an element of downright insincerity.

This same unctiousness appears to the extent that the school, under popular pressure, tends to supplant the home in the training in manners and morals. Here also the average person gets very little, yet tends never to outgrow the childish fixations of his early schooling. I think this is the case with most that the public school teaches in its efforts to equip children to live in our machine world. It might be better if we concentrated our efforts on the task of giving children the elements of a scholarship which, by the time they had mastered the elements, would open to them a grown-up world to be met with mature judgment and not childish sentimentality and idealization. I am sure there would be a larger number of really educated people if we did this.

We are beginning to see the result of the attempt to teach children a smattering of everything presented in terms of their inexperience and tender years, while neglecting to give them the essentials of learning. Dumping a little of everything into the school makes of education intellectual garbage. Short cuts to specific knowledge are delusions. Knowledge of means without knowledge of ends is animal-training. The throwing of emphasis on practical advantage rather than on scholarship tends to deprive our people of that respect for scholarship without which a high civilization is impossible. To divide attention among a multitude of subjects only superficially presented results in a lack of thoroughness which is notorious in our entire educational system from primary grades to graduate university courses.

The infantile sentimentality, lack of thoroughness, scattering of attention, and superficial interest in a thousand things without mastery of anything—these are the psychological deposits of our education in the public mind. The school cannot evade responsibility for the present low level of mental life in this republic. This people can read, and the school may be judged by the reading habits of its human output. The people have been taught by the school to read; they prefer to read trash, and they act in important situations just as people would be expected to act who read that sort of thing. The school was forced to try to do everything; hence it could do nothing well.

## XI

IT would seem that the destiny of Western civilization is bound together with the most ambitious and perhaps utopian programme of popular education ever contemplated. Not only is there an attempt to take over from custom and rule of thumb all kinds of human activity and make proficiency everywhere a matter of special training; in addition the entire population is to be enlightened, drilled, regimented, and initiated into the ways of modern life by means of compulsory attendance at school.

The considerations which led our predecessors to attempt universal education and today justify the enormous expense of the enterprise are the commonplace of contemporary thought. Is not every child entitled to his share in our cultural heritage? Society owes it to all its members to equip them to perform the tasks which it will require of them. Popular education is the best safeguard of democratic institutions. Industry has need of trained men and women. Moreover since training is of advantage to the individual in the struggle for preferment and personal advancement, the democratic dogma of equal opportunity requires that the State extend educational opportunity to all. We like to believe that in our civilization any youth, however poor, may "get an education if he really desires it," and that, once he has it, his humble origin is no barrier to him. He may rise to any position and move in any circles to which ambition may inspire him and to which his ability and industry may entitle him. Thus universal education at once asserts that equality of opportunity demanded by democracy and justifies the inequalities of competitive industrialism. All the arguments are in favor of the widest possible extension of education.

But when we turn from argument to consideration of the actual situation, we may question whether in the attempt to educate everybody we are really educating anyone. In their en-

thusiasm over equal opportunity—a splendid ideal—men forgot
to inquire whether all persons could be educated; whether what
they thought.they wanted was really education; whether the material conditions under which so vast an experiment must necessarily be conducted could ever be made conducive to the learning process.

There are almost insurmountable difficulties in trying to teach
large numbers of students in crowded class rooms, where there is
little opportunity for personal contact between the teacher and
the individual student. Inevitably a vast educational system
emerges which tends to become an end in itself and in which appear the tendencies to bureaucracy, the emphasis on externalities
to the point of neglect of original aims and values, the standardization, uniformity, and spirit of quantity production which commonly defeat the ends of human organization.

The idea of equal educational opportunity—even with the best
we can do—remains something of a fiction. The realization of
this ideal is everywhere defeated by facts of economic, domestic,
and psychological nature. The greater portion of students in
the public school stop their lessons and go to work before they
have had opportunity to learn much of anything. One person in
a little less than three hundred in the population enters college or
university. This number which represents an enormous increase
in recent years is so unprecedented that institutions of higher
learning are obliged to decline admission to many candidates.

In the common school—notwithstanding the occasional efforts
of psychologists to isolate the unusual children for specially super-
vised instruction—the presence of large numbers of dull and poorly
prepared children retards the progress of learning and makes thoroughness in teaching difficult. In the colleges a prevailing social
custom requires the sons and daughters of families of wealth and
position to attend. These young people may have little inclination toward scholarship or possess only mediocre ability. Many
are first subjected to a distasteful and often painful process in preparatory school where the chief end of man is a passing grade in
the college entrance examinations. The presence in a college of a
large number of students who have come not out of love of learn-

ing so much as for social reasons gives rise to the idea that there can be education without scholarship, and that as an agency for broadening culture the fraternity house is preferable to the library. It is a charming picture to be sure and who can say that good does not come from that confusion of adolescent activities and interests known as undergraduate college life? But is this education? Are not the dominant spirit and present intellectual level of school and college very much what one should expect when the attempt is made to educate a large number of people who have no interest in scholarship?

Universal education must proceed with the disadvantage of having to overcome the cultural influences—or lack of them—of the early home environment. Psychologists recognize the great importance of the early years of childhood in the family circle. Generally speaking it makes a great difference for the success of education whether the home from which the student comes to school is an ally of culture or is indifferent or hostile. The older "class education," limited as it was chiefly to the favored few, could assume that the students had a similar background of cultural interest. The child had early associated with people for whom books, travel, art, and good manners were a part of daily existence. The task of education was half done before it was given over to the school master.

Universal education unfortunately has in most cases no such pre-school training to give it a running start. It must begin at the beginning. It must deal with social groups in whose daily existence culture has little place. The home of the average student in the public school may be—usually is I think—one in which there is a spirit of love, industry, self-respect. Sometimes there is also some training in manners. But generally speaking, in these homes books are few and usually of little educational value. There is little interest in art. There is little political philosophy beyond that of the editorial page of the newspaper.

Many a promising student enters school—even university—never having voluntarily read one of the world's great classics in literature—often with no developed reading habits at all—never having heard, except in recent years over the radio, a symphony of Beethoven or Brahms, never having seen a good painting or work of sculpture or of architecture better than the rural county court house or small town post-office—never, in a word, having known the fellowship of people of easy cultured habits or broad intellectual interests.

The school often tries frantically to make up for this common lack of cultural background. In some cases it succeeds. But it is doubtful if the effort is often very successful. Thus it is easier to give needed information in specific subjects than to develop in the student an educated person's outlook on life, or intellectual curiosity beyond that stimulated by some specific material interest. Librarians today are making a study of the reading habits of the public. They wish to learn why it is that, although the people have learned in school to read, they do little serious reading and show almost no interest in the great literatures to which it is the aim of the school to introduce them. I think that a study of home influence would throw much light on this problem. An interest in reading observed in those about him by a small child becomes part of daily existence and is retained after school days as life-long habit. Interest in reading acquired in school is likely to be thought of as something required, a part of an irksome discipline, something extraneous which belongs to the school, not to the home life. People read the tabloid papers because they think that these papers deal with "real life," with sensational stories taken from the uncouth environment to which they were "conditioned" in pre-school days and after. Poetry they do not read because poetry belongs to the world of the school, a world from which they have returned to real life bringing back very little. Even on those occasions when they do bring home from school something more than practical knowledge with the promise of material success, it is a difficult matter to adapt the newly acquired knowledge to the old environment. I fear it will be a long time before universal education finds in the daily environment, from which it draws the majority of its students, an ally which prepares them to be receptive to instruction or cordially welcomes any cultural change that the school makes in their habits.

The situation is somewhat similar for institutions of higher

learning. Few students enter undergraduate study really prepared and few leave college with a passion for truth and with
habits of study which make any great difference either in their
personal lives or in the general spirit of the communities to
which they return, aspiring to positions of leadership. Illustration
of this fact may be seen in the influence on almost any educational
institution of the organized alumni. Such influence is seldom
on the side of scholarship. The loyalty and generosity of the
alumni are of great value to a college and are quite genuine and
universal. But it is said that gifts from alumni increase and
fall off each season in proportion to the success of the college
football team over its rivals. Most alumni are business men and
there has grown up a psychology of business, a psychology of the
fascination of publicity and efficiency. Football and schools of
business "put a college on the map."

There is confirmation of this point in the fact that the large
women's colleges of America have been obliged to unite in an
appeal for funds. These institutions in which athletic contests
and schools of business are not part of the tradition of education
have little of spectacular method of appeal and are neglected by
that portion of the public which commonly supports higher education.

### XII

THE advance of learning is in America almost confined to those
who have completed courses of graduate study. It is such persons who make up university faculties, carry on research and experimentation and, in a word, give to modern education such ultimate standards as it has. Graduate study makes for proficiency
in the subjects studied. But for reasons I have pointed out it
is often pursued by those who in school and undergraduate days
have failed to gain a general cultural background. Graduate
study, which for many students is the first real study they ever
experienced, is not necessarily culture. It is rather the mastery
of the technique of a profession. It is less a culmination and
flowering of a growing, deepening, and broadening cultural interest, than a narrow specialization superimposed upon such gen-

eral knowledge and cultural background, or the lack of it, as the student may have gained in earlier years. Expert information may or may not become integrated with one's intellectual life as a whole. It is a question moreover whether the combined influence of minds trained in one-sided specialization can provide a community with the balanced and well-rounded leadership it needs. It is only in providing such leadership that education performs successfully its social task.

Lacking this leadership of education, Western civilization makes shift to find such temporary and plausible leaderships as it can, and seeks its valuations of events in whatever has sentimental appeal. Interest centres in the immediately practical. The utilitarian spirit becomes dominant and presses into its service all cultural agencies, education included. Education serves this interest well and in the future we may expect it to serve even more effectively. Knowledge of engineering will be perfected and disseminated as never before. Business methods will be developed, devices of salesmanship and the psychological technique of propaganda will doubtless be carried to a subtilty quite beyond our imagination today. Men will have mastered the techniques of their several tasks in numbers far beyond anything we have yet known.

In all this, education will have merged itself more and more completely in the immediate needs and passing interests of the time. Men have always wrestled with the forces of nature and have struggled with one another for position and power. But there have been leaders, not content that the struggle be intensified or carried on with sharper weapons, who have sought to humanize it, to view it in the light of larger experience and wider sympathies. Such as these have given to human life some meaning beyond the struggle for material ends; these are they who have changed the accidents of history and the conflicts of the hour into a somewhat continuous advance of civilization. Out of their efforts have come to us something more than clever ways of doing things—a certain emancipation of the mind from routine, a set of interests which belong not merely to one time but to all time. Is not this the proper task of education in any civilization? The following passage quoted from a letter pub-

lished in a liberal journal sums up the aim of liberal education and
the failure to achieve that aim:

> In the words of G. Stanley Hall, is it not the true aim of college edu-
> cation to "break down prejudices, religious, political, philosophical, lit-
> erary, social, and to postpone discipleship to any school or view in every
> field where there are many held by intelligent and sincere men"?
>
> We must admit that the present system of education is not doing very
> much toward the accomplishment of this task in the liberalization of the
> minds of American youth. In raising the standard of work along tech-
> nical lines, in enlarging programs of endowment and equipment, and in
> the great increase of attendance, it would seem that education has made
> progress, if these things are counted the same as education. But in
> modernization of the curriculum and humanizing of knowledge to free
> the minds of the youth from superstitions and prejudices, little progress
> is being made. If education is to provide the source of liberalization, it
> must be a new type of education.

I have tried to show that the "new education" must be something
different from the technology which today is supplanting an outworn classical tradition. It must be an adventurous quest for
meaning and for that which is important, a disposition to think
things through similar in spirit to that which once created classical
education and gave it vitality. That education today has so
generally accepted the subordinate position assigned to it by the
utilitarian interest is, I think, a result of the confusion of educators
as to their task at the time we entered the industrial age. It is
absurd to suppose that intellectual leadership will be permanently
left behind in an industrial civilization which is itself, in its
various elements, a product of intelligence. The time must come
when educators, instead of trying meekly to meet any demand the public may make upon them, will have something to say
on their own account. And instead of giving all their attention
to social service, pedagogical methods, and administration detail
will again approach their task in a philosophical spirit. Many
people now see the need, not of some new educational trick, but
of a well-considered philosophy of education. I am thinking of
the ancient Greeks who also felt the need. Perhaps we of the
Western World are just beginning to be civilized.

## XVI—LITERATURE

### By CARL VAN DOREN

S O FAR as literature is concerned the machine age began with the invention of printing in the fifteenth century. Before that time all the forms of literature were limited to more or less special audiences. What the orator had to say seldom reached beyond the ears of those persons who were within range of his rostrum or his pulpit. The poet or historian or man of science might write books, but the cost of making copies of them by hand kept the number of even the most popular books down to what now seems relatively negligible. Even the dramatist, though his work might be both heard and read, had nothing to compare with what has come to be known as a general public. And the journalist, whose work in its various aspects has done more to condition modern literature than any other of its forms, may be said to owe his very existence to the printing press.

In the twentieth century, of course, it is no longer possible to look upon the invention of printing as the last great step taken to enlarge the audiences which men of letters may expect to reach. There are other steps beside which the mere printing of a writer's words seems to belong to an old fashion. If George Bernard Shaw, for instance, sends a witty letter to a London evening newspaper, his words may be cabled to the United States and may appear the next morning in other papers of which millions of copies have been printed. The telegraph thus extends the uses of the printing press. A still more recent invention, the radio, partly supplements and partly supersedes them. How these different machines can be united in a single purpose would lately have been shown if a certain plan, never thinkable before the present century, had been carried out. That plan was to entice Shaw to New York Harbor, to show respect for his prejudice against the United States by not asking him to leave the ship in which he had crossed the Atlantic, to install the necessary apparatus on board, and to allow him to speak his mind through the air to as many Americans as might have radios and care to listen. This, it was argued, would have given him the largest audience ever addressed by any man of letters.

Socrates might have had to content himself with a few inquiring citizens in the Agora, and Cicero with those Senators who would find time to leave the routine of their committees, and Abelard with the students who could make their way to him from the parts of Europe to which his fame had traveled. But the comic dramatist of the machine age, only incidentally an orator, could without effort or delay have had an audience of millions. Machines would have brought him across the ocean, would have informed a continent as to the precise hour at which he was to speak, and would have conveyed his very accents to the ears of his listeners, sitting at home almost as peacefully as if literature had never been devised to carry human speech farther than the unaided human voice could send it. Not in a thousand years did Socrates address himself to as many minds as Shaw could have addressed while his voice was still sounding.

Let it be at once admitted that mere numbers do not make an important audience, nor does an audience, important or unimportant, by itself make an art. Nevertheless, the literature of the machine age cannot be studied without reference to the machines which have led to the creation of new literary functions and the development of new forms. These functions and forms may have been imposed from without. They may be shown to have had little or no effect upon the essential processes of the creative artist. Poetry is still poetry, drama is still drama, story-telling is still story-telling, persuasion is still persuasion, logical argument is still logical argument. The principal themes of the earliest writers continue to be, with but few outward differences, the prin-

cipal themes of the latest writers. But the part played by literature in civilization at large has steadily changed ever since printing was invented, and it goes on changing with each mechanical
device which serves to bring writer and reader into closer and
more immediate relationship.

Possibly the radio, bringing the voice of the speaker to the
ear of the listener, may be held to have no connection with literature, because nothing has been written. But suppose another
case. Suppose there were in New York a poet as characteristic
and as eminent among the poets of the city as Villon was of Paris.
Villon read his ballads and testaments to his companions in this
or that tavern, and allowed manuscript copies to be made. Not
till after his banishment, and in all likelihood after his death,
were they printed. Consequently the audience most fitted to
enjoy him, to recognize his topical allusions as well as to enjoy
his art and wit, had but few chances to know of him until he
was already a legend. A Villon of New York, however, might
read his poems over the radio, might make records of them for the
gramaphone, and might thereby give a special delight to innumerable hearers. It is by no means certain that he would. Such an
outlet is ordinarily given only to work in which music has a
part. But there are the machines which in a few days might
spread such a vogue for a poem as is now spread for a song.
That the vogue, as vogue, would yield the next month to another, does not matter. In the long run, naturally, the poem
would have to take its due course among the perils of oblivion.
Yet the machines would have added to its career, during its month
in court, something that the poems of the actual Villon did not
have. And literature would have done something to the machine age which literature was not able to do to the fifteenth
century.

The tavern reading of the actual Villon of Paris and the radio
appearance of the imaginary Villon of New York mark the extreme limits of the change brought about by the machine age.
The intermediate steps, which must be traced, have been most
of them taken by the printing press. Viewed strictly, this has
meant nothing beyond the rapid multiplying of the number of

copies of any book which might be given to the world. That multiplying, however, has meant many other things. So long as books remained as expensive as they were when they had to be copied out by hand, they were necessarily available to few persons, and only a few persons took the trouble to learn to read. But as books became more readily available they stimulated the desire which they were produced to satisfy, precisely as does any other commodity when introduced to a new market. Because there were more books there were more readers, and because there were more readers there were more books. By 1600 the better part of the literature of ancient and mediæval Europe had found its way into print. By 1700 there were few contemporary writers of merit, in Europe or the Americas, who had to remain long in manuscript. By 1800 journalism had passed through its preliminary stages and was entering into competition with the more artful forms of writing. By 1900, after a century of enormous expansion, printing had become one of the major industries, and literature had been elaborated and subdivided and extended until what had once been called by that name seemed now but a more or less permanent island in the midst of an unquestionably ephemeral sea of printed words. Since 1900 there has been evident a tendency to move, in several of the forms of literature, beyond printing: in oratory, with the radio; in drama, with the moving picture; in journalism, with the illustrated newspaper. Dark prophets, here and there, insist that literature is near its end and that the future will drift into illiteracy as the past struggled out of it.

For the present it is enough to study what the machine age has actually done for literature. Most of all it has brought about, as in other forms of activity, such a division of labor and such a specialization that something very like a system of castes has arisen. For example, literature and journalism are often spoken of as distinct, if not antagonistic. Oratory has almost ceased to be classed with literature, as have all of science and a good deal of history. Moreover, the spoken drama has drawn a little to one side, and the moving picture contentedly inhabits another sphere. Even the bulk of verse and prose fiction not too resentfully accepts a sub-literary rank. The term literature, in a world in which nearly everybody is literate, is as a rule held to apply, not to whatever is written to be read, but only to what is written in certain ways for the benefit of those who will read it in certain ways. Nor does this suggest a mere technical status, like that of a Roman citizen among non-citizens. It springs from the fact that all the conceivable facilities for making writers known do not, apparently, increase the number of those who are gifted. The ratio of genius to population remains much the same. Literature, in the special sense, goes on being produced as rarely as ever. But so great a demand has been created that it is supplied, and often no doubt satisfied, with inferior productions. And when these sub-literary or extra-literary productions are not precisely inferior, for the reason that they do their special tasks as well as could be expected, they are nevertheless thoroughly subordinate to literary masterpieces. The literature of the machine age, dividing its labor and growing more and more specialized, has distinguished itself from the literature of previous ages by adding to itself what it does not, in its exacter moments, consider to be literature at all.

Conditions might have been different if the printing presses had confined themselves to masterpieces issued by the million, but there have always been obstacles to such a program. Publishers, for one thing, do not invariably know masterpieces when they see them. Furthermore, there has steadily been a demand, beyond the strength of publishers or writers to resist, for written matter which would serve various purposes not served by the classics. Easy instruction, entertainment, news—these have been the demands most frequently insisted upon. These demands, indeed, are not peculiar to the machine age. They are perfectly universal. Before writing was invented, no less than between that and the invention of printing, men were eager for easy instruction, entertainment, news. And it is not to be wondered at that the machine age, able to meet the demand as no previous age was ever able to do, has given over its printing presses so largely to manuals of information, prose fiction, and newspapers. A Babylonian shepherd might consult a soothsayer about a disease which had harmed his flock, might listen to a legendary tale at the camp-fire, and might ask a traveling merchant what had recently happened in the capital. An American farmer reads a government bulletin, a novel, and a newspaper, and obtains the same satisfactions. Printing makes the only difference.

The familiar temptation, customarily yielded to, is to brush aside all the inferior or subordinate aspects of literature and to consider, in serious discussions, only that literature which is produced with deliberate art for what it is hoped will be eternity. A discussion of the sort, however, is not broad enough to take into account all the theoretical elements involved. After all, literature is whatever is written to be read, a device to carry human speech farther than the unaided human voice can send it. Nor is such a discussion, practically, altogether precise. Between permanent masterpieces and temporary ventures it is not always possible to draw a line which will unmistakably distinguish them. Moreover, they may stand in some respects so close together that neither can be estimated by itself. Don Quixote was created as a parody on innumerable gentlemen whose chroniclers, too much attached to a passing fashion even to notice that their heroes were mad, wrote, in that fashion, books which would be entirely forgotten except that they must be vaguely remembered in any explanation of the book which smiled at them and which outlasts them. Robinson Crusoe may have been created for what literary historians call eternity, but he too emerged from a fashion which at the time ran to lost travelers and shipwrecked sailors and which led to the production of many books now investigated only by the curious. Nor can it be said with assurance that Cervantes and Defoe undertook deliberately to add art and permanence to models which they saw lacked these qualities. Being writers of genius, they went beyond their models; yet without these models they would not have written these masterpieces; and they may even have been unaware that they were doing what their competitors could not do. Posterity has decided, in these as in all instances, which books to keep alive and which to let die, but the making of literature continues to be a general process, to be understood only if the failures are thought of along with the successes.

The influence of the printing press upon the matter printed appears nowhere more clearly than in connection with the novel, which in the machine age is the outstanding literary form. Without the printing press, indeed, the novel would hardly exist at all, and certainly not on the scale on which it exists now. Though the form itself had been invented long before printing came to its aid, it could never have prospered as it has if it had been obliged to depend upon the slow labors of men copying novels by hand. Even with printing to depend upon, the novel had to wait for more than three hundred years to reach its maturity. It might be, as it is, the most easy, natural, flexible, and varied of the forms of literature, but it could not exhibit—or perhaps discover—all its qualities until there was a body of readers large enough to offer it progressive encouragement. The printing press had developed such a public. The antagonism which the novel aroused in several quarters was symptomatic. The novel was, its enemies declared, nothing better than entertainment. They thus implied that reading ought to be confined to what was clearly useful or edifying. They could not so confine it. Men and women who had learned to read for use went on to read for pleasure. Grown accustomed to books, they did not need to take them solemnly, but could regard them as entertainment, as mere pastime. There followed an immense increase in the demand for novels, and consequently in the supply. During the nineteenth century the novel left all the other forms behind. It drew into itself the chief function of the narrative poem, because prose is easier to read than verse. It did more than a little damage to the drama, because it is easier to send a thousand miles for a book than it is to go a dozen miles to see a play. The novel became a school of manners, a forum of debate, a picture of history, and a pocket theater. It brought imaginative literature closer to more people than any other species of writing had ever done. It is, in literature, a triumph of the machine.

Whatever may be said of the novel may be said still more emphatically of the newspaper, which without the printing press could not be imagined. Though the hunger for news is age-old, it took the newspaper to make clear how great the hunger is and how much news there is. Whether the news makes the news-paper or the newspaper makes the news is a nice point which need not be decided. Plainly, however, the greater part of what is printed is trivial. The whole world does not produce enough important events in a single day to fill a newspaper. But the machines which have been invented and developed to play their indispensable part in the gathering, transmitting, printing, and distributing of news are not lightly to be kept idle. They go on like the changes of day and night. No matter how trivial their news may be, it must be abundant. And indeed a news-paper with hundreds of thousands, or millions, of readers can hardly find an item of information which some one will not wel-come. Because so many readers are to be served, the sheer bulk of a twentieth-century newspaper, particularly in the United States, is enormous. And because all this is intended to last for only a single day, everything is arranged and written for the bene-fit of those who may want to read with a hurried, glancing eye. Quickly written, quickly read, quickly forgotten. Machines have made newspapers possible; machines set the pace for them and de-termine their qualities. And though the machines actually start and stop under human guidance, they themselves seem to be cre-ators. Or rather, the element of creation is lost sight of. The style throughout a newspaper is as uniform, or nearly so, as the typography. Special writers sign their names in order to lay claim to whatever touches of personality may have crept in among the even columns. The general aim of the newspaper is a vast im-personality, mirroring the world day by day. Often the men who direct the machines are less impersonal than irresponsible, but somehow it has come about that the machine age has a mirror in words which nothing in any other age can match. It may be doubted whether all the surviving literature of Athens furnishes a picture of Greek life as complete as the picture of American life which is furnished by a single issue of a New York Sunday paper.

The drama, a literary form much older than the novel or the newspaper, has fallen no less than they into the multiplying hands of the machines. To say nothing of Greek or Latin plays, the plays of Shakespeare and Molière, early in the machine age, were produced by hand as truly as they were written by hand. Not till the nineteenth century did the theater discover and employ the methods of lighting, of changing scenery, of raising and lowering curtains which have turned the stage into an intricate machine in the midst of which the play itself is sometimes displayed with a fresh brilliance of effect, and is sometimes lost. It might be possible ingeniously to point out various effects which the mechanized theater has had upon the drama, in the way of shortening the action, limiting the scene, sharpening the exits and entrances; but these are not strikingly important. Plays have remained plays and actors have remained actors. Shaw, after all, is more like Euripides than Tolstoi is like Homer. The conspicuous novelty in the drama of the machine age is the moving picture. What the printing press was to the book the camera has been to the drama. It has multiplied copies of it. A play when acted can reach only one audience at one performance. A play when photographed can then be presented to as many audiences as there are copies of the film. Within a few weeks after a moving picture is released it may have been shown throughout the world. Language is no barrier, because pantomime is a universal language. Charlie Chaplin might never leave his California studio and yet be, as he is, the most widely-known human being now alive. The moving picture is perhaps the form of literary art most completely characteristic of the machine age, and it is the form which is, on the whole, most dependent upon machines. In it may be seen the full extent to which machines can liberate an art and the full extent to which they narrow it. By means of the camera the drama has been set free to choose any spot on earth for its scene. The top of a mountain, a ship at sea, the interior of a factory, an airplane at high altitude, a city street, the middle of a desert: these things not merely painted on a swaying curtain at the back of the stage, but really present in the picture. The action may be larger than any stage in a theater could ever find room for, more dangerous, more exciting, more picturesque, more realistic. Since the photographs are made in private, with time for endless repetition and correction, nothing reaches the public except the best performance ever given, and that exactly repeated on every film. On the other hand, the moving picture, aiming always at the eyes of so many millions, notoriously prefers being below the few to being above the many. As a rule its plots are conventional, its characters stereotyped, its sentiments banal. Machines can photograph better than they can think.

It may be thought that emphasis is here unduly laid upon the literature, and sub-literature, of the present century, to the neglect of what lies between this and the century in which printing was invented. The answer is that printing had little effect upon the place of literature in western civilization until it had helped bring into existence a large literate public. Reading had to be made a normal habit of mankind, as common as, say, the wearing of shoes. Until that was accomplished, printing was chiefly a convenience for the learned. After literacy ceased to mean the same as learning, the changes were very rapid. And they are still going on. Tides of printing sweep over and through the world. Rumor never sped as fast or as far. The information, news, and entertainment which once had to make their way slowly by word of mouth may now reach millions of readers in a single day. The result has been to accelerate and to extend all the influences brought about by the spread of ideas and emotions. A continent can be roused as quickly as could an ancient city. A hero can be made over-night, a movement started in a week, a crusade got on its way in a month or so. So can divisions be engineered and hostile parties founded. And the most trivial forms of entertainment may be borne in all directions on the same swift tides. With the radio, the moving picture, and the newspaper, western civilization may be represented as a man sitting in a whispering-gallery, watching a play, and holding on his lap a book of which the pages continually turn of their own accord.

So much for what literature has done to civilization. But what has civilization, in the course of the process, done to literature? On this point the various schools of taste are bound to disagree. For once, however, it ought to be possible to look beyond them—beyond either the school which holds that literature has been debased from something high and noble or the school which holds that literature has been rescued from something haughty and difficult. Neither argument covers the whole ground. Most of what has happened is that a great deal which formerly was only spoken and then allowed to die on the wind has come to be put into type. Though it may seem less temporary than random speech, it is not much less so. It should be taken into account not for itself but for the influence which it exerts upon the literature which is produced with deliberate art for what it is hoped will be eternity. That sort of literature remains, age after age, surprisingly the same. Perhaps there ought to be no occasion for surprise in this fact. The stature of men is still much what it was when it first occurred to their ancestors that writing, as well as serving a use, might also be an art; so are their intellects and passions, their sense of tragedy and comedy, their modes of eloquence, their supply of images, their rules of discourse. Great writers occur, as if by accident, where and when they occur, and their native gifts vary from individual to individual, not from century to century.

The machine age has done little to writers of genius, but even to them, and certainly to writers as a whole, it has given an impulse to productivity which did not exist before printing came into vogue. When machines wait, men hurry. Or, to express it in less pictorial terms, the knowledge that an audience is readily accessible, and may be eager, has a strong tendency to stimulate the literary mood, especially when a writer's living depends upon it. Whereas in the manuscript age a good many writers, conscious of only a small, like-minded audience and hopeful of profit only from some patron, might work for years on a single masterpiece, in the printing age a good many more writers keep frequent appointments with their audiences and leave a miscellaneous bulk of writings to be remembered by. Somewhere in almost everything now written there is a sense of the audience. But that sense of an audience shows itself in more ways than has ordinarily been noted. It may lead to simplicity of language, to the avoidance of controverted themes, to the repetition of literary devices so often tried that they can be certain of effect, to a concession to vulgar prejudices. A writer whose audience has been brought close to him may fall into such sympathy with it that he loses himself in its mass, and thereby loses distinction. But there is another consequence of such proximity. That is a kind of fear of the vast, uncritical, undiscriminating body of readers whom every writer has to face. The fear is essentially modern. A Greek or Roman might, as a citizen, dread the mob; as a writer, however, he did not dread it, because it could not read. The modern mob does read. Doubtless the writers who are afraid of it, grow self-conscious about it, suspect those writers who can please it, and in their own work turn away to intricate, eccentric modes, are in no great danger. The reading mob travels along straight lines. But the fear obviously exists, generally disguised under the pretense—often, it may be, the self-delusion—of independence and contempt. From this comes the presence in modern literature of numerous figures who voluntarily, even violently, reject the special advantages which the machine age has to offer them. They will not live by it, and can hardly bear to live in it. They furnish one member of the antithesis in which the effect of the machine age upon literature may be summed up: It has drawn author and audience closer together, it has driven author and audience farther apart.

In some future century, when the effect of the machine age upon literature shall have become history and shall not still, as at present, remain a debatable item of speculation, historians may well wonder at what they will presumably regard as the thanklessness of writers toward the machines which served them. For it cannot be denied that the common attitude of men of letters toward machines is that of resentment toward a new and ominous dynasty. Among the writers of inferior novels, newspapers, and scenarios this attitude does not appear, but they, being sub-literary, have not formulated their gratitude and so have not strikingly influenced opinion. The writers of a prouder rank for a hundred years have steadily complained of the machines which, brought in to serve as slaves, have turned into masters. This mechanical dynasty, the complaint runs, has shaped mankind to mechanical patterns, has dimmed its natural colors, has forced the intricate dance of life into a dull march in a single direction. There were freedom and grace under the old régime, they say; there can be no such things under a régime which thinks in geometrical designs and which feels as with instruments of precision. Such writers seem like royalist poets in a republic, still longing for the good old days of the monarchy and drinking toasts to the king over the water. Negligent, even scornful, of the benefits which have come to them, they go on polishing up their loyalty and elaborating their memories. Literature lags while life moves forward.

The phenomenon, however, is by no means peculiar to the present age. The human imagination, which exists in men at large but which finds words in men of letters, has always been slow to grasp its new materials. There must have been a time when the trireme to a Roman poet seemed a hulking craft, without charm. But one by one the trireme and the viking longboat and the galleon and the clipper ship were absorbed into the imagination and took a place there. Metaphors were fitted to them. Romance was built up around them. No longer merely timbers and sails, they became homogeneous to the mind and could there easily find harbor and sea room. Exactly the same process is now at work upon the ocean liner, though it has not yet gone far enough to make men generally aware of it. Men generally, perhaps, but not the poets. And until the poets have found the words, it is difficult to say whether the thoughts behind those words are actually in existence. Thoughts without words are vague and shaggy. A boy watching a liner put out to sea may be visited by an ache like that which has sent thousands of other boys to venture on salt water. A novelist, trying to define that ache, slips into confusion because he inherits an archaic vocabulary of towering masts and creaking cordage, tarry trousers and marlin-spikes, when he should be writing about propellers and oil-burning engines, radio antennæ and gyroscopic compasses. Nor does the confusion lie wholly in the writer. The reader, too, inherits the archaic vocabulary. Poetry and fiction seem to him to be associated with the objects with which he has often seen them associated, for in literature, familiarity breeds anything but contempt. It is more likely to breed glamor. Towering masts are glamorous because they have been made so; radio antennæ are not, because they have not been.

Neither the writer nor the reader does justice to the impulse in the boy. The liner is still too large and complex, too glittering and novel, to have been absorbed into the human imagination.

So with all the machines of which the liner is a convenient example. However much they may be used, however customary they may have become in daily life, men still walk warily among them. The imagination can far more readily throw a glamor around the figure of a medieval scribe illuminating a manuscript by a dim candle than around a twentieth-century printing press performing its tasks with punctual ingenuity in a thunder of noise and a blaze of light. What poet has celebrated the modern printing press as Whitman celebrated the broad-axe? Is it to be concluded, as it is often said, that the brain with its tender cells cannot master, for the purposes of imagination, the complicated, powerful, irresistible machines which give a special character to the industrial age? Must the human imagination, that is to say, forever remain agricultural? It is too early to decide. Nor has the recent cult of the machine, which has won followers in every art, done much to bring about any notable change. The imagination does not take a step because the will has commanded it to. It appears rather to evolve in accordance with the laws, not yet discovered, of a growth which is virtually organic. Centuries may have to pass before machines can fall into their due place, whatever it turns out to be, among human circumstances. And then, it is safe to prophesy, they will not be, as the cult of the machine would like them to be, the direct objects of literary scrutiny, but something which, like weather and landscape, can be taken for granted. Then only will the imagination be free to turn naturally to its perennial subjects for literature, making merely such use of the machines as this or that subject may call for.

For, machines or no machines, the functions of literature will be the same. To store up knowledge and transmit it to other places and other times; to catch sight of some kind of order in the chaos of appearances and to represent that order in forms so concrete that they suggest reality even to those for whom reality itself is chaos; to create characters of such validity and substance that they become inhabitants of the world like the creatures of genuine flesh and blood; to pluck drifting thoughts and swirling emotions out of the stream of consciousness and to fix them, as precisely as possible, to the words which alone can give them outlines: these are the functions which literature seeks to perform in all ages. It can be nothing but the representation in words of experience endured or experience desired or experience feared. But these are everywhere intrinsically the same. Men endure birth and growth and labor and grief and death. They desire food and fortune, love and joy, adventure and peace. They fear loneliness and poverty and frustration, accident and torment, premature annihilation or life drawn out too long. The special or local conditions in which they live, and in which books represent their lives, are merely an idiom, merely a setting of the stage. One of the most effective writers of melodrama now living has pointed out that of all his hundred plays there is not one that does more than play some variation upon the story of Cinderella or of the Prodigal Son. And less conventional writers find it difficult to escape from fairly conventional themes, not because more unusual themes cannot be invented but because the important human experiences fall into simple patterns. In only one essential respect does modern literature differ from the various older literatures: in the variety of minor personages, often with special, even trivial experiences, who are admitted into the imagined world of books. This difference, of course, has been brought about by machines. By multiplying books, they have multiplied readers; by multiplying readers, they have multiplied the number of persons desirous of seeing experiences like their own mirrored in literature; and by multiplying this demand, they have caused the supply to be multiplied. The enormous banality of many popular novelists is a result of the development which, no less logically, has also resulted in the enormous subtlety of James Joyce and Marcel Proust.

Perhaps the final sense, after a survey of the literature of the machine age, is a sense of waste. Innumerable printed pages flutter in the wind. Libraries of unopened volumes lie like heaps of slag. Myths, with the help of journalism, spring up almost over night, so that a few weeks can do for Lindbergh what it took centuries to do for Galahad. And if various literary processes have been accelerated, so have the processes of oblivion. It seems necessary to borrow a term from the language of industrialism and to say that the turn-over in literature has reached a point without precedent in literary history. Yet this hardly justifies the consternation which it often rouses in timid spirits. It is another condition of the machine age, like the use of railroad trains instead of stage-coaches. Men have accustomed themselves to walking in crowded streets continually in danger from motor cars almost as swift as missiles, and more deadly. So must readers of taste accustom themselves to moving with security among the rush of books, unconcerned by the mass of traffic, their intent fixed upon their particular goals. For there still are masterpieces, as safe in a crowd as in a desert.

## EPILOGUE

### By CHARLES A. BEARD

FROM this appraisal of modern civilization what grand conclusions emerge?

*First:* Science and the machine have changed the face of the earth, the ways of men and women on it, and our knowledge of nature and mankind. They break down barriers before us and thrust us out into infinity. Not even the Living Buddha escapes their impact, for ships, railways, motors, and airplanes carry visitors to disturb the calm of his contemplation. If St. Peter's chair is still planted on a rock, the rock itself has moved; by no possible stretch of the imagination could the Syllabus of Errors be written now in the terms of 1864. Even pure Idealists, who disdain all reference to reality, must give heed when they breathe and stir. It might be even respectfully suggested that Kant could not write to-day without making reference to the discoveries in physics, chemistry, biology, and psychology which have been made during the past hundred years. If the categorical imperative still stands unimpeached, the execution of its commands must reckon with the bewildering variety of choices offered by that revolving kaleidoscope called modern society. While adherents of ancient creeds may continue to recite in unison the words of their professions, they differ violently among themselves with respect to applications, thus becoming assimilated in practical affairs to pagans and unbelievers. Old rules of politics and law, religion and sex, art and letters—the whole domain of culture—must yield or break before the inexorable pressure of science and the machine. Women, perhaps even more than men, find it difficult to steer by ancient headlands. Accustomed by long necessity to functions that conserve life, they suddenly discover that the modes of conservation are multiplied by science and the machine into endless complexity. They too confront the peril of taking thought.

*Secondly:* Through the preceding chapters, with varying emphasis, runs another theme, namely, that by understanding more clearly the processes of science and the machine mankind may subject the scattered and perplexing things of this world to a more ordered dominion of the spirit. This is the paradox of the symposium. Nowhere in these pages is there a signal for surrender or retreat. The effects of science and the machine upon human life are often metallic and oppressive, sometimes terribly cruel to our hopes and conceits; but in dealing with these engines of modern thought and work, our authors consider quality as well as quantity—development, ends, and values as well as numbers. They are not oblivious to the evils of the modern order, but they do not concede that any other system, could it be freely chosen in place of machine civilization, would confer more dignity upon human nature, make life on the whole richer in satisfactions, widen the opportunity for exercising our noblest faculties, or give a sublimer meaning to the universe in which we labor. On the contrary. With some skepticism (perhaps not more disheartening than could be found in many a Jesuit Seminary) they express a belief that there is in the new order of affairs a prospect for life on higher levels, more emancipated from vain imaginings and conquerable sufferings, freer to make flights into the realm of the imagination, and, at all events, devoted to better uses than lamentation and propitiation.

In attempting to evaluate modern civilization and understand its drift, our authors do not arrange themselves on the side of the Materialist in his ancient battle with the Idealist. If those accustomed to taking refuge in occultism discover little consolation in these pages, the materialist of the old school, who reduces all things to terms of matter, organization, and motion, will find little aid and comfort in any of the arguments here presented.

Indeed the Chinese philosopher, Dr. Hu Shih, insists on reversing the tables; instead of admitting that modern civilization is materialistic as compared with the heritage of antiquity still surviving, especially in the Orient, he flatly declares that it is the machine age which rightly deserves the appellation "spiritual." He knows the East and the West, their languages, institutions, philosophies, and practices.

As he goes about in the Far East, seeing sickness that elementary medicine could cure or prevent, starvation due to defective transportation, and appalling poverty near undeveloped resources, Dr. Hu Shih cannot look with amused indifference on well-fed persons gathered in comfortable drawing-rooms to deplore the materialism and black despair of science and the machine. Far from it. Instead of conceding that they may have some right reason on their side, he boldly denies the correctness of their terms, demonstrates the shallowness of the old antithesis between matter and spirit, turns the customary conceptions of the East and the West upside down, and comes out with the firm conclusion that inventors, scientists, and producers of goods deserve the blessings of mankind as spiritual leaders, while the mumblers of mystic formulas are to be set down as the slaves of circumstance, themselves fundamentally materialist in their surrender to starvation, misery, and darkness, called fate. Naturally this will be shocking, particularly to those Westerners who, pained by the hardness of the machine and baffled by the inconclusiveness of science, seek refuge in one or more of the two or three hundred varieties of religious exercise given to the world by the fruitful Orient.

It is clear from these pages that modern scientists, in spite of the doubts and uncertainties which assail them, are not willing to be made partisans of materialism in an ancient theological battle concerning the ultimate constitution of the universe. The very idea of subjecting the scattered and perplexing things of this world to a more ordered dominion is itself born of the spirit, marks mankind off from animals and inanimate nature, and requires for its realization the practice of the grand virtues usually ascribed to religion.

Indeed, effort to reduce the confusion of the modern age to

principles of control, whether in matters of business, labor, health, family life, economy, the arts, government, or international relations, is no mere excursion in mechanics, no mere question of arranging material objects. It involves habits, customs, morals, and the appreciation of values. It requires all the services which psychology can render. It functions not only through regimentation, but also through individual understanding and co-operation. In becoming parts of a greater organism, men and women do not shrink either in the range of their knowledge or the sweep of their imagination. Never before was there a larger opportunity for the exercise of their creative faculties, a more urgent need for intelligent leadership, or a wider variety of choices in enterprise. The transformation of chaos into order is a work of the mind, not a mere function of mechanism.

The process of subjecting the things of this world to a more ordered dominion of the spirit, here revealed as an outstanding characteristic of the modern age, makes short work of the doctrine of anarchy-plus-the-police-constable celebrated in the writings of Herbert Spencer. Nowhere in these pages is there a display of faith in the unlimited beneficence of "the acquisitive instinct" let loose among machines and test tubes. Business enterprise discloses co-operative effort on every hand. Even finance is international. "We are passing," declares Mr. Herbert Hoover, "from a period of extremely individualistic action into a period of associated activities."

The tendencies revealed in business are also found in government. There has been a reaction in Europe against state socialism, but nevertheless it appears that "the field of government ownership and operation will slowly widen." This will come about gradually as a necessity of the machine system, as a part of the process of introducing order into industrial economy. Economic regions to which government ownership does not extend will be invaded by regulation, and that regulation will be administrative rather than judicial. Laws will multiply rather than diminish. Where courts of the state fail in speed and justice, courts of private conciliation will supplement the tribunals of government. The establishment of collective interests functioning through the state, instead of reducing always the freedom of the individual, often enlarges it by placing on his side the services of a Leviathan, Government, a clumsy and frequently a tyrannical agency, but still one very useful in holding at bay the powerful private associations which flourish in our civilization.

The great schemes of modern society for raising the standards of those who work for wages under the hazards of accident and poverty rest on collective foundations, public, private, and semi-public. Their existence is a fact, standing four-square in law, custom, and organization. However they may be curtailed or extended in the future, the wheel of time will not turn back again to the epoch of Manchesterism. The dominant issues of the modern age are, in this respect, matters of means in detail, not of high policy. The debates over the ten hours bill in England sound like echoes from a forgotten age.

Even in the arts, intensely individualistic as they sometimes seem to be, collectivism has a significant rôle to play in the process of subordinating machinery to ideals of beauty. Especially do the grandest projects of technology—bridges, factories, and office buildings—which in these later days are coming under the dominion of artists, require for their fulfilment and flowering the development of city and regional planning. Indeed the movement is well under weigh with enormous practical interests behind it. It gathers momentum. It extends beyond narrow city limits to regions, beyond regions to the countryside, promising to transform the hideous aggregations of the machine city into efficient unities of use and beauty. Of course, no one can be sure of the future; wars and the psychology of patent-medicine salesmen may yet spoil the picture, but there is no inherent necessity in folly. The spirit of intelligent control is here; it has a fighting chance to prevail.

Associated enterprise leaps beyond national boundaries. Innumerable international organizations, economic, scientific, and cultural, afford signs of a transition. If the devastations of war are to be prevented, threatening a dissolution of modern civilization as a fruit of the science and the machine which created it, then nations must associate themselves in understandings and guarantees. No doubt, the magnitude and difficulties of this undertaking are immense, but the League of Nations and treaties of renunciation already indicate what the strategy of peace may be. Men (who have been great destroyers) and women (who conserve life) will do well to make a common reckoning.

Yet, while the collective note in this volume is strong, it would be a mistake to conclude that the individual under the machine is being reduced from a former high estate as an independent thinker and free creator to the level of a cog. Indeed most of our authors are inclined to doubt whether the altitude of his estate ever was as lofty as generally represented and they agree that, notwithstanding the collective invasions, his capacity for liberty and the enjoyment of it are, on the whole, greater, not less, than in the feudal age. What appears to be an "invasion" is, in fact, often merely the recognition of a standard established by science and its application as a means of comfort, convenience, and safety for the community at large. If there are individual losses, at all events, the terminology of the old debate on Man *vs.* the State seems hopelessly obsolete in the presence of revelations respecting bacteria, ignorance, and accidents.

Whatever criticism may be advanced against these pages, in gross or in detail, it will surely be conceded that they present the challenge of science and the machine to modern thought. They set a task for philosophy—the task of affording illumination and direction to "our confused civilization." In a way, all divisions of this book are but departments of philosophy, truly considered, and it would seem not too much to say that strength and glory will come to modern civilization just in proportion as philosophy attends to the business of living under the necessities imposed by technology, and the business of living itself is inspired by an effort to see things whole and steadily, relating means to the highest imaginable ends, making use of reality rather than attempting to escape from it.

Printed in the United States
41661LVS00006B/45